STEPHEN FOSTER,
AMERICA'S TROUBADOUR

Stephen Collins Foster
Water Color by Walter L. White from an ambrotype in Foster Hall Collection

STEPHEN FOSTER,
AMERICA'S TROUBADOUR

BY

JOHN TASKER HOWARD

AUTHOR OF
"Our American Music"

TUDOR PUBLISHING COMPANY
NEW YORK

TUDOR PUBLISHING CO., 1939

COPYRIGHT, 1934, 1935
BY JOHN TASKER HOWARD

PRINTED IN THE UNITED STATES OF AMERICA
BY MONTAUK BOOKBINDING CORPORATION

To one who is truly a
"Dear Friend and Gentle Heart"
JOSIAH KIRBY LILLY
The Laird o' Foster Hall

PREFACE

THE biographer or historian, in writing for the public, may choose one of two methods. He may write a narrative in story fashion, or he may present his readers with a guide to the sources of his information through the use of liberal quotations and by full documentation of each statement he makes in his text. By the first method he aims to compose a book for the casual reader; by the second, a work for reference and for the student.

In writing the life of Stephen Foster it has been a temptation to use both methods. Foster was such an intensely human figure, one whose personal traits are so apparent in his music, that any biography which deals with the events of his life should tell the story to the lay reader through a narrative not overloaded with contributory references and documentation. Yet there has been so much misunderstanding of Stephen Foster, so much controversy over the facts of his career, that it is but fair to the student of American music that he be given proof of assertions, and shown where the sources of data may be found.

I have attempted, therefore, to write both a narrative and a guide to source material, hoping that I have made it possible for the reader who wants only the narrative to read the story, leaving the references and citations to those who are concerned with proof of facts.

It is obvious that the time is at hand when a new biography of Stephen Foster should be written. Morrison Foster's book, published in 1896, is no longer available and cannot be procured in book-shops. It has passed into the category of a collector's item.

In the case of Harold Vincent Milligan's biography of

Foster, published in 1920, the author encountered obstacles that it has been my good fortune to avoid; the information that was made available to him was in many respects meagre, and various of the obstructions he met proved insurmountable. It was impossible for him to know all the story, and it was inevitable that inadequate evidence should lead him to several assumptions that have since proved incorrect. Yet in spite of hindrances Mr. Milligan accomplished valuable pioneer work and wrote a touching, sympathetic narrative of Stephen Foster, one which told the story to many who had never heard it before.

All of which brings us to the man who has made it possible for the complete story of Stephen Foster to be written, Josiah Kirby Lilly, to whom it has been my privilege to dedicate this book. The final chapter of this volume tells of Foster Hall, and its founder, Mr. Lilly—a project which I believe to be unique in the annals of collecting and of research. Mr. Lilly has accomplished something that had never been achieved before. Through fair dealing and frankness, and by pursuing his objective solely for the love of it, he has won the confidence of the relatives and descendants of Stephen Foster, who have put in his hands documents and records that had previously lain hidden in family archives. Through his own generosity, and his love of sharing his abundance of Foster material, he has made Foster Hall a clearing house to which all interested in the composer may turn.

Of Mr. Lilly's helpfulness to me in compiling this volume, anything I might write would prove inadequate. Everything he has done has been vouchsafed with a friendliness and graciousness that have rendered my own labors a memorable experience.

The staff of Foster Hall has been equally generous. Mr. Fletcher Hodges, Jr., has been unstinting and tireless in his efforts to help, especially with the compilation of the bibliography. Others to whom I am indebted are Mrs.

Hodges and Miss Ruth Clifford Hodges. The Washington representatives of Foster Hall, Mr. Walter R. Whittlesey, and his daughter, Mrs. Katharine W. Copley, have been of great assistance in supplying information on first editions of Foster songs. Nor must I omit mention of Miss Dorothy J. Black, secretary at Foster Hall, who has been extremely helpful in providing transcripts of documents and letters.

I am also indebted to Mr. Harry T. Richards, of River Forest, Illinois, and Mr. Jules T. Richards, of Struthers, Ohio, for data respecting Foster's short residence in Warren, Ohio. Officials of the Pennsylvania Railroad have aided greatly in supplying information on the career of William B. Foster, Jr. I am especially grateful to Mr. E. S. Vogel, of the Personnel Department.

Members of the Foster family have been a particularly valuable source of first-hand information. Mrs. Evelyn Foster Morneweck, a niece of Stephen, supplied transcripts of the family letters and documents preserved by her father, Morrison. In addition, she has read the entire manuscript of this book, checking all references to dates, events and persons. Mrs. Marion Foster Welch, aged daughter of Stephen, has been a living link between the composer and posterity. Her daughter, Mrs. Alexander D. Rose, who lived in her childhood with her grandmother, Stephen Foster's widow, has supplied interesting reminiscences. I have also had the pleasure of meeting a grandson of Stephen, Matthew Wiley Welch. Others of the relatives who have been helpful are Miss Henrietta Crosman, the eminent actress, and Mr. Sedley Brown.

There are several persons in Pittsburgh to whom I am indebted—either for actual information or for indicating places where material was to be found: Mr. George M. P. Baird, Miss H. Marie Dermitt, Dr. and Mrs. Will Earhart, Mrs. Maria Leech Lynch, Professor John W. Oliver of the University of Pittsburgh, and the librarian of Carnegie Library.

In Kentucky there were many who offered to assist in my search for Foster data: Mrs. J. W. Arnold, hostess at "My Old Kentucky Home" at Bardstown; Mrs. R. H. Vaughn, of the "My Old Kentucky Home" Commission; Dr. L. G. Crume, of Bardstown; Mr. and Mrs. John B. Thomas of Bloomfield; Mr. Rowan Hardin of Louisville; and Mr. John Wilson Townsend of Lexington.

In seeking to locate information and documents dealing with Foster's residence in New York I am grateful for the help given me by Mr. Joseph Muller, of Closter, New Jersey, an authority on *Americana;* and the officials of Bellevue Hospital, where Foster breathed his last.

Others whom it is a privilege to thank are: Mr. Elmer Steffen, of Indianapolis; Mr. Frank J. Metcalf, of Washington; Mrs. Robert W. Page, of Glen Ridge, New Jersey; Mrs. Julia Welles Murray, of Athens, Pennsylvania; and finally my collaborator in my recent radio series, Mr. Innis G. Osborn, the playwright, who prepared the dramatizations of episodes of Foster's life.

Nor can I close this long list of acknowledgments without mention of the hundreds of correspondents who responded to that Foster series of broadcasts, always with friendly comments, at times with valuable information. I have already acknowledged these letters privately and only regret that space does not permit me to do so publicly. They have proved not merely a continual encouragement in this arduous, though pleasant task; they have demonstrated in no uncertain manner the deep and abiding interest in Foster and love for his melodies, which has permeated into the most remote corners of the world.

J. T. H.

Glen Ridge, New Jersey
January 1, 1934

PREFACE TO FOURTH PRINTING

SINCE the original publication of this volume a number of events have occurred which should be chronicled in order that the records of Fosteriana may be made complete. Little has been discovered or has occurred which would change any statements or surmises in these pages, but several disclosures have been made which throw added light on matters that had been obscure.

When this book was first published only twenty-two letters written by Stephen Foster were known to modern students of the song-writer's life. Recently several additional letters have come to light and have been added to the Foster Hall Collection at Indianapolis. Some of them are discussed in detail in an article by the present author, "Newly Discovered Fosteriana," which appeared in *The Musical Quarterly,* of January, 1935. Two of the letters were addressed to Stephen's sister, Ann Eliza Buchanan. The first, dated September 15, 1845, was written from Pittsburgh. It shows that Stephen was considering taking Henry's place temporarily in the Land Office at Washington. This plan presumably was never carried out. The second letter dated Pittsburgh, July 16, 1850, informs his sister that he is to be married "on Monday next to Miss Jane, daughter of the late Dr. McDowell of this place." He tells of his plans for a wedding trip: "We will start on the same evening for Baltimore and New York. The trip will be on business as well as for pleasure, as I wish to see my publishers in the east as soon as possible. . . ."

The "publishers" were undoubtedly F. D. Benteen of Baltimore and Firth, Pond & Company of New York. Stephen's statement about his forthcoming trip is important because it further discredits the theory that he and his bride visited the Rowan home at Bardstown, Kentucky, on their honeymoon. (See page 165.)

Of equal importance to letters written by Stephen himself are two letters written by Henry Foster after Stephen's death, telling the details of his accident and fatal illness and corroborating in almost every detail the verbal account given by George Cooper to Harold V. Milligan. One of the letters was written to Mrs. Susan G. Beach (January 23, 1864) and the other to Ann Eliza Buchanan (February 4, 1864). Perhaps the most important item in the second letter is the statement that "we found everything connected with Stevey's life and death in New York much better than we expected, he had been boarding at a very respectable hotel and did not owe the landlord a cent or any one else that we knew of. . . ."

Of greatest importance to students of Stephen Foster's life is the revival of the controversy regarding the song-writer's birthplace, discussed in this book on pages 70 to 73 inclusive. This dispute was again brought to the public attention in May, 1934, when Mr. Henry Ford purchased the "House at the Forks" and moved it to Dearborn, Michigan, where it was restored and dedicated in Greenfield Village as the birthplace of Stephen Foster, July 4, 1935. The publicity attendant upon Mr. Ford's purchase of this building brought to light a number of documents which were not available when this volume was first published.

Through the efforts of several Pittsburghers and Foster relatives, notably Mrs. Evelyn Foster Morneweck, niece of the composer,[1] careful searches of the titles render it possible to trace the history of both properties in the dispute to the time of their original ownership by William B. Foster, Stephen's father.

Referring to the plan of Lawrenceville facing page 70, the reader will find lot no. 9 corresponding in location to

---

[1] The author is indebted to Mrs. Morneweck for the privilege of examining her exhaustive monograph on the subject: *The Birthplace of Stephen C. Foster.*

the present Stephen C. Foster Memorial Home, now maintained by the City of Pittsburgh as the site of Foster's birthplace. Lots no. 6 and 7 correspond to the location of the "House at the Forks," the building which Mr. Ford purchased.

It is now known that William B. Foster lost all the property on the south side of the Turnpike Road by foreclosure to the Bank of the United States, May 6, 1826, a little less than two months before Stephen was born. This included lots 2, 3, 4, 5, 6, 7, 8 and 9. On September 6, 1827, when Stephen was a year and two months old, the Bank of the United States sold lot no. 9 to Malcolm Leech for a consideration of $4,000. The deed to Leech described the property as "now in the tenure occupancy of William B. Foster."

Malcolm Leech's administrator sold the property to Andrew Kloman, August 9, 1864. Kloman held it until April 7, 1883, when it was sold to Dr. W. S. McIntosh. It next passed to Andrew J. Lee in 1884; then to Katharine McKee (October 2, 1884), and from Mrs. McKee to James H. Park, who presented it to the City of Pittsburgh in 1914.

The history of lots 6 and 7 (the site of Mr. Ford's house) has also been traced. After they had been acquired by the Bank of the United States they were sold to William Toman for $500, January 8, 1828, when Stephen was a year and a half old. At the same time lots 3, 4, and 5 were sold to other purchasers. The total acreage of the five lots was about four acres, almost the same acreage as lot 9. The total price of the four acres of lots 3, 4, 5, 6 and 7 was $1,250, while a few months before the four acres of lot 9 had brought $4,000. It seems reasonable to attribute the difference in value to the fact that there was a building on lot 9 and none on lots 3, 4, 5, 6 or 7 when Stephen was born. The subsequent history of lots 6 and 7 is traced through deeds of transfer to successive ownership by Thomas Howard, Leopold Vilsack, Patrick Conwell, Patrick McCabe, the Rt. Rev. Richard Phelan, and to Henry Ford.

This evidence seems to make an almost conclusive case for the City of Pittsburgh in claiming that the museum it maintains at 3600 Penn Avenue (lot no. 9) is on the site of Stephen Foster's birthplace, and to remove the matter from the realm of speculation it occupied when it was first discussed in earlier editions of this book. (See pages 70-73.)

When the house that had been moved to Greenfield Village at Dearborn was dedicated (July 4, 1935), the principal address was delivered by Mr. W. J. Cameron. Mr. Cameron is quoted as saying: [2]

The Stephen Foster House, which we are today dedicating at Greenfield Village here at Dearborn, is known in the Foster family as the birthplace of Stephen Foster. There still survives Stephen Foster's only child, a daughter, Mrs. Welch of Pittsburgh, now eighty-four years old, who had this old cottage frequently pointed out to her by her father as his birthplace. . . .

Whatever Mrs. Welch may have said when she was eighty-four years old I do not know, but what she is reported to have said on the subject, eleven and a half years earlier, when she was seventy-two years old, is a matter of record. The following sentences are taken from an article in the Pittsburgh *Gazette Times*, January 10, 1924:

Memories of her father, Stephen C. Foster, in the happy years when he lived in Pittsburgh and she as a child played at his knees, came back clearly yesterday across the span of years to his only daughter, Mrs. Marion Foster Welsh [sic], aged 72, in the Foster Memorial Home, 3600 Penn Avenue [the museum maintained by the City of Pittsburgh]. . . .

She spoke of the controversy as to the correct location of the old Foster homestead where her father was born. "All the records that I have been able to find," she said, "show that this was the spot where the old home stood. It was the only house in this district at the time, and the fields sloped from the house to the Allegheny River."

[2] In *Ford News*, August, 1935.

Shortly after the dedication of the house at Dearborn, Mrs. Welch died, July 9, 1935. This removed one of the few remaining links between Stephen and the present. The little old lady was eighty-four when she passed away, and she was still living, with her daughter, Mrs. Rose, in the Stephen Foster Memorial Home in Pittsburgh, the spot which seems so surely to be the site of her father's birthplace.

Several new memorials to Stephen Foster have been planned or installed. The Eastman School of Music at Rochester has named one of its dormitories "Stephen Foster Hall." Because of Foster's association with Cincinnati, a group of citizens of that city have planned a memorial which will be placed in a large room in the main library of the University of Cincinnati. Mr. J. K. Lilly, founder of Foster Hall in Indianapolis, has presented facsimiles of letters, manuscripts and other documents in the Foster Hall Collection, as well as magazines, broadsides, books, sheet music, and other items pertaining to Foster.

As for Foster Hall itself, Mr. Lilly has announced that when the new Stephen C. Foster Memorial Building in Pittsburgh is completed on the Cathedral of Learning Quadrangle, he will present the entire Foster Hall Collection for installation in a special wing which will be part of the building. Thus all of the material which has been collected in Indianapolis, representing the most complete collection of Fosteriana in existence, will be returned through Mr. Lilly's generosity to Pittsburgh, from which so much of it originally came.

J. T. H.

September, 1935.

CONTENTS

LIST OF ILLUSTRATIONS

STEPHEN FOSTER

America's Troubadour

I

"DEAR FRIENDS AND GENTLE HEARTS"

I

Ward 11, Stephen Foster, Died January 13.
Coat, pants, vest, hat, shoes, overcoat, January 10, 1864.

Recd. of Mr. Foster [a brother] ten shillings charge for
Stephen C. Foster while in Hospital, Jany. 16, 1864.
WM. E. WHITE, *Warden, Bellevue Hospital*

SO READ the inventory of personal possessions, and the
receipt for hospital charges of the late Stephen Foster,
almost unrecognized, a patient in a charity hospital. But
there was one item in the coat, pants, or vest that escaped
official notice—a little purse, containing thirty-eight cents
in bills and coin, and a slip of paper with five pencilled
words,—"Dear friends and gentle hearts." No doubt
this was to be the title of an unwritten song, but whatever
its intent, the phrase describes quite perfectly the dear
friend and gentle heart who added "Old Folks at Home,"
and a dozen other immortal songs to the world's spiritual
riches.

The significance of Foster's songs has been appreciated
only in recent years. In his own day they were sung all
over the world, but then they were looked upon as mere
popular songs of the moment, destined to the early oblivion

that awaits most of our current balladry. The prospect of immortality for his songs never occurred even to Foster himself. When "Old Folks at Home" had been published for six years and had paid him some sixteen hundred dollars in royalties, he estimated that the song was probably good for another hundred, and he was willing to sell his entire interest in it for that amount.

Many of the songs are now eighty years old, and the best of them are more alive than ever. Within the last quarter of a century musicians, as well as laymen, have come to realize that they are a genuine folk expression, that Foster assimilated the native influences with which he was surrounded, and gave them an expression that was natural and unaffected, spontaneous and unmanufactured. He wrote for a market, but when he was himself, the market never soiled his work—it merely gave him a voice that would be understood.

Nor are Foster's best songs merely a folk expression. They reflected the character and temperament of the man who wrote them, and in that sense they are truly an art product. The two hundred songs and compositions that Foster wrote, the best and the worst, form an autobiography of the man who composed them. The finest of the sentimental songs were lyrics of home. With Stephen Foster the love of home and the companionship of his parents, his brothers and sisters, was his strongest emotion. He was thoroughly miserable when he was away from the friends of his youth. The nonsense songs, "Oh! Susanna," "De Camptown Races," and others of their kind, show a laughing Stephen, convivial and buoyant, sometimes a leader and sometimes led. The man who understands Foster's songs will have no difficulty in understanding Foster.

Yet there has been a persistent misunderstanding of his life and character, caused largely by irresponsible and ill-informed journalists who have so exaggerated his failings and his improvident ways that it is commonly supposed that his life was a continuous debauch, and that Stephen was at all times penniless. He did drink heavily, it is true, constantly in the last four years of his life, but it was only in these last years that his weakness really got the better of him and made him a vagabond. He died in poverty; but for eleven years—from 1849, when he became a professional song-writer, to 1860, four years before his death—his income from songs averaged over thirteen hundred dollars a year, a small sum to-day, but an amount that may be multiplied several times in making comparisons with present values.

Since love of home was Foster's dominant passion, the character of that home, and its family background, provide the key to the man and his work. The Fosters were, and their descendants still are, a clannish lot—devoted, suffering perhaps their own differences with each other, but presenting to the outer world a united and loyal front, especially in concealing anything which they feel discreditable, or, in the case of Stephen, disgraceful. It has been said, and often, that Stephen was deserted by his family in his last years. This is only partially true, his living alone was his own concern, and when he died his wife and two brothers rushed to New York as soon as they were notified of the tragedy.

The family never stopped loving Stephen Foster, and helping him when he needed aid; it merely failed to understand him, which was at most a sin of ignorance, rather than intent—an ignorance that came from environment and tradition, not from lack of intelligence. Even though the failure to understand a sensitive, creative temperament was probably the basic cause of Stephen's ultimate downfall, it is difficult to see how the Fosters could have acquired such an understanding in the frontier surroundings they lived in.

2

The family belonged to the pioneer aristocracy of Pittsburgh. The father, William Barclay Foster, had come there in 1796, when the future city was little more than a settlement. Born September 7, 1779, in Berkeley County, Virginia, he was the third son of James Foster, himself the eldest son of Alexander Foster, an emigrant from Londonderry, Ireland, who settled in Little Britain Township, Lancaster County, Pennsylvania, about 1728.

James Foster, Stephen's grandfather, served in the Revolutionary War, and was present at the surrender of Cornwallis. Shortly after the war he settled near Canonsburg, Pennsylvania, nineteen miles from Pittsburgh. When he died at his daughter's home in Poland, Ohio, April 7, 1814, James left a substantial inheritance to his children. His wife, William's mother, was Ann Barclay, a relative of the Barclays and Rowans of Kentucky, the kin who figure so prominently in the Kentucky episodes of Stephen Foster's life. Judge John Rowan, at one time a United States Senator, was the owner of Federal Hill, the homestead at Bardstown, Kentucky, now maintained by the State as "My Old Kentucky Home." We shall examine the claims in behalf of this "shrine" later.

William Barclay Foster deserves a biography for himself alone. Previous accounts of Stephen's life have told of his father, and have painted pictures of him that are faithful as far as they go, but they present only one aspect of his many-sided nature. His son, Morrison Foster, in his biography of Stephen,[1] shows his father as the man of substance he actually was at one time; the public-spirited patriot who dipped into his own pocket to help equip the troops and boats in the War of 1812, who donated a burying ground for soldiers, and who was a man active in local

[1] *Biography, Songs and Musical Compositions of Stephen C. Foster,* by Morrison Foster: Pittsburgh, 1896.

and state and, to a limited extent, in national politics. It was natural that his son should be content with that much of the portrait. Yet, a later historian, Harold V. Milligan, admittedly impartial, was able in his biography of Stephen Foster [2] to go but little further, and to give his readers only the prosperous merchant and man of affairs.

A much more lovable and human figure emerges from the family letters and other documents pertaining to the Fosters—an able, industrious man, but an impractical vision-ary whose frequent errors of judgment reduced his depend-ents almost to poverty on several occasions. Had he not been so anxious to turn things up for himself, he might have been a Micawber. On one occasion he did actually take Stephen to call on Dickens at Pittsburgh's Mononga-hela House in 1842. No doubt this was a mere coincidence, for it is surely too much to claim that his visitor suggested the character Dickens was to create in a future book, espe-cially when the author was concerned chiefly with the un-pleasant things he was planning to say about America in his *American Notes* and *Martin Chuzzlewit*. Moreover, "Boz" was suffering from an indisposition for which he was treated by Dr. Andrew N. McDowell, whose daughter Jane the young Stephen was later to marry.

Starting his career as a merchant and trader with sub-stantial success, William Foster finished his days on the edge of the political scene, forced to be content with minor appointive or elective offices. When his friends, the Demo-crats, were out of office, he had to wait until something turned up, or make a desperate attempt to turn it up him-self by reviving old claims against the federal government, and against a transportation company he had managed in his earlier years.

He thought and acted in the grand manner, literally. He was far from being a strutter or an idle boaster; he

[2] *Stephen Collins Foster, a Biography,* by Harold Vincent Milligan: New York, G. Schirmer, 1920.

actually had the temperament as well as the bearing of a man of affairs, but he met two obstacles which prevented him from continuing as he started—his own faulty business judgment and the several financial panics which swept the country between the years 1825 and 1850.

William Foster had his schooling at the "Log College," the Canonsburg Academy which later became Jefferson College. His father was one of its first trustees. When he went to Pittsburgh, sixteen years old, William entered the employ of Denny and Beelen, dealers in general merchandise. Anthony Beelen and Ebenezer Denny were merchants of considerable scope, and their business called for trading with as distant points as New Orleans. As William Foster learned the business he was sent away on long trips, to sell and to buy. Twice a year he would take charge of the flatboats loaded with fur, pelts, whiskey, flour, and other products of the surrounding country, and sell their cargo in New Orleans, either for money or in exchange for sugar and coffee. Generally he returned by ship to Philadelphia and New York, where he was commissioned to buy goods for the store at Pittsburgh. Sometimes he returned from Louisiana by land, with companions strongly armed for skirmishes with Indians. Once his ship was surrounded by pirates off Cuba, and rescued by Spaniards.

How much the father of the Foster family was able to amass from his connection with Denny and Beelen is uncertain, but at one time his fortune must have been of respectable size. In 1814 he purchased a tract of land, one hundred and twenty-three acres, located on the Allegheny River about two and a half miles from Pittsburgh. The deed to the property was signed April 5, and the price was $35,000. It is not certain whether he was still connected with Denny and Beelen at this time, but the probability is that he was not, for there are no contemporary references to the firm in the family documents.

Nor is it known whether the purchase was made with

money he had earned from his business activities. When his father died two days after the execution of the deed (April 7) William inherited his share of the father's estate, but unless he had received an advance from his father before the latter's death, he could hardly have used this inheritance to buy the property. Moreover, James Foster's estate was divided among the several children, and William B. Foster's share would have been relatively small.

Foster acquired the land chiefly as a real estate venture, although it was there that he built his own home. On April 9 he sold thirty acres to the government as a site for an arsenal, a building used by the United States until 1901. Its gate is still standing. For this tract Foster received $12,000—a sum that yielded him a proportionate profit at the very beginning. Then he proceeded to lay out the rest of the land as a town which he named Lawrenceville, in honor of Captain James Lawrence of "Chesapeake" fame, the man who is credited with the saying "Don't give up the ship." Perhaps it was to appease his conscience for the profit he had made from the sale to the government that Foster donated a piece of land, one and a quarter acres, as a burying ground for soldiers.

It was some time in 1815 or 1816 that the Foster family moved into the White Cottage that Foster built in Lawrenceville. It was there that Stephen was born and the family lived until Foster lost control of the property and it passed into the hands of the Bank of the United States, some time after 1830.[3] Financially, the investment in land proved almost disastrous, for many of the lots, sold partly on credit, came back to Foster when those who had bought them were unable to complete their payments.

[3] See pages 70-71.

3

At the time he established Lawrenceville, William Foster was in his heyday as a man of importance, even though his patriotism and enthusiasm got the better of his caution. During the War of 1812 he offered his services as a volunteer commissary to the Pennsylvania brigade. This body of troops suffered intense hardships from cold and stormy weather at the outbreak of the war, and the government was slow in providing adequate equipment. Foster advanced his own money for its supplies on several occasions.

In 1814, April 18, he was officially appointed Deputy Commissioner of Purchases, with headquarters at Pittsburgh, and in the following December he came to the rescue with his own funds and his individual credit when it was necessary to equip the "Enterprise" for its famous trip to New Orleans under the command of Captain Henry M. Shreve. The boat was loaded and dispatched from Pittsburgh December 15, and reached New Orleans January 5, 1815, just in time to help Andrew Jackson win the battle three days later, a battle which was fought almost a month after the peace treaty had been signed, before word of the war's ending had reached this country.

Foster never collected the full amount he advanced for the government. On February 18, 1815, the War Department instructed the Treasury Department to transmit to him $21,308.08, "being the amount of Warrant No. 2057 issued by the Secretary of War on account of the Quarter Master Depart. of the Ordnance Department and of Clothing of the Army—which sum is the Balance found to be due to you on settlement of your accounts to the 31st. December, 1814."

This settlement covered many of the expenditures, and Foster's salary, but it was $2,704.90 short of the amount of his claim, filed April 30, 1815. In 1823 he won a ver-

The White Cottage at Lawrenceville, Birthplace of Stephen Foster

From a painting in the possession of the Foster family

dict in the United States Court at Pittsburgh, under Judge Walker, who said, in his charge to the jury:

Terminate as this cause may, Mr. Foster has established for himself a character for zeal, patriotism, generosity and fidelity which cannot be forgotten, and has placed a laurel on his brow that will never fade.

These words may have impressed the jury, but not Congress. Foster received only $1,107.89 of the twenty-seven hundred he claimed. Congress held that when no official requisition was issued, and goods were bought on individual responsibility, a dangerous precedent would be established if generosity was thus recognized. Foster was left with $1,597.01 still unpaid, at a time when he needed it badly. He made a number of attempts to collect. On one occasion (March 2, 1836) he wrote his wife:

As I intimated to William in my last letter from Washington, all my exertions fail'd in procuring my just dues from the Government, but as I had made the attempt, I determined to persevere to the last, and did everything that was expected, or required of me to set the equity of the claim in full view of the Committee; but all in vain. I found it useless to remain any longer.

In 1846, his friend, Colonel John H. Eaton,[4] did his best to get payment for Foster, and presented to Congress the claim which attorneys' fees and interest had increased to $4,820. Nor was this allowed, and the last time that Foster pressed his claim, in 1850, the amount had grown to $5,218.60. The only settlement he obtained was a land grant, in 1851, given generally to veterans of the War of 1812.

Litigation against the government was not the only matter that took William Foster into court. After his work for the army in the War of 1812 he became manager of a turnpike transportation company, a concern that operated

[4] Secretary of War in Andrew Jackson's cabinet, and Minister to Spain, 1836-40.

stage-coaches and Conestoga wagons between Pittsburgh and Philadelphia. Foster held this position from 1815 until the firm went out of business in 1818, but its dissolution was by no means the last that Foster heard of it. The company failed for some hundred thousand dollars, and the manager had a proportionate liability for its obligations. The matter dragged along for many years, and in a letter to William, junior, Foster explained the situation in detail (December 7, 1834):

> You may perhaps remember that I have had since the year 1818, a claim against [Messrs. X, Y and Z] for two Bonds, put into their hands as collateral security, contingent on my settlement of my accts. as agent for the old Philada. and Pittsburgh Transporting Company, and for which they were my security in a bond with me, for $5000 dollars. A suit on the Bond was entered against us all in 1822—and I never could find any one to settle my accts. with, although I went twice to Philada. for the express purpose. . . . Determined at last to know the result, I urged my Lawyer (Mr. Biddle) about three months ago, to push the business to a close, which he did, by taking out a rule to arbitrate, and gave notice to the compy's. attorney, who did not attend on the day of the trial; and a verdict was rendered and filed in our favour; no appeal being taken, the matter is now at rest forever, and my three Bondsmen are relieved from any liability on my account.

So much for Foster's liability; he now had a case against his bondsmen. The letter continued:

> In the mean time, they had sued the bonds I gave them, received the money and applied it to their own private purposes; I now call on them to refund, which they do not pretend to deny; the amount will be upwards of 3000 dollars, for which they are all individually and collectively bound; they are amply able to pay. . . . Mr. [X] recd. out of the spoil from 1500 to 2000 Dollars, [Y] the balance. . . .
>
> I have already drawn on [X] at 6 months for 150 Dollars, which he has accepted & which is proof positive, (if necessary) of the justice of my claim. . . . I can do nothing with [Y] until his return from Russia. . . . Mr. [X] is expected here in a few days when I expect to make an amicable arrangement for his part by giving him time & perhaps deducting a part of the interest, etc. etc.

Like the government claims, the disputes regarding the
old transportation company dragged along in the courts
for many years, and at least provided Foster with occupation, if not with immediate cash. In 1837 he learned that
a tract of land in Erie, Pa., owned by one of the direc-
tors of the old company, was to be sold by the sheriff.
Foster immediately went to Erie to enter his claim. He
left home in high hopes, with definite plans for spending
the money he was to get. If he received only a thousand
dollars, he would send his son Dunning to a school for
civil engineers, and put Dunning's brother, Henry, in a
business of his own. These were hard times, and Henry
had been dropped from his position with a local firm. The
financial panic of that year caused a ten million dollar deficit
in the national treasury, and as Foster wrote to William,
junior, "the banks all refuse specie, and nothing but shin-
plasters for change."

But there were several others who had moved a little
faster than Foster, and had reached Erie before him.
Their claims came first, and when they were satisfied, there
was nothing left from the sale of the land. When Foster
returned to his home he probably needed the diversion that
was provided by a pioneer balloonist:

Clayton made a splendid ascension in his Balloon from the East
Common of our town, within twenty rods of our door. It was the
most beautiful sight I ever saw. . . . He landed near Johnstown, and
return'd yesterday by the Canal, Balloon and all, safe and sound.
He goes up again on Monday next. (September 5, 1837)

After the 1837 trip, there were many visits to Erie. By
1840 the defendants' property had passed into the hands
of an agent of the Bank of Pennsylvania, and the suit was
pressed against him. In 1841 the case was transferred to
the Erie courts, and finally Foster settled for $2,000, two-
thirds of his original claim. His travelling expenses alone
had amounted to $500, to say nothing of attorneys' fees.

4

After the failure of the transportation company it was some time before William Foster held another position. His fortunes declined sharply, although he did manage to keep the White Cottage at Lawrenceville for a number of years. From 1825 he served two terms in the State Legislature, and became an ardent supporter of Andrew Jackson. During the 1828 campaign his enthusiasm and his hopes mounted high. As early as June 26 he wrote his daughter Charlotte, visiting in Louisville:

Tell my Jackson friends that we cannot get a single bet on the final result of the Presidential question against the old *Ginneral.*

As election grew nearer, he wrote again to Charlotte (September 7):

Tell our friends that Kentucky has done her part nobly in her late vote for the Jackson ticket, far beyond what the Hero's friends here expected, and places the election of General Jackson beyond all doubt; tell them that they need not fear Pennsylvania, if we do not give a majority of 25 thousand votes for the Jackson electors, I shall be more disappointed than I ever was in my life in an election; notwithstanding all the noise about great changes in favour of Adams. I have no doubt that the Generl. will pass through Pittsburgh in January or February next, when I flatter myself with the expected pleasure of hearing you play to him "Hail to the Chief."

A later paragraph in this letter bore important news:

I have declined a re-election to the Legislature, in consequence of the arrangement made with the Board of Canal Commissioners.

This inaugurated an episode in William B. Foster's career that not only nearly ruined him, it almost cost him his character and reputation for honesty.

The new canal, Blairsville-Pittsburgh, had been planned and discussed for a number of years. In 1826 (August 16), a cousin had written from Cincinnati:

I understand there is great dissension among the gentlemen of Pittsburg conserning [sic] the canal. I am clear for the Pittsburgh side, and am as much interested as if I were there.

Foster, too, was "for the Pittsburgh side," and his support of the project was so hearty that when the canal was finally built he was rewarded by the "arrangement" with the commissioners which made him Collector of Tolls at Pittsburgh.

Although he had received, or been promised the appointment in 1828, it was almost four years before he was actively in office. On June 22, 1829, Foster wrote to Charlotte:

The water in the canal reached Allegheny Town last night, and in a few days, if no accident happens, boats will be passing from Blairsville to Pittbg. a distance of 70 or 80 miles by water.

Yet, three years later, June 17, 1832, he wrote to William, junior:

The water is expected to be in the canal in about ten days, when I must take my post at the office.

The position was difficult and financially embarrassing even before the actual work had begun. In the June 17, 1832, letter he confided to William, junior:

Mr. Lynch has return'd from Washington without a Dollar of money; although the Sectr'y gave us the credit of having furnished the most satisfactory returns and report on the subject of manufactures that he had recd. from any part of the U. States. We must wait for our pay until an appropriation can be made by Congress, which places me in a very disagreeable situation, having been constantly on expenses, generally traveling, and having made considerable advances to different of our assistants, makes me very hard run.

By August 7 both the canal and Foster's office were functioning:

The canal is in good order and a great deal of freight to come down, principally Iron Blooms and Salt.

In the same letter (to William) he shouted his applause of Jackson's veto of the bill renewing the National Bank charter:

Thanks to Providence, Old Hickory has put his veto on that *vilainous* [sic] *mammoth Bank cal'd* the United States, in which there has been more fraud, in favouritism, corruption and oppression than in any monied institution in the world. We are all veto men now, or nearly so; we have gained more than we lost by it, although we are immediately under the guns of their *Corrupt Battery,* which keeps some poor Devils quiet.

Stephen Foster's niece, Evelyn Foster Morneweck, in her book on the Foster family,[5] has explained the difficulties of the collectorship:

He [Foster] soon found that Collector of the Tolls was not the ideal position he hoped it would be. The "Corrupt Battery" under which he labored held up his salary and that of his subordinates on every trifling technicality they could invent. While he was compelled to handle large sums of money in tolls collected, he was not permitted to pay off the workmen with any of the money until an accounting had been forwarded to Harrisburg, and a voucher returned, which took two weeks if everything was found correct, and much longer if any item were questioned. This continual bickering kept him in a state of ferment and irritation; his men were always in arrears of wages, unless he paid them out of his own pocket, which he was seldom in a position to do.

Owing to the scarcity of cash all over the country, it was the general practice for business men to pay their obligations with notes owed them by others. When a borrower and his bondsmen signed a note, they never knew who would present the note for payment when it fell due. If, after it passed through a dozen hands, it matured in the possession of some one who was willing to renew, all well and good; but if the holder of the note was being pressed by his own creditors, and could not extend the term, the signers were in a very bad way. For a sale amounting to as little as $200, one might receive three or four notes drawn on as many different persons, each falling due on a different date. This medium of exchange required a great deal of careful bookkeeping, and a watchful eye on

[5] *Chronicles of a Foster Family: From Which Came a Great Genius,* to be published by Foster Hall, Indianapolis.

one's own liabilities. It is not strange that so many business failures resulted—many a man thought his notes were safe in the hands of his friends, and woke to find the Bank holding them all, and demanding payment.

Foster kept his spirits high in spite of his difficulties. The White Cottage had been disposed of, and the family had moved from a near-by summer resort at "Harmony" to a house in Allegheny City. Finances were far from what they should have been, but William, junior, was proving helpful with various advances of cash, and frequent gifts.

It was at this time, too, that Foster took a decisive step in joining the Temperance Society, a circumstance which throws some light on the possible hereditary influences on Stephen Foster's weakness. Politics was a convivial profession, and William Foster was active both in the profession and in its social amenities. That these troubled his family, and his own conscience, is evident from a letter to his wife, written from Harrisburg while he was a member of the Legislature, January 20, 1826:

I just happened to be at Mr. Wilson's when the stage arrived, and we sat down and dined to-gether. I found him so friendly and polite, I stretched a point and bot [sic] a pint of wine, the only one I have bot since I came to Harrisburgh.

Then, perhaps to forestall the question this would raise, he continued:

I continue to enjoy, thank God, good health, and am always at my post, where I feel much encouraged to remain firm, by numerous flattering letters, approbatory of my conduct since I have been here from persons of different parties. . . . I mention this for your own eye, knowing it will be pleasing to you.

In 1833 he made a definite decision, and informed William, junior (February 8):

I know you will be pleased to learn that I joined the temperance society, and sign'd the constitution some time before I left home, since which I have touched not, nor handled the poisonous article, and trust I never will.

He became almost a fanatic in the temperance cause, to the dismay and discomfiture of the local clergy. Reforming was their province, and one of the ministers spoke of "men who have hardly yet opened their eyes from the drunken doze of years, exalted to the rank of public teachers, to rebuke the Christian ministry and reform the church."

Foster kept right on, and eight years after he first joined the society, he wrote (September 3, 1841):

The cause of temperance continues to flourish throughout our Western Country. . . . We have a Washington total abstinance [sic] society in Allegheny, in which I am a member, with others numbering in all about 150 members. We receive many calls from different parts of the country to send out members to address conventions on the subject of temperance. Yesterday, six of us addressed in succession upwards of one thousand persons assembled agreeably to previous arrangements. I was call'd upon first to address them, and thought I did it pretty well; was followed by John D. Mahon, Esqr. in a thrilling appeal to the feelings of considerable length. The people appear'd well pleased, and upwards of three hundred subscribed the teetotal pledge.

Meanwhile, matters in the Collector's office had become so difficult that something drastic had to be done about it. If William, junior, had not stood by and helped, there might have been a tragedy. There was a hint of trouble in Foster's wife's letter to young William, July 9, 1833:

Your Father says with your liberal assistance he has been enabled to close his accounts with the state to his satisfaction.

Yet in Foster's next letter to William (October 5) there is nothing but optimism:

I was very glad to know that my letter inclosing my note reached you in safety, and in good time. . . . Our election compaign grows

warm. . . . What do honest Republicans of your county think of
Gen'l Jackson's second veto? . . . Our bankites give up all hope of
a recharter since the exposure of their Hellish Depravity and Corruption. . . . The canal is in good order, and doing a pretty good
business. A great quantity of Merchandise is daily arriving by the
Boats.

The following year brought a less cheerful prospect. On
February 24, 1834, Foster wrote William that he was in
Harrisburg, where his first business was to settle his ac-
counts.

As I have nothing positive as to my fate here, I will write you in
about a week. . . . I feel in fine health, and strong in the confidence
you so much desire. My old friends receive me with great cordiality; and I feel quite happy.

Adieu, my dear boy—that God may prosper and preserve you
many years after I shall be laid low in the dust is the prayer of your
father.

In March Foster resigned his position as Collector of
Tolls, and on the following July 14 he wrote William, fully
explaining the whole affair:

You mentioned in a former letter that you regretted I had resigned my office. I promised to give you some explanation for quitting
the public business. On the opposite side of the leaf, you have a
statement of our expenses during the last five years, which is I feel
confident entirely within bounds, and not one cent of my own private
expenses is included in it except my clothing; by this you will see that
it was impossible for me to live on my salary, which would now
have been $720 dollars, and while I was handling money *it must be
had,* no matter where it was to be replaced from; so that I was
kept in eternal misery between Constables on one hand, and the fear
of involving my Bailsmen on the other, and blasting my reputation
forever by being dismissed from service for using public money. In
this dilemma I was happy in closing my business and quitting the
dangerous precipice on which I was standing. You will see for the
last six years, it has cost us $7366.00, an average of $1227.00 per
ann. To make up the annual deficit, I sacrificed the coal in the out
lot, drew on you, etc. etc. so that strange as it may appear, I am now

not more than about $1200 in debt. I feel totally at a loss to know what to turn my attention to, I expect to receive two or three hundred dollars this summer, a sort of a windfall. If it comes, I will tell you all about it.

5

After this episode Foster groped about for something to do. The family moved to a frame house on the bank of the Ohio River, a quarter of a mile below Allegheny Town, where the rent was $125 a year.

Foster ran for assembly on the Jackson anti-bankite slate, and was defeated along with the rest of the ticket. He devoted himself to buying and selling land, and there was some talk of going on a farm, sharing its purchase with his son-in-law, Edward Buchanan.

Late in the following year, 1835, he entered on another ill-starred project, a partnership with a man named Hall, in a store at 106 Market Street, Pittsburgh. William, junior, invested in the firm, and Foster's wife, with three of the children, including Stephen, went to Youngstown to live with this eldest son, who at that time had his headquarters there.

Hard times soon finished the business for the Fosters, and William had to help in closing out the family interest in the enterprise. It happened that the man who finally bought their share of the concern had a number of suits standing against him. The Fosters learned this only after the deal had been closed, when the new owner asked them to continue the use of their names as proprietors to keep his own creditors from taking over his newly acquired business. William let him use his name for two months, and by that time the purchaser had fortunately collected enough money to pay off his threatening creditors.

It was all very complicated, and in spite of the careful records he kept, books that are still preserved in the family, Foster never knew exactly where he stood. He was

Eliza and William Barclay Foster,
Stephen Foster's Parents

again unoccupied for several years, except for small deals in land and coal lots. The family moved for a time to Poland, Ohio, where they boarded with Foster's brother-in-law, John Struthers.

In 1841 Foster received an appointment to a minor office in the Treasury Department at Washington. His friend, Walter Forward, had been made first controller of the Treasury, and had room for a number of clerks at a salary of a thousand a year. Foster was in Washington for only a few weeks. He took office early in December, but soon he was back in Allegheny, where he was elected mayor. In this office he served for two years. He wrote William that his duties were not laborious, but that his office afforded him "about enough business to keep from desponding." It at least gave him a chance to further the temperance cause.

Our temperance cause is prosperous. I think I have redeemed one miserable drunkard, our first acquaintance being a commitment by me, to the jail of the County 24 hours for drunkenness and abuse of his family. . . . After he came out, he call'd on me and sign'd the pledge, and has remain'd since (about two weeks) a sober, decent man, for which I received the thanks and prayers of a wife and three daughters. (March 14, 1842)

And again:

[My office] is painful in many respects, to witness as I do, the awful depravity of poor human nature, in many cases of female intoxication and prostitution, is truly lamentable. (March 30, 1842)

After the mayoralty he held no position for about five years, although financial matters were eased by some favorable investments he made in Youngstown, in 1846. In 1849 he secured a license to act as Soldier's Agent in Pittsburgh, in charge of pensions and land grants. Although he was an invalid from early in 1851 he was able to continue his duties for some time with the aid of his younger sons, including Stephen, who went on his errands for him and secured the affidavits and receipts of those who were awarded the land warrants.

William Foster lived to be almost seventy-six years old. He died July 27, 1855, scarcely more than six months after the death of his beloved wife, Eliza.

6

This Eliza, the mother of Stephen, was indeed a devoted and loving wife. Born Eliza Clayland Tomlinson, in Wilmington, Delaware, January 21, 1788, she was her husband's junior by some eight years. Her father was Joseph Tomlinson, whose relatives, like Foster's, had distinguished themselves in the War of the Revolution. Her mother's ancestors, the Claylands, had come to America from England, and settled on the shores of Maryland in the early years of the Colony. According to Morrison Foster,[6] "they [the Claylands] were generally accomplished, both men and women, highly educated and refined. It is believed that much of the musical and poetic genius of my brother Stephen was derived from this branch of the family. The ladies were distinguished in Baltimore society for their musical and artistic ability."

William Foster probably met his future wife on one of his business trips through Philadelphia, where Eliza Tomlinson used to visit her aunt, Mrs. Oliver Evans, in her home on Race Street. Evans was the genius who invented the first high-pressure steam engine and the first steam dredging machine used in the United States. It was he who was responsible for the first actual steam propulsion of a carriage on land in America, and Eliza Foster often told her children that she watched the inventor walk beside his machine as it moved out of his yard and into the street.

William and Eliza were married by the Reverend David Denny, November 14, 1807, when the groom was twenty-

[6] *Op. cit.*

eight and the bride not yet twenty. The wedding was held in Chambersburg, Pennsylvania, where Eliza had relatives, and the bridal trip to Pittsburgh was a journey over the mountains on horseback. Years later, when she compiled a book of reminiscences at the request of her children, Eliza described that trip and her first reception into Pittsburgh:

The journey was slow and monotonous, and it was not until the fourteenth day that I hailed with delight the dingy town of Pittsburgh, my future home, where every joy and every sorrow of my heart since that bright period have been associated with the joys and sorrows of its people. It was evening when, weary and faint with travel, I was conducted, or, rather, borne, into the hospitable mansion of my husband's partner, the benevolent Major Denny, a dwelling in the centre of the town, where I was received and treated with the most extreme kindness. After resting and changing my apparel I was shown into an apartment below stairs where blazed in all its brilliancy a coal fire, casting its light upon the face of beauty clothed in innocence in the person of little Nancy Denny, at that time five years old. The well-cleaned grating of the chimney-place, the light that blazed brightly from the fire, the vermillion hearth, the plain, rich furniture, the polished stand with lighted candles in candlesticks resembling burnished gold, made an evening scene that fell gratefully on my pleased sight. Upon a sofa lay the tall and military figure of the Major, a gentleman of the old school, easy and dignified in his bearing, a soldier who had served his country well under Washington at Yorktown, and Harmar, St. Clair and Wayne in the subsequent Indian campaigns.

Eliza and the fine-writing of her journal! In spite of her formal attempts to be literary, she could never avoid being quite herself when she wrote. She described a funeral she attended the year she was married:

The resplendent sun had risen in his gladness, but through whose lattice did he shed a beam upon a being whose heart was deeper sunk in sadness than that of the fair young bride who late had smiled, but with a foreboding smile, upon her worshipped groom.

The borough could only boast of two double carriages ready for use. . . . I think there were other carriages, but like old pianos, they were out of use. . . . Be that as it may, the company in attendance all walked, except the mourners. The procession moved without pomp; not even a pall covered the coffin. The pride of these people did not lean to vain glory. In those days, strangers were few, consequently all knew the amount of wealth owned by every person. It was not necessary to impose external show upon the eye of the beholder to affect his senses with a false respect. Their frequent associations, kindnesses bestowed by the rich upon the poor whose services they schooled themselves to value, mutual exchanging of benefits, pecuniary and otherwise, made confidence and friendship go hand in hand among them.

There was but one usurer; too contemptible to be named in these pages. A few of his descendants lived to reap the benefits of his extortions. Some of them have been visited with the just retribution of God's wrath. But, I should not bring him in with the people of whom I am now writing. He could not then be welcome even at a funeral such as that which left the house of O'Hara on the forenoon of that remembered day. . . .

Tender, patient Eliza! Bearing children with clocklike regularity; loving them and sending them into the world with her fondest blessing. Ten she bore, and four she lost —three of them as infants, one her firstborn, and then her eldest daughter, the brilliant Charlotte, in the full bloom of her youth. Eliza never quite recovered from Charlotte's death. When the daughter was away at school, the mother's letters had always carried the deep affection and motherly concern she felt for all her brood.

I wish in all your letters you may be able to say in the usual childlike manner, I am well, even if you think proper to omit the next common sentence, and I hope you are the same? We save your letters in your little red morocco trunk because they are as precious as the absent child is always the darling during her exile. . . .

I wish you would tell me in your next letter how your eyes are, as I frequently think of them; and how you progress in music. Learn some handsome pieces of sacred music. . . .

God be with you my love, and protect you from all evil, be patient and meek and lift your thoughts to Heaven, and rough paths will become smoother to you and confinement and disappointment will only seem the retirement of peace, and the cloister of happiness. The days of good children are guarded, and their pillows watch'd by night by the angels of Providence. (Nov. 2, 1821)

When Charlotte's voice was stilled, and little James, the youngest, died the following Spring (May 19, 1830), Eliza was crushed. She wrote few letters for several years, and when she finally took up her pen, it was without much effort at literary production. Her heart was bared. She made no attempt even to spell correctly. In 1832 (May 14) she wrote to William, junior:

As I have written one letter to Ann Eliza the only time I have had a pen in my hand that I can recolect, for two years or more, in fact I felt fearful of making unpardonable mistakes, which prevented me from makeing the attempt when my inclination led me to communicate by letter with an absent friend.

Besides the very many perplexitys of house keeping, there was the weak and tremulous state I was left in after the death of your ever to be lamented sister Charlotte and equally interesting little brother James, that my body has only recovered strength, since my mind was restored to that tranquility which a perfect reconciliation to the will of that omnicient power which regulates and rules, and although the vessels are all broken which I hew'd out to hold the sources of my earthly joys, and all my goneby hopes are nothing but a dream, the song of joy, the delightful cottage, and the sound of the deep toned instrument still comes danceing on in the arrear of memory, with pain, and sorrow, at thought of how it closed, with the departure from this transitory stage of her we loved so dearly. . . .

That we may be all together again when it pleases God the unseen influence that directs our ways is the sincere prayer of one who proudly clames the name of Mother to the best of sons.

Devoted, faithful Eliza! When her daughters' first children were born, she was always on hand to lend aid and encouragement. Their joys and their sorrows were hers also. When her fingers became stiff and for a time her sight failed, she never let her husband close a letter to any of their children without the fondest message from herself.

And she understood her husband as none other knew him. In the trying months of 1841, when he was waiting for the appointment to the Treasury Department, Eliza confided to William, junior (August 12):

Pa continues as you left him; whilest he is so, I will not thwart his plans, believing them to be wiser than my own. Indeed I am but a dependent being in every respect, being too timmid to contradict one so cute as your Father, for if I made a devided house and led off to something of my own invention, he would be sure to overthrow it all, so that I will ever and annon train myself into the first great necessary lesson of resignation, and raise my thoughts morning and evening to Jehovah for my daily bread, and to forgive me my trespasses as I forgive those who trespass against me.

Unquestioning Eliza! Surely her husband was not taking too much for granted when he wrote his son that his mother was "quite contented"; and on another occasion (March 24, 1840):

Your mother is quite composed and resign'd to her destiny, and I still look forward to the time when we can have a permanent situation, where we may "Totter doon the Hill together" in peace and quietness, and sleep together at the foot, and be forgotten by all the world except our dear children.

This wish was partially fulfilled, for from 1850 they lived in Allegheny in a house belonging to William, adjoining their former home on the East Common. Living with them were Stephen and his wife, and two other sons. Eliza's death was sudden; she was stricken on Marbury Street, Pittsburgh, and died in a nearby house where she went for refuge, January 18, 1855. Three days later she would have been sixty-seven years old. The inscription on her tombstone reads: "Her children shall rise up and call her blessed."

7

In their joys and in their sorrows, and above all, in their financial difficulties, the entire family turned to Brother William for counsel, and for the material aid he never failed to furnish. The story of William, junior, is one of the most beautiful episodes in the annals of the Fosters. Although Eliza loved him as her own, and told him that

Eliza Foster's Sampler

he was "one among the few that can feel conscious of being a son in every acceptance of that truly noble title," he was not her real son. He was actually a young relative of William Foster, senior, who came to live with the family shortly after the death in infancy of the fourth child, William Barclay Foster, junior, in 1815. The newcomer was given the name of the dead child, and as he was older than the other children, he became the eldest son of the family.

In 1826, the year Stephen was born, the young William left home to join a party of engineers, and thus started the career that was to bring him honor and fame. When he died, March 4, 1860, he was a vice president of the Pennsylvania Railroad, and had been one of the three engineers who built the section of the railway that crossed the Alleghenies.

His rise was rapid from the very beginning of his career as a surveyor and engineer. Within two years after he left home, the family letters tell us that he had been promoted from an assistant to an assistant engineer, and his pay raised to $3.50 a day. Even at this time he had already contributed much to the expenses of the family in Allegheny. On March 17, 1828, his sister Charlotte wrote him that she wished he could spare her enough to go to Cincinnati, but that "it is hard to ask you when I know you have sent so much to Pa."

He made frequent gifts to the family—on one occasion a piano; to Ann Eliza, the second daughter, fifty dollars as a wedding present; and during the father's difficulties as Toll Collector, William as usual stood by and averted disaster.

In the Spring of 1834 he was made principal engineer on the Green River Improvements in Kentucky. In the following year he became principal engineer of the Eastern Division of the Pennsylvania and Ohio Canal Company, with headquarters at Youngstown. (This was the year he invested in his father's partnership with Hall.) When he

left Kentucky the Commissioners regretted his departure
with an official resolution, stating that they took "great
pleasure in bearing Testimony to the very satisfactory manner in which he has discharged his duties." They added
that "his official conduct has been marked by firmness of
purpose, and by sterling integrity." (June 19, 1835)

1836 found William back in Kentucky, with a romance
started that was soon to end in the first real tragedy of his
life. In Youngstown he met Mary Wick, sister of the
Thomas Wick who married William's sister, Henrietta.
William fell in love with Mary, and they were soon engaged to be married. The formalities and inhibitions of
early Victorian courtship were strictly observed in those
days, otherwise it would be hard to believe that William
and Mary were engaged when Mary wrote him this letter
on June 9, 1836:

> The account you gave me of your itinerant cavalcade gave me much
> pleasure, as I believe I can from that form a tolerably correct idea
> of your situation. Imagination pictures you moving along, followed
> by Assistants, Rodmen, Axmen, Wagons, &c.—I would be happy
> if those "sundry gentlemen" whom you mentioned would not again
> take it upon themselves to monopolize the time set apart for absent
> friends, especially if they have no other duty to perform than that
> of drinking a bottle of Champagne. You will discover from this
> that I advocate the cause of "total abstinence." . . .
>
> My health remains much the same. I spend some of my time
> practicing upon the piano, some I devote to my friends, and some
> in performing domestic duties. . . . I could write on an hour to
> come in the same uninteresting manner, but fearing I shall weary
> your patience, I will bid you farewell, though not until I have
> sent the respects of my father and mother, and beg you to believe
> me your very sincere and faithful friend.

The postscript carried Mary's real feelings:

> do write soon

The reference to her health had its special significance,
for when William married Mary Wick, in November or

December, 1837, she was so far from well that William had to return to his work in Kentucky without her. There were frequent references to Mary's health in the family letters. Two months before the wedding, Henrietta wrote William:

Mary has been to Pittsburgh for a week, but got home on Friday last. She does not look so well lately, poor little dear. She got her wedding dress and a great many little nice things when she was in town. I think you had better come as soon as you can for if you were here it seems to me she would be better. . . .

I do not want you to be alarmed about Mary for she may be no worse than when you left.—When she is here she talks all the time about you. She says "it will not be long till you come now." (September 7, 1837)

The plans for the wedding went forward, and in September William wrote his father in Pittsburgh, asking that he order his wedding clothes from the tailor. His father replied that the clothes would be ready when he arrived, "a most beautiful suit, black coat & Pants and *white* vest. Lee [the tailor] says he will make you a black sattin vest also, which you may take or not as you please. Blue overcoat; they are costly, but the best in Pittsb'g."

The couple were married in Youngstown, and though William had to go back to Kentucky alone, Mary was to join him in the Spring, when she would be better. But she failed to improve, her malady was the consumption that no doctors understood in those days, and William was left a widower, January 9, 1838.

He stayed in Kentucky for another year, and then, in the Spring of 1839 he went to Towanda, Pennsylvania, to become the principal engineer of the canals and railroads of Eastern Pennsylvania. To the Pennsylvania commissioners he was recommended by no less a person than James Buchanan, the future president of the United States, whose brother Edward married William's sister, Ann Eliza. Buchanan told the commissioners that William had been "an excellent son to his father and mother throughout their reverses of fortune," and that he had always understood he was an excellent engineer. (January 31, 1839)

This was the railroad-building era, and surveyors and engineers were playing a major part in the development of the nation. It was only a few years before that railroads had first been started: the Mohawk and Hudson in 1825; the Boston and Albany, 1827. In 1830 the Baltimore and Ohio opened the twenty-three miles of track that it had commenced in 1828. By 1840 the original twenty-three miles in the United States had increased a hundredfold.

Back in 1833, William Foster, senior, had been apprehensive of the effect of the railroads on canals. He wrote William, junior (February 8):

The Improvement Bill has passed the lower House, and this morning passed through Committee of the whole in the Senate, as it was reported with the addition of 400,000 dollars, to make a double track of railroad from Columbia to Philada. I can't say how the grand committee gets on with the Canal Commissioners, but hope that justice may be done and the comiss'ers have nothing to fear.

At that time William, senior, was Collector of Tolls on the Pittsburgh canal.

It was in Towanda that William took the young Stephen to live with him, in 1840, so that the boy might attend the schools at Towanda and nearby Athens. We know that Stephen loved William, for after he had returned to Allegheny, his father wrote that "Stephen says he would like to be in brother William's sun shine." (March 14, 1842)

It worried Eliza Foster that William did not have a wife. Three years after Mary Wick's death, she wrote him that she had no doubt that as a husband he would not "lack in that first of all gifts, the capability of making a wife happy." (August 12, 1841) Again she wrote in October of the same year, "If you give up settling in Towanda, I have a charming girl here for you, Ann Eliza

Anderson. Every time I see her, I think how happy she would make you, I know of none who will compare with her."

But William was able to choose his own wife, for on September 22, 1842, he married Elizabeth Burnett, a widow with one son. William was prosperous in those days, he owned a barouche and two horses, and when he married, his home was the scene of frequent parties and entertainments. Mildred Rahm Smith, a resident of Towanda, recalls hearing of the Fosters from her older relatives. In a letter of reminiscences she writes:

Louise Overton was invited to a party given by Mrs. Barclay Foster. She was, girl fashion, greatly interested in Mrs. Foster's gown and thought it very low in the neck. The fashion at that time was off the shoulders. . . . The house where the Barclay Fosters lived still stands on the River Bank at Weston Street and River St. When the Fosters lived there in 1842-3 I understand it was very attractive, the lawns running to the river.

William's second wife lived for thirteen years after their marriage, and bore him three children, yet none of his descendants are living to-day.

We may be certain that Elizabeth made William happy, for there are a number of references to this wife in the family correspondence. Eliza Foster visited them often, particularly after William went to Harrisburg as Canal Commissioner in 1844. Although Eliza once wrote that William lived "very grand," she told her son Morrison that she would never forget "how respectfull the dear child [Elizabeth] was to me."

It was in the Spring of 1847 that William was appointed one of the chief engineers of the Pennsylvania Railroad, and a few years later (1853) he was elected vice-president. During his last years, when he lived in Philadelphia, his health failed, and he had to live principally in the South until the time of his death, March 4, 1860. He was honored and respected, and one of his obituary notices spoke of him as "an upright, amiable gentleman, a good engineer, and an excellent officer of the railroad with which he was so long connected." [7]

8

The first born of Eliza and William Foster was Ann Eliza, who came into the world November 2, 1808, and died December 23 of the same year. The next child was Charlotte Susanna, born on the fourteenth of December, 1809. It is from Charlotte, more perhaps than from any other member of the family, that we learn of the surroundings into which Stephen Foster was born.

The Fosters had many relatives in near and distant towns, and both parents and children paid extended visits to their aunts, uncles and cousins. When they were away from home, the members of the family wrote many letters to each other, letters which bore news of their doings as well as their views on current happenings. From these documents it is possible to draw a faithful picture of the early days of the Foster family.

The first we learn of Charlotte is that in 1818 she was studying with a Mrs. Brevost. Eliza Foster's diary records a conversation concerning this lady.

"Mrs. Brevost is quite competent to the task of instructing young ladies, I believe," said the Captain.

"She is an accomplished French lady," said Miss Denny, "and deserves much credit for supporting her aged parents so handsomely by her efforts. She instructs her pupils in everything that will improve and polish. The old gentleman, her father, lost his estates by his adherence to Bonaparte. She has been educated in Paris, and presented at the Court of Louis 16th and Marie Antoinette. They came here well recommended from Baltimore by Mr. Carrol and others."

"Mrs. Brevost has already effected wonders with my little Charlotte," said Mrs. Foster.

[7] *Vincent's Semi-Annual United States Register,* Jan.-July, 1860.

"Charlotte is a prodigy," said the younger Miss Denny. "Mrs. Brevost will bring forth all her powers if she stays with her another year."

Charlotte herself was apparently put on exhibition after this conversation, for the diary continues:

"Come, Charlotte," said Mrs. Feebarton, "before I ride, sing and play some of those favorite little airs of yours."

Charlotte lifted her soft blue eyes and looked sweetly at Mrs. Feebarton. She did not whine, nor look affected, nor did she undertake to excuse herself by saying she had a cold, or other such reprehensible device, but walked modestly to the piano, and seating herself, sang "There's nothing true but heaven" in a manner that touched the feelings and moved the hearts of all those present.

"It is alas the case," said Mrs. Woolley, "that we are continually deceived with the glitter of a delusive world. My dear little Charlotte, there is so much pathos in your song, do not leave the instrument until you have given us another."

Charlotte immediately complied, then rose, and slightly curtsying, with a gentle "Good night" left the room.

I have before me an old and yellow copy of "There's Nothing True but Heaven, A Favourite Song from Moore's Sacred Melodies, Composed by Oliver Shaw," published about 1810. Here is what the nine-year-old child sang for her mother's guests:

This world is all a fleeting show, for man's illusion giv'n;
The smiles of joy, the tears of wo,
Deceitful shine, deceitful flow . . .
There's nothing true but heav'n!

And false the light on glory's plume, as fading hues of even;
And love, and hope, and beauty's bloom
Are blossoms gathered for the tomb . . .
There's nothing true but heav'n!

Poor wand'rers of a stormy day, from wave to wave we're driv'n;
And fancy's flash, and reason's ray,
Serve but to light the troubled way . . .
There's nothing true but heav'n!

Charlotte remained under Mrs. Brevost's tutelage for more than another year. She studied with the French lady until 1821, when at the age of twelve she was sent to a convent—St. Joseph's, near Emmitsburg, Maryland. Even though her letters show the formality of expression required by the critical inspection of the good Sisters, the messages nevertheless reveal a very human little girl. One of them was written in 1821:

DEAR MA,

I am very happy here. The teachers are all so kind to me, and the Lady Superior notices me a great deal. I have never once been corrected since I have been at school, but have been praised for everything I do. I have received many tokens of approbation from the Superior for my proficiency in music. . . .

I am quite well and rosy, and feel as contented as I look. I rise early, and I sometime fancy myself at home with Ann Eliza,[8] skipping along the lane, leading to the barn yard. . . . The tears sometimes for a moment fill my eyes, but I brush them away, for every one looks so sweetly and kindly on me here, that I drive from my mind the beauties of home and devote myself to taking pleasure out of what I find here. . . .

The family missed Charlotte as much as she missed her parents, her sisters and her brothers, for her mother wrote her:

Your father has been drawing a few tunes on the violin for your little brother and sister to dance, this evening. They have not forgotten the danceing tunes you used to play on the pianno. Henry whistles and henrietta sings them yet. . . . (November 2, 1821)

The next we hear of Charlotte is in 1825, when she was visiting in Meadville, Pennsylvania, and her father wrote:

We are all much pleased, my dear child, to learn by your letter that you had reached Meadville in safety. . . . Remember that I have many old and good friends there both male and female, make yourself happy with them. . . . (July 29, 1825)

[8] Charlotte's younger sister, who was given the name of the first child, who died in infancy.

Most of the letters from Charlotte date from the last year and a half of her life, when she was eighteen and nineteen. They show a brilliant young lady, prim and inhibited with the conventions of the early 19th Century, yet withal a vivacious young belle whose accomplishments attracted friends, admirers, and even her rightful share of marriage proposals.

In May of 1828 Charlotte left Pittsburgh on the steamboat "Waverley," bound for Cincinnati and Louisville. In Louisville she visited the Barclay cousins, and on June 13 wrote her brother William:

It is almost a month since I left home. I spent two weeks in Cincinnati delightfully, it is the most beautifull city in the western country. To me who had been accustom'd to see houses look black [and thus spoke a young lady from Pittsburgh] it appeard to have been all built in a week. The country around is very pretty, I went 10 miles up the canal and pass'd through several locks. I think on a long journey it would be tedious—I should prefer a steamboat although it is more dangerous. . . .

I left C. two or three days before Mr. & Mrs. Baldwin with Mr. Barclay and am very much pleasd with my relations, they are the most hospitable and friendly people you could wish to see, indeed it appears to be the Kentucky character.

When I arrived here the Misses Rowans (daughters of John Rowan a member of Congress) were in Town, they claim connection with Pa, and say I must spend some time with them at Bardstown if I am in this country all summer. It is very healthy now and if it continues to be so, I will perhaps stay until Fall. Mr. Barclay has bought a new piano, and as I have none at home now that will be one inducement.

That was before William had presented the family at home with a new piano, in August. On June 21st Charlotte wrote her father that she had been in Louisville almost three weeks, and had come to feel quite at home there.

I have made a number of very agreeable acquaintances, all the young ladies of first respectability have calld on me and a number of married ladies. . . .

I was at a delightfull party at Mrs. Matthews this week, she is a lady who came from Philadelphia here last fall to teach school and has two of the most accomplished daughters, they play delightfully on the Piano and Harp, understand several languages and are altogether most interesting young ladies. They live in the same street I do and at no great distance. The temptation of taking Harp lessons was so great that I could not resist it. . . . I only intend to take a few weeks' lessons and what money I have will pay for it. I would much rather do without some gegaw and make a little improvement of some kind while I am away. . . . I have only taken three or four lessons on the Harp and can play, Come rest in this bosom, Flow on thou shining river, and I have Loved thee. They say I learn very fast. . . .

Ma did not know if I had received everything she sent, I have mentioned them all but the letters may have miscarry'd, I will mention them again; a lace cap, pocket handkerchiefs, silk dress, pair of stockings, stuf for collar, and lace to trim it, musling for peticoat, neck ribbands, I think that is all.

In August Charlotte was still in Louisville, and in a letter to her mother, written on the 12th of the month, she referred to the piano that William had bought.

I received a letter from Brother William telling me about the piano. You, my dear Mother, who know almost my thoughts on every subject can imagine how delighted I was, not from merely selfish views which would be sufficient to delight me, but now my dear Sisters will have the advantage of learning and practising—it must have been a day of rejoicing when it was brought home. It is well I was not there, I should have behaved like a fool. Ann Eliza must practice a great deal. Although so many young ladies learn to play, I have seen only two or three who you would like to hear; while I was at Mrs. Pearces they kept me playing constantly and singing. . . . The girls think Go, my Love, and Like the Gloom of Night Retireing more beautifull than any they have ever heard, and would you believe it, they think I sing delightfully.

The same letter mentions several admirers, one of whom, Mr. Prather, was later to win the fair Charlotte.

I think a Kentucky farmer's life is very happy, those who are rich and have their negros and overseer as Mrs. Pearce has; when the gentlemen come from Town, they never think of returning, but have their horses and themselves provided for, sometimes we had more than a dozen to breakfast. Mr. Prather and Churchill came out almost every day, and Mr. Nicholas Grason and others; it reminded me of the happy times I used to spend in the country at home.

The guest was quite evidently welcome with her visitors:

Mrs. Pearce seems to have taken a fancy to me, she took me in her arms and hug'd me saying at the same time she did not know what made her love me so much. I think if I could be spoild I would have been, the girls every night bespoke who would sleep with me, and always express that warm affection that is easily distinguished from incincerity.

It was in referring to her coming visit at the Rowans' in Bardstown that Charlotte showed her respect for the conventions.

I mentioned in my last letter my intention of going to Bardstown, I shall go as soon as convenient for Mr. Barclay. The day before I went to Mrs. Pearce's the last time, Miss Louisa Bullet came with her brother and Captain Hopson to ask me to go to Bardstown with them. I was to go in a gig with her brother, and she with Capt. H. but I declined going; perhaps I was a little prudish on the subject, I did not like the idea of two young ladies and gentlemen traveling without a married person. Miss Bullet might have gone as she had her brother, but I was a stranger, and *Prudence* said stay. I will perhaps go with Mr. B. this week or next.

9

In the meantime Charlotte's father had been writing her to come home, or at least to return as far as Cincinnati, where she could wait until the water was high enough for boats to navigate the rest of the trip. This was the "fever and ague" season in the South, and the parents were anxious about the health of their eldest daughter.

Charlotte replied that she had left Louisville, as her father had requested. She had, however, departed for a town farther south.

Your letter in which you express a wish that I should leave Louisville was duly receivd. I left that place on Tuesday week last with

Judge Rowan and his daughter; I mentioned in my last to Ann Eliza my intention to come, they claim me as a relation and treat me as such. Judge Rowan insists upon my staying with his family until he goes to Washington City and he will be my escort home; but that I could not think of doing, although I am grateful for the invitation. He will go in November and it is very probable I will return with him if the River is in order, it will be an excellant opportunity. There is another young lady going to Baltimore under his protection; we came up in the stage.

Bardstown is a beautifull vilige—its Catholick institutions deserve some celebrity, the Cathedral is the finest publick building I have seen, since our own Church. I have not yet visited the Nunery and Coldge, but intend to do so soon. I have two beaux who are ready for our commands, Mr. Rowan's sons; his family consists of four daughters, three sons, one married, and three grandchildren, and there are always visitors. They live in a plain, farmerlike way, just in sight of town. . . . I never met a man so aggreeable to be a great man as Judge Rowan is. I sometimes listen to his conversation until I am lost, and fear to draw a breath lest I should lose a word. (September 16, 1828)

This is a truly important letter, for it is one of the few family documents that touch on historic Bardstown. So many traditions have become associated with Stephen Foster's later connections with the place that true facts concerning family visits to the "Old Kentucky Home" are enlightening.

John Rowan, the elder, had come from Pennsylvania to Kentucky after the Revolution, and in Bardstown he built his home, "Federal Hill." As a lawyer he won a large practice, and election first to the House of Representatives in Washington, and later to the Senate. As a Kentucky gentleman he dispensed true Kentucky hospitality, aided by his slaves and the product of his spreading fields.

When the senior Rowan died in 1843 he was succeeded on his estates by "Young John," a handsome youth who was at one time (1848-1850) minister from the United States to the two Sicilies. The Rowans would have had a still closer connection with the Fosters if young John Rowan

Judge John Rowan
From a painting

John Rowan, Jr.
Sketch by Joseph Muller in the Foster
Hall Collection

Federal Hill
Sketch by Joseph Muller in the Foster Hall Collection

had been allowed his way, for though he later married Rebecca Carnes of Baltimore, and reared a family of ten children on Federal Hill, he first wanted to marry Charlotte Foster. He proposed to her during her first visit to Bardstown. Read Charlotte's letter to her mother (October 12, 1828):

On Wednesday last I return'd home [to Louisville] from Judge Rowan's where I spent three weeks very pleasantly. . . . I left the girls all in tears and I may have the vanity to think the young gentlemen were not a little grievd at my departure. . . .

I believe I am to be an old maid, I am too hard to please, but is it not better to be one than marry without loving? I will tell you a secret about my late visit to Federal Hill. I tol'd you Mr. R. had two sons at home, the eldest is about 25, a Lawyer, very clever and generally considered handsome; now it must remain between you and I if I tell you he wish'd me to engage myself to him, but as usual I could not love him, and would not do him or myself the injustice to make promises I was not inclined to perform. You may conclude I was glad to get to Louisville again. I suppose he would think I might be glad to get the son of a Senator of the United States and so distinguished a man as Judge Rowan, but I cannot let considerations of this kind influence me when my happiness for life depends on it. . . .

When Charlotte returned to Pittsburgh she was sorely missed by those she had visited. Her cousin, J. G. Barclay, wrote her from Louisville (November 30, 1828):

We were all disappointed in not receiving one short line from you by the return of the "Waverley" but I cannot believe it was neglect —you were so overjoyed at meeting your relatives and friends that you had not time. On the news of the Waverly's arrival, I hastened to the River, and who do you think I overtook going there also,— if you cant guess—it was Mr. Prather and Mr. Rowan making the same inquiries that I was. . . .

We are very lonesome since you left us, we want you back again, so make your arrangements to return with me. . . .

Charlotte spent the Winter and early Spring at home, and then in May left with Ann Eliza to attend the wedding of Matilda Prather in Louisville. Sometime in this year

Charlotte became engaged to Prather, "the dignified Mr. Prather" she wrote about in one of her letters. The exact date of her accepting his suit cannot be established, for there are a number of gaps in the letters that have been preserved. In June, when Charlotte was planning the return journey home, a trip she was never to take, her father wrote her:

We have concluded that you might just exercise your own judgment about coming home yourself with Mr. P—— We can see no impropriety in it. . . . (June 22, 1829)

Yet by August Charlotte does not seem to be engaged to any one, for in a letter to her mother she refers to attentions that may have been shown by her future fiancé:

Your and my dear Father's kind advice in a letter I received at Bardstown with regard to a certain person I try to abide by, but I think you have mistaken his politeness in thinking it anything more than a passing compliment; for my own part, I do not look upon him as anything more than a friend and am very certain he is that, as well as the rest of the family. (August 12, 1829)

In June, when Charlotte wrote her family from Louisville, she reported her own doings, as well as her care of her younger sister.

Ann Eliza is getting tired of company. There is not an evening without three or four, and sometimes half a dozen beaux, and most of them come to see her, but there is not one I believe she likes as well as *Cornelius* [probably Cornelius Darragh, a suitor in Pittsburgh], except our Cousin John [Rowan?]. . . .

The celebrated Mr. E. Forrest of the American boards will be here to-morrow when the theatre will open.

Henry Clay will be here next week and is to have a dinner given him.

Judge Rowan will leave for home on Sunday—he says they have a grudge at me for not coming up to Federal Hill; that it was as much as to say, I have been there once and that is enough. Since Ann Eliza came home [from Bardstown] I persuaded her to take an emetic—she was not sick, but complained from a headache. It relieved her. She is perfectly well, and very glad she took it as it was the means of her getting a splendid edition of *Byron's works;* Cousin Hill Rowan [a younger son] came up—I told him she was not well, and when he went to his boarding house, he sent a present to her of the above mentioned works. . . . (June 22, 1829)

By August Ann Eliza had left Charlotte in Louisville and had returned to her home in Pittsburgh. Charlotte had yielded to the persuasion of the Rowans and had visited Bardstown once more, in spite of the hesitancy that may have been caused by the presence of her rejected suitor.

The last chapter of Charlotte's life is brief and tragic. On October 13, 1829, G. M. Barclay wrote her father:

Charlotte is very much indisposed and I think you had better come to Louisville immediately. Mrs. Joshua G. Barclay has been and still is extremely ill, and from fatigue sitting up with her no doubt is the cause of Charlotte's indisposition.

The father immediately dispatched Ann Eliza on the steamboat "Sylph," but she arrived too late to see her sister again, for Charlotte died October 20. Her death was a blow to her family and to her many friends, and there are still in existence letters that lament her passing. Shortly after Ann Eliza had returned to Pittsburgh, A. Hill Rowan, John's younger brother, wrote her a long letter. He had been visiting the Barclays when Charlotte died there, and he described both her illness and her death.

. . . I cherish the memory of Charlotte; and if one agony more could have been wrung out of my heart than that which her sad, sad fate inflicted, it would have been for that Sister and those parents who have sustained in her untimely death a bereavement so heavy and so lamentable. The truth is I knew not, and I know not, *what* to write. . . .

I have in former letters already told you that I believed her distemperature was superinduced by fever, anxiety of mind for Mrs. Barclay, and individual apprehensions of death from sickness in Louisville. I do not believe there was any other cause, if there was, it was perhaps a deep melancholy, not perceivable when she was in health, and which could not be traced to any *certain* cause in sickness, as it indicated its seeming existence *alone* in the wild, plaintive and touchingly tender songs which she always sang; for she was generally cheerful, animated, vivacious & witty in her remarks and in her deportment throughout. She preserved her complexional beauty, suavity and simplicity of manners, and except to a few, whom I regret to say she could never tolerate, she was either bland & affable, urbane & polite, or gentle, affectionate and caressful, in the proportion which she loved them, for she was even to her friends, discriminating in her marks of attachment . . . but Ann Eliza, I must stop the description, the review of such scenes is too painful. I will tell you of her death.

The night of the morning which she died, I sat up and was frequently in her room. She was more tranquil, yet did not sleep, but seemed as attentive as at any time during her illness to the movements of her friends, occasionally speaking to them, and about an hour before day, when all were silent, she sang a song preserving with much melody & great accuracy, every note, but her voice was then so thickened that she did not articulate sufficiently plain for the words to be heard, or for the song to be recognized. It soon however, became more distinct, and she called for Josephine. . . . She was sent for and came, and Charlotte, taking a ring from her finger, gave it to her. Josephine asked her . . . if she must give it to Ann Eliza, she immediately and with eagerness replied *Yes*. She then gave her some messages of an affecting character to her Father, Mother, yourself & sisters & brothers. There were prayers for blessings upon you all . . . never, never have I seen any one die so easy, no convulsions, not the writhing of a feature . . . the ravages of disease were scarcely perceptible on her face . . . for there she lay serene, placid & quiescent . . . so lovely, that would her last breath have been observed by her friends, they could not & would not have believed that her gentle spirit had flown.

Such, my dear cousin, were the last moments of the lovely & beloved Charlotte. The fell influences of an infuriating malady could not make her do violence to that gentleness, delicacy and propriety of conduct which characterized her life. . . . (November 19, 1829)

The death-bed scene or "exercises" must have been discussed widely, for back in Pittsburgh, a friend, George W. Buchanan, wrote to his sister:

The recent death of Miss Charlotte Foster has cast a shade of sorrow over our whole society. . . . She was amiable, handsome and intelligent. With truth she might have been styled "the pride of our society." So fleeting is everything human. A few weeks ago, I was her partner in the gay dance; now, her spirit is in eternity. From the intelligence received by her friends, the exercises of her death-bed were of the most encouraging character, & they have the only consolation a dying friend can leave, a reasonable hope that she is now in heaven. (October 31, 1829)

Charlotte died when Stephen Foster was only three years old, and while the oldest sister often referred to "dear little Stephen" in her letters, he was too young to have been influenced by her evident brilliance, or by her musical talents. Yet it is important to know of this sister, and to realize that the surroundings which could produce Charlotte would also produce Stephen; to know that the type of songs which Charlotte sang were of a kind that Stephen was soon to write himself, and that the "deep melancholy" of Charlotte's singing was later to find poignant expression in the works of her little brother.

10

The third child of the Foster family was the second to bear the name Ann Eliza. The Ann Eliza who lived to grow up, and to be an old lady, was born January 12, 1812, when Charlotte was one month more than two years old. Some of Ann Eliza's early education was gained from the Episcopal minister, Mr. Hopkins, who had a boarding-school for a number of young ladies at his home. Ann Eliza must have been a serious-minded maiden in her youth, for none can doubt the earnestness and sincerity of a letter she wrote her father when she learned that he had recovered from the results of a slight accident. When Ann Eliza again saw this letter, fifty-five years after it was written, she remarked that "it takes a long life to get all the nonsense out of us," and she thought that there were probably few persons who "could look over the effusions of their early life with any satisfaction." The letter was written March 23, 1828, when the young lady was sixteen. Her father was in Harrisburg, at the House of Representatives.

I was very aggreeably surprised yesterday at receiving a letter from you, for I confess that I was growing a little impatient. I hope that the injury you received is not a serious one, but however trifling, do dear father be careful of it, for you know from what a slight cause the loss of your left hand proceeded. In this very instance, I have often thought that we have cause to be abundantly thankful that a Merciful Providence has preserved the hand that is of so much importance to you in the support of the family which has been lent you. As far as I can see back, we have been the especial care of our Maker otherwise we never could have stood, for you know my dear father that you have surmounted difficulties which beforehand it seemed impossible to overcome, and I can ascribe it to no other cause than that of the Lord of Hosts watching over us and guarding us from all the perils that seemed to await us. . . .

Ever since I can recollect every coming year had a more formidable aspect than the preceeding one, and it seemed almost impossible to withstand the storm any longer, but all difficulties were cleared and at its end when we looked back we scarcely knew how we had passed over them. The Eye that rules the Universe was upon us and the strong arm that reaches through Eternity upheld us; and with such stays we could rest secure, though misery in its new & hideous forms was staring us in the face. . . .

I will have to bid you good bye rather abruptly, dear father, for Ma has just sent Henry [a brother] out to know if I would not come home to spend the night with them, and as Mr. Hopkins has given his consent, I intend accompanying him immediately. . . .

Like Charlotte, Ann Eliza had her admirers, and we have already learned of the "Cornelius" who Charlotte thought should be encouraged.[9] Ann Eliza was not yet seventeen when Charlotte, in one of her letters from Louisville, asked her mother:

Does Mr. Cornelius come to see Sis Ann now? She will be a very foolish girl if she slights him, I think him one of the finest little fellows in the world, you do not meet one in a thousand with a mind like his. . . . (October 12, 1828)

[9] See page 38.

Then there was the time when Charlotte wrote that there was not one man in Louisville whom her sister liked as well as Cornelius, even when Hill Rowan was accompanying his attentions with a set of Byron to counteract the emetic Charlotte had administered.

When Ann Eliza had returned to Pittsburgh, the summer before Charlotte died, her sister wrote their mother:

Ann Eliza writes me Cornelius is gone to the Eastward, I hope she did not look cool at him on her return. . . . (August 12, 1829)

But Ann Eliza married neither Cornelius nor her cousin Rowan. She finally accepted the hand of a young Episcopal clergyman, Edward Y. Buchanan, brother of the James Buchanan who was later to become President of the United States. The couple were married April 9, 1833, when the bride was twenty-one, and her little brother Stephen was not yet seven. The next day Ann Eliza's father wrote Brother William:

As you will naturally expect, I have the satisfaction to inform you of the marriage of your dear Sister last evening, at half past six o'clock, it took place in Christ's Church in the presence of all our family, and a very respectable collection of friends and acquaintances. The ceremony was performed by Dr. Upfold. Dear Ann Eliza is gone from us, but it is a source of great consolation that she is under the protection of a most amiable and worthy man. They set out in a carriage to Greensburgh to visit Mr. Buchanan's mother and sister, they will return on Monday, remain a few days with us and set out on Friday week for their residence at Meadville. Your very kind present of 50 dollars to Ann Eliza came in good time to enable her to complete her wardrobe comfortably. . . .

The Buchanans were not in Meadville for long, for it was in Allegheny, just one day after her father and mother had moved into a frame house opposite Smoky Island that Ann Eliza's first child was born, May 3, 1834. The child was a little boy, named James, for his uncle. Edward Buchanan's health was a source of worry, and when the

Fosters considered going on a farm after William the senior's experience as Toll Collector, the Buchanans thought that Edward might benefit by going there too. For a time he had not been preaching, but had been travelling as a missionary agent through Pennsylvania. His physicians thought it was "necessary to save his life that he should travel."

Finally Buchanan was advised to live in Florida, but a doctor in Philadelphia put an end to all his troubles. Foster, senior, wrote to William, junior:

Mr. Buchanan proceeded as far as Philada. with the view of going by Sea to Florida, but on his arrival there, consulted Doctr. Harris, the most celebrated Physician in the city, who informed him that his complaint was not produced by affection of the lungs, but was owing to too great an extension of the palate of the throat. He performed an operation by cutting a piece off it, and Mr. B. has since remained with his brother James at Lancaster, still under care of the Doctor, and by a letter recd. from him yesterday we are informed he is almost entirely restored; the Doctor says his lungs are perfectly sound, and he need not go to the South. (December 7, 1834)

Sometime in 1835 or 1836 Buchanan was assigned to a post in Pequea, Pennsylvania. The family lived in a lonely spot, a mile from the nearest neighbor, and a half mile from the public road. It was Buchanan's task to establish Episcopal missions in new places, and he was gone from home for many days at a time. Ann Eliza had a woman to help her, and a man who hung about and helped with the chores. In 1836 the second child was born, a daughter named Annie, and Eliza Foster came to stay with her daughter.

We have another glimpse of Ann Eliza's family in a letter that Brother William wrote in September 1843. The Buchanans were living in a place called Paradise, and William and his wife Elizabeth took their little daughter, Charlotte Frances, to be baptized by the Reverend Buchanan.

It was quite a family meeting at the christening of our little Charlotte Frances. You know the prayer book requires for a female, two god-mothers, and so Elizabeth and Sister Ann Eliza stood up along with me, and the dear little thing behaved admirably. She was entirely quiet. . . . She was the sixth baptized by Mr. Buchanan on that day, and at the same (afternoon) services. . . . Ann Eliza looks in much better health than when I saw her last fall. . . . Her youngest child, Edward, is a prodigy for size and a beautiful boy. . . . Mr. Buchanan looks more robust and healthy than I ever saw him, and all their children look healthy and well. . . . James is a large boy, and can take the horse to water, besides has made good progress with his books. . . .

The Edward to whom William referred was Ann Eliza's third child, and there were yet to be five more little Buchanans—eight children in all. In 1855 the family was living in Olney, Pennsylvania, and later they moved to Philadelphia, where Ann Eliza died at the age of seventy-nine, in April, 1891. The operation on Mr. Buchanan's palate was most surely of permanent benefit, for he survived his wife by almost four years.

II

After Ann Eliza, the next entry in the Foster family Bible records the birth of William Barckly (sic) Foster, "born 7th May 1814, 6 oClock P.M." This was the William, junior, who died the following March 26 (1815), and it was soon after his death that the adopted William, junior, joined the family.

The next child was Henry Baldwin, born March 23, 1816, at eleven o'clock in the morning. Henry was named for a friend of his father's, the Henry Baldwin who in his day was a prominent lawyer and jurist.

Elected to Congress in 1816, Baldwin was appointed an associate justice of the United States Supreme Court in 1830 as a reward for his active support of Jackson in 1828. He was an erratic person, said to have been insane in his later years when sometimes he became uncontrollable in his conduct on the bench.

There are frequent references to Baldwin's namesake, Henry Baldwin Foster, in the correspondence of the Foster family. When Charlotte was visiting in Meadville, Ann Eliza wrote her that "Henry minds the pigs every day," and there are other accounts of the boy's part in the family life and routine. When he was sixteen he was sent to Basenheim, a sort of manual training institute at Zelienople, Pennsylvania. It was thought that such work would improve his health, for his family feared he would have consumption.

Henry's health was a frequent topic of discussion among the members of the family. In 1833 we learn that "Henry is going up to-morrow to learn to be a tanner with Mr. Singer, and I am in hopes it will be the means of restoring him to perfect health" (Henrietta's letter to Brother William, October 27). In 1834, after William Foster, senior, had resigned as Canal Collector, he hoped to put Henry in a partnership with William, but the following year Henry had employment of his own, as a clerk with a local Pittsburgh firm, Hutcheson and Ledlie. He evidently travelled for this concern, for in 1836 (March 10) he wrote his mother, who was then in Youngstown:

We have at length arrived here [Pittsburgh] after an absence of nearly 2 months and have enjoyed excellent Health during my absence.

While at Nashville the barkeeper and myself (for want of a better companion) hired a horse and rode out to the Hermitage, which is a very neat Building much the form of Mr. Avery's in Allegh. surrounded by 1200 acres of land and worked by 100 Negroes. From thence I procured a Hickory Staff for pa, and some Rose Roots from the gardener for Etty. . . .

Tell Mit and Stevy [10] to be good boys and go to school regularly and when they have time, what kind of fellers they have for play-

[10] Morrison and Stephen Foster, aged 12 and 9.

mates and how they spend their time, will be thankfully recd. in a
letter from either. . . .

During the hard times of 1837, when conditions were so
bad that William Foster wrote William, junior, that "our
country is in a terrible state of depression" and that "the
countryman, when he looks at a *shinplaster* for 25 cts. to
take the price of a quart of cherries, damns all banks and
hurrahs for Jackson," Henry was dropped from the payroll
of Hutcheson and Ledlie. Afterwards, sometime in 1838,
his father was able to help him enter partnership with a
Mr. Skinner in a general store in Warren, Pennsylvania,
and in 1840 he joined Brother William in Towanda.

Henry was always socially inclined, and like his father,
optimistic and guileless. When he was young he often
fancied himself in love, though his affairs never lasted for
long. He frequently unburdened himself of his thoughts in
letters to Brother William. On March 25, 1842, Henry
wrote his brother:

Selina and I got up quite a flirtation and there is no Knowing
where it may end, as both of us manifested pretty strong symtums
of attachment for each other.

And again, the following April 24:

I received a very affectionate letter from Selina and wrote her a
very friendly one in answer. I do not know as yet what course to
pursue until I hear what Pa thinks about it. What say you, brother?
Had I better go the whole figure?

It is not known whether Pa, Brother William, or Henry
himself vetoed Selina, or whether, perhaps, Selina herself
was consulted with negative results. At any rate Henry
remained a bachelor until he married Mary Burgess, January 12, 1847.

It was in the Fall of 1841 that Foster, senior, received
his appointment to the Treasury Department from Walter
Forward. Henry also went to Washington, where he was

given a position in the Land Office of the Treasury. Although his father soon returned to Allegheny, where he had been elected Mayor of the city, Henry stayed in Washington for eight years.

The letters that Henry wrote from the Capital tell not only of his own doings, they contain also numerous pictures of the life in mid-century Washington. One of the early letters written from Washington, addressed to William, tells of Henry's own coming to the city, and of his father's leaving. It is dated December 20, 1841.

Pa left this [place] on the 15th inst. for Pittsb. I found him when I arrived here busily engaged in the Treasury Building writing. After the usual Salutations, he accompanied me to Fuller's Tavern and had my baggage removed to his boarding house, which I found to be a very Comfortable one, situated on Pennsylvania Avenue between 10 & 11 Streets, and kept by an elderly Gentleman by the name of King, who has a very agreeable family & ten boarders, among whom is General Stokely, member of Congress from Steubenville, Ohio. Price of board per week, $4, as low as any respectable boarding house in the Citty. . . . Some of the members of Congress pay as high as $14 per week! Now I don't consider this any great scratch of a place after all. There is one thing certain that it contains about as many fools as any place I ever was in. It appears as if the Government was the whole and only Support of the Place, and yet the members of the most dependent families carry their heads so high that you could scarcely touch them with a ten foot pole.

The same letter told of the work at the Treasury Department, and its Land Office which was later to be organized as a separate unit of the government, the Department of the Interior.

We keep bank Hours at the Treasury, working from nine in the morning until three in the afternoon, Really! The building is a magnificent one, built of solid stone four stories high, with Thirty Three Tremendous columns in front. There are four clerks in the room I write in, two of whom are Gentlemen with nine & ten in family, and receiving the same salary as Pa ($1000). We are all engaged in the same business, which is very simple, recording certificates of land sales, and making out patents, which I can do as well as any of them. I dine at three o'clock (it being the fashionable hour throughout the City) after which I generally take a stroll out to see the fashions, up to the Capitol, down to the Steamboat landing, out to Georgetown, or round the President's house.

Henry's opinion of Washington as not "any great scratch of a place" probably changed, for subsequent letters to William tell of parties and gayety in profusion. On March 25, 1842, Henry wrote:

About a week after you left, the President [John Tyler] had another Levee, which by far surpassed the one you attended, as he had the East Room thrown open and splendidly illuminated by five large Chandeliers, attended by a large concourse of People & a fine band of music. Gen. Patton & I hired a hack between us, and took Ma & Mrs. Patton. [This was the time when Henry's mother, Eliza Foster, was visiting in Washington, and later in Baltimore.] . . .

Henry missed one of the most important "levees" at the White House.

There has been one during my absence which was attended by Charles Dickens and Washington Irving, so I missed the best one of all.

On April 24, 1842, Henry wrote William of the scene that followed Henry Clay's resignation from the Senate.

Mr. Clay took his leave of Washington City this afternoon and I understand it was quite an imposing sight, all the members of the Senate and several from the House being present. They all took off their hats and held down their heads.

A letter dated June 30, 1842, told of the political situation.

I presume you [William] have heard of the Veto of the Postponement Bill by the President & have no doubt there is considerable confusion to-day in Congress in consequence of it. I enquired of Irwin yesterday how they received it, to which he replied that it was expected he would Veto it. I understand the President agrees to sign a bill should the duty be 50 pr. ct. provided that amt. is necessary to support government, if they will repeal the distribution bill, but will not agree to distribute the proceeds of the public lands among the states and increase the Tariff to make up for it. . . . Huzza for John Tiler! [sic] I say he is not so easy headed, or beheaded as they think for. Too much old Hickory in him.

There is also an account of Washington's diversions in this letter.

The principal amusement at present is promenading in the Capitol & Presidents grounds to the music of the Marine Band, on every Thursday & Saturday Evening at 6 o'clock, and as I want to go up to the Capitol this evening I am writing this in a great hurry it being about the time the music commences. . . .

Mrs. Patten's daughter is here, a very pretty girl, jet black hair & eyes. I visit Mrs. Eaton's frequently and find her and her two pretty Daughters extremely agreeable. Ex-Vice Presidentess, you know.[11]

In a letter to William, written the following August 2 (1842) Henry told William of his own advancement.

In a report made by an investigating committee to Congress of the number and qualifications of the clerks, my name stands thus— Henry B. Foster, Salary $1000, attentive and a good clerk.

Henry held his position in the Land Office until the accession of Zachary Taylor to the presidency, and the appoint-

[11] There was no Vice-President named Eaton. It is possible that this sentence may refer to the former Peggy O'Neill, wife of John Henry Eaton, Secretary of War under Andrew Jackson, and from 1836 to 1840 Minister to Spain. It was Eaton who presented Wm. B. Foster's government claim to Congress in 1846. Mrs. Eaton was herself a colorful figure in Washington. The daughter of a Washington tavern keeper, a noted beauty, she had first married a purser in the United States Navy, a man named Timberlake, who committed suicide in 1828. Gossip regarding her conduct toward Eaton while she was still married to Timberlake caused Washington society to refuse to recognize her for several years. Andrew Jackson, while President, endeavored to break down the hostility toward Mrs. Eaton, because of his friendship for both her husband and herself. Partly for this reason Jackson almost completely re-organized his cabinet. It is said that this episode helped to strengthen the cordiality between Jackson and Martin Van Buren, who himself had befriended Mrs. Eaton, and to alienate Jackson and Calhoun, then Vice-President, whose wife had refused to recognize Mrs. Eaton socially.

By the time Henry was in Washington, this Mrs. Eaton had become popular in the society of Madrid, where she lived from 1836 to 1840, while her husband was Minister to Spain.

ment of Thomas Ewing as Secretary of the newly created Department of the Interior. The Pittsburgh *Morning Post* commented on Henry Foster's removal from office (August 13, 1849):

When THOMAS EWING was called to take charge of the "Department of the Interior," it was not to be expected he would retain Democrats in office, especially when they were appointed by, or at the instance of, MR. FORWARD. The speculator in land scrip has an undying antipathy with every man who was connected with President TYLER, and of course could not think of retaining in office clerks appointed during that administration. Accordingly it was resolved upon that a work of wholesale proscription should be commenced. To carry this out with greater expedition *blank letters of dismissal* were printed, which were easily filled up by writing names and dates. One of these beautiful whig epistles is now before us, addressed to Mr. FOSTER. . . . Its brevity is only surpassed by the celebrated dispatch sent by Cæsar to the Roman Senate. . . .

It will be observed that no charge whatever was preferred against Mr. FOSTER, affecting his fidelity or capacity. The "Secretary of the Interior" had reason to suspect that he was a Democrat, which was a great *crime* in the eyes of Z. Taylor & Co., who obtained the places they now hold by extravagant professions of no-partyism.

In a few years the Democracy will be in power again, when the Goths will most assuredly be driven from the Capital. Tom Ewing and every other proscriptionist at Washington, will be hurled from power without much ceremony. . . .

Henry had meanwhile married Mary Burgess, January 12, 1847, and when he left Washington, he took his wife to Allegheny, where they lived for a time with his father's family—father, mother, Morrison, Stephen, and two servants. The rest of Henry's life was spent around Pittsburgh. He had a strong attachment for the place, and often he would be seen walking around the scenes of his childhood in the Lawrenceville section.

His death was sudden and tragic—he was killed in the fire of 1870. On June 28 lightning struck the plant of the Eclipse Oil Works, and Henry Foster, an employee, was in the office, which caught fire as soon as the first oil tank burst. The Pittsburgh papers lamented the tremendous destruction of property caused when the fire extended to six adjoining oil plants, and stated that the "saddest incident connected with this most disastrous conflagration was the death of Mr. Henry B. Foster." [12]

12

The next of the Foster children was Henrietta Angelica, born September 14, 1818, at twelve o'clock. There was another birth in the Foster household on that day, for the family Bible shows that Thomas Hunter, "a bound boy," was born on that same fourteenth of September. Tom's mother was one of the Foster servants, married to a philandering soldier from the Arsenal, a man who one day before Tom's birth threw his wife down a flight of stairs, and thinking he had killed her drowned himself in the Allegheny River. The boy stayed with the family until his sixteenth year, when he left for the West and was never heard from again.

Henrietta lived to be sixty years old, until March 13, 1879. She married twice, bore seven children, and is survived by a goodly company of grandchildren and greatgrandchildren, among the former the beloved Henrietta Crosman, who, among her many achievements as an actress, made the character of Shakespeare's "Rosalind" a living and vital figure to her generation.

Henrietta Foster played a major rôle in the Foster family affairs. She was a witty person, yet almost fanatically religious, and her comments on the views of her brothers and sisters are always illuminating, even though they may have caused argument and controversy. "Etty" was only eight years older than Stephen; she was closer to him than was Ann Eliza, and more of an influence on his early life. In May, 1833, the month after Ann Eliza's marriage, Hen-

[12] *Pittsburgh Evening Chronicle,* June 29, 1870.

rietta and Stephen were taken by their mother on a trip
to Augusta, Kentucky. Eliza Foster described this journey
in a letter to William, junior:

It has been one week this day since I return'd from a long journey.
In the first place, your Father conducted me with Henrietta and
Stevan aboard the Napolian and placed me under the care of Captain Stone. . . . We landed on the fourth night at eleven o'clock at
Augusta, a beautiful village on the bank of the Ohio in Kentucky
where I have two brothers living very neatly. Joseph [Tomlinson]
the eldest, where I stayed three weeks is President of the Colledge,
and a fine, amiable, gentlemanly little man. Henrietta had a fine
opportunity of practicing on the piano at his house. When we left
Augusta, my brother pay'd my passage, and put me on board the
Champlain, a daily packet which convey'd me to Cincinnati, where
I remained a week at Mr. Cassilys on Broad Way, handsomly
treated. It is scarcely necessary to tell you how beautifull that City
is, which I left in such great stile, you would have thought it was
Mrs. Webster, the statesman's lady, as he was on a visit there at the
same time I was. Mr. Cassily gallanted me down to the water in
his new state coach, where Captain Stone again received us and we
went to Louisville on the Napolian. Captain Erwin, partner of
Cockran, was passenger on her, he very politely waited on George
Barclay and inform'd him of my being at the landing. He brought
a hacenny coach down for me and escorted me up to his house. He
lives delightfully on Market Street. I made a visit of a week at his
house and saw many people, and left in fear and trembling lest the
Cholara Asphyzia should overtake us. But Bless God, ever mercifull
and gracious to one of the least deserveing of so many kind provi-
dences—after spending a tedious week on the river, we arrived at
home in good health where I found the destroying angle yet a
stranger. (July 9, 1833)

In October, Henrietta herself wrote to Brother William:

I have never written to you, my dear brother, and therefore I feel
almost ashamed to write now, but to begin, we are all very well except
that ma has had a very bad toothache for two or three days, but she
is getting quite well again, and little Stephy had his eye bitten by a
spider, and it was very much swolin indeed, but he is getting well
too. . . . I am going to school to Miss Parry and am very much
pleased with her indeed, but as my quarter is nearly up I shall soon
quit. Henry and I have had a delightful visit up to Springdale. . . .

I must go and get ready to go to church and therefore must make a stop. (October 27, 1833)

In 1835 when part of the family moved to Youngstown, Henrietta went there to live with her mother and her two youngest brothers, Morrison and Stephen. The father stayed in Pittsburgh to manage the store he had established in partnership with Hall. From a letter Henrietta wrote William in the following year, it is evident that she paid a visit to her father in Pittsburgh:

> I have received your letter by Mr. Hall on yesterday evening and was very sorry to hear that you have such a cold. Pa is going home next week, and he says that I may go with him. Do write soon and tell me about the little boys. Oh! I do want to see them so badly, poor little fellows, they must be as lonely as I am. Sometimes I get so homesick (when I see any person from Youngstown particularly), that I do not know what to do with myself. . . . Mr. Mahon is as attentive as ever, only a little more so. He comes only once a day now—that is, he comes in the morning and stays all day. I am in an awful pickle about it. . . .
>
> I was at the theatre on Monday with Mr. and Mrs. King, La Tour de Vesle was played. Mrs. Pritchard making her first appearance as Margaret of Burgundy. She is a splendid actress, but that is all I can say of her. . . .
>
> I have learned a beautiful new song since I saw you, My hopes are departed forever, is the name of it. . . .
>
> Cousin Jane sends her love to you and Tom Wick. . . . (April 30, 1836)

It was Tom (Thomas L.) Wick whom Henrietta married, on October 20 of that same year, 1836. He was the brother of Mary Wick, who married William Foster a year later. The couple made their home in Youngstown, where the first baby, Mary Wick, was born July 28, 1837. Henrietta wrote Brother William that her daughter "is a sweet little creature (at least I think so): she has deep blue eyes and black hair." It was this blue-eyed baby who later became the mother of Henrietta Crosman.

In 1840 the Wick family moved to Warren, Pennsyl-

vania, and Foster, senior, told of the moving in a letter to
William.

> Thursday morning after you left us, Thomas Wick and myself
> set out with his Horses and Sleigh to Warren in Pennsylvania, with
> the view of ascertaining what encouragement he could have in re-
> moving his Store and Family there for a permanent establishment.
> We made the journey in two days, 100 miles. . . . Thomas made a
> conditional bargain . . . and immediately on his return . . . ob-
> tain'd his father's approbation, packed up his goods, loaded up two
> sleds with them, and rigged up a large sled with carpeting around
> it in which he placed himself and family. . . . They took only a few
> trunks of clothing with them, left the House and furniture here just
> as it was. The furniture we are packing, and if the sledding re-
> mains good, will send one or two loads, the balance by canal and
> Steam Boats via Pittsbg. when the navigation opens. . . . (January
> 27, 1840)

Thomas Wick did not enjoy robust health, and the store
in Warren was evidently not prosperous, for in another
year the family was back in Youngstown. For a time in
1841 they lived with the Fosters in Allegheny, where they
paid "one dollar per day for boarding and lodging, including a hired girl," while Foster, senior, went to Warren to
wind up his son-in-law's business.[13]

In 1842, May 24, Thomas Wick died, leaving Henrietta
a widow with three children: Mary, Eliza ("Lidie") and
Thomas, a baby one month old. In the following August
Eliza Foster and Stephen went to stay with Henrietta
for a few months at Youngstown, and when the mother returned to Pittsburgh in November she left Stephen with
his sister.

Four years later, January 5, 1847, Henrietta married
her second husband, Jesse Thornton of Youngstown, where
her mother reported—"Mr. Thornton has Etty nicely
pack'd in cottage stile, with a nigro to wait on her." (August 23, 1847) Henrietta bore Thornton four children.

[13] See page 109.

Sometime before 1859 the family moved to Warren, Ohio,[14] and it was there that Stephen Foster and his wife visited Henrietta before he went to New York in 1860. Thornton became a major in the Union army during the Civil War and saw active service.

It is from Henrietta's extreme religious views that we learn of the church connections of the other members of the family. William Foster, senior, was active in the Episcopal Church. At one time he was a vestryman, but he never became a church member. This worried his daughter Etty, and she frequently urged him to be confirmed. In 1859, June 10, she wrote a letter to her brother Morrison, thoroughly typical of her religious zeal.

Your very affectionate letter of the 1st of this month was received. . . . You need not be afraid of my being dispirited, I have no fears but that my Heavenly Father will provide those things which are needful for me. . . . As to all these things, and indeed every thing that relates to me, either bodily, or spiritually, "I know in Whom I have trusted," and am persuaded that nothing shall ever separate me from His love. It is of Him who has been so much to me that I would venture again to speak to you, my very dear brother. I owe it to you, I owe it to my God, and I owe it to myself, to speak to you out of the abundance of my heart. He alone knows the deep love I have for you, He alone knows how my poor prayers go up to him daily, for my precious Morrison and Stephen. William and Henry are already in the Ark of Safety; for them therefore my prayers are calm, knowing that they have put themselves voluntarily into His fold, the Church, and that if they but continue faithful, he will bring them into His fold at last. But you, my dear brother, and dear Stephy, are wilfully remaining out of His Church, keeping yourselves away from those holy influences, which course you must know is calculated to grieve away the gentle spirit of God entirely. So, after I have presented my own children, my husband, dear Siss Annie, William and Henry before the Savior for His blessing and protection, there comes up the names of my sweet brothers, Morrison and Stephen, and it seems as if my very soul would burst away and

[14] The distinction between Warren, Ohio, and Warren, Pa., should be noted. It was in Warren, Pa., that Henrietta and Thomas Wick lived in 1840, and where Henry entered a partnership in 1838. When Henrietta married Thornton she moved from Youngstown to Warren, Ohio.

lay hold on my Saviour's garments, that I might detain Him until
he would promise to bless you and save you.

I hope you will forgive me if there is anything in this letter that
looks like preaching to you, you know I seldom say anything on the
subject, though indeed it is always the subject nearest my heart.

Good bye, my dear brother, remember that while I live, and you
live, you have the sincere love and earnest prayers of your sister,
Henrietta.

13

The two brothers nearest in age to Stephen, Dunning
and Morrison, were the ones most closely associated with
his active career, and Morrison was his companion in childhood. Dunning McNair Foster was born on the afternoon
of January 26, 1821, at three o'clock. When he was still a
young boy the family reverses had begun, and as early as
1833, when he was twelve years old, his father wrote to
Brother William:

> Could you get Henry or Dunning a situation as a rod bearer on
> the Canal? They must go to business this spring. I can't keep them
> together, they are both good boys. (April 10)

Dunning did not become a rod bearer, but in June found
employment in Hogan's book store in Pittsburgh. The
following year, August 1834, his father "engaged a situation for Dunning with Mr. George Cochran in his domestic
warehouse." Three years later Foster hoped to send this
son to a school for civil engineers, but his plans were
thwarted when the trip to Erie for settlement of his claim
against the transportation company proved in vain. Shortly
afterwards Dunning was given the position with Hutcheson
and Ledlie that Henry had lost because of hard times.
When conditions improved Henry had gone to Warren,
Pennsylvania.

Two years later we learn that "Dunning is still at his
labors with Hutcheson and Ledlie; he made a long tour
of collecting for them in Tennessee this spring" (Father's

letter to William, July 25, 1839). Soon after Dunning must have changed his profession, for less than a year later, March 24, 1840, Foster, senior, wrote William that "Dunning is still on a steam boat as clerk."

From that time Dunning was closely associated with river boats, and a few years before his death was captain of the "Norma," a steamboat in the Mississippi trade. In 1846 there was an interruption in his career of navigation. He entered partnership in a firm named Irwin and Foster, commission merchants of Cincinnati. It is well that Dunning's career in Cincinnati can be thoroughly documented, and that the city directories of those years record the existence of Irwin and Foster, first at No. 4 Cassilly's Row, and later at 22 Broadway, between Pearl and Second Streets. Also that Dunning M. Foster lived first at the Broadway Hotel and then at the boarding house of Mrs. Jane Griffin. By that time Mrs. Griffin had two Fosters for boarders, Dunning and Stephen.[15]

It was to Dunning that Stephen Foster came as a clerk and bookkeeper late in 1846, and remained until early in 1850. We shall hear much about this period in Stephen's life, for it was in these years that he gained his early successes as a song writer, and finally decided that composing would be his profession. The contemporary documents show what actually occurred during these years, and disprove many of the false statements that are made about Stephen's life—such absurd traditions as the one which pictures him working in the grocery store of a brother, who was constantly driving him to his work and always fretting because Stephen preferred writing songs on wrapping paper to waiting on customers. There was no grocery store, and Stephen learned to be a good bookkeeper.

While Stephen was in Cincinnati Dunning enlisted for service in the Mexican War. Under date of June 9, 1847, he made his will. In the form of a letter to his brother

15 See pages 135-136.

Morrison, he wrote a list of moneys due him, amounting to $1,276, and then proceeded:

In case any accident should befall me, I wish all the resources I have in this world settled up as soon as possible and converted into cash the whole amount to be invested for the benefit of our dear Mother, as long as she lives, after her death to be applied to the benefit of our dear Father, as long as he lives, should he survive Mother. After the death of both let it go as the law directs, as I have no preference among my brothers and sisters. . . .

All my clothes you can have—my watch give to Stephen, in case it should ever reach you. Any small trinkets that may be found in my personal baggage, distribute as you may see proper to the different members of the family. The emerald gold ring I have left with Stephen give to Ma. . . .

In case I should die in Mexico, I wish my body brought home if it can be found; pay the expenses out of any property I may leave. I hope however that it will not be found necessary to comply with the last wish expressed, as I expect to be able to bring my own body home. . . .

This hope was fulfilled, though when he returned to Cincinnati a year later (June, 1848) he was in exceedingly poor health, and never fully recovered. He actually contracted the consumption that the family had feared for Henry, and died March 31, 1856, thirty-five years old.

Shortly after Stephen left Cincinnati for Allegheny, Dunning gave up his business. The Cincinnati Directory of 1851 shows that the location at 22 Broadway was occupied by his partner alone, as Archibald Irwin, Jr. & Company, commission and forwarding merchants and steamboat agents. In 1854 Dunning was travelling near Vicksburg as captain of the "Norma."

On March 17, 1856, he wrote the following letter to Morrison:

Since the change of weather I have been obliged to keep my room at the Broadway Hotel [Cincinnati] and am quite weak. . . .

I don't feel ill enough for any of you to come here, and hope by care and attention to be strong enough to see you again. I made a fatal mistake in remaining here this winter.

The mistake was indeed fatal, for he died a few days later, March 31. Henry, Morrison and Stephen reached him before he died, and brought his remains to Allegheny, where the services were held in Stephen's home. Dunning was the only member of the Foster family to grow up who never married.

14

Morrison Foster was next in age to Stephen, and because he was so closely associated with his younger brother in both childhood and his later years, we shall meet him often. The world owes a great debt to Morrison Foster. It was he who preserved most of the family letters that are now in existence, and when he gathered material for his biography of Stephen,[16] he obtained from other members of the family the letters in their possession. He also kept a scrap book, in which he pasted newspaper accounts of events that occurred during his long life, as well as obituary notices of his relatives, and many items about his brother Stephen.

Morrison lived to be almost eighty-one years old, and he provides the link between Stephen and the present generation. He followed the Foster tradition in his political activity, and was a prominent Democrat in the several cities he lived in. In 1882 he was elected a state senator in Pennsylvania, but the election board gave the seat to his opponent on a technicality. Foster engaged counsel, and finally won a decision in a contest that took over two years. By that time the senatorial term had expired, yet the next Legislature recognized the justice of the case, and voted Morrison his full salary for the term, and all his expenses in the contest.

The family Bible records Morrison's birth as occurring at 1 P.M. on the 10th of June, 1823. His business career started when he was sixteen, and his father wrote to Brother William:

[16] *Op. cit.*

Morrison Foster in 1849
Photograph in Foster Hall Collection

William B. Foster, Jr.
Sketch by Joseph Muller in Foster Hall Collection

Morrison is to go into the warehouse of Wrenshall & Co. cotton factory at Pttsbg. on the 1st of Septr. Mr. McCormick one of the partners took a great fancy for him. (July 25, 1839)

September came and the plan was carried out. On the 29th Henrietta wrote William:

Pa is in Pittsburg, having gone there to get Mitty fix'd at Mr. McCormack's [sic].

Mitty, and sometimes Mit, was the family nickname for Morrison. He stayed with McCormick for over ten years, and became a buyer who travelled on the river boats between Pittsburgh and New Orleans, purchasing cotton for the Pittsburgh factory and for export. His start with the firm was humble, but entirely satisfactory to his mother, who told Brother William:

Morrison is place'd for two years with Mr. McCormack, as clerck, and Messenger, boarding and washing found, and 100 dollars a year, he was applied for, and is highly pleased, having a fine little Poney to ride on when he is sent out. He has no lamp-lighting, shutting up, ware house cleaning or anything to abuse his clothes, and is treated with much respect, as he performs his duties promptly and well. (August 7, 1840)

It is evident that Eliza Foster had no particular favorites among her children; she loved them all. That Morrison had his full share of her affections is apparent from a number of her letters, particularly one she wrote from Washington, when she was staying with Henry after her husband had left the Treasury Department to take up his office as Mayor of Allegheny.

I sit down after night to write you a few lines for the purpose of encloseing five dollars for your own private use, either to buy a hat with or any other usefull purpose as regards your clothing. I would be glad that you would not mention to any one the having received the hatte or the money, but write to me as soon as possible everything that has transpired since I left you; have you been any where, and how are you content? . . . is all right with Pa and Stephen? William is gone and Henry and I have it all by ourselves; we take a walk up the Pennsylvania Avenue every afternoon to see the fashions. Arch Street in Philadelphia is nothing to it. I have been once at the Capitol and at one levee. On Sunday the day was so wet I did not go to church. I saw Harmar Denny at the Presidents, he is now at New York. . . .

Tell the Evanses that black velvit spencers with short sleeves and white thin scirts for the evening is the latest trick, and small parisols in a cold winterry day with clocks and muffs. I saw at least one hundred on the Avenue the day I went to the Capitol.

Good night, my dear son, take care of your precious health. I will write to you shortly again a letter that you can shew to the rest. Remember that I am your own affectionate Mother. (February 16, 1842)

Although Morrison stayed with the McCormick firm until he joined the Penn Cotton Mills as general manager, in 1851 or 1852, he was at least tempted by the California gold rush in 1849. On January 13th of that year, Dunning wrote:

I am very glad to learn that you have abandoned the California gold speculation as I feel confident that it is not an undertaking that would yield profit enough for the deprivation of comfort that you would naturally be subjected to. I agree with a letter written in those parts that a full stomach of good food is better than full pockets of gold dust.

In 1857 Morrison resigned from the Penn Mills to join Brother William in Philadelphia.

William's health was failing and he asked Morrison to come and help him. Morrison stayed with William for two years and then went to Cleveland to enter the iron and steel business, with a Major W. F. Carey. From this firm he went to the Juniata Iron Works, of Pittsburgh, as manager of the Cleveland office. When he returned to Pittsburgh in 1869, it was to enter business for himself, in the operation of coal mines located at Salineville, Ohio. This occupied him until within a few years of his death, which occurred May 14, 1904.

Morrison's first wife was Jessie Lightner, herself a friend of Stephen, and a singer who took part in many of the musical evenings to which Stephen brought his new songs. A few years after her death, November 5, 1882, Morrison married a second time, when his bride was Rebecca S. Snowden, granddaughter of the John M. Snowden who was mayor of Pittsburgh in the year that Stephen Foster was born.

Morrison was to Stephen what Brother William had been to the entire family. Of all the Fosters, Morrison was probably the only one who really understood this dreaming, seemingly drifting, and thoroughly lovable brother. It was beyond his power to save Stephen from his tragic fate, yet we shall see how it was Morrison who stood by him in his time of greatest need, and who tried to take him away from the surroundings that proved his undoing. It was to Morrison, too, that Stephen's wife turned when she felt she was misunderstood, and it was to him she appealed when she thought that Stephen might still be spared the end that awaited him.

***

These then, are the dear friends and gentle hearts who produced Stephen Foster, and who form the background for a career that is difficult to understand unless we know them all. Their attitude towards Stephen was in many ways unfortunate. Had they known what modern psychologists teach us to-day about the development and training of children, they might have known that the idle, dreaming ways of Stephen's youth were in themselves an indication of where his outlet lay; that his strange talent for music was the secret of his future, and not a mere distraction from the serious business of life.

Yet the ignorance of the Fosters was not an ignorance peculiar to them, it was a nineteenth century attitude that was tragically common to all Americans. Up to the present day it has been our business to settle and cultivate a continent, and such settlement has of necessity meant the cultivation of material things, the physical necessities of life. To this end, the making of money through the accepted channels of business became by tradition the greatest of virtues. With this as the national creed, how could it be expected that the Fosters of pioneer and frontier Pittsburgh would be endowed with an intelligence and an enlightenment that would have been an anachronism?

That would surely be asking too much, and we must rest content with the knowledge that they were kindly gentlefolk who had their share of the culture of the time, who loved their strange genius even if they could not comprehend the significance he was later to achieve.

II

STEPHY

I

WHEN Stephen Foster was born, men in Pittsburgh shouted mighty cheers, sang lusty songs, and drank so many toasts that some of them were tipsy. Bands played "Hail Columbia," "The Star Spangled Banner," "Yankee Doodle," and "Hail to the Chief," while cannon with their noisy salutes shook the ground so heavily that some were afraid they would disturb the delicate, though accustomed operation at the White Cottage.

Stephen's father aided the Mayor of Pittsburgh, John M. Snowden, in the conduct of the celebration, but unfortunately for Stephen's biographers, none of the salutes, none of the toasts, and not any of the singing had anything to do with Stephen. It was not that seers or astrologers had been able to predict the newcomer's fame, but rather that the occasion was the fiftieth anniversary of the signing of the Declaration of Independence, July 4, 1826.

Had Stephen been the first, rather than the ninth child his wife had borne him, William B. Foster might not have felt as free to absent himself from his home at noon on that 4th of July. Surely by the time the celebration started, he must have known that the little fellow was soon to be born, for according to the family Bible, Stephen came into the world at exactly twelve-thirty.

The *Pittsburgh Mercury* of July 12 tells of three celebrations on the 4th—one on the west side of the Allegheny River, by the Pittsburgh Light Artillery; another at Elliot's Spring where the jubilee was conducted by the

Democratic Republicans of Pittsburgh and vicinity; and the third at "Foster's Grove," a jubilee celebrated by another group of Democratic Republicans, who had the distinction of attendance and participation by the Mayor.

It was the Foster Grove jubilee that had first place in the *Mercury,* perhaps because the Mayor was its editor.

At 12 o'clock the Declaration of Independence was read by Mr. *N. R. Smith,* after which an excellent oration was delivered by *Samuel Frew,* Esq. *John M. Snowden,* Esq. Mayor of the City, acted as president of the day, supported by *Wm. B. Foster,* Esq. and Mr. *Alba Fisk* as vice presidents, and *David B. McLain* and *Wm. Bryant, jr.* as secretaries.

The company sat down to an excellent dinner, prepared for the occasion by Mr. William Gillespie; and spread with much taste and elegance. At the head of the table was placed the portrait of WASHINGTON, the father of his country, and at the foot, the portrait of LAFAYETTE, the distinguished friend of America, and of universal liberty.

The toasts were reserved until "after the cloth was removed," and then came a series of thirteen, from such general subjects as "the fiftieth anniversary of our Independence," "our country's rights," "the national government," "American invention," and, of course, the ladies as "the daughters of Columbia," to such specific notables as Washington, Jefferson, General Jackson, and the Governor of Pennsylvania. It may be noted that John Adams was omitted from the honors of the Democratic Republicans, an omission that might have been a little too pointed had it occurred a few days later, for it happened that not only Jefferson, but John Adams as well, died on that same Fourth of July.

After the thirteen prepared, planned-in-advance toasts, the volunteer toasts were given. How long the capacity of the celebrants held out through the twenty-three that followed is not told in the newspaper account. William Foster proposed his toast while the company was still reasonably sober, for he came second, as first vice-president of the day, following the Mayor, who drank to "The United States of America." Foster toasted "The independence of the United States" . . . "acquired by the blood and valour of our venerable progenitors. To us they bequeathed the dear bought inheritance; to our care and protection they consigned it; and the most sacred obligations are upon us to transmit the glorious purchase, unfettered by power, to our innocent and beloved offspring." Was he thinking of his latest offspring, of whose coming by this time he must have known?

After the second vice-president, Alba Fisk, as well as N. R. Smith, Samuel Frew, and the secretaries of the occasion, Messrs. Bryant and McLain, had offered toasts, the meeting was open to a miscellaneous assortment of suggestions, largely repetitions of those already presented. Finally, after the presiding officers and the host had been honored, the jubilee came to an end with three cheers.

2

In the meantime matters had been progressing smoothly enough at the White Cottage, and the cannon had failed to disturb so experienced a mother as Eliza Foster. Ann Eliza, then fourteen, remembered the occasion vividly. Years later, in 1872, she wrote to Morrison:

The mention of the "fourth" in 1818, of which our father was President, brought forcibly to my mind the one which occurred on the day of Stevy's birth, in the woods back of our house. I remember so well how we children were seated at the table and saw and heard all that went on, taken there for the purpose, as I now understand, of keeping the house quiet for our dear Mother. I also have a distinct recollection of the anxiety expressed by those in attendance at the house, lest the cannons of the national salute should deafen the little infant, not more than an hour or two old. In that celebration, also, Pa, of course, bore a prominent part. . . .

The baby was named Stephen Collins, for the son of a neighbor and childhood friend of Eliza Foster, a little boy who had died just before Stephen was born. There were those who thought that the association with John Adams and Thomas Jefferson, who both departed this world as the future song-writer entered it, should have been recognized in naming the newest Foster. In August a relative, Susan Clayland, wrote to Charlotte from Cincinnati:

How does your Ma do, my dear Charlotte, and the little Hero, for I prophecy he will be one being born on so great and eventful a day. You certainly ought to call him Jefferson or Adams and no other name. . . .

And in closing the same letter:

Give my love to your mother and father and Ann Eliza and kiss little Jefferson Adams for me. . . .

But such a merging of Federalist and Democratic-Republican parties could scarcely be conceived by such staunch Democrats as the Fosters, so the non-partisan Stephen Collins stood as originally planned.

It is possible to trace little Stephen's babyhood and his early years closely through the family letters. He was loved and petted, and as one of the babies of the family he was the object of much solicitude. On the 22nd of April, 1827, he was baptized at Trinity Church. He had the usual childish ailments. When he was not yet two Charlotte wrote Brother William that "Stevy is not quite well—he is still very weak" (March 17, 1828). In the following September his father wrote Charlotte:

Dear little Stephen was very unwell a few days ago, your mother took him out to Gillespie's a week; the mosquitos being very troublesome at our house. He is now quite well, as are all the family.

To which Charlotte responded:

How is dear little Stephen? I am uneasy about him. I suppose it is the summer complaint, and teathing. Do write now and tell me how he is. Kiss the dear little pets all for their affectionate Sister.

If the cases were diagnosed correctly Stephen had whooping cough twice. When he was three his father added a postscript to a letter to Charlotte (July 29, 1829):

Nothing new, except the little boys, Stephen and Jim, have the whooping cough.

In William B. Foster's scrap book there was pasted a "cure" for whooping cough. It was probably inserted in the book about this time, so it may have been the mixture that was administered to "the little boys."

20 grains salt of Tartar
10 grains Cochineal
  1 oz. refined sugar dissolved in 1 gill warm water
  1 Teaspoonful three times a day, for a child 4 to 5 years old; and
    a little every time the cough is troublesome

When Stephen was almost eleven his mother wrote William, under date of June 16, 1837, that "Stephen has recovered from the whooping cough." While it is possible that the boy was twice afflicted with the same malady, the second attack may rather have been a chronic cough, indicating a tubercular tendency that possibly developed in later life, one which would explain, if it actually existed, some of the happenings of his last years.

There were other references to infant sicknesses when members of the family wrote each other—sore throats, and the spider bite Henrietta told William about. Altogether, Stephen appears to have been reasonably healthy, if not actually robust and sturdy.

Jim, who had the whooping cough at the time of Stephen's first attack, was his little brother, James Clayland, born when Stephen was two and a half years old, February 3, 1829. James died May 19 of the following year (1830), so except for the year and three months when he had a younger brother, Stephen was always the youngest of the Fosters.

3

How long Stephen lived in the White Cottage at Lawrenceville is not certain. It may have been for six years after his birth, for it is said that William Foster disposed of the house and some of the land in 1832. The date, however, is open to question, as is the exact location of the Foster homestead. This matter was thoroughly discussed when the city of Pittsburgh accepted the present Stephen Foster Memorial Home as a gift from James H. Park, the building that is now maintained as a museum, and the home of Stephen's daughter and two of his grandchildren.

At the time the site was purchased for the city (1914) discussion centered around two houses: one, the building which is now the museum, at 3600 Penn Avenue, and the other an old frame house resembling vaguely a contemporary painting of the White Cottage, and located at a place called the Forks of the Road, opposite the present junction of Penn Avenue and Butler Street. There were those who claimed that the house at the forks was the actual White Cottage in which Stephen was born.

The house which was finally purchased resembles the actual White Cottage in no particular, but is supposed to be located on the original site and to have assumed its present form through the addition of wings which have changed its shape and its size. This house stands on Penn Avenue several hundred yards above the house at the forks, at the junction of Penn Avenue and Denny Street. This is the location of lot No. 9 in the plan of the Town of Lawrenceville shown in the illustration, a copy, made in 1847, of the original plan laid out by W. B. Foster and attested by him in 1836. The house at the forks is situated in what would have been lots No. 6 or 7.

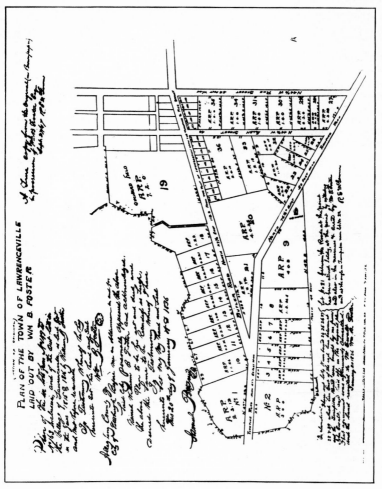

Plan of Lawrenceville, as Laid Out by William B. Foster

Courtesy Sims Visual Music Company

It seems plausible that William Foster would have built his own home on the spacious lot No. 9 rather than on the smaller 6 or 7, a supposition supported by the fact that the name W. B. Foster is printed under the diagram of the house in lot No. 9.

Testimony on the site was given to the Pittsburgh *Sun* (February 17, 1927) a number of years ago by Maria Leech Lynch, granddaughter of the Malcolm Leech who is supposed to have purchased the property.

It seems strange to me that any doubt should exist as to the birthplace of Stephen C. Foster, so firmly have family traditions fixed the locality in my mind.

It is pretty generally known that the village of Lawrenceville grew up on a 300-acre tract of land owned 100 years ago by Stephen Foster's father, and that he built a cottage, four rooms and basement, on his land, in 1814 in which 12 years later Stephen was born.

About ten years after this the Foster family moved to Allegheny. My grandfather, Malcolm Leech,[1] purchased this cottage and some 30 acres adjacent, situated on both sides of Penn Avenue and extending from Penn to Butler and from Allen Street, now Thirty-eighth Street, nearly to the forks of the road. Adjoining the cottage he built a brick house (the main part of the house as it now stands), leaving the white cottage as a wing, and here he lived until his death in 1862.

The property was then divided and placed on the market, the home passing into the hands of Andrew Kloman [one of the early partners of Andrew Carnegie in the iron, and later in the steel business], who tore down the original cottage, erecting on the exact spot a brick wing.

Strangely enough, when I called on Mrs. Lynch, April, 1933, a number of years after her article was written, she completely reversed her opinion, and stated emphatically and repeatedly that the house her grandfather had bought was not the original Foster home; that the White Cottage was actually the house at the forks. This testimony is probably not altogether reliable, for when I saw Mrs.

[1] Malcolm Leech acquired the property from the Bank of the United States to whom William Foster had lost it by foreclosure.

Lynch she had reached the venerable age of eighty-seven, and many years had passed since she had made her original statement.

It is further said that Morrison Foster was called upon in his old age to lend his aid in settling the controversy. He was taken first through the house at the forks, where he found no familiar landmarks. Then he went to the other house, at Penn Avenue and Denny Street, and though the house itself revealed nothing, the timbers in the roof of the spring house, in a corner of the grounds, brought back childhood memories that caused the aged man to burst into tears.

Lest this evidence seem too conclusive, there is another document to keep the controversy alive. There has recently appeared in Pittsburgh a letter, in the possession of Mr. George M. P. Baird, written by Anthony Kloman, son of Andrew, to his own son, Charles A. Kloman, December 17, 1927. This letter denies that the property Andrew Kloman purchased from Leech was the Foster birthplace, and it contains the statement that the spring house Morrison Foster identified was erected by Kloman in 1866. None of this, of course, comes within the realm of contemporary documentation. Like the statement of Mrs. Lynch it offers only recollections written in later years.

The nearest approach to documentary evidence is found in the plan of Lawrenceville, in which the name of W. B. Foster is noted directly under a house that stands in a spot corresponding with the site of the present memorial home. To this may be added a paragraph from Eliza Foster's diary, written in 1818.

It was on a summer morning, early in the month of June, when a plain, square-bodied carriage turned slowly up a shady road two miles from Pittsburgh. The fresh breeze fanned the foliage of the locust trees that grew along the white fence which surrounded the grounds belonging to a beautiful Cottage that stood upon an elevation, retired from view: for the road wound half circularly round the base of the hill.

This was Eliza's description of her own home. It will be seen from the plan of Lawrenceville, that the half turn of the road is at lot No. 9, the road is straight at Nos. 6 and 7 where the house at the forks now stands. This is by no means proof, but it lends weight to the claim in behalf of the site of the present memorial home.[a]

4

Whatever the exact site of the White Cottage, and however dreary and sordid that closely-built section of Pittsburgh is to-day, the birthplace of Stephen Foster was once a charming spot, where the pleasant home, high on a hill, looked out on the village of Lawrenceville and the winding Allegheny below.

When Stephen was a child the family moved often, in fact throughout his whole life he was never in one place for many years in succession. After the White Cottage the family went to Harmony, Pennsylvania, to a summer home they enjoyed, not far from Pittsburgh. Then, in the Autumn of 1832, when Stephen was six, they moved into a house in Allegheny, which may have been provided by the State because of William B. Foster's position with the Canal Commission. A year and a half later, in May of 1834, the Fosters occupied a frame house in Allegheny, facing Smoky Island in the Ohio River, where the rent was $125 per annum. The following December they moved again, this time to a three-story brick house in the heart of Allegheny.

According to Morrison Foster,[2] Stephen had his first schooling when he was five, and was sent with the other children to an "infant school" conducted by a Mrs. Harvey

[a] For further discussion of the controversy, revived by Henry Ford's purchase of the "House at the Forks," see *Preface to Fourth Printing*.

[2] *Biography, Songs and Musical Compositions of Stephen C. Foster,* op. cit.

and her daughter, Mrs. Morgan. Morrison wrote that Stephen was never, in all his life, a methodical student, and that his "erratic symptoms" in the class-room were apparent at an early age. The first time he was called upon to recite at Mrs. Harvey's he started on the letters of the alphabet, but before he had gone very far "his patience gave out, and with a yell like that of a Comanche Indian, he bounded bareheaded into the road, and never stopped running and yelling until he reached home, half a mile away." [3]

The little primer which was used at this school is still in the possession of the Foster family, and even a casual study of its pages causes wonder and admiration that Stephen's patience held out at all. First come the alphabet jingles: "In Adam's Fall, We sinned all," through to the bitter end—"Zaccheus, he did climb the Tree, His Lord to see."

At the end of the alphabet lesson lies the warning to the indolent and the unwilling:

He that loves God, his School, and his Book, will no doubt do well at last;
But he that hates his School and Book, will live and die a slave, a fool, and a dunce!

Morrison said that the Foster children used this book as long as they attended Dame Harvey's school.

Sister Ann Eliza also had a hand in Stephen's early tutoring. When the family was in Harmony, she wrote her father on June 16, 1832:

On arriving I found all the family perfectly well, though the boys [Morrison and Stephen] had just recovered from the sore throat. Ma has thought it best that they should cease going to school, as the weather is so intensely warm, and their walk was long. I employ myself by assembling them together every day and putting them through the usual exercises, with which arrangement they appear well pleased. . . .

[3] *Biography, Songs,* etc., op. cit.

When you . . . come, will you let me trouble you to bring a few articles. . . . My pink calico wrapper in the second drawer, and if you will trouble yourself to rummage among the books, I should be very glad to have "Plutarch's Lives" and the first two volumes of "Hume's History"—these I wish partly for the children.

When Stephen was not quite seven he went to Augusta, Kentucky, on the trip with his mother and Henrietta when they visited the uncles John and Joseph Tomlinson, who Eliza said "lived very neatly." We have already learned how Eliza and her two children boarded the "Napolian," and how they were royally treated both on shipboard and ashore. They visited in Cincinnati and Louisville, and the entire trip lasted some six weeks. The travellers returned to Allegheny July 2, 1833, just two days before Stephen's seventh birthday.

It has been said that Stephen suffered from cholera during this trip, but that belief is seemingly disproved by Eliza Foster's gratitude that they arrived home in good health, before the "Cholara Asphyzia" had overtaken them.[4]

After Mrs. Harvey's school, Stephen was entered at the academy of the Reverend Joseph Stockton, in Allegheny. Stockton was the pastor of the First Presbyterian Church, and during the week he conducted his Allegheny Academy. Exactly when Stephen first went to Mr. Stockton is not certain, but it is evident that he was there by the time he was eight, for on July 14, 1834, his father wrote William:

The boys are going to school. . . . Little Stephen is learning very fast. Mr. Kelly says that he and Morrison are the most sensible children he ever saw in his life.

Mr. Kelly was Stockton's assistant, a man to whom Stephen in later years seems to have written a poem[5] in tribute. Morrison Foster, in his biography of Stephen,[6] tells of these school days.

[4] Eliza Foster's letter to William, page 53.
[5] See pages 242-243.　　　　[6] *Op. cit.*

This academy was a model institution for the education of youth, and was attended by the sons of nearly all the most prominent citizens of Pittsburgh and Allegheny. Mr. Stockton was a perfect tutor. He was learned, he was firm, he was amiable, and he was thorough and practical. His acquirements were numerous and general. In addition to the classics, he was master of the grammar of the English language, and was also a profound mathematician. . . .

Mr. Stockton had with him an assistant who was his equal as a scholar except in knowledge of the classics, Mr. John Kelly, an Irishman, of wonderful accomplishments. He had been a tutor in the family of Sir Rowland Hill, and brought with him letters of introduction from people of the most excellent sort in the refined city of Dublin. Mr. Kelly was a thorough disciplinarian. While he was of genial disposition and out of school played ball and prisoner's base with the boys, and excelled in every manly athletic exercise, in school he required rigid attention to business.

Elocution was also taught as a separate branch by Mr. Caldwell . . . and penmanship by Mr. Egerton. . . .

After the death of Mr. Stockton the Academy in Allegheny was continued by Mr. Kelly, and the same thorough system of education was kept up. Lindley Murray was the standard authority on grammar, and the "English Reader" by the same author was used for instruction in reading. Walker's Dictionary was the recognized lexicon. Hutton's Mathematics and the Western Calculator were relied on for arithmetic. These constituted the sources of primary education for the youth of Western Pennsylvania. . . .

In 1837, when Stephen was almost ten, the family letters show that he was "going to school with Morrison to Mr. Todd" (June 16). According to Morrison,[7] the Reverend Nathan Todd was

a learned professor, who gave much attention to instruction in Latin and Greek, as well as in the English branches. Under the tutorship of Mr. Todd, Stephen made very satisfactory progress. Mr. Todd was not so rigid a disciplinarian as Mr. Kelly, but Stephen's conduct was always satisfactory. His sense of honor raised him above the meanness of taking advantage of leniency in his tutor. Mr. Todd remarked to my father that "Stephen was the most perfect gentleman he ever had for a pupil."

[7] *Op. cit.*

5

Stephen was musical from the time he was little more than a baby. Probably the earliest musical anecdote that has been told of him is related by Morrison, telling how Stephen, when he was two, used to lay Ann Eliza's guitar on the floor and pick out harmonies from its strings. He called it his "ittly pizani," translated by Morrison to "little piano."

Milligan was inclined to doubt that story, for in his biography of Foster [8] he wrote:

There may be some truth in this pretty legend as far as the guitar is concerned, but it is extremely doubtful if "Little Stephy" at the age of two, had ever seen or heard a piano. It was not until twenty years later that the first "upright" piano was brought across the mountains to Pittsburgh, and "grand" pianos were certainly not familiar objects there in 1828. At any rate, we know that the Foster family did not possess one at that time.

The family letters that have come to light since Mr. Milligan wrote his book prove that pianos were indeed "familiar objects" to the Fosters and their neighbors. As early as 1815 there was a piano maker in Pittsburgh, Charles Rosenbaum. Whether he made grand, upright or square pianos is uncertain, but at any rate they were pianos. The Fosters had one as early as 1818, for it was in that year that Charlotte entertained her mother's guests with "There's Nothing True But Heaven." There were of course periods when the Fosters were without an instrument. In 1825 Ann Eliza must go "every day to Mrs. Mallory's to practice on the piano," and again, in 1828, Charlotte wrote Brother William that "Caroline Grace is still with us. I do not know what I shall do when she and her piano are gone" (March 17). Visitors brought their own pianos in those days!

It was in that same year that Charlotte visited Louisville,

[8] *Stephen Collins Foster,* op. cit.

and wrote that the Barclays' new piano was an inducement to prolong her visit, for there was none at home. That was in May, but the following August Brother William made the family in Lawrenceville a present of a new piano.

Another story about Stephen's precocity in music has had wide circulation. This anecdote was also told by Morrison. When Stephen was about seven, he was taken to the music store of Smith & Mellor in Pittsburgh, where he picked a flageolet from the counter and though he had never before handled either flute or flageolet, in a few minutes played "Hail Columbia" to the delight of clerks and customers. It was not long after this, according to Morrison,

that he learned, unaided, to play beautifully on the flute. He had the faculty of bringing those deep resonant tones from the flute which distinguish the natural flutist from the mechanical performer. Later he learned to play remarkably well on the piano.

The general supposition that the Fosters were unmusical is flatly contradicted by fact. We have already noted the numerous references to the musical activities of the family. Yet outside of the mention of William Foster, senior, "drawing a few notes on his violin," [9] all of these musical references apply to the women of the family. There is no indication that indulgence in music was in any way a masculine diversion. While he was still a little boy, Stephen's musical leanings were probably interesting and amusing to his family, but it is hardly to be doubted that when he grew older his talents and preoccupation with music caused doubts and dismay.

He was not quite six when his mother wrote William:

Stevan . . . has a drum and marches about . . . with a feather in his hat, and a girdle about his waist, whistling old lang syne. . . . There still remains something perfectly original about him. (May 14, 1832)

[9] Eliza Foster's letter to Charlotte, Nov. 2, 1821, quoted on page 32.

The earliest letter, now in existence, that Stephen ever wrote shows that his thoughts were largely centered on music. This was written when he was not yet eleven, January 14, 1837, when the children were with their mother in Youngstown, and the senior Foster was conducting his business with Hall in Pittsburgh.

MY DEAR FATHER

I wish you to send me a commic songster for you promised to. if I had my pensyl I could rule my paper. or if I had the money to by Black ink But if I had my whistle I would be so taken with it I do not think I would write atall. there has been a sleighing party this morning with twenty or thirty cupple. Dr. Bane got home last might and told us Henry was coming out here I wish Dunning would come with hin tell them bothh to try to cone for I should like to see them both most two much to talk about.

I remane your loving son

STEPHEN C. FOSTER.

William Foster, the elder, apparently had his own ideas on music, in addition to his ability to draw a few notes on the violin. In his scrap book was pasted a clipping from an 1830 issue of *Gale's National Intelligencer*. No doubt he concurred heartily in its views.

MESSRS. EDITORS:—Music is, doubtless a delightful accomplishment, it "hath charms to soothe the savage breast, soften dull rocks," and so forth. All this I believe and acknowledge to be true. But, I would humbly submit to the young ladies of this precocious, intellectual and highly accomplished generation, that all sounds which are producable from a piano are not Music! Oh! is it not a torture to "sit with sad civility" and listen to that disease (excuse the bull) called a popular song? Why, the thing is more contagious than the cholera. Every amateur catches a popular tune; and one has to listen to it for the thousand and first time, varied only by the blunders and affectation of the player. Oh! parents! why will ye, in despite of Gall, and in contempt of Spurzheim, make your daughters learn music as a *mantrap,* whether they have the organ developed on their pericrania or not? Oh! Satan, what a sad blunderer you were to kill Job's daughters! why did you not teach them to play on the piano, and sing, "Come Rest in this Bosom!" Your business would have been done at once, you silly fiend. Job could not have stood it —he would have cursed and died. M.

Even in this bit of irony all reference is to daughters, none to sons. Yet William Foster had his sentimental side, and his scrap book is filled with bits of poetry, many of them by Mrs. Sigourney, "the Sweet Singer of Hartford." There is also that immortal gem to which John C. Baker, of the Baker family of singers, set the music:

> Tell me, ye winged winds, that round my pathway roar,
> Do ye not know some spot, where mortals weep no more,
> Some lone and pleasant dell, some valley in the West,
> Where free from toil and pain, the weary soul may rest?
>
> The loud winds dwindled to a whisper low—
> And sigh'd for pity as they answered No! No!

Such things may have been quite all right for leisure moments, and Stephen was no doubt cunning when absorbed with music as a little child; but with a boy growing into manhood preoccupations of this sort were cause for concern. True, his mother, soft-hearted as she probably was, asked if he got a "clarionette" when Brother William took him through Harrisburg in 1840, on his way to school near Towanda. Yet it was probably William's indulgence for a home-sick little brother that prompted him to take Stephen to "a fine concert in Haresburg," [10] for in spite of such indulgences, William's real attitude toward Stephen's devoting his thought and time to music is probably indicated in a letter Stephen wrote his elder brother, promising to study hard, and "not to pay any attention to my music untill after eight Oclock in the evening." [11]

In 1841, September 3, his father wrote William:

[Stephen] is at school, now, with Mr. Moody, a first rate teacher of mathematics in Pttsbg. and it is a source of comfort to your mother and myself, that he does not appear to have any evil propensities to

[10] See page 91.   [11] See page 93.

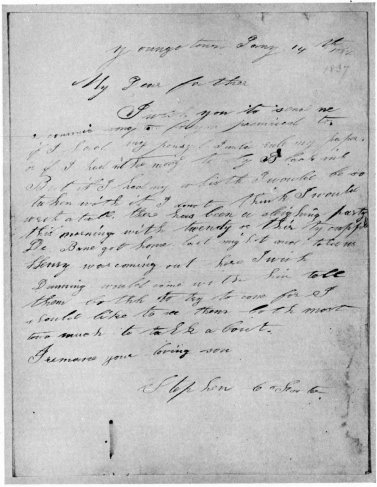

Letter Written by Stephen Foster at the Age of Ten and
a Half Years

indulge; he seeks no associates; and his leisure hours are all devoted to musick, for which he possesses a strange talent.

Was there perhaps a note of relief in his mother's voice when she wrote William, the following October 18?

[Stephen] is not so much devoted to musick as he was; other studies seem to be elevated in his opinion. He reads a great deal, and fools about none at all.

Pity indeed that Stephen lived in a time when native talents were not recognized as pointing the way to vocational guidance. With modern training he might have become a musician equipped to develop fully the vital musical thoughts that sang their way from his heart. Had he been trained at an early age to bring them from his heart through his mind, the world might have lost the unaffected, simple speech in music that was Stephen Foster's greatest charm, but his own road would have been far easier to travel.

6

For personal glimpses of Stephen we must rely principally on Morrison Foster. According to this brother, Stephen, "from earliest childhood, was noted for his courage, coolness and skill in the combats which continually occur among boys of the same town. . . . He was known as one who must be let alone, and was held in high respect accordingly." [12] His aversion to rigid class-room discipline has already been noted; yet "he had a faculty of reaching far ahead and grasping the scope of a lesson without apparent effort, which was remarkable and sometimes startling. He preferred to ramble among the woods and upon the hills by the three beautiful rivers of his home with his books and pencil, alone and thoughtful. Here the rustling of the leaves, the twitter of birds, the falling twigs and the rippling waters accorded harmoniously, and fell in grateful

[12] *Biography, Songs,* etc., op. cit.

melody on his sensitive ear. He was always perfect in his recitations, however, and his shortcomings in discipline were pardoned by my mother and father, who appealed to his tutors for forbearance in his case." [13]

All of which was penned by a loving brother, but it doubtless presents a reasonably faithful and accurate picture.

There have been so many misconceptions of the influences that shaped Stephen Foster's so-called plantation songs, that it is well to know exactly what memories he may have carried with him from childhood. It is true that he saw little of the real South. The trip to Augusta, Cincinnati, and Louisville, with his mother and Henrietta, is the only known journey he took to any part of the South until he reached manhood. He could hardly have known actual plantation life at first hand.

Yet Pittsburgh lay at the head of the Ohio River, and boats travelled regularly from there to New Orleans, and they must have brought with their cargoes and passengers, to say nothing of their crews and deckhands, something of the flavor of the far South. Then, when Stephen later went to Cincinnati for a few years, he was still closer to Southern life, particularly on the wharves and docks where goods for his brother's warehouse were landed.

Although Stephen wrote many Northern songs during the Civil War, the Fosters were ardent Democrats and hated the Abolitionists. In a sense they were slave owners to the extent of using the services of Thomas Hunter, the "bound boy," as well as a "bound girl" named Olivia Pise. It was probably Olivia who gave Stephen his first impressions of Negro singing.

She had evidently been with the family for some time when Stephen was born. As far back as 1821 Charlotte wrote from Emmitsburg that she pictured "Lieve passing along with her pails of frothing milk, on her way to the

[13] *Biography, Songs,* etc., op. cit.

spring house." In 1828 Eliza Foster wrote Charlotte that "Leave is lying in a billious fever."

Olivia was said to be the illegitimate daughter of a West Indian dancing-master, possibly the same who was listed in the 1815 Pittsburgh Directory as "Henry G. Pius, dancing academy, w side of the Diamond." Morrison tells of the daughter's influence on Stephen's future songs.

"Lieve" . . . was a devout Christian and a member of a church of shouting colored people. The little boy [Stephen] was fond of their singing and boisterous devotions. She was permitted to often take Stephen to church with her. Here he stored up in his mind "many a gem of purest ray serene," drawn from these caves of negro melody. A number of strains heard there, and which, he said to me, were too good to be lost, have been preserved by him, short scraps of which were incorporated in two of his songs, "Hard Times Come Again No More" and "Oh, Boys, Carry Me 'Long." [14]

This statement is important in showing how far Stephen's "Ethiopian" songs were shaped by the singing and songs of actual Negroes, and how much they were influenced by the songs of minstrel performers, the white man's conception and imitation of the Negro.

Stephen's later association with minstrel shows came naturally to him, for in his boyhood "playing theatre" meant imitating the songs and antics of black-face comedians. Stephen later came to be associated with the leading performers of his day, but it was in childhood that he first showed his fascination for anything connected with the stage. Morrison tells of an incident in this connection. [15]

When he was nine years old a Thespian company was formed, composed of boys of neighbor families, Robinsons, Cuddys, Kellys and Fosters. The theatre was fitted up in a carriage house. All were stockholders except Stephen. He was regarded as a star performer, and was guaranteed a certain sum weekly. It was a very small sum, but it was sufficient to mark his superiority over the rest of the company. "Zip Coon," "Long-tailed Blue," "Coal-Black Rose," and "Jim Crow" were the only Ethiopian songs then known. His per-

[14] *Op. cit.*   [15] *Ibid.*

formance of these was so inimitable and true to nature that, child as he was, he was greeted with uproarious applause, and called back again and again every night the company gave an entertainment, which was three times a week. They generally cleared enough to enable the whole party to buy tickets to the old Pittsburgh Theatre on Saturday nights, where they could be seen in the pit listening to the acting of Junius Brutus Booth, Augustus A. Addams, Edwin Forrest, Oxley, Conner, Logan, Proctor, William and John Sefton, Mrs. Drake and Mrs. Duff.

7

In 1837, after the father's interest in Foster and Hall had been closed out, Eliza Foster brought her children back from Youngstown, and the family again lived together in Allegheny, this time in a house on the East Common, at the corner of Gay Alley. This was the period of the "terrible depression," when the "silk stocking gentry" were all damning Jackson, and the elder Foster needed the help of William to keep his household afloat.

In the summer of that year Stephen and his mother went on a visit to Uncle John Struthers, in Poland, Ohio, from the middle of July to the last of August. Visits to Uncle Struthers were ever a delight. The old man gave the children the run of his place, and he always let Stephen do exactly as he pleased. Struthers was the husband of William Foster's sister Mary, and it was at his home that James Foster, Stephen's grandfather, died in 1814.

John Struthers had been a surveyor, hunter and Indian fighter in the settlement of pioneer territory, and even though he was past eighty when Stephen visited him, he was always ready to welcome the children. Morrison tells of these visits.

Old Uncle Struthers had dogs and rifles, and himself would lead the hunt at night for 'coons, opossums, and such like nocturnal game. It was tame work to the old pioneer, who had been used to bears, panthers and hostile Indians. These hunts and the stories of adventure told by his aged relative, of course gave great pleasure to

Stephen, and kindled the flame of his vivid fancy. One cold day, he was missed from the house, and was hunted for everywhere outside. At last his uncle discovered him sitting up to his neck in a pile of chaff, watching the movements of the chickens and other barnyard animals—"just thinking," as he briefly explained. The old gentleman always prophesied that Stephen, who even then displayed great originality and musical talent, would be something famous if he lived to be a man.[16]

The family stayed in the house at Gay Alley for only two years. Times were terribly hard, and Foster, senior, failed to get his full claim from the old transportation company. In addition to his financial troubles, he suffered from the 1837 election, when the Democrats were overwhelmed by the "combined enemy, Whigs and anti-Masons."

In 1839 the Fosters left the Allegheny house and stayed for a time near Uncle Struthers. On July 25, William Foster wrote William, junior:

We are still in Poland, that is your mother and myself. Uncle Struthers has not yet got his house in order, but will in a week or two when we will go there. We have excellent board and lodging here for 2 dollars each per week. . . .

Morrison and Stephen board at Mr. Reno's [in Youngstown], going to free school at $1.50 per week for boarding. . . .

Later that summer there was further reference to Stephen at Uncle Struthers'. Henrietta, who by that time was married to Thomas Wick and living in Youngstown, wrote Brother William, September 29:

Thomas has just taken the Buggy and horse down to Uncle's for Ma. She has not been up to see us for some time, and we thought she must be very lonely there now, with no one but little Stephy, as Pa is in Pittsburgh. . . .

Stephen enjoys himself finely at Uncle Struthers—he never appears to have the least inclination to leave there, and don't seem to feel at all lonely. Uncle just lets him do as he pleases with the horses and cattle, which makes him the greatest man on the ground.

---

[16] *Op. cit.*

The Fosters stayed in and about Youngstown and Poland for over a year. February 7, 1840, Eliza wrote Morrison:

When your Father and myself will go to Pittsburgh I cannot inform you. We are very happy here [in Youngstown], having a pleasant room and good boarding and a kind family in that of Mr. Richards. . . .

In August Eliza was still writing her letters from Youngstown, but she was back in Pittsburgh by November, when her husband wrote William, "we are boarding at Mrs. Paul's, a widow lady, no boarders but ourselves."

In her February 7 letter, Stephen's mother added a significant sentence:

I feel quite contented about Stephen, believing that William will take good care of him.

William had taken his thirteen-year-old brother to be near him at Towanda, where he could attend the neighboring Athens Academy, at Tioga Point. This marked a definite epoch in Stephen's life, a period that showed some of the traits he was to exhibit in manhood, and developed some of the problems that were later to trouble his parents. It also marked Stephen's first appearance as a composer of music.

III

TIOGA POINT

I

WHEN Stephen went to Towanda with William, in 1840, the Academy at Athens had been in existence for some twenty-six years. Originally planned in 1797, when the little village, fifteen miles from Towanda at the junction of the Susquehanna and Chemung Rivers, was known by its original name of Tioga Point, the school opened its building in 1814. During its first twenty-six years the Academy enjoyed, or endured, at least twenty principals. The first of them, Sylvanus Guernsey, taught for ten months and then asked for a discharge because of ill health. In 1817 (May 27) the board inserted an advertisement in the *Bradford Gazette,* Towanda:

ATHENS ACADEMY

(At Tioga Point, Pa.)

The public are hereby respectfully informed that the summer term in the Athens Academy will commence on the twenty-first day of April. Terms of tuition for Latin, Greek and Mathematics will be, $5. Geography with use of maps and globes 4-50, Rhetoric and Logic, $4. English grammer [sic] and Punctuation, $3-75. The students will also have frequent exercises in Oratory, composition and history. . . .

The location of this seminary is very eligible and pleasant. It stands on the west bank of the Susquehanna a few yards from the channel of the river, where the water glides sweetly along in a smooth still current a considerable distance, nearly opposite the building the river inbosoms a small island which with other rural prospects, meets the eye very agreeably. The salubrity of the air, conveniences for bathing and pleasure grounds for exercise, conspire

87

not only to preserve the health of youth, but to exhilirate [sic] their spirits in prospecting their studies. Here likewise youth are secluded from scenes of riot and dissipation which are frequently to be met with in cities and other populous places. . . .

. . . [The preceptor] considers it his indispensible duty not only to instruct youth in literature, but in the correct principles of morality and religion; and strenuously to enjoin it upon them to observe a suitable decorum among their associates and in society. E. WELLINGTON, Preceptor.

Mr. Wellington lasted for only a year, and was followed in quick succession by several others who found that the "salubrity of the air" did not insure permanence for the preceptor. In 1840 John G. Marvin was appointed principal, and it was he who was in charge of the school when Stephen Foster came there as a pupil.

A description of the Academy during Marvin's administration is afforded by Raymond M. Welles in an address delivered before the Bradford County Historical Society, February 11, 1905.[1] According to Welles, Marvin's education was somewhat defective, and it was necessary for him to study continually to keep ahead of his advanced classes. Nevertheless, the school was successful under his administration, and enjoyed such a large enrollment, two hundred pupils, that three assistants were necessary. One of these was Edwin C. Marvin, John's younger brother. It was in the Spring of 1841 that the first and only catalog of the school was published. It contained the names of 130 males, and 70 females—among the former, "Stephen Collins Foster, of Pittsburgh."

A handbill issued August 10, 1840, tells of the courses taught during the time Stephen was at the school. After listing the names of the Marvins as principal and assistant, and of a "Miss Stevens" as teacher of music, and calling to the attention of the reader "the beautiful and healthy location of the Academy," and "the morality and intelli-

[1] Printed in pamphlet Number Five, *Bradford County Historical Society Annual.*

gence of the citizens," it stated that "measures are being taken to procure several hundred dollars' worth of Philosophical, Chemical and Astronomical Apparatus, which will make the Institution one of the best in the country for acquiring an intimate knowledge of the Natural Sciences." The courses offered were Reading, Writing and Spelling ($1.50); Arithmetic, English Grammar and Geography ($2.50); Rhetoric, History, Logic, Mathematics and the Natural Sciences ($4.00); Latin, Greek, and the Modern Languages ($5.00), and Music, *extra charge*. Board could be obtained at one and a half to two dollars a week.

The school building was a two-story affair that suffered many vicissitudes before it was finally used for its intended purpose. According to the original regulations, adopted in 1797,[2] the plans for the schoolhouse were elaborate.

The building contemplated to be erected . . . in the township of Athens, on Tioga Point . . . shall be forty-two feet in length, and twenty-four feet in width; and to consist of two stories, the height of the posts to be twenty-two feet. The second story shall be formed into one entire hall, to be arched and finished in a handsome manner; a chimney shall be built at each end; an elegant balcony shall be erected on the middle of the roof; and venetian blinds shall be made to all the windows of the first and second stories. . . .

Although the frame was soon erected and enclosed, the work was not completed at that time, and after the building had been used as a grain storehouse, it was advertised for sale, in 1808. Public interest was again aroused, and although the house was not yet used for school purposes, the project was refinanced, and arrangements were made with the Masonic Lodge to finish the upper story "as an arched hall, according to the original design," and to use it for the Lodge's own purposes. The Masons occupied these upper premises until 1835.

In 1813 the Pennsylvania Assembly appropriated $2,000

[2] As transcribed by Guy Maxwell, and now in the Museum of the Bradford County Historical Society.

for establishing the Academy, with the proviso that the present owners relinquish all claims to the building, and that the school educate without charge four poor children annually. Thus in 1814 the building was completed, the lower floor used as a school, and the Academy commenced its varied career.

2

Brother William went to Towanda in the Spring of 1839. The previous Winter he had been recommended to the Pennsylvania Canal commissioners by James Buchanan, and he had been appointed principal engineer of the canals and railroads of Eastern Pennsylvania. Towanda was his headquarters for five years, for it was there that work must be done on the North Branch Canal.

William was becoming a man of substance by this time. He was helping the family liberally. By 1841 he owned a barouche and two horses, and when he married a second time, September 22, 1842, his wife was able to become one of the social leaders of Towanda.

These were the years when matters were hard for the Foster family. Although Stephen was boarding at Mr. Reno's and going to free school in Youngstown, the education to be obtained there was probably far from what was desired for the youngest of the Fosters. So Brother William suggested that the lad go with him to Towanda, and attend school in that neighborhood.

William Foster, senior, wrote of Stephen's departure to Morrison, then in Pittsburgh.

We have concluded to let Stephen go with William, who will put him to school at the Academy in Towanda, where William's Office and Headquarters are. I think it an excellent chance for the dear little fellow to get education. I expect they will leave this [place] on Tuesday, and will arrive at Pittsburgh some time on Wednesday; you will of course be ready to receive him and take him home with you to stay while William remains in town, and I need not tell you to be kind and affectionate to him; the gun which you bought for him I will take in when I go to town and give it to you. You can buy some little trifle for a keepsake, and give it to Stephen. Tell Dunning to do likewise. . . . (January 12, 1840)

What Stephen's feelings may have been on leaving his father and mother will never be known, but everything possible was done to keep him from being homesick. Morrison Foster, in his biography of Stephen [3] tells that

William drove him all the way to Towanda in his own sleigh, drawn by two horses. The distance travelled was over three hundred miles, but the sleighing was good, and, of course, it was a jolly journey for the little boy, especially as brother William was a man of great personal popularity, and had many friends and acquaintances everywhere along the road.

As they passed through Pittsburgh on the way from Youngstown they visited Morrison and Dunning, and no doubt the brothers gave Stephen the keepsakes their father had suggested. Back in Youngstown Eliza Foster thought constantly about her youngest. On January 20 she wrote to Morrison:

Tell me little particulars about Stephen while with you. Did he get a clarionette? And did you see him when he started—was he well wrapt up?

As they passed through Harrisburg Brother William took Stephen to the House of Representatives, and to call on the Governor. He also treated him to the "fine concert" his mother referred to in her letter of February 7.[4] By January 27 they were in Towanda, and Stephen was probably at school, for on that date his father wrote William:

We received a letter this morning from Morrison, which informs us of your doings at Pittsburgh and your departure. Surely Stephen must feel grateful to you for your brotherly kindness to him at Pittsburgh, and will I trust, exert himself by carefully pursuing your

[3] *Op. cit.*   [4] See page 80.

advice and instructions, and returning to you kindness for kindness. You will please to shew him this letter and tell him I will write to him after we hear from you, which we now daily expect.

It is difficult to trace exactly Stephen's goings and comings from school during the year and a half he was with William. We know that he was at Athens in November of 1840, for on the ninth of that month he wrote his brother a letter which is still in existence. It appears that he was boarding at the house of a Mr. Herrick, who evidently had a noisy family and did not consider it his responsibility to keep his boarder warm.

DEAR BROTHER

As Mr. Mitchell is going to start for Towanda today, I thougt I would write you a line concerning my studies as he says you will not be here for more than a week.

My Philosophy Grammar & Arithmetic not being enough to keep me going I would ask your permision to Study either Latin or Book-keeping.

I have no place to study in the evenings as the little ones at Mr. Herricks keep such a crying and talking that it's imposible to read. There is a good fire place in my room and if you will just say the word I will have a fire in it at nights and learn something. When you come dont forget my waistcoat at the tailors. there are several little articles which I need though I have no room to mention them. I must stop writing as I am very cold.

Your affectionate Brother
STEPHEN.

It is a pity that another letter from Stephen to William is undated, for if we could know when it was written it would show more about Stephen's career at Athens. This letter indicates that Stephen was in Towanda, and anxious to stay there, nearer to William; that he was homesick at Athens. Because of the reference to Mr. Herrick in the postscript, it appears that this letter was written some time after that of November 9, 1840.

Towanda Thursday

My Dear Brother.

As you wish to have me go to Athens for fear I will not learn enough in this place, I will tell you what my ideas were on the subject.

Mr. Vosberry is a very good mathematition, and as he has quit keeping school, he is going to ocupy a private room in the house of Mr. Elwell.

Mr. Kettle will be here tomorrow and will stop at Bartlett & Fords. he will have a room there but will not be in it in the day-time as his paint room will be at another house. Mr. Ford says he will board me and give me as good a room as I wish for $2.00 per week.

If you will let me board here (while you stay) and room with Kettle I will promise not to be seen out of doors betwen the hours of nine & twelve A.M. and one & four P.M. Which hours I will attribute to study, such as you please to put me into. I will also promise not to pay any attention to my music untill after eight Oclock in the evening after which time Mr. Kettle will probably be in the room as he cannot paint after dark. I dont se how I could have a better chance for study. & the above price is as cheap as I could live in Athens that lonesome place—I can go over to recite in the forenoon at about 10 oclock and in the afternoon at 4—do please consent.

Your affectionate & grateful brother

STEPHEN.

Please pay Mr. D. Mitchell $3.00 which I borowed from him to pay for pumps, subscription &c for the exhibition. I allso owe Mr. Vandercook a very small amount.

Dont pay Mr. Herrick for fire in my room as I have not had any since you payed him last.

Meanwhile the father and mother in Youngstown, and later in Pittsburgh, were always solicitous. Eliza would invariably add to her letters such a line as "Poor little Stephen. How is he? I think of him very much of late," or "Give much love to my dear boy Stephen." She had the utmost confidence in William's ability to take care of his little brother, and in her letter of August 7, 1840, wrote:

As to Stephen, I leave every thing regarding the future for him to your own judgment, West Point, or the Navy, I have no choice; you are not only his brother, but his Father; and I trust all his feelings will ascend to you as his patron.

We shall hear more later about West Point and the Navy.

Stephen's father adopted a sterner tone in his letters. On March 24, 1840, he wrote William:

We think it time to receive another letter from Stephen. I hope he is attentive to his studies, give much love to him from his mother and myself. Tell him his old Uncle Struthers looks to him to become a verry great man. He says he is confident that he is possess'd of superior talents for one of his age. I hope Stevy will not disappoint the fond hopes of so good an old man.

A month later, April 27, his father wrote again to William:

I wrote to Stephen on the 18th inst. and scolded him pretty smartly for not having written us more frequently, but he is not quite so much to blame, as I then thought, for on the evening of that day (the 18th) I rec'd a letter from him which was dated on the 27th of March, and must have been 21 days on the way. I wish you to tell him of this; I presume letters would come with more certainty by way of Harrisburgh if you have a daily mail from there to your place. . . . Give much love to Stephen for your father.

3

As nearly as can be determined from existing records, Stephen stayed with William for about a year and a half, from January 1840 until the late Spring or early Summer of 1841. How much of this time was spent at Athens, and how much in Towanda, may never be determined. We have learned from Stephen's own pen that he was homesick at Athens, "that lonesome place," and that he begged William to let him stay in Towanda.

There is evidence to show that Stephen attended the old

Towanda Academy as well as the school at Athens. Milligan, in his biography of Foster,[5] quotes a reminiscence of Stephen written by W. W. Kingsbury, a schoolmate. Milligan speaks of Kingsbury as one of Stephen's friends at Athens, but this is not correct; William Wallace Kingsbury, who later became the first United States Senator from Minnesota, was a schoolmate of Foster's at the Towanda Academy, not at Athens, and the reminiscence is quoted by Kingsbury's brother, A. H. Kingsbury, in a paper on *The Old Towanda Academy*,[6] read before the Bradford County Historical Society March 25, 1905, a little over a month after R. M. Welles delivered his address on the Academy at Athens.[7] (February 11, 1905)

The Towanda Academy was a younger institution than the school at Athens. Founded in 1836, it occupied a two-story brick building that had been erected the year before. A number of its teachers later became distinguished in political as well as educational fields; Henry M. Hoyt became governor of Pennsylvania, Orville H. Platt was for many years United States Senator from Connecticut; and Frederick W. Gunn established the famous Gunnery, a school for boys at Washington, Connecticut.

It is impossible to know how long, or when, Stephen attended the Towanda Academy, but it is certain he spent some time there during the year and a half he was with William. The Kingsbury reminiscence establishes this fact conclusively, for the landmarks mentioned are at Towanda rather than Athens.

Well do I remember the inimitable Stephen C. Foster. He was my special friend and companion; being a year older than myself and considerably larger, he used to defend me in my boyhood antagonisms with belligerent schoolmates. We often played truant together, rambling by shady streams or gathering wild strawberries

[5] *Op. cit.*
[6] Printed in pamphlet Number Four, *Bradford County Historical Society Annual.*
[7] See page 88.

in the meadows or pastures, removed from the sound of the old academy bell. One mutual luxury, in which we jointly indulged in those excursions without leave, was in going barefoot and wading pools of running water that meandered through Mercur's farm and down Mix's run, in the village of my nativity. Foster wore a fine quality of hose, and I remember how it shocked me to see him cast them away, when wild [soiled?] by perspiration or muddy water. His was a nature generous to a fault, with a soul attuned to harmony. His love of music was an all-absorbing passion, and his execution on the flute was the very genius of melody, and gave rise to those flights of inspired pathos, which have charmed the English-speaking world with their excellence from cabin to palace. Genial, well remembered friend, how proud I have been in the thought that it was my good fortune to have been the boyhood comrade of a character, commanding such world-wide fame as you have established in the hearts of a song-loving people.

There are two anchors to which we can fasten definite dates connected with Stephen's career at Athens. First, the letter of November 9, 1840,[8] in which he wrote of the children at Mr. Herrick's, and his need for a fire in the evenings; and second, the Academy Catalog, issued in the Spring of 1841, which contained Stephen's name as one of the pupils.

If the dates in reminiscences are reliable, there is added evidence to indicate that Stephen was at the Athens Academy from the time of his November 1840 letter to the following Spring. R. M. Welles, in his paper on the Athens Academy,[9] stated that he met Foster at the school in January, 1841. In the same paper Welles quotes an address by John A. Perkins, of Fresno, California, a former pupil at the Academy, delivered at its hundredth anniversary in 1897, in which Perkins recalled an exhibition held by the school at the old Presbyterian church, April 1, 1841. It was for this exhibition that Foster wrote his "Tioga Waltz."

It is also possible that this was the exhibition that Stephen

[8] See page 92. [9] *Op. cit.*

referred to in the postscript of his undated letter to William,[10] where he told his brother that he had borrowed three dollars from Mr. Mitchell to pay for pumps, subscription etc. "for the exhibition." If this reasoning is sound, the guess may be ventured that the undated letter was written after April 1, 1841; that Stephen was at Athens, possibly during the first Winter and Spring he was with William (1840), surely for most of the season 1840-1841; and that he left Athens after April of that season, begged William to let him stay in Towanda, and that William then entered him at the Towanda Academy. R. M. Welles states that Stephen spent some time at Towanda after leaving Athens. If this was the case, he was not at the Towanda school for long, for Morrison Foster does not even mention it in his account of Stephen's stay with William.[11]

It is worth noting, however, that the letter of William Foster, senior, written when Stephen first went with William [12] (January 12, 1840), states that William "will put him to school at the Academy in Towanda." This might indicate that Stephen was there, rather than at Athens, during his first season with William, and that he went to Athens the following Summer or Autumn.

Evidence to support this theory is found in the handbill of the Athens Academy, issued August 10, 1840.[13] This announced that "the Trustees of this Institution . . . have *re-opened* their commodious building for the reception of Students." It is possible that the Academy at Athens was closed when Stephen went to Towanda, that he went first to the Towanda Academy, and that when the Athens school reopened William decided to send him there.

Following this reasoning, it might be guessed that the undated letter was indeed written after April 1, 1841 (the date of the exhibition), but that inasmuch as Stephen's suggestions for continuing his studies involved only an indi-

10 See page 93.
11 *Op. cit.*
12 See page 90.
13 See page 88.

vidual teacher (Mr. Vosberry), he planned to pursue his work under a tutor, rather than at an institution. This theory may be further supported by the fact that Stephen was with William for only a few months after April, 1841, by July he was at the Jefferson College in Canonsburg, Pennsylvania, again making excuses for his troubles with routine and curriculum. If Stephen, in a year and three months, had tried two schools and been able to adapt himself to the ways of neither, it is entirely possible that William found the problem of a young genius too much for him, and that he decided to ship him back to his parents.

4

While personal reminiscences may not succeed in establishing an absolute chronology, they nevertheless afford a portrait of Stephen during his years with William. These accounts are interesting and important, for they concur on a number of points. They all speak of Stephen's absorption with music, they agree that he was shy, and though he may have been studious, they imply that he was not enough of a social mixer to fit comfortably into the life of a boarding school.

R. M. Welles wrote of Foster: [14]

He was at that time [1841] in his 15th year; his complexion was rather dark; his face and head . . . of uniform width, neither wide nor narrow, but well proportioned; he had a tall, large head, which was covered with fine, nearly black hair, that lay flat upon the scalp, and if I recollect correctly his jaws were somewhat square—indicating firmness. . . . He was studious and according to my recollection, kept much to his room and did not join with the boys in their sports. . . . Stephen C. Foster evidently was rather delicate in health, mainly, I think, because of lack of physical exercise, and later in life was somewhat nervous, not being able to sleep at night except in perfect quiet. . . . He was a good penman, and made fine ornamental letters. . . .

[14] *Op. cit.*

John A. Perkins, in his recollection of Foster,[15] spoke as follows:

Stephen C. Foster, of minstrel fame, was at the academy about this time, and showed some of the genius he displayed in later years. I can see him speaking "Lord Ullins' Daughter," as though it was yesterday; at the close he would fold his arms, throw back his head and tragically exclaim, "My daughter, oh, my daughter!"

Welles also quotes another schoolmate, Joseph Powell, who reminded him that Stephen played a great deal upon the "clarionet" while he was at Athens. Was this the "clarionette" that his mother had asked about in her letter to Morrison, January 20, 1840? [16]

By far the most important event at Athens was the composition of Stephen's "Tioga Waltz," according to the record his first known musical work. Robert Peebles Nevin stated [17] that a song, "Sadly to Mine Heart Appealing," was written in the same year.[18] This cannot be authenticated, for the song was not published until 1858, and moreover, Nevin errs in the date of the "Tioga Waltz" by stating that it was composed in 1839, when Stephen was thirteen. No original copy of the waltz apparently exists today, but years later Morrison Foster wrote it down from memory and included it in his biography of Stephen, published in 1896.

It is an innocuous little piece, without any particular individuality, but nevertheless it has a certain charm, a verve and sparkle, and represents a highly creditable initial effort. Morrison stated that it was written for the commencement at Athens, and that Stephen arranged it for four flutes. At the performance he played the leading part himself, while three other students played the remaining parts. According to Morrison "its performance was very satisfactory

[15] *Op. cit.*
[16] See page 91.
[17] In an article in *The Atlantic Monthly*, November, 1867.
[18] See pages 285-286.

to the audience, and was rewarded with much applause and an encore."

Recollections of schoolmates, who were present at the performance, differ from Morrison in some details. Welles states that the waltz was composed in February or March of 1841, while John A. Perkins, quoted in the same article,[19] tells of its performance at the school exhibition in the Presbyterian church, April 1 of that year. He says:

> Foster composed and wrote his first piece of music, I think, expressly for the exhibition, and with James H. Forbes and William F. Warner, the three practiced the piece, which Stephen named "Tioga Waltz," and played it upon the stage with their flutes—not "four flutes" as stated by his brother, Morrison Foster.

According to another historian, Louise Welles Murray,[20] the "Tioga Waltz" was dedicated to Frances Welles, daughter of Henry Welles, and a cousin of R. M. Welles, Stephen's schoolmate. The suggestion that Stephen mingled enough with townsfolk to have friends to whom he would dedicate a composition is interesting in view of the statements that he shunned society; yet the school was co-educational, with "70 females," and Frances may have been a schoolmate too.

No contemporary documents have appeared to establish Stephen's whereabouts between March 24, 1841, when his mother wrote William, "Poor little Stephen, how is he?", until July 24 of the same year, when he himself wrote William from Canonsburg, stating that he had arrived at that place four days before. Some time between April and July William's guardianship of his youngest brother came to an end.

Henry also had been with William during some of this period, presumably as a rod-bearer on the survey work of the canal. He had for a short time been in Warren, Pennsylvania, but the father's letter to William, November 16,

[19] *Op. cit.*
[20] *A History of Old Tioga Point and Early Athens* (1908).

1840, said: "Give my love to Henry and Stephen when you see them." On May 15, 1841, William Foster, senior, wrote his eldest son: "I am happy to know that you will be in employment for some months yet, and hope you will be able to keep Henry employ'd also." Henry was with William until late in that year or early in 1842, when he went to join his father in Washington, and secured for himself an appointment in the Land Office of the Treasury Department.

While Stephen was with William the family had moved back to Pittsburgh from Youngstown. First they boarded at Mrs. Paul's, at the corner of Second and Smithfield Streets. On August 12/14 (no year given, but presumably 1841), Eliza Foster wrote Brother William:

Mrs. Paul has removed to Pen Street, where every thing is very delightfull, a fine house pleasantly aranged, good table and a respactable neighborhood, but all this cannot be afforded, therefore I think we will go into your house on Monday. I can get a house for one hundred and fifty in town where Duning and Morrison could board with us, but your Father seems afraid to attempt it.

Accordingly the Fosters moved into a house owned by William, on the East Common in Allegheny, next door to the house they had occupied before they went to Youngstown.

Whatever happened to bring Stephen's days at Towanda and Athens to a close may never be known, but it is apparent that they ended in a vague, indeterminate fashion that characterized all but a few years of Foster's entire career. His talent was evident at this time, it found expression in at least one composition, but there seemed to be no one to point the way, none who really understood what this strange contradiction of a lad was best fitted for. As a result he drifted, for the checks and reins, and the formula for bringing up a Pennsylvania youth in the 1840's failed to provide for a personality as unusual as that of Stephen Foster.

IV

THE END OF SCHOOLING

I

THE events immediately following Athens and Towanda are easily determined, for the family letters provide a complete record. On July 20, 1841, Stephen entered Jefferson College at Canonsburg, Pennsylvania, of which his grandfather, James Foster, had been one of the first trustees, and where his father had gained his schooling when it was the "Log College," or Canonsburg Academy. Stephen was at Canonsburg for not more than seven days; the town was probably too near home (eighteen miles) for the homesick lad to stay away. The story is told in full by several letters, and the reasons and excuses for the shortness of his residence at Canonsburg offer light on the reactions of Stephen's home-loving nature.

William probably brought Stephen back to Pittsburgh the latter part of June, 1841, while his father and mother were still boarding at Mrs. Paul's, Second and Smithfield Streets. On July 24 Stephen, in Canonsburg, wrote this letter to William:

My Dear Brother,

I arrived here on last Tuesday, and found among the quantity of Students of this institution, several of my old acquaintances.

This is a very pretty situation where I board as it is on an elivation of about four hundred feet. We have about two hundred and thirty students here at the present time, and a library of about 1500 volumes.

Pa left this [place] on Wednesday last and is now at Warren I believe. [It was at this time that Thomas Wick, Henrietta's husband, had his business at Warren, Pa.]

The tuition instead of being $5.00 amounts to $12.50 and boarding $2.00 per week.

Pa paid my tuition bill in advance, as is customary at this place. Their is several other bills which I have not paid as I have not the means. Such as 2 or $3.00 for joining one of the literary societies, as all of the studens belong to them I was requested to joiin one and put it of for a couple of weeks, for as Pa has not much more than the means of geting along I thought I would write you this letter that you might considder over the matter. I will also have to pay boarding bill at the end of every month which will amount to $8.50 that is at the end of four weeks and a half which generally makes a month, and if you see fit to send me a little of the bino. once in a while I will insure you their is no inducements here to make me spend any money unnecesarily. I will allso have to pay about $1.25 per week for washing as I have to keep myself very clean here.

I would inform you in the meantime I need another summer coat or two and especially for Sunday.

The Ohio river is very low and falling gradually. The boats have ceased runing.

As I have made out a mideling long letter and am clear out of information (news) I would only say, wishing you a safe journey home and through life, and that I may some day be fit to render thanks to you for your unceasing kindness to me. I remain your ever grateful and affectionate brother

STEPHEN.

The August 12-14 letter from Stephen's mother to William,[1] telling him of the proposed move from Mrs. Paul's to William's house in Allegheny, contains also this important information:

Stephen will not stay at Cannonsburg—he says he has lost conseat of himself because he was once in his life a great fool, and that was when he did not go back with brother William. He begs me to ask you to say that he must board with Ma and go to day skool: . . .

Then follows a mother's plea for her youngest:

indeed, if I am in Allegheny Town I shall be almost too lonely without one child with me, for if I should be ill, I would be in a bad way.

Two weeks later Stephen himself wrote William, seeking to explain his action. The letter is dated August 28.

[1] See page 101.

My Dear Brother,

I suppose you are surprised and probably displeased at me for not being more punctual in writing to you every fortnight, as you wished to have me do. I will therefore proceed to make my best excuses.

When I wrote to you from Canonsburg I did not tell you whether I liked the place or not (if I remember aright) but now I will take the liberty of telling you that I became more disgusted with the place as long as I stayed in it. It is not a good time to begin college in the middle of the Session as I could not get into any class for three or four days after I went there, and when I did get started into a recitation it was in irregular hours.

If I had went [sic] as a regular student I might have been examined and got along very easily, but going as I did just to stay a session or two, I suppose they did not care much whether I was attended to or not. Besides, when I had been there but five days I took sick (from a disiness in my head occasioned by an overflow of the blood) and was confined to bed for two days.

To give emphasis to the seriousness of this episode, Stephen added a footnote at the bottom of his letter, connected with the original account by an asterisk.

When ever I would go to raise up out of bed I would become so dizy that I could scarcely see.

The main portion of the letter concludes the story of his illness.

In the night of of the second day of my Sickness, my nose took to bleeding which made me feel better the next morning.

Then follows an account of leaving Canonsburg.

It so happened that one of the students was coming in to town that day (Samuel Mongomery of Pittsburg) and I concluded I would come in with him, as he asked me to.

When I left Canonsburg your letter had not arrived. So that I wrote to Mr. Mercur (brother to the Mercur's in Towanda) to forward it on as soon as it arrived, but nevertheless I did not receive it untill about two weeks after won [you?] wrote it. Although you told me not to wate for your letters when I wrote, still I expected it every day so that I was put of beyond the regular time.

The next paragraph tells of the move to William's house in Allegheny, and also of the "day skool" to which Eliza referred.

When I did get it [William's letter] we were just preparing to move over here, which kept me buisy [sic] for two or three days, and as soon as we got partly moved I commenced going to School to Mr. Moody—So that I never got a fair chance to write untill to-day.

I hope you will pardon me for writing to you so extensively on the money subject. But at the same time I will let you know that a boy comes out mighty thin in Canonsburg without some of it in his pocket.

Pa had not told me that he would furnish me with as much money as I needed, or I would not have troubled you on that subject.

The letter also shows that there had been earnest family conferences on what Stephen should do with himself.

As were were all talking over different subjects the other evening among others the subject of the Navy was talked of. Now a midshipman is just what I fancy.

Stephen, the dreamer as a middie—perish even the thought! The letter concluded:

Pa is away in Washington County at a temperance meeting and will return this evening I think.

With these few lines I will bring to a close by stating that we are all well and in good spirits. Hopeing that you will ever be blessed with the same qualities I remain your ever affectionate and justly dutiful brother

STEPHEN.

I will try hereafter to come up to the mark in the letter writing line. . . .

If there was any witness to what Stephen's father said to his son when he left Canonsburg, such an observer failed to record what he may have heard. Lacking direct evidence, we may hazard a guess that the senior Foster's remarks were somewhat the same as those contained in a letter to William, September 3, 1841, less than a week after Stephen himself had written his brother.

I regret extremely that Stephen has not been able to appreciate
properly your generous exertions in his behalf, by availing himself
of the advantage of a college education, which will cause him much
regret before he arrives at my age; and he will no doubt express
those regrets in much sorrow to you both should you both live, long
after I shall be no more.

Then comes a paragraph which has been quoted earlier in
these pages.[2]

He is at school, now, with Mr. Moody, a first rate teacher of
mathematics in Pittsbg. and it is a source of much comfort to your
mother and myself, that he does not appear to have any evil propensities to indulge; he seeks no associates; and his leisure hours
are all devoted to musick, for which he possesses a strange talent.

2

The house William had built in Allegheny stood in a
pleasant spot. It lay next to the house the family had occupied before moving to Youngstown, and it faced directly
on the East Common of Allegheny. Near at hand was the
Allegheny River, with Pittsburgh on the opposite bank.
Next door to the Fosters' was the home of the Pentlands,
with a connecting gate in the fence that separated the two
houses. Across the Common was the home of Andrew
Robinson, who was later to marry the Pentland daughter,
Susan. Few of the old landmarks of this section are standing to-day, the several houses the Fosters occupied have
been replaced with new dwellings, but the church that stood
next door on the East Common is still there. The inscription on the present building reads:

FIRST M. P. CHURCH
BUILT A.D. 1831
REBUILT A.D. 1843

Stephen must have watched the rebuilding.

[2] See pages 80-81.

In his biography of Stephen,[3] Morrison fails to mention the Mr. Moody with whom Stephen went to study after he left Jefferson College. Morrison speaks of a Captain Jean Herbst, and states that Stephen studied French and German with this Belgian gentleman at about this time. The brother also claims that Stephen acquired proficiency in both languages.

It also appears from the same source that "Stephen became a creditable artist in water colors as an amusement, and some of his pictures are yet preserved with pride by his friends." Pity it is that a search for pictures by Stephen has failed to yield any specimens, either in the possession of his family or among the descendants of his friends.

What music study Stephen was able to accomplish is not definitely known to-day. Among the reminiscences of his friends and family there are frequent references to Henry Kleber, a Pittsburgh musician and teacher who is supposed to have had considerable influence on Stephen's career. Morrison states that Stephen studied with Kleber, but exactly when, and for how long, is not known.

Kleber was born in Darmstadt, Germany, in 1816, and was brought to Pittsburgh by his father in 1830. About five years later, when he was nineteen, it is said that he became the music instructor in Dr. Lacey's seminary, "the élite female school of the city." In 1845 Kleber, with his brother, established a piano and music store, H. Kleber & Bro., and it is fairly certain that Stephen spent considerable of his time on its premises.

It may be that the future composer had some lessons with Kleber in these early years after he left Canonsburg, but it is not probable that he had many of them. It seems more likely that when Stephen later started to compose songs, Kleber helped him put them in final shape.

Morrison [4] has the following to say about Stephen's musical studies, a statement that can be somewhat tempered by

[3] *Op. cit.*   [4] *Op. cit.*

the knowledge that it was written years later, and in memory of a beloved brother:

Stephen . . . needed only elementary instruction, for his rapid brain and quick perception scorned the slow progress by the beaten path, and he leaped forward to a comprehension of the whole scope of the instrument [piano] by the force of his great musical genius.

But he was not content to rely on inspiration alone for his guidance in music. He studied deeply, and burned much midnight oil over the works of the masters, especially Mozart, Beethoven and Weber. They were his delight, and he struggled for years and sounded the profoundest depths of musical science. The simple melodies which he gave to the public were not the accidental rays from an uncultured brain, but were the result of the most thorough and laborious analyses of harmonies, and when he completed them and launched them on the world, he knew they would strike favorably the ear of the most critical as well as the unlearned in music.

We may admit that Morrison was sincere in that paragraph, even though he could scarcely have spoken higher praise had he described the workmanship and faculty for self-criticism of Brahms or Hugo Wolf!

Stephen's father wrote that the boy's "leisure hours are all devoted to musick," and Morrison [5] tells how

He would sit at home in the evening at the piano and improvise by the hour beautiful strains and harmonies which he did not preserve, but let them float away like fragrant flowers cast upon the flowing water. Occasionally he would vary his occupation by singing in plaintive tones one of his own or other favorite songs. Of the latter class he much admired the "May Queen" of Tennyson, and the music as composed by Mr. Dempster. His rendering of the verse "To-night I saw the sun set, he set and left behind," etc., was truly pathetic. At times tears could be seen on his cheeks as he sang this song, so sensitive was his nature to the influence of true poetry combined with music. I usually sat near him on these occasions and listened quietly with profound delight. Sometimes he would whirl round on the piano stool and converse a few moments with me, then resume his improvisations and his singing.

Another anecdote by Morrison relates to these years.

[5] *Op. cit.*

It was difficult to get him to go into society at all. He had a great aversion to its shams and glitter, and preferred the realities of his home and the quiet of his study. When he was eighteen years old, a lady who was an old friend of the family, gave a large party, and invited us all, and added, "tell Stephen to bring his flute with him." That settled it so far as he was concerned. He would not go a step. He said, "tell Mrs. —— I will send my flute if she desires it." This dislike to being classed as a mere performer characterized him during his whole life, though he was not at all unsocial and willingly sang or played for the enjoyment of himself or others, if the occasions were spontaneous and not set up. He, however, often sang in chorus with others, upon occasions of concerts for charitable purposes, in Pittsburgh.

3

The letter that Foster, senior, wrote William on September 3, 1841, regretting Stephen's leaving college, tells of the household and its finances.

Your kind letter to your mother of the 23rd. ult. covering a ten Dollar Bank Note, came duly to hand, as also Henry's letter to her of the 20th ult. covering a like sum of ten Dollars. For these kindnesses you both deserve and receive our kind thanks and blessing.

The money came in good time, as we had two weeks ago, scraped our little plunder together, and your mother with Stephen and myself commenced keeping house in the old place. Thomas [Wick] and Henrietta with their little ones, soon after joined us, and we are now all together. Thomas pays us one Dollar per day for boarding and lodging his family, including a hired girl—they talk of returning to Youngstown in a week or two; I expect I shall be obliged to go to Warren in a day or two, in order to wind up (if I can) his business there. They will remain until my return.[6]

A month and a half later, October 18, Stephen's mother wrote William:

Thinking you would be crowded with letters from home, your Father writing and Stephen, I defer'd answering your last kind letter acknowledging the receipt of ten dollars untill now, Pa having written you immediately. He left this [place] for Erie on Thursday last. I expect him back on Monday.

[6] See page 55.

This was the year when Foster's case against the old transportation company was transferred to the Erie courts, and he finally settled for two-thirds of his original claim. Eliza's letter continues with intimate details of the household.

Stephen and I have the house to ourselves and lonely enough it is, so much so that it has induced a very pretty (girl, you think I am about to say, no, they like gay places where there is some stir on foot) tortoise-shell colour'd cat to take up her boarding and lodging with us. . . . Stephen gives her all the little bits he is permited to gather for the sake of her company. . . .

Then a statement we have quoted before:[7]

He is not so much devoted to music as he once was; other studies seem to be elevated in his opinion. He reads a great deal, and fools about none attall.

On November 14 Eliza sent her husband news of the neighborhood.

Everything around our neighbourhood looks natural and perfectly harmonizes with the very pleasant association of home. The Robinsons have been to see us, looking as cheerily as they could to welcome us back.

The new Christ Church takes up most of our attention at this time, as it is now completely under way; fine preacher, fine musick, fine stoves, plenty of room, and people flocking in. Mr. Woodward, our minister is indeed an indefaticable person, and is the agent in the hands of the Lord to make every thing prosper that he finds to do.

In one paragraph of this letter Eliza heaved a sigh of contentment.

What will I tell you about myself; a haknied stale story. You know what I am doing very well at this season, turning old clothes into new ones, looking after the baking and the cooking, and brushing about the house, and sometimes taking a comfortable rest in a rocking chair, by a pleasant coal-fire to read the Cronicle in the forenoon, and the daily American at four o'clock in the afternoon, going to bed at nine o'clock that I may rise at six to have breakfast

[7] See page 81.

for Morrison who is off to his business the moment it is over. We have ever and anon a quiet and peacible and temperate house, exactly such a one as I have always been looking for.

Although William Foster, senior, was busying himself with Thomas Wick's affairs, his own claim against the transportation company, and with temperance meetings, the principal object he was seeking was an appointment at Washington from Walter Forward, recently named as first Controller of the Treasury in the Harrison-Tyler administration. As early as March 30, 1841, when Stephen was still at Athens or Towanda, Foster had written to William:

On March 28, Mr. Forward received the appointment of first controller of the Treasury, salary $3500 per annum—12 or 15 clerks in office, and he assures me that I shall in future make one of them, at least $1000 per ann. and added that it was unnecessary for me to hawk about a petition on the subject. I cannot doubt his sincerity, and as soon as he gets fairly into the harness, and gets his clerks ranked and sized, he will write me. I don't know how we are to get off and pay expenses to Washington, but "sufficient for the day is the evil thereof"; I am pretty good at financiering and with an office in view, I will put forth all my genius, to go ahead.

Foster had a long wait for his office. April 28 he wrote William: "I have heard nothing from Mr. Forward yet"; on May 15: "If I should hear anything from Mr. Forward before you come out, will write you immediately"; and again September 3: "I have not a word from Washington City yet."

It was not until November that Foster finally reached Washington. On the 30th of that month he wrote William from the capital:

I arrived here to-day at 12 oclock and have just been to see Mr. Forward, who received me very cordially, and asked me to dine with him to-day—to-morrow he says he will put me in office.

It is evident that Henry, still with William, was to join his father immediately, and that plans for his entering the Land Office were already under way.

If Henry should not have left when you receive this letter, tell him to come on as soon as he pleases, tell him when he arrives at Washington to come to Fuller's hotel, on the Pennsylvania Avenue, and near the Treasury Office, he can get a Hack to bring him here with his baggage for 25 cents—from the railroad depot.

Foster planned that Stephen's mother was to come too.

I have thought that if you have your Barouch and two horses, that if you would bring them down to Harrisbg. with you that I would go that way and take them out to bring your mother over the mountains, I fear the journey by Stage in January would fatigue her exceedingly. I could go any time after Henry would be here a few days, but must be at Pittsbg. before Christmas Day.

4

But Eliza did not go to Washington just then. She stayed in Allegheny with Stephen. The father's November 30 letter to William said:

Stephen seems inclined to join you again if you remain there [Towanda], and go to school at Athens, but more of this hereafter.

Foster, senior, was not long at Washington. He left December 15 for Allegheny, where he was elected mayor of the city. Eliza later went to Washington to visit Henry, and a question in her letter of February 16, 1842, addressed to Morrison—"is all right with Pa and Stephen?" —shows that Stephen was with his father.

Eliza made an extended visit. By March 14 she had been in Baltimore, for on that date her husband wrote William:

We are getting along very well, but feel very lonesome in the evenings without your mother. but as she will probably not cross the mountains again shortly, I wish her to visit all her friends. She was in Baltimore at the date of her last letter a week ago.

And again on March 30:

. . . the boys and myself get along very quietly, but we are wretchedly lonesome without Mother—the days are getting very long and the evenings very dreary without her company, but as she is there, I wish her to see all her friends. I have not heard from her for two weeks, and do not know whereabouts she is, she last wrote us from Baltimore.

Meanwhile the Mayor of Allegheny, whose office afforded him "about enough business to keep from desponding," and who was pained from the necessity of witnessing "the awful depravity of human nature," [8] was doing his best to understand his youngest son. The father's letters to William show the situation clearly. On March 14:

I wish you could make a target bearer of Stephen, and find emplymt. for him, that you would take him through the summer. . . . He is uncommonly studious at home, but dislikes going to school, he says there is too much confusion in the school. I dislike to urge him, so long as he discovers no evil or idle propensities. . . . He says he would like to be in brother William's sun shine.

Again, on March 30:

I wrote you, on the subject of Stephen, and expect to hear from you soon; he is a very good boy, but I cannot get him to stick at school, he reads a good deal, and writes some in the office with me.

No thought or hint appears at any time that Stephen should follow his natural outlet and study music seriously.

The March 30 letter concludes with a statement that would provide an interesting anecdote if we only had details.

"Boz" is here, Morrison call'd on him to-day; Stephen and I will go to see him to-morrow.

Pity it is we cannot know what Dickens said to the future composer of "Old Folks at Home," if the plan for the visit was actually carried out!

Eliza returned in May. On the 24th of that month

[8] See page 19.

Thomas Wick, Henrietta's husband, died in Youngstown.
The family letters deal extensively with his death, and tell
of the plans for Henrietta and her three little children.
On the 27th of August Eliza took Stephen to Youngstown
for an extended visit. Her letter to William is interesting,
not only because it tells of the visit to Henrietta, but also
because of its account of the Foster household at Allegheny
during the previous summer.

I left home this day week, in company with Stephen, to stay some
time with Henrietta, in order by degrees to reconcile her to living
here. I believe your father has closed the house as to the living
part, and will only sleep in it. The additional expence of three
persons [two women, cousins, and a little boy from the South] living
on us for the last three months has made it necessary to close up for
awhile. Indeed, I do not know how long they would have hung
on if we had not come to that determination. Henrietta and her
children are charmingly fixed as to comfort and good health. While
we are here, we pay her two dollars a week a peace board. I will
stay with her untill the weather becomes colder than is good for me.
I understand that you intend to be out in September; if so the time
is nigh at hand. Henrietta anticipates considerable pleasure from
your visit. (September 3, 1842)

It was in September that William married his second
wife, Elizabeth Burnett.

By November Eliza Foster was back in Allegheny, while
Stephen stayed with his sister in Youngstown for another
month. On December 3, Morrison noted in his diary:

Pa returned from Erie by way of Youngstown, bringing Etty and
Stephen with him.

5

During these years, except for the periods when Morrison was away on business trips, Stephen and this brother
who was nearest him in age were constant companions.
While Stephen was in Youngstown Morrison went to New
Orleans, visiting every town and city along the Ohio and

Mississippi. What tales of Southern life he must have told the future writer of plantation songs! When they were both back in Allegheny in December the brothers went many places together. They saw "Mr. Booth perform Richard III, King Lear, and John Lump"; [9] at five o'clock on Christmas morning they attended the services at the Catholic church; and early in 1843 they went to hear Henry Russell, the famous ballad singer, composer of "Woodman, Spare That Tree," "The Old Arm Chair," and other songs that must have made a deep impression on Stephen, and doubtless exerted some influence on his own later songs.

During these months Morrison and Stephen were constantly borrowing from each other and trading among themselves. In Morrison's notebooks are numerous entries of frequent loans, all of them conscientiously repaid and the payments recorded. Although Stephen was not yet seventeen in February, 1843, and Morrison was approaching his twentieth birthday, the two boys were evidently of about the same size, for on the 22nd of the month, Washington's Birthday, Morrison bought Stephen's "good blue coat" from him for $10.

Stephen was now becoming increasingly absorbed in his music. That he was beginning to write songs is evident not only from the recollections of those who knew him, but also from the fact that his first song to be published was issued in December of 1844. Exactly when it was written is not known definitely, some say when Stephen was sixteen, two years before it was published. The words of the song are not Stephen's—only the music. The poem was written by George P. Morris—"Open Thy Lattice, Love"—and it appeared in a supplement to the *New Mirror* (volume of 1843-44), a Saturday paper edited in New York by Morris and Nathaniel P. Willis.

The poem had been set to music by another composer

[9] Entry in Morrison Foster's diary.

several years earlier, a fact noted under the title of the poem when printed in the "New Mirror." Joseph Philip Knight, the English song-writer who composed the music to Emma Willard's poem, "Rocked in the Cradle of the Deep" while he was in America in 1839, made a setting of "Open Thy Lattice," published in 1840. It is interesting to compare Knight's music with the song Stephen composed. Knight's setting is more musicianly, more resourceful in the development of its melodic idea. Stephen's song is far more spontaneous, and is often sung to-day, while Knight's is forgotten.

An idea of Stephen's musicianship at this time may be gained from comparison of the original manuscript of "Open Thy Lattice" with the first edition of the published version. The voice part—the melody—is identical in both, but the accompaniment differs materially. In some cases the harmonization has been changed, and often the accompanying figuration has been altered. Some of Stephen's elaborations in the piano part were fussy and awkward, and these are removed in the published copy.

Whether Henry Kleber had a hand in preparing the manuscript for publication, or whether the publisher's editor made the revisions, we cannot know, but the song was issued by George Willig of Philadelphia as a two page song, without title page, with this heading on the first page:

OPEN THY LATTICE LOVE
Composed for and dedicated
to
MISS SUSAN E. PENTLAND
Of Pittsburgh
by
L. C. FOSTER
Lines from the New Mirror

Poor Stephen, the publisher failed to print his name correctly on his very first song!

The dedication to Susan Pentland is interesting. This

pretty little miss was the daughter of the Captain Ephraim Pentland whose house adjoined the Fosters'. It is known that Stephen spent much time at the Pentland home, and it has been often suggested that there was a love affair between Susan and the young Stephen. This is hardly possible, at any rate during the period when Stephen wrote the song. Susan was very young then,[10] and as soon as she was grown up, she married Andrew Robinson, who lived across the East Common—in 1849, while Stephen was living in Cincinnati.

How the song ever came to be published by Willig in Philadelphia may never be known. Whether Stephen sent it to him, or whether it came to his notice through some one else is a mystery. Nor do we know how much, if anything, Stephen was paid for "Open Thy Lattice, Love." All we know is that it is a charming song, with no little individuality, and that it marks Stephen's début as a published song-writer.

There is another manuscript that seems to date from these years, a sixteen measure waltz, without title, dedicated to Miss Maria Bach. This piece has a pleasant flow of melody, but it is awkward and clumsily put on paper. It appears to be an exceedingly amateurish attempt to write out an idea improvised at the keyboard. If this waltz was actually written by Stephen Foster, it indicates the struggle he was waging. Musical ideas kept coming into his head, and there was no one to understand that he must learn now what to do with them. Nobody seemed to realize that here was a lad intended for a single purpose, one who would be a misfit as long as he tried to do anything else.

Morrison, in his book,[11] tells of musical gatherings that

---

[10] When the song was published (1844) Susan was thirteen. If, as Morrison Foster and Robert P. Nevin believed, the song was written when Stephen was sixteen, two years earlier, Susan would have been only eleven at the time.

[11] *Op. cit.*

occurred frequently in these years. He tells how starting in 1845 a club of young men met twice a week at Foster's home. Among the members were Susan Pentland's future husband, Andrew Robinson, J. Cust Blair, Robert P. McDowell, and Morrison and Stephen. Known as "The Knights of the S.T." (Square Table?), the club was most secret in its proceedings, and the meetings were marked by semi-burlesque rituals of the most formal sort. The sign of the order was a fish, and the watchwords were "Heroes, Fail Not." Each member had a fraternal name—Morrison was addressed as "Sir George Armstrong" and his office was "Grand Pantler and Commissary."

Five of the members were described in a poem written by Stephen. The manuscript (now in the Foster Hall Collection) is dated May 6, 1845.

THE FIVE "NICE YOUNG MEN"

First, there's Charley the elder, the sunday-school teacher,
    Who laughs with a groan,
    In an unearthly tone,
    Without moving a bone
    Or a feature.   (CHARLES P. SHIRAS)

Then Charley the younger, the Illinois *screecher,*
    Who never gets mad,
    But always seems glad
    While others are sad;
Though his face is so long that it wouldn't look bad
    On a methodist preacher.   (CHARLES RAHM)

There's Andy, who used to be great on a spree,
Whose *duds* (as he calls them) all fit to a T:
    But people do tell us
    He's got just as jealous
    Of Latimer as he can be.
    They say that he wishes
    The sharks and the *fishes*
Would catch him and eat him when he gets out to sea.
      (ANDREW L. ROBINSON)

And Bob, that smokes seventeen *tobies* a day,
He's liberal, however, and gives some away.
   Bob's been to college
   Picking up knowledge
But now he's got home and I hope he will stay.
                    (ROBT. P. MCDOWELL)

We will wind up with Harvey, the *bluffer,* the gay.
He can play on the fiddle (or thinks he can play)
   Harvey's mind
   Is inclined
   To all that's refined,
   With a count'nance so bright
   That it rivals the light
Of the sun that now cheers us in this sweet month of May.
                    (J. HARVEY DAVIS)

Writing personal poems was not the most important outgrowth of Stephen's connection with the "Knights of the S.T." According to Morrison, the group practiced songs at its meetings, and when the singers had learned all the current pieces then popular, Stephen tried his hand at writing songs for them himself. First he wrote "Lou'siana Belle." Morrison states that the group liked this song so much that at the next meeting Stephen produced "Old Uncle Ned," and Ann Eliza, his sister, later claimed that "Oh! Susanna" was also composed for the club.

6

The type of songs Stephen wrote at this time indicates the predominant influence that affected his early creative talents; in fact, it was not only the force that moulded the characteristic Foster song, it provided the outlet through which his songs attained their amazing vogue. And moreover, while it was an influence that affected Foster profoundly, it was a medium that Stephen himself completely reformed. He found the songs of the current minstrel shows crude, vulgar ditties that struck the popular fancy, but which were nevertheless lyrics and songs that in spite of their vulgarity actually represented something definitely American. Stephen made of this class of music a literature that is well worth preserving—he brought artistry and sincerity to a medium that before his entry had reeked of the alley and the barroom.

We have already learned that in his childhood Stephen was an able performer in a neighbor's carriage house, when as the star member of a group of playmates he earned "uproarious applause" singing "Zip Coon," "Long-tailed Blue," "Coal-Black Rose," and "Jump Jim Crow." The minstrel shows were in their infancy then, but "turns" in "black face" had already become enormously popular.

There are records of black face performances occurring even before 1800. Negro slaves were depicted on the stage at least as early as 1769, when Lewis Hallam delighted an audience in New York with his imitation of a drunken darkey. It is sometimes claimed that Gottlieb Graupner, the musician who organized a Philharmonic orchestra in early 19th century Boston, became the "father of Negro minstrelsy" by singing "in character," with the accompaniment of a banjo, a song called "The Gay Negro Boy" between the acts of a play at the Federal Street Theatre, Boston, December 30, 1799.[12]

The early years of the 19th century saw such pioneer performers as "Pot Pie Herbert," an ambitious vendor of pies who promoted the sale of his commodity by blackface advertising skits; "Hop" Robinson, who sang "Negro Philosophy" at a performance in New York; and the long-forgotten Andrew Jackson ("Dummy") Allen, who played the part of a Negro in *The Battle of Lake Champlain*.[13] There was also Bob Farrell, who in company with George Nichols disputed the authorship of "Zip Coon" with George Washington Dixon. Dixon made his début in a circus at

[12] See Howard, *Our American Music*, p. 138.
[13] See Carl Wittke, *Tambo and Bones*, Durham, N. C., Duke University Press, 1930.

Albany in 1827, and in the next year appeared at the
Chatham Theatre in New York. He was one of the first
to sing "Coal-Black Rose" and "Long-tailed Blue."

Few if any of the performances by these early song and
dance artists were organized into anything resembling the
minstrel shows of a decade or two later. The first performers would generally black up for a single turn and
appear between the acts of plays. Often in circuses clowns
would sing Negro-like songs from the backs of horses as
they cantered around the sawdust rings.

It must be borne in mind that the darkey of the minstrel
show was a figure exaggerated to the extent of caricature.
Francis Pendleton Gaines has described the genuine darkey
as "the folk-figure of a simple, somewhat rustic character,
instinctively humorous, irrationally credulous, gifted in song
and dance, interesting in spontaneous frolic, endowed with
artless philosophy." [14] Carl Wittke comments further on
this point.[15]

In the process of adapting this type to the theatre, the stage Negro
became quite a different person from the model on which he was
formed. More specifically, the plantation type which got into minstrelsy apparently was calculated to give the impression that all
Negroes were lazy, shiftless fellows, careless of the morrow. The
stage Negro loved watermelons and ate them in a peculiar way. He
turned out to be an expert wielder of the razor, a weapon which he
always had ready for use on such special social occasions as crap
games, of which the stage Negro was passionately fond.

In minstrelsy, the Negro type had all these characteristics and
many more. He always was distinguished by an unusually large
mouth and a peculiar kind of broad grin; he dressed in gaudy colors
and in a flashy style; he usually consumed more gin than he could
properly hold; and he loved chickens so well that he could not pass
a chicken-coop without falling into temptation. In minstrelsy, moreover, the Negro's alleged love for the grand manner led him to use
words so long that he not only did not understand their meaning,
but twisted the syllables in the most ludicrous fashion in his futile

[14] F. P. Gaines, *The Southern Plantation: A Study in the Development and
Accuracy of a Tradition*, New York, 1925.
[15] *Tambo and Bones*, op. cit.

efforts to pronounce them. This, in the main, was the Negro of the joke-book tradition and more especially of the minstrel tradition, and undoubtedly he was a somewhat different individual from the one to be found in real life in the Southern states. But it was this type of darky that the white minstrels strove to imitate or, better stated perhaps, created and perpetuated.

Pittsburgh, at the head of the Ohio River, enjoyed its full share of these "Ethiopian" performances. In fact the city is one of the claimants for the honor of being the scene of "Daddy" Rice's first performance of the "Jump Jim Crow" song. Thomas Dartmouth Rice was undoubtedly the man who "gave the first entertainment in which a black-face performer was not only the main actor, but the entire act," [16] and it was he who actually brought such performances to a vogue that produced many imitators. Rice, born in New York in 1808, served his apprenticeship in New York theatres and by travelling as an itinerant performer along the Ohio valley and among the frontier towns. In 1828 he was a member of Drake's company at the theatre in Louisville.

The origin of the "Jim Crow" song has become a legend in American folk-lore, and so many versions of the story have been told that it is impossible to learn the actual facts. Yet the myths all correspond in essential details, and it seems to be agreed that the event took place sometime between 1828 and 1830. Some say that the episode occurred in Louisville, others in Cincinnati, and there are those who hold that it took place in Pittsburgh.

Robert Peebles Nevin gave as colorful a version of the story as any that have been written.[17] According to his account Rice was walking along a street in Cincinnati when he heard an old Negro singing a song with this refrain:

> Turn about an' wheel about an' do jis so
> An' ebery time I turn about I jump Jim Crow.

[16] Wittke, *op. cit.*
[17] In an article, "Stephen C. Foster and Negro Minstrelsy" in *The Atlantic Monthly*, November, 1867.

As he trolled his song, the darkey lolled lazily on the box of his wagon. Rice was a shrewd enough showman to sense the value of this scene. Some versions of the story claim that the actor tried it out on an audience that very night, but Nevin says that he waited until his engagement in Cincinnati had closed and he had moved on to Pittsburgh. The date, according to Nevin, was in the Autumn of 1830. Rice was engaged for the old theatre on Fifth Street.

There was a negro in attendance at Griffith's Hotel, on Wood Street, named Cuff . . . who won a precarious subsistence by letting his open mouth, as a mark for boys to pitch pennies into, at three paces, and by carrying the trunks of passengers from the steamboats to the hotels. Cuff was precisely the subject for Rice's purpose. Slight persuasion induced him to accompany the actor to the theatre, where . . . Rice . . . ordered Cuff to disrobe, and proceeded to invest himself in the cast-off apparel. When the arrangements were complete, the bell rang, and Rice . . . waddled into view. The extraordinary apparition produced an instant effect. The crash of peanuts ceased in the pit, and through the circles passed a murmur and a bustle of liveliest expectation.

The orchestra played a short prelude, and then Rice sang the song he had learned from the Negro in Cincinnati. He aped his model in every respect. The audience went wild. Encore after encore was demanded, and Rice had to use his wits by improvising new verses with references to local events and persons.

The story has a sequel. Nevin continues:

Now it happened that Cuff, who meanwhile was crouching in dishabille under concealment of a projecting *flat* behind the performer, by some means received intelligence . . . of the near approach of a steamer to the Monongahela Wharf. Between himself and . . . a certain formidable competitor called Ginger, there existed an active rivalry in the baggage-carrying business. For Cuff to allow Ginger the advantage of an undisputed descent upon the luggage of the approaching vessel would . . . cast a damaging blemish upon his reputation. . . . After a minute or two of fidgety waiting for the song to end, Cuff's patience could endure no longer, and, cautiously hazarding a glimpse of his profile beyond the edge of the flat, he called in a hurried whisper: "Massa Rice, Massa Rice, must have my clo'se! . . . steamboat's comin'!"

Rice paid no heed, or else he did not hear the desperate Cuff, even when the Negro put forth his whole head. The applause was too much for Rice to miss one second of his advantage. Finally:

Driven to desperation, and forgetful in the emergency of every sense of propriety, Cuff, in ludicrous undress as he was, started from his place, rushed upon the stage, and, laying his hand upon the performer's shoulder, called out excitedly: "Massa Rice, Massa Rice, gi' me nigga's hat,—nigga's coat,—nigga's shoes,—gi' me nigga's t'ings! . . . STEAMBOAT'S COMIN'!!"

This was the final touch; the applause was so deafening that the curtain was dropped and the exits thrown open to show that the performance was over.

7

Some light on the date and place of Rice's début as "Jim Crow" may be gained from the whereabouts of William Cumming Peters, the musician and music dealer to whom Rice is said to have taken the song, and who put it in shape and published it. And who, incidentally, was a man we shall hear more of in connection with Stephen Foster.

Peters was born in England (in 1805) and came to Texas in the early 1820's. From 1825 to 1828 he taught music in Pittsburgh, and in 1829 moved to Louisville where he opened a music store. In 1839 he started a branch house in Cincinnati, and ten years later another branch in Baltimore. If, as the story tells, Rice took the song to Peters immediately after its first performance, the date must have been some time in 1828, if the episode occurred in Pittsburgh. Peters, however, did not become a music dealer until he went to Louisville. It was there that he first opened a music store. This furnishes strong evidence to support the claim of the Kentucky city, particularly as most of the accounts of Rice's performance give the date around 1829 and 1830. Cincinnati is eliminated because the incident is known to have occurred long before Peters opened his branch there in 1839.

Wherever it happened, the initial "Jim Crow" performance launched Rice on a career that brought him enormous fame and made him one of the highest paid performers of his day. He became a favorite in all the American cities, in Washington he launched Joseph Jefferson on his career by introducing him from a burlap bag as a miniature Jim Crow. In 1836 Rice became a sensation in London.

Rice himself appeared in very few minstrel shows. He was at his best alone, or as an added feature appearing between the acts of a play. His imitators, however, soon came to form themselves into groups, and by the 1840's the Virginia Minstrels, organized by Dan Emmett, the author and composer of "Dixie"; the Christy Minstrels, whose leader, E. P. Christy, was to play such an important part in Foster's career as a song-writer; the Bryants and many others had organized themselves into travelling troupes, and had made interlocutors and end-men, jokes and conundrums, as well as gaudy parades from the railroad station an American institution—certainly the most individual contribution America has ever made to the theatre.

Even if T. D. Rice's début was made in Louisville rather than in Pittsburgh, he was well known in the Pennsylvania city, and there is testimony to the fact that Stephen Foster knew him well. Rice's grandson has written of the association between Stephen and Rice.[18]

Foster as a mere boy had seen Rice on the stage at Pittsburg, and had been carried away by the "Jim Crow" craze of the time, to the

[18] Dean J. Rice, in the foreword to *Two Stephen C. Foster Songs,* New York, J. Fischer & Bro., 1931.

extent of trying his even then somewhat practiced hand at writing some farcical negro songs. He submitted some of these to Rice with the hope of their acceptance, but as Rice at that time composed his own songs, the boy's only reward was the praise and encouragement of the minstrel, and a promise that perhaps some other time he would consider some likely songs. However, this first meeting between the celebrated burnt cork comedian and the promising song writer was the foundation for a friendship between them which was only broken by T. D. Rice's death in 1860—a friendship of Foster's part that it was the high privilege of Thomas C. G. Rice, the minstrel's only son, to inherit after his father's death.

Thus we learn that in his 'teens Stephen not only heard the minstrel shows in Pittsburgh, he probably wrote his earliest songs for them. And it is apparent also that he raised his courage to the point of taking his songs to the leading performers and asking them to sing them.

Pittsburgh not only enjoyed the visits of travelling minstrel troupes, it also had the advantage of resident companies. One of the early troupes that often visited Pittsburgh appeared under the leadership of Nelson Kneass, a musician later to win fame as the composer, or at least as the adapter, of "Ben Bolt." In 1845 the manager of the company decided to enter another business, and the troupe was disbanded. Robert Nevin tells what happened next to Kneass.[19]

A certain Mr. Andrews, dealer in confections, cakes, and ices, being stirred by a spirit of enterprise, rented, in the year 1845, a second-floor hall on Wood Street, Pittsburg, supplied it with seats and small tables, advertised largely, employed cheap attractions— living statues, songs, dances, &c.—erected a stage, hired a piano, and, upon the dissolution of his band, engaged the services of Nelson Kneass as musician and manager. Admittance was free, the ten-cent ticket required at the door being received at its cost value within towards the payment of whatever might be called for at the tables. To keep alive the interest of the enterprise premiums were offered, from time to time, of a bracelet for the best conundrum, a ring with a ruby setting for the best comic song, and a golden chain for the

[19] *Op. cit.*

best sentimental song. The most and perhaps only really valuable reward—a genuine and very pretty silver cup, exhibited night after night, beforehand—was promised to the author of the best original negro song, to be presented before a certain date, and to be decided upon by a committee designated for the purpose by the audience at that time.

Nevin, of course, wrote largely from memory in his accounts of these early days, but the existence of Mr. Andrews' establishment can be established by contemporary evidence, particularly by an item of extreme importance to our own story. An advertisement in the Pittsburgh *Daily Commercial Journal*, September 11, 1847, announced the program to be rendered by the "Vocalists" at "Andrews' Eagle Ice Cream Saloon." The singers were Kneass and others announced as Mrs. Phillips, Mrs. Sharpe, Miss Bruce and Mr. Holman. One of the numbers on the program was "SUSANNA—A new song, never before given to the public."

That, of course, was in 1847, a little ahead of our present story, at a time when Stephen had gone to Cincinnati. It shows, however, that Foster had begun to associate with minstrel performers before that time and that he was showing them the songs he was writing.

We may further jump ahead of our chronology to finish the anecdote Nevin commenced in his account of Mr. Andrews' establishment. Morrison also told this story, but he was kind enough to omit names. When Stephen had gone to Cincinnati his brother persuaded him to send to Pittsburgh a song which Morrison could enter for him in the Andrews competition. After some persuasion Stephen forwarded the manuscript of "Away Down Souf, Whar de Corn Grows." The song, together with other entries, was duly performed by the company. The audience, by its applause, voted conclusively and unmistakably for Stephen's song, but the judges, no doubt according to their coaching, awarded the prize to a song written by a member of the performing company.

It is possible that "Wake Up Jake, or the Old Iron City" was the song that won first prize. The song was first published by W. C. Peters with several of Foster's songs, but the music itself credits the authorship to George Holman, and gives the information that "A magnificent Silver Cup was awarded to the Author of this song by A. Andrews, Esqr., of the Eagle Saloon, Pittsburgh, Pa."

Nor is this all of the story. The morning after this performance Morrison took Stephen's song to the United States District Court to enter it for copyright. Who should be there for the same purpose but Nelson Kneass, asking for a copyright on the song in his own name! Such treatment happened frequently to the songs Stephen handed to minstrel singers for performance.

Before leaving the minstrel performers we may conclude the account that Rice's grandson has written of his grandfather's relations with Foster, even though this too puts us ahead of our own account of Stephen. The younger Rice writes: [20]

It was at Cincinnati in 1851 [21] that the young American song writer presented himself again to Thomas D. Rice. . . . The later meeting . . . resulted in Rice's not only purchasing the song "Long-Ago Day" from Foster, but in Rice's requesting Foster to compose an air to some verses written by a G. Mellen (or Mellon) which Rice treasured for their sentiment. So the song "This Rose Will Remind You" came to be.

According to Foster's account of the songs related to Thos. C. G. Rice, the minstrel's son, after his father's death, the song "Long-Ago Day" was never brought to public attention by reason of the fact that a close associate of T. D. Rice advised the minstrel that its sentiment was a little anti-slavery and for that reason Southern audiences would receive it with coldness. This seemed hard to imagine and Foster resented the criticism. It was his desire to repossess the song after T. D. Rice's death and have it published but an embar-

[20] In the foreword to *Two Stephen C. Foster Songs*, op. cit.
[21] The date was probably earlier, for Stephen left Cincinnati early in 1850.

rassment in Rice's estate, at the time, prevented this. Rice had re-served the song "This Rose Will Remind You" for a production he was not destined to complete, so it likewise found oblivion.

The two songs were finally published in 1931, sixty-seven years after Stephen's death.

8

In 1846 Stephen received further encouragement as a composer; another song was published. Peters & Field of Cincinnati (the same Peters who had issued Rice's "Jump Jim Crow") brought out Stephen's "There's a Good Time Coming," and copyrighted it October 9, 1846. This is not a Negro dialect song, the music was composed to a poem Stephen had found in the *London Daily News*. Although the song does not mention the name of the author, the verses were written by Charles Mackay, who also wrote the words of Henry Russell's "Cheer, Boys, Cheer." Musically Stephen's music for "There's a Good Time Coming" is inferior to "Open Thy Lattice, Love," but never-theless it has a pleasant melody, its introduction brings a reminder of the schottische, and its accompaniment is con-siderably more elaborate than some of Stephen's later songs.

"There's a Good Time Coming" was dedicated to "Miss Mary D. Keller of Pittsburgh," one of the group of young ladies to whom the Knights of the S.T. were constant beaux. Others of this social set were "Ginny" and Annie Crosson, Annie and "Lib" Ogden, Julia Murray (in whom Morrison was much interested), Jane McDowell (who later became Stephen's wife), Caroline Denny and the young Susan Pentland. Mary Keller was the sister of Rachel Keller, who later married Harry Woods and went to live in Hazelwood, where it is claimed Stephen first played "Old Folks at Home" on the Woods piano, an instrument still preserved in Pittsburgh. It was to Rachel, as Mrs. Harry Woods, that Stephen dedicated "Farewell Old Cottage" (1851), and the song Robert Nevin claimed was written in 1839, but which was not published until 1858 —"Sadly to Mine Heart Appealing."

The parents of the Keller girls, Samuel and Prudence Keller, lived on Penn Street in Pittsburgh, and they were close friends of the Fosters'. Mary died in December of 1846, two months after the song Stephen dedicated to her was published. After her death Stephen composed "Where is Thy Spirit, Mary?", said to have been written in 1847 but not published until 1895, thirty-one years after Foster's own death.

Two anecdotes related by Morrison [22] offer light on Stephen's character. No dates are given, and they may or may not have occurred at this time, but they afford a portrait nevertheless. The first shows that he was tender hearted.

His sympathies were . . . always with the lowly and the poor. Once on a stormy winter night a little girl, sent on an errand, was run over by a dray and killed. She had her head and face covered by a shawl to keep off the peltings of the storm, and in crossing the street she ran under the horse's feet. Stephen was dressed and about going to an evening party when he learned of the tragedy. He went immediately to the house of the little girl's father, who was a poor working man and a neighbor whom he esteemed. He gave up all thought of going to the party and remained all night with the dead child and her afflicted parents, endeavoring to afford the latter what comfort he could. [23]

The other episode also probably occurred later, but it may be told here.

And yet this sensitive man had the nerve and courage of a lion physically. . . .

[22] *Op. cit.*
[23] It has been said that Foster's song, "Gentle Annie" was inspired by this episode. This song was first published in 1856.

One night as he was returning home from Pittsburgh to Allegheny, he found at the end of the bridge two brutes abusing and beating a drunken man. He of course interfered, and fought them both, rough and tumble all over the street. He managed to pick up a board in the scramble, with which he beat one almost senseless and chased the other ingloriously from the field. A knife wound on the cheek, received in the encounter, left a scar which went with him to his grave.

9

It is not to be assumed that Stephen's association with minstrel performers and the encouragement he may have received from some of them solved the problem of the young man's future for his family. In fact, such contacts with "Ethiopian" actors probably intensified the situation, for it is hard to imagine the Fosters looking on passively while Stephen held converse with those who exhibited "living statues" in a saloon, even though the place was merely an "ice cream saloon." And it is quite in line with the theory that Morrison understood and sympathized with Stephen that he should have been the one who urged his brother to enter a song in the Andrews-Kneass competition. It is significant, too, that if this episode occurred in 1847, while Stephen was in Cincinnati, it was at a time when the parents were away from Pittsburgh. Eliza Foster was living in Youngstown for a while, and her husband was travelling.

During this period Henry was still in the Land Office at Washington, and a letter he wrote to Morrison, March 16, 1846, shows what had been planned for Stephen.

I received your acceptable letter of the 12th inst. & it seems that the appointment to West Point resulted (I can scarcely believe that there is so little justice in our Government) in that of young McK. & had I not been under the impression that you would be informed of that fact by some of his friends, I should have informed you some time since. However, I make no complaints, hoping that it may result for the best, as I doubt very much whether Steve's health would have permitted him to remain at the point, had he received the appointment. . . .

It is doubtful that "young McK." knew the good turn he was doing Stephen by winning the appointment from him, nor is it pleasant to think what might have happened when Stephen's dislike of discipline and routine had irritated a few army officers. We can imagine that there were several voices in the discussions on Stephen's future, for Henry's concluding sentence—"With much love to Ma, Etty, Steve, Pa & the children"—shows that Henrietta was in Allegheny at the time.

Further light on the family attitude is furnished by another sentence in Henry's letter.

Tell Steve not to be discouraged & to try & get at some employment as soon as possible.

It is clear from that statement that the Fosters did not consider writing songs as "employment."

A further document shows that Stephen was still in Allegheny October 31, 1846. On that date his father wrote Morrison a letter from New Castle, telling that Henrietta's children had been left an annuity of $30 a year until they became of age. To this letter he added a postscript— "With much love to Ma & Stephy." We know then that it was after the date of this letter that Stephen went to Cincinnati.

As far back as 1840 brother Dunning had gone into steamboating. We have already learned that on March 24 of that year his father wrote William; "Dunning is still on a steam boat as clerk." [24] On August 7 Eliza Foster wrote William:

Dunning and Augustus Anshutes have purchased and loaded a keel boat and have been seven days under way to Louisville.

And on February 13, 1841:

[24] See page 58.

Dunning has gone on a Steam Boat in the Mississippi trade at 75 dollars per month and found.

By 1846 Dunning had left steamboating for a time and had entered into his partnership with Archibald Irwin, as Irwin & Foster, commission merchants on Cassilly's Row in Cincinnati. Having failed to get an appointment to West Point for Stephen, and anxious to get him "at some employment as soon as possible," the family quite naturally thought of Dunning, just as they had turned to William when Stephen went to Towanda.

Dunning accordingly agreed to have Stephen come to Cincinnati as his bookkeeper, and so the twenty-year-old "idle dreamer," in the eyes of his family a drifter, sailed down the Ohio from Pittsburgh, bound for a place where he would learn how to make an honest living, according to the standards of pioneer commerce.

V

OH! SUSANNA

I

CINCINNATI has considerable justice on its side when it lays claim to an important part of Stephen Foster's career. While we may not be certain which of his early songs he wrote in Cincinnati, he nevertheless had his residence there when these works achieved their rapid and amazing success. Moreover, it was during these years that Stephen decided definitely to abandon bookkeeping, or any other form of conventional business activity, to make the writing of songs his profession.

It was not that he was a failure as a bookkeeper. Morrison has told that his penmanship was excellent, and for proof of this claim we need only consult the many letters that Stephen wrote, and other documents which are written in a handwriting that for legibility and regularity might well cause envy in the heart of many a professional copyist or draftsman. The decision to give all of his time to music was made rather because when Foster came of age it was apparent that he could write songs that would be successful commercially. With that proof in hand, he had an argument to convince his friends and family that he could earn as good a living in music as others could in the accepted channels of commerce—perhaps better.

We do not know exactly when Stephen went to Cincinnati, it was probably late in 1846 or early in 1847. He did not go to an absolutely strange place. He had visited the Ohio city before, and in those days the Ohio River and the steamboats bound Pittsburgh, Cincinnati and Louisville closely together. Not only was there a constant interchange of commerce between the towns, the society of the three cities mingled frequently. Stephen's brother Dunning, young and unmarried, was a member of the social circles of Cincinnati, and Stephen himself had many friends in the city before he went there to live.

E. Jay Wohlgemuth has written a delightful account of the place of Cincinnati in Foster's life,[1] and while the author himself admits that some of his material is taken from verbal narratives without any attempt at verification, he has made a valuable contribution to data on Foster through his examination of Cincinnati directories. He also provides local color in his description of the place where Stephen did his work as bookkeeper.

In the Forties the Public Landing was the most conspicuous and important center of the city. The firm of Irwin & Foster were steamboat agents and commission merchants, at first located at No. 4 Cassilly's Row and afterwards at 22 Broadway, between Pearl and Second streets. A picture in Dr. Goss's history shows this old row, which in later years was known as "Rat Row." But in Foster's time it was the pick of locations, especially for a river business. There were sixteen steamboat and commission agencies listed in the city directory of 1846 and they were nearly all in this section. Old residents no doubt recall this row of buildings which was torn down some years ago to make way for the L. & N. railroad tracks. Only the rear of the row was on East Front street, but the offices and stores extended through from the real front, which was known as Giffin street. These stores were four stories high on the river side and three stories high on the Front street side. Number Four was presumably the fourth store from the corner of Front and Broadway.

The river front of course presented the most lively and varied appearance imaginable. From Main to Walnut it used to be known as Gilmour's Landing and from Broadway to Ludlow it was Wiggins' Landing. The Public Landing was between. There were no wharfboats, but "stages" were rigged and thrown out from the boats to the shore to form a gangway.

We have already learned that both Dunning and Stephen boarded with Mrs. Jane Griffin.[2] In 1846 the directory

[1] *Within Three Chords,* by E. Jay Wohlgemuth: Indianapolis, 1928.
[2] See page 58.

shows that Dunning lived at the Broadway Hotel, corner
of Broadway and Second Street. In that year Mrs. Griffin
had her boarding house at the corner of MacAllister and
Fourth Streets. When Dunning and Stephen lived with
her (1849-50 directory) she had her establishment on the
south side of Fourth Street between Broadway and Ludlow.
The entries in the later directory show:

Foster Stephen, b.k. Irwin & Foster, bds. Mrs. Griffin

Dunning is listed at the same address.

2

It is not likely that Stephen wrote "Lou'siana Belle" or
"Oh! Susanna" in Cincinnati. They were probably composed before he left Pittsburgh. We have already learned
that some persons claim these songs were written for the
"Knights of the S.T." We know also that Stephen had
given manuscript copies to various minstrel performers.

It is only from the many, almost simultaneous editions
of "Oh! Susanna" and a few letters, that we can reconstruct
the events of these years. William C. Peters, the publisher
who had issued "Jump Jim Crow" some fifteen years
earlier, had his music store in Cincinnati by this time as
well as in Louisville, and he probably divided his time between the two cities. The Cincinnati directories give the
following addresses for the Peters firm:[3]

1846—Peters & Company . . . South side of Fourth Street between
    Main & Sycamore
1849—Peters, Field & Company . . . 12th and Walnut Streets
1851—William C. Peters & Son . . . Melodian Bdg. cor. Fourth
    and Walnut

From one of Stephen's letters, which we shall quote presently, we know that Foster gave Peters several of his songs

[3] See page 124.

to publish.   Undoubtedly the songs were being sung in
public from manuscript and were meeting with the approval
of audiences.

Here is Morrison Foster's version [4] of Stephen's relations with Peters:

> While in Cincinnati he wrote "Oh, Susanna," a song which soon
> became famous. [The place of writing, I believe, is open to question.]
> There was then in Cincinnati in the music business, W. C. Peters,
> whom Stephen had known in Pittsburgh, and who had taught music in
> our family. [Peters left Pittsburgh in 1828.] Stephen had no idea at
> this time of deriving any emolument from his musical compositions,
> so he made a present of "Old Uncle Ned" and "Oh, Susanna" to
> Mr. Peters. The latter made ten thousand dollars out of them, and
> established a music publishing house which became the largest in
> the West. The fame of these two songs went around the world, and
> thousands sang and played them who never heard the name of the
> author or knew whence they came.

The "ten thousand dollars" that Peters made from
Stephen's songs may have enabled Peters to expand his business, but it was of course "established" as a publishing
house long before Stephen came along. It is true that in
1849 Peters opened another branch in Baltimore, and for
a year published a musical magazine in that city—*The
Olio*. It is possible that the earnings of Foster's songs
helped him start his new venture.

Robert Peebles Nevin tells a story that is substantially
the same as that of Morrison's,[5] except for the matter of
Peters' payment for the songs. Nevin, in his article, is
slightly mixed in his chronology, for according to his account the incidents occurred after Stephen had returned
to Pittsburgh from Cincinnati. Possibly this is why Morrison himself later made the error of stating that Stephen
returned home from Cincinnati in 1848, when contemporary documents show that he was there until 1850. Nevin's

[4] *Op. cit.*
[5] "Stephen C. Foster and Negro Minstrelsy," *The Atlantic Monthly*, Nov.,
1867.

account starts with the story of the club of friends in Pittsburgh, for which Stephen wrote "Lou'siana Belle."

The piece elicited unanimous applause. Its success in the clubroom opened to it a wider field, each member acting as an agent of dissemination outside, so that in the course of a few nights the song was sung in almost every parlor in Pittsburg. Foster then brought to light his portfolio specimens, since universally known as "Uncle Ned," and "O Susanna!" The favor with which these latter were received surpassed even that rewarding the "Lou'siana Belle." Although limited to the one slow process of communication—from mouth to ear—their fame spread far and wide, until from the drawing-rooms of Cincinnati they were introduced into its concert-halls, and there became known to Mr. W. C. Peters who at once addressed letters requesting copies for publication. These were cheerfully furnished by the author. He did not look for remuneration. For "Uncle Ned," which first appeared (in 1847) [The correct date was 1848.], he received none; "O Susanna!" soon followed, and "imagine my delight," he writes, "in receiving one hundred dollars in cash! Though this song was not successful," he continues, "yet the two fifty-dollar bills I received for it had the effect of starting me on my present vocation of song-writer."

It is difficult to imagine that Stephen, or any one else, would make the statement that "Oh! Susanna" was not successful. Not only did it appear immediately in the repertoire of every minstrel show, it became the national anthem and marching song of the forty-niners on their way to California.

3

While the accounts of Morrison Foster and Nevin are probably accurate in essentials, the story of "Oh! Susanna" and the other early songs is far more complicated than these versions. We have already learned that "Oh! Susanna" was sung, possibly for the first time, at Andrews' Eagle Ice Cream Saloon in Pittsburgh, September 11, 1847. In regard to Peters, here is the chronology of his publishing of Foster's songs:

1846—Oct. 9—"There's a Good Time Coming" entered for copyright by Peters & Field, Cincinnati.

1847—Oct. 18—"Lou'siana Belle" and "What Must a Fairy's Dream Be?" entered for copyright by W. C. Peters, Cincinnati.

1848—May 16—Peters advertised "Uncle Ned" as "this day published."

    July 15—Peters advertised "Stay Summer Breath" as "just published."

    Sept. 6—Peters advertised "Susanna Don't You Cry" as "recently published."

    Dec. 30—"Away Down South," "Susanna," "Uncle Ned," "Santa Anna's Retreat from Buena Vista," and "Stay Summer Breath" entered for copyright by W. C. Peters & Co., Louisville.

1849—Nov. 21—"Summer Longings" entered for copyright by W. C. Peters, Baltimore.

1850—Feb. 12—"Soirée Polka" entered for copyright by W. C. Peters, Baltimore.

This appears simple and straightforward, but actually the question of who first printed "Oh! Susanna" and "Uncle Ned," and where the manuscripts that fell into the hands of publishers came from, is a tangle that would delight the heart of any detective in Scotland Yard. For example, there was the New York publisher, William E. Millet, who issued printed copies of both "Uncle Ned" and "Oh! Susanna." Millet entered "Uncle Ned" for copyright May 16, 1848 (by coincidence on the same day that Peters advertised the song as "this day published"), and although he claims copyright on his edition of "Oh! Susanna," there is no copyright entry in the Library of Congress. It appears that Millet addressed a letter to Foster asking who had the right to publish these songs, for on May 25, 1849, Stephen wrote from Cincinnati:

Mr. Wm. E. Millet

Dear Sir

    I hasten to acknowledge the receipt of your favor of the 21st inst. and to give you what information I can touching the subject of your inquiry.

I gave manuscript copies of each of the songs "Lou'siana Belle"—"Uncle Ned"—& "Oh, Susanna" to several persons before I gave them to Mr. Peters for publication, but in neither instance with any permission nor *restriction* in regard to publishing them, unless contained in a letter to Mr. Roark accompanying the m.s. of "Uncle Ned"—although of this I am doubtful. Mr. Peters has my receipt for each of the songs.

The only information which I can give you in regard to dates, as my memory does not serve me, must be in copying the years named on the title-pages of the Cincinnati publications, from which I infer that "Lou'siana Belle" was copy-righted in 1847—the others in 1848.

If I see Mr. Roark (who lives in our city) I will give you further information in regard to the letter which I wrote him. I have the honor, sir, to subscribe myself

Very Respectfully Yours
STEPHEN C. FOSTER.

The reference to "Mr. Roark" is illuminating. William Roark was a minstrel performer, belonging to the troupe whose members called themselves the "Sable Harmonists." Roark himself was the gentleman with long curls whose picture appears in the lithographs of the company. It is something of a temptation to picture him nightly as he made up in blackface tucking these curls under the edges of his kinky wig.

The Peters editions of "Lou'siana Belle," "Uncle Ned," "Away Down South" and "Susanna" were issued by Peters under the collective title-page of "Songs of the Sable Harmonists." Nelson Kneass had been a member of the troupe before he settled in Pittsburgh. It is important to know that the Sable Harmonists were in Cincinnati on September 2, 1847, and that on September 15 they were advertised in Pittsburgh. It was on September 11 that "Susanna" was sung by Mr. Kneass at Mr. Andrews' establishment.[6] This suggests a possibility, an extremely slender one, that the song came to Kneass from Cincinnati, brought by his former associates, the Sable Harmonists, who had

[6] See page 127.

Edwin P. Christy   William Roark

Sketches by Joseph Muller in Foster Hall Collection

obtained it from Foster in the Ohio city. In that case it is possible that the song was composed in Cincinnati after all.

Stephen's letter to Millet indicates the cause of so many editions of the songs. Foster was generous with manuscript copies. In that day common law copyright, protecting the author of a manuscript until publication, was apparently not yet established, and the first to present a work at the district copyright office was allowed to take out a copyright. Not only did publishers print editions from the manuscript copies that Stephen handed out to minstrel performers, others who had only heard the song wrote out versions of their own which were published. This fact is apparent from the differences, musical and poetic, between the various editions.

Mr. R. W. Gordon of Washington, D. C., has conducted extensive research into the chronology of "Oh! Susanna" editions, and through shrewd deduction and exhaustive comparison of many issues has arrived at a list that is as accurate as can be made from existing records. I give the list in full, principally because the information on the title pages shows what minstrel companies were singing the song. The Millet edition does not appear on this list, because this New York publisher apparently did not enter the song for copyright.

1. C. Holt, Jr.[7] . . . . .February 25, 1848
   Oh! Susanna Sung by G. N. Christy of the Christy Minstrels
   Copyright deposited in Southern New York

2. Joseph F. Atwill . . . . .August 28, 1848
   Susanna don't you cry for me. Re-Written and Arranged by William Clifton.
   Copyright deposited in Southern New York

[7] It is possible that Stephen and Morrison attempted to secure some interest in Holt's edition of the song, for when Morrison took a business trip to New York in October, 1848, he entered in his notebook the names of various persons he was to call on. Among the entries was: "N. Y. 260 Broadway, C. Holt, Published Susanna."

3. Elias Howe.........................September 12, 1848
   The Ethiopian Glee Book . . . No. 2.
   [This contains Oh Susanna on page 88, "By permission
   of C. Holt, Jr., proprietor of the copyright."]
   Copyright deposited in Massachusetts

4. William Vanderbeek, Agent.................:Oct. 30, 1848
   The Gems of the Christy's
   [The title page contains the titles of 25 songs, among
   them Oh Susanna.]
   Copyright deposited in Southern New York

5. Wm. Vanderbeek, Agent.....................Nov. 4, 1848
   Julius Quadrilles Arranged from the celebrated Christy
   Melodies By John Casper Scherpf—Second Sett.
   > Happy are we
   > Oh Susanna
   > O carry me back
   > Rosa Lee
   > De Bold Nigger Boy
   Copyright deposited in Southern New York

6. F. D. Benteen [8]...........................Nov. 21, 1848
   Oh! Susanna an Ethiopian melody composed with variations
   for the Piano Forte by J. Hunter.
   Copyright deposited in Maryland

7. Oliver Ditson............................Nov. 22, 1848
   Oh Susanna! With Easy Variations composed for the
   Piano Forte By Edward L. White.
   Copyright deposited in Massachusetts

8. Oliver Ditson............................Nov. 22, 1848
   Oh! Susanna Quick Step. In which are introduced the
   favorite airs of Oh! Susanna & Oh! Carry me back &c.
   Arranged by Edward L. White.
   Copyright deposited in Massachusetts

9. W. C. Peters...............................Dec. 30, 1848
   Songs of the Sable Harmonists
   Susanna as sung by Mr. Tichnor of the Sable Harmonists.
   Copyright deposited in Kentucky

---

[8] On Dec. 16, 1848, Benteen also copyrighted "Old Uncle Ned," an Ethiopian melody arr. with symphonies and accompaniment for the voice and piano by R. O. Wilson.

10. George Willig, Jr............................Jan. 8, 1849
    Susanna Polka composed for the Piano Forte by J. E. Muller.
    Copyright deposited in Maryland

11. F. D. Benteen..............................Jan. 11, 1849
    Susanna Polka for the Piano Forte as played with unbounded
    applause by the Steyermark Musical Company composed by
    Francis Rziha Leader of the Company.
    Copyright deposited in Maryland

12. F. D. Benteen..............................Feb. 8, 1849
    Oh Susanna Quick Step, composed and arranged for the
    Piano Forte. By R. O. Wilson.
    Copyright deposited in Maryland

13. Firth, Pond & Co..........................April 23, 1849
    The Popular Melody Oh Susanna   Arranged with intro-
    duction & brilliant variations   By Henry Herz.
    Copyright deposited in Southern New York

14. Lee & Walker............................April 24, 1849
    Oh Susanna   A popular Ethiopian Song arranged for the
    Guitar   By F. Weiland.
    Copyright deposited in Eastern Pennsylvania

15. Lee & Walker.............................June 30, 1849
    à Mademoiselle Emma Virginia Welsh   Salut à Washing-
    ton or Gems of the South   Six Favorite Melodies with
    Variations for the Piano Forte   By Charles Grobe.
        No. 1   Oh Susanna
    Copyright deposited in Eastern Pennsylvania

16. C. Holt, Jr...............................April 30, 1850
    The Celebrated Ethiopian Song   Oh! Susanna or "Don't
    you cry for me."   As a Quick Step   Introducing also "Stop
    that knocking at the door."   Arranged for the Piano Forte.
    Copyright deposited in Southern New York

17. C. Holt, Jr...............................April 30, 1850
    Susanna Quadrilles   Arranged from Christy's Melodies for
    the Piano Forte   By Henry Chadwick.
    Copyright deposited in Southern New York

18. C. Holt, Jr...............................April 30, 1850
    Oh! Susanna.   "Don't you cry for me."   One of Christy's
    Melodies   Arranged for the Guitar   By Henry Chadwick.
    Copyright deposited in Southern New York

19. C. Holt, Jr................................April 30, 1850
   Susanna Polka Arranged for the Piano Forte and Dedi-
   cated to Miss Julia Westlake By Henry Chadwick.
   Copyright deposited in Southern New York

20. W. C. Peters...............................Feb. 14, 1851
   Susanna
   Copyright deposited in Maryland

On some of these many editions of his early songs Foster
was credited with authorship, but on most of them there
was no mention of his name. Probably the publishers in
many cases had no idea who wrote the songs. The Holt
edition of "Oh! Susanna" gives merely the information
that the song was "sung by G. N. Christy of the Christy
Minstrels" and offers no light on who may have composed
it. Peters' edition of "Oh! Susanna" gives Foster's name
as the author and composer, as does the same publisher's
issue of "Old Uncle Ned," but in the edition of "Lou'siana
Belle," issued by Peters the preceding year, Foster's name
is omitted entirely and the song is published as "written
for and sung by Joseph Murphy of the Sable Harmonists."
"Away Down South" (thus on the title page and "Away
Down Souf'" above the first page of music) gives due
credit to Foster.

4

"Oh! Susanna" is a glorious bit of nonsense, and it shows
a side of Stephen Foster's nature that became less apparent as he grew more introspective in his later years. Here
is a love of boisterous fun, of rollicking good humor that
may contain nothing of subtlety, but nevertheless shows a
wealth of jovial good spirits that will ever prove highly
infectious. The very lilt of the song was catching, so contagious that almost every one in America was singing it
before he realized what he was singing. The song travelled
to foreign lands. The Germans sing "Ich komm von Ala-
bama, Mit der Banjo auf dem Knie" and many nations have

their version of the song. Bayard Taylor, writing in 1853,
tells how he heard a wandering Hindoo minstrel sing "Oh!
Susanna" in Delhi.[9]

But what has made the song most typically an American
folk-song is the use that was made of it by the forty-niners.
In January of 1848 gold was discovered in California.
February second of the same year the United States signed
a treaty with Mexico, and California and New Mexico
were ceded to us. By 1849 the trails were almost choked
with westward travellers, and their favorite song en route
and around their camp-fires at night was "Oh! Susanna."
Maybe it was the carefree, jaunty lilt of the song that made
it so appropriate, but whatever it was that endeared it to
these pioneers, "Oh! Susanna" is always considered the
"theme song," the "leitmotif" of the California gold rush,
whether it is pictured in books, the movies or on the radio.

"Oh! Susanna" is a quite different affair from "Jump
Jim Crow." The earlier song is catchy in its refrain, but
it has not the absolute command to join in the chorus that
lies in "Oh! Susanna." And while the words of Foster's
song are nonsense, and the humor slapstick, there is fun
in such foolishness as

> It rained all night the day I left,
> The weather it was dry,
> The sun so hot I froze to death;
> Susanna, don't you cry.

And then the refrain—everybody, please!

> Oh! Susanna, don't you cry for me,
> I've come from Alabama wid—(long hold)
> My banjo on my knee.

The list of pirated editions of the song shows something
of the variety of uses to which it was immediately put—in
minstrel shows, of course—by the Sable Harmonists, the
Christy Minstrels, and in such collections of "Negro" songs

[9] In *A Visit to India, China and Japan.*

as "The Ethiopian Glee Book" (published, incidentally, in New England). Then it appeared in many versions which took it to mid-century parlors, where we may be sure it was played by many a young miss as the "Susanna Polka" or in the numerous arrangements with "easy variations for the Piano Forte." It was used at parties as a quadrille, by bands as a quick-step, and the fact that it also reached the concert halls is shown by the published variations (characterized as "brilliant" on the title-page) of Henry (Henri) Herz. Herz was a French pianist who came to America in 1845 to repair his fortunes, and it was he who really started the vogue, in Europe as well as in the United States, for variations, fantasias, and the florid runs and trills that were so characteristic of a certain type of nineteenth-century piano music.

We find also on our list the "Susanna Polka . . . as played with unbounded applause by the Steyermark Musical Company." This was a little orchestra that came to America in 1846, and although its concerts did not prove successful financially, it accomplished valiant pioneer work. The leader and the composer of this "Susanna Polka," Francis Rziha (later spelled Riha), afterwards became second violin of the Mendelssohn Quintette Club, one of the first chamber music organizations in America.

"Susanna" was adopted by both the high and lowly within a few months of her birth, and bold tom-boy though she was, she has had also those qualities that win the hearts of all who have ever known her.

5

The dedications of Foster's songs tell of his associates during the periods in which the songs were written. "Stay Summer Breath," copyrighted by Peters (Louisville), December 30, 1848, is dedicated to Sophie B. Marshall. Sophie's mother, Ann Cassilly, had been a schoolmate of

Stephen's sister Charlotte at St. Joseph's Academy, the Convent in Emmitsburg, Maryland. Sophie's father was Dr. Marshall of Cincinnati, and her grandfather on her mother's side was Michael P. Cassilly, probably a member of the firm of C. & W. Cassilly, for which Cassilly's Row was named.

Michael Cassilly had lived formerly in Pittsburgh, where he had been a friend of the Fosters'. It was his home that Eliza Foster, with Stephen and Henrietta, visited in Cincinnati on their six weeks' trip in 1833.[10] They "remained a week at Mr. Cassilys on Broad Way, handsomly treated," and it was the same Mr. Cassilly who, when they left, "gallanted" Eliza "down to the water in his new state coach."

When Stephen came to Cincinnati the Cassillys were still living on the west side of Broadway, between Third and Fourth Streets, and when Stephen boarded at Mrs. Griffin's he lived just around the corner from these friends. He was on the south side of Fourth Street, between Broadway and Ludlow. It can well be imagined that Stephen was welcomed at the Cassilly home, and that he went there frequently, particularly as Sophie Marshall's soprano voice provided a common interest. Morrison Foster wrote that her voice was beautiful, and that she sang with much grace.[11]

Something of Stephen's acquaintanceship with music, and of his taste, may be learned from a bound book of music now in the Stephen Foster Memorial Home in Pittsburgh, a volume that apparently dates from this period. This was Stephen's own book, and his name is printed in gold letters on the cover. It may be approximately dated by the fact that all of Stephen's works that it contains are those that were published while he was still in Cincinnati or before he went there—"Santa Anna's Retreat from Buena Vista" (a quick-step for piano), "Stay Summer Breath," "What Must

---

[10] See page 53.　　　　　[11] *Op. cit.*

a Fairy's Dream Be?" "Open Thy Lattice," "There's a Good Time Coming," "Away Down South," "Susanna," "Uncle Ned," and "Lou'siana Belle."

The music by others, bound in the first half of the book's contents, consists of the following pieces:

Sounds from Home—Valse Styrian, as performed by the Steyer-markische Company, by Francis Rziha (published 1848)
La Miranda, Valse Brillante, by Henry Kleber (published 1848)
Valse Brillante, pour le Piano Forte . . . par Th. Döhler (published before 1844)
L'Invitation a la Valse, . . . C. M. de Weber [sic]
Nocturne, pour le Piano Forte par Theodore Döhler (published between 1844 and 1849)
Trois Reveries pour le Piano Forte par Henry Rosellen
    No. 1 Le Tremolo

There is nothing about such a list that shows any re-markable familiarity with the classics, or even with the best music of the period. It is, however, a highly representa-tive, average group of pieces that might be expected to ap-pear in the collection of any music lover or amateur musi-cian of that day. The Weber piece has proved its lasting merits, and even though the others are seldom heard nowa-days, they were considerably in vogue during Stephen's early manhood. Döhler was a composer of salon pieces which proved highly popular; of Rziha we have already learned; Kleber was the Pittsburgh musician with whom Stephen may have studied; and Rosellen was a pupil and imitator of Herz who composed many pieces of a drawing-room character. If Stephen played these pieces himself, as may be assumed from the fact that he owned copies of them, he must have been a reasonably accomplished per-former on the pianoforte.

It is known, too, that Stephen attended concerts in Cin-cinnati, and associated with musicians who visited the city. One of these associations is recounted in a letter to Mor-rison, April 27, 1849.

DEAR MIT,

You must be tired waiting for an answer to the many favors which I have received from you, not the least welcome of which was that introducing to my acquaintance Signor Biscaccianti and his accomplished lady. I called on Madame Biscaccianti and was as much delighted by her conversation and agreeable manner as I was subsequently by her singing at her concerts. She spoke very affectionately of you and the ladies who accompanied you on the occasion of your visit to her, as if you had been her own brother as well as mine. Her concerts were very well attended, indeed such was her encouragement, notwithstanding the formidable opposition carried on at the theatre by Mr. Macready, that she expressed an intention to return after she should have made a visit to Louisville, where she is now singing.

Eliza Ostinelli Biscaccianti belonged to a family that has a prominent place in the annals of early American music. Her grandfather was the James Hewitt who before he came to America in 1792 had been leader of the orchestra of George III. In this country he was active as a composer and leader of orchestras in theatres. His eldest son, John Hill Hewitt, has been called the "father of the American ballad," a contemporary of Foster's who, when Stephen in 1850 and 1851 published his songs, "I Would Not Die in Spring Time" and "I Would Not Die in Summer Time," responded with an "answer" song, "I Would Not Die At All."

Madame Biscaccianti's mother was Sophia Hewitt, herself a musician who married Louis Ostinelli, a violinist prominent in the organization of one of the first orchestras that ever played in Boston. Eliza, daughter of the Ostinellis, studied at the conservatory at Naples; at one time she was one of the prominent prima-donnas of Europe. Her husband, Biscaccianti, was a 'cellist who was supposed to be an Italian count. He proved to be something of a rascal, for it is said that he appropriated one of the Hewitt family's proudest possessions, the 'cello that George the Fourth, then Prince of Wales, had given to his wife's grandfather, James Hewitt.

6

The chronicle of Foster's years in Cincinnati must of necessity be somewhat sketchy, yet there are sufficient documents to construct at least an outline of what he did there, and what his family at home was doing meanwhile. On January 5, 1847, Henrietta married her second husband, Jesse Thornton of Youngstown. It was in that Summer that Eliza Foster visited Henrietta, and found that her husband had her "nicely packed in cottige style, with a nigro to wait on her." [12]

It was in that Summer, too, that Dunning went to the Mexican War, and drew up his will, June 9.[13] Stephen was left in charge of his brother's interest in the business. Also, in April of that year Brother William became one of the three principal engineers of the Pennsylvania Railroad, and started to construct the line over the Alleghenies.

Eliza Foster's letter from Youngstown, August 23, 1847, expresses concern for both Dunning and Stephen. It was written to Morrison:

Poor dear Duning, what perils is he going through by this time. . . . Have you seen any one who has seen Stephen since you came home?

Dunning was gone for a little less than a year. He returned to Cincinnati in June, 1848, in poor health. Morrison also was ill in Cincinnati in the Summer of 1848; on one of his visits to the city he was stricken with the cholera, and Stephen helped take care of him. There was always fear of the cholera when the weather was hot.

Stephen himself contracted a year later (Summer of 1849) the "fever and ague," possibly a malarial condition, from which he never wholly recovered. It may have been that this was the beginning, or the signs, of tuberculosis, but for this assumption there is no proof.

[12] See page 55.   [13] See page 59.

In January of 1849 Stephen evidently paid a visit to Allegheny, probably to attend the wedding of Isaac Pennock. On January 13, Dunning wrote Morrison:

> We have not the slightest apprehension about cholera here, it is all a bugbear. Stephen need not stay away on that account. I should have liked very much to have been at the wedding of Isaac Pennock and Lizzy Grant, as they are both friends whom I highly esteem. . . .

The next paragraph of Dunning's letter refers probably to Sophie Marshall, to whom Stephen had dedicated "Stay Summer Breath."

> We had quite a time last night at Mrs. Marshall's where we had a masked party, and an interesting and amusing one it was. All characters from the Roman Senator to the bat in the play of "Fair One With Golden Locks" were there to speak for themselves. My character was a Mexican soldier with the last remnants of a uniform and less of a face, all of which gave us a most pleasant evening and most agreeable entertainment. I have entered considerably into the fashionable world again, and may now be put down as one of the beaux (not b'hoys!) of Cincinnati; which reputation I do not covet, but as I am amused, I shall not quarrel about names. . . .

By February Stephen was back in Cincinnati, but he returned to Allegheny in June for two more weddings. It was then that Susan Pentland married Andrew Robinson, and J. Cust Blair, one of the "Knights of the S.T." married Anne Robinson. In July Stephen visited Henrietta in her new home at Warren, Ohio, and by the Fall he was again in Cincinnati.

7

It appears, then, that Stephen was frequently absent from his post as bookkeeper, and for almost two months on at least one of his visits. By this time bookkeeping and business had no doubt become secondary considerations, for he already had seven or eight published songs to his credit.

And one of them was not alone published, it was internationally famous.

In the Autumn of 1849 Stephen received the following letter, dated New York, September 12:

S. C. FOSTER, ESQ.

DEAR SIR

Your favor of 8th inst. is received and we hasten to reply.

We will accept the proposition therein made, viz. to allow you two cents upon every copy of your future publications issued by our house, after the expenses of publication are paid, of course it is always our interest to push them as widely as possible. From your acquaintance with the proprietors or managers of the different bands of "minstrels," & from your known reputation, you can undoubtedly arrange with them to sing them & thus introduce them to the public in that way, but in order to secure the copyright exclusively for our house, it is safe to hand such persons printed copies only, of the pieces, for if manuscript copies are issued particularly by the author, the market will be flooded with spurious issues in a short time. [To which Stephen no doubt cried "Amen!"]

It is also advisable to compose only such pieces as are likely both in the sentiment & melody to take the public taste. Numerous instances can be cited of composers whose reputation has greatly depreciated, from the fact of their music becoming too popular, & as a consequence they write too much & too fast, & in a short time others supercede them.

As soon as "Brother Gum" makes his appearance he shall be joined to pretty "Nelly," & your interest in the two favorites duly forwarded to your address, say 50 copies of each.

We remain in the hope of hearing from you soon.

Very truly yours,
FIRTH, POND & CO.

This letter requires some explanation. Stephen's letter to Morrison referring to the Biscacciantis (April 27, 1849) had contained this paragraph:

In writing to Gil Smith, please say that I am very much grieved at having been the cause of so much trouble and humiliation to him on account of a miserable song, and tell him that if he has not already burned the copyright, as I certainly should have done, he may give it to Messrs. Firth & Pond any time that he may be in the neighborhood of No. 1 Franklin Square. If they will give him $10, $5, or even $1 for it, let him make a donation of the amount to the Orphan Asylum, or any other charitable or praiseworthy institution. Mess. F. & P. have written to me for the song.

Morrison, in later years,[14] threw light on this incident.

The song Stephen refers to had been sent to Gilead A. Smith, Esq. a connection of ours in New York, to be delivered by him to a person who had requested Stephen to send him a song for public performances. Mr. Smith, after calling several times, failed to find the person, and so informed my brother. Hence the latter's irritation. I well remember that this very song was "Nelly Was a Lady," one of Stephen's best compositions. It afterwards sold in immense numbers and to a profit of several thousands of dollars.

These letters enable us to piece together the facts of an important event in Foster's career. "Nelly Was a Lady" was published by Firth, Pond & Company of New York in 1849. There is no copyright deposit in the Library of Congress to establish the day and the month of publication, but it was presumably issued between the time of Stephen's April 27 letter, and the letter Firth, Pond wrote him on September 12. Moreover, the Library of Congress records show that "My Brudder Gum" was copyrighted October 1, a few weeks after the date of the Firth, Pond letter.

It is apparent that Stephen started his relations with this New York publisher with these two songs. It is evident, too, that although the firm opened these relations themselves, by asking for "Nelly Was a Lady," Stephen was willing to sell them all his rights in both "Nelly" and "My Brudder Gum" for fifty copies of each. The reference to "your interest in the two favorites . . . say 50 copies of each" is by no means surprising. Some publishers, even to-day, try to obtain all rights in a song by an unknown writer for a few printed copies. When we examine Stephen's later royalty statements, we shall find that he apparently had no financial interest in either of these songs.

[14] In a letter to Louis J. Cist, St. Louis, Mo., February 27, 1865.

When "My Brudder Gum" was about to be published, Stephen evidently managed to get a royalty agreement on all future publications the firm might issue. This fact is not only established by this Firth, Pond letter, it is also confirmed by later contracts which we shall examine in future pages. The terms proposed in the September 12 letter were embodied in a formal contract dated December 3. No copy of this document is known to be in existence, but there are references to it in later contracts.

On November 14 Firth, Pond published the first song to be issued under the two-cent royalty arrangement, "Dolcy Jones." It did not prove particularly successful, for by January, 1857, it had earned the composer only $21.46 in royalties. Had Foster had a similar interest in "Nelly Was a Lady" it would have paid him a large amount.

By the end of 1849 Stephen had entered into a thoroughly businesslike arrangement with one of the leading publishers in New York, and according to Morrison Foster he made a similar contract with F. D. Benteen of Baltimore. This was probably negotiated at about the same time as the Firth, Pond contract, for starting with "Oh! Lemuel!", January 7, 1850, Foster published nine songs and one instrumental piece with Benteen in the year 1850.

Stephen had by this time proved his ability as a song writer who could find a market for his wares. He could burn his bookkeeping bridges behind him, and definitely announce to his family that he himself had found his own place in the scheme of things. With contracts in his hands, he could show that what he was able to do would produce actual money. His work had already earned something of a fortune for others—now it would bring a fortune to himself.

He accordingly left Cincinnati and returned to Allegheny and Pittsburgh. The exact time of his return has never been established until recently. All that was known was that he was in Cincinnati in the Autumn of 1849, and that by February 23, 1850, he was back in Pittsburgh. On that day he wrote a letter dated from his former home. Recently there has been uncovered at Foster Hall in Indianapolis two items in the *Olio*, the magazine published by W. C. Peters in Baltimore. In the January issue of the magazine the following note appears under the column headed "To Correspondents":

"S.C.F." Cincinnati.—"Summer Longings" will appear in our second number.

"Summer Longings" was a song by Foster which Peters copyrighted November 21, 1849.

The other item of interest appeared in the February issue of the *Olio*, this notice too under the "To Correspondents" heading.

"S.C.F." *Pittsburgh*—It is too late to make the alteration as you requested. It is very popular in its present state. The Soiree P—a will appear next week.

Foster's "Soirée Polka" was copyrighted by Peters February 12, 1850.

It is evident then that Stephen was back in Pittsburgh by the time the February issue of the *Olio* went to press, and that a month before he had still been in Cincinnati.

Although the family at home had been boarding at various places in Allegheny during the previous Summer, with Mrs. Lynch, Mrs. Thompson and Mrs. Hart, in April they settled again in a home of their own on the East Common, in another house belonging to William, next door to the one they had occupied before. Henry, with his wife, was in Allegheny living with the family, for it was in the Summer of 1849 that Thomas Ewing, Secretary of the Interior in the Taylor-Fillmore administration, had caused the dismissal of Henry Foster and all other appointees of previous administrations in Washington.[15]

---

[15] See pages 50-51.

William Foster, senior, again had occupation, and after his five years of enforced idleness following his two terms as Mayor of Allegheny, he had opened an office in 1849 as Soldier's Agent in Pittsburgh, in charge of pensions and land grants. So when Stephen went back home to live, it was to a reunited household, numbering as its occupants the father and mother, Henry and his wife, Morrison and Stephen, and two servants. Contributions sent by Brother William and Dunning helped no doubt to assure payment to the servants. After his years in Cincinnati Stephen returned to the old, familiar scenes of his boyhood, to a family once more established, and with the knowledge that he was on the way to justifying his own choice of a profession.

VI

JANE

I

DUNNING'S letter to Morrison of January 13, 1849, contained other news than an account of the party at Mrs. Marshall's.

> Jane McDowell appears to enjoy herself at Mr. Stewart's very well and does not complain in any way. She is, by the way, a very sensible and interesting young lady. I have a good deal of sport out of her and Lidia, and give them some strong doses of news from Pittsburgh, which they swallow with a good grace. They often sigh over their friends at Pittsburgh and wish to be with them, but as yet I have not heard them set a time to go up. They say they will go up when I do, but as that is a very indefinate [sic] period, it is not very conclusive as to the time they will be in Pittsburgh.

This was written while Stephen was away from Cincinnati, visiting in Pittsburgh. Another letter, written in 1849 by a friend, Mary Anderson, reports Jane as engaged to "some chap near Lisbon."

Jane Denny McDowell was the daughter of Dr. Andrew N. McDowell, one of the physicians of Pittsburgh. It was he who attended Dickens when the celebrated English novelist was ill at the Monongahela House at Pittsburgh in 1842. There were three of these McDowell girls—Jane, Agnes, and Marion. Agnes later married a Dr. Cummings of Lewistown, Pennsylvania, and Marion became the wife of John D. Scully, a banker who lived in the Hazelwood section of Pittsburgh.

It is a pity that none of the contemporary letters that have come to light contain any word of Stephen's acquaintance with Jane McDowell before 1850. In fact, what is apparently the first time their names are connected in any way is in a little notice that appeared in the Pittsburgh *Daily Commercial Journal* of Wednesday morning, July 24, 1850.

MARRIED

In Pittsburgh, on Monday evening 22nd inst. by Rev. T. H. Lyman, Stephen C. Foster and Jane D. M'Dowell, daughter of the late Dr. A. N. M'Dowell.

There are no letters to show when the courtship started, or how rapid or slow its progress may have been. All data on Stephen's relations with the young ladies of Pittsburgh, Allegheny and Cincinnati are exceedingly vague, if not entirely lacking. His granddaughter, Mrs. A. D. Rose, speaks of Mary Keller as an early sweetheart. She was the girl to whom Stephen dedicated "There's a Good Time Coming," and after she died in 1846 he inscribed "Where Is Thy Spirit, Mary?" to her memory. According to tradition, Stephen visited Mary Keller's grave many years later, and finding it unmarked, himself ordered erected the headstone that now stands in Allegheny Cemetery.

All of this is undocumented, as are any other friendships that Stephen may have enjoyed with the young ladies of his acquaintance. It is apparent that there could have been no serious love affair with Susan Pentland, for even though Stephen's friendship with Susan lasted through his whole life, she was only a little girl when they were neighbors. As soon as she was grown she married Andrew Robinson.

Stephen's biographer is entirely unable to weave a romance about his hero, for as far as women are concerned the records are dismally silent. If he was a gay Lothario, there is no evidence to prove it to-day. I doubt extremely that he was such, or that he "had a way with women." He was sentimental, and his feelings ran deep, but I do not think he was a highly sexed individual. With him true friendship was one of his strong emotions; many of his

Photograph Left by Foster at the Gaskill House, Warren, Ohio, in 1860

The center figure is said to be Stephen's wife, Jane. Her companions have not been identified. (See page 300.) Acquired by Foster Hall from descendants of proprietor of the Gaskill House.

friends were women, but I think he enjoyed their companionship more than their feminine charms. But more of this later.

2

It is from Mrs. Rose, Stephen's granddaughter, that we may learn whatever is known of Stephen's courtship. Mrs. Rose was brought up principally by her grandmother, and after Mrs. Rose herself was married, Stephen's widow, then Mrs. Matthew Wiley, lived with her until she died at the age of seventy-two.

Mrs. Rose has written:[1]

In the last years of her life, when she had much leisure, her mind seemed to hark back to her girlhood days and early married life, and she talked to me almost daily of my grandfather—as often as I would listen. It was like a shower of gold that she was letting fall upon me, but with the heedlessness of youth, I tossed much of it away, allowing many of these precious memories of hers to roll into the limbo of forgotten things.

Nevertheless this granddaughter has remembered much that was told her, and her recollections are informative and interesting. How much is seen through colored glasses, and tempered by intervening years, will of course never be known. Mrs. Rose writes that Jane was a renowned beauty in her girlhood, with auburn hair and eyes to match. Stephen once told her that he first fell in love with her hair.

At the McDowell home there was an old Negro named Joe, who drove the doctor on his rounds for many years. Mrs. Rose writes:

He [Joe] also had some household duties, such as admitting visitors in the evenings. All through the sweetheart days, Joe watched Foster come and go, presenting to "Miss Jenny" with much shuffling

[1] In an article—"My Grandmother's Memories," which appeared simultaneously in the *Pittsburgh Post* and Louisville *Courier-Journal,* July 4, 1926. A manuscript of the same article, with amplifications, is in the Foster Hall Collection at Indianapolis.

of feet and many broad grins, his and other admirers' bouquets, so stiff and starch in their tin foil and embroidered paper frills.

"Some day I am going to put you in a song," he [Stephen] told Joe, and with Foster, a promise was a promise. The old man was gone when the day of inspiration came, but to-day and perhaps always, Old Black Joe lives again. [Foster's "Old Black Joe" was first published in 1860.]

Since Stephen was in Pittsburgh when Jane was in Cincinnati, and because of the suggestion that she was at that time engaged to another man ("some chap near Lisbon"), it seems probable that Stephen's courtship did not start seriously until he had returned to Pittsburgh permanently, in January or early February of 1850. In that case his courtship was rapid, and lends authenticity to an anecdote related by Mrs. Rose,[2] a story which shows his uncompromising handling of a situation that might otherwise have been long drawn out.

Foster, although mild and gentle of disposition, was known to his family and friends, to be the possessor of an iron will, when he chose to exercise it. His very proposal of marriage to his wife was typical of this.

At the same time Foster was courting her, she [Jane] had another attentive admirer, Mr. Richard Cowan. Mr. Cowan was a lawyer, wealthy, handsome, and distinguished in appearance. Foster suffered somewhat from the contrast, as he was small in stature, and although his features were regular and pleasing, he was not of the type which women call handsome. The two of them continued, each to pay court. One evening, owing to some miscalculation on Miss Jane's part, both called at Dr. McDowell's home at the same time. Steve came first. When Richard was ushered in by Old Black Joe, Steve promptly turned his back upon the pair, took up a book and read the evening through. . . .

At ten-thirty calling hours were over in those good old days, and Richard, punctilious in all things, arose, wrapping his military broadcloth cape about him elegantly, he bid the forbidding back of Stephen a low, sweeping "Good-evening, sir." No answer from Stephen. Jane accompanied Richard to the door, feeling in her heart that a crisis of some kind was impending. She often laughingly said that

[2] *Op. cit.*

when she came into the parlor that night, she scarcely knew where
her sympathies lay, whether they had departed with Richard, or were
present with Stephen. At any rate, she had small time for speculation—Steve had arisen, was standing by the table, pale and stern as
she came in.

And now, Miss Jane, I want your answer! Is it yes, or is it no?
And Grandma, nineteen in years, unused to quick decisions, made one
then and never regretted it.

Richard Cowan had been a member of the Knights of
the S.T. Whatever rivalry he and Stephen may have had
for the hand of Jane McDowell quite evidently failed to
mar their friendship, for Stephen and his wife saw much
of Dick Cowan during the following years.

The statement of Mrs. Rose that Jane McDowell never
regretted her decision to marry Stephen may be accepted as
something told her by her grandmother—in later years.
No doubt as time passed Stephen's widow could forget
many things that had happened when Stephen was still alive.
But even though this loving granddaughter termed Foster's
wife "buoyant and sunny in disposition, attractive and lovable and full of the joy of living to the last day of her life
. . . in truth a very mate for Stephen C. Foster," it is all
too apparent that Jane was not the perfect spouse for
Stephen. Not that Foster proved an ideal husband—far
from it. Disregarding entirely the fondness for drink, and
the weaknesses that developed during the last years of his
life, Stephen was not altogether fitted for married life.
Although he was thoroughly masculine, it is doubtful that
the love for woman, as a physical, male emotion, was in
any way a dominant passion of his existence. He loved
home, his songs show that, but to Foster home meant his
parents, his brothers and sisters, and the surroundings of
his youth. His wife and the daughter that was born the
year after marriage were included in that home, but I do
not believe that they were by any means the first and only
consideration of Stephen.

As for Jane, she no doubt put up with a great deal of nonsense, and it would have required something of a saint to have become the perfect wife for the dreaming Stephen Foster, gentle soul though he probably was. Yet some say that though Jane sang, and had been a member of a church choir, she did not care particularly for music, that she talked during performances at concerts, which irritated Stephen almost beyond endurance. Nor does it appear that she sympathized with his decision to make song-writing his profession. It is highly improbable that Stephen's associations with the theatre, and particularly the black-face song and dance men of the minstrel troupes, were regarded as an ideal environment—at any rate not in the 1850's.

When they were married Stephen had already taken the definite step of abandoning commercial pursuits for his career as composer, and Jane accepted him as a musician rather than as a business-man. Yet there is reason to believe that she did not realize how seriously Foster took his music, that she expected to persuade him to return to some sort of business, especially when the added responsibility of little Marion came to the household. It is probable, too, that she nagged him. There is evidence that she was an efficient person; later she learned to make her own living as a telegrapher. If she bustled about the house in businesslike fashion she could easily have interrupted many a reverie of Stephen's. It is said that Stephen became more moody and introspective after his marriage.

The common supposition that Stephen and his wife became permanently estranged is not true. Even though they separated on at least two occasions, they were reunited. It is not accurate, either, to say that Jane deserted Stephen in his last, miserable years. She left him because she had to earn her own living, and even though his ways were improvident and careless, and although drink had taken its hold of him, she saw him and wrote him often, and it was she who came to New York with Morrison and Henry when Stephen died.

It is not to be doubted that Stephen loved Jane—at least as much as his temperament would allow of such an attachment. The several songs in which he used her name bear witness to his affection. It may be observed that all of these songs were published, and probably written and composed, after his marriage, none of them were issued during courtship—"Jeanie with the Light Brown Hair" (1854), "Jennie's Own Schottisch" (1854), "Jenny's Coming O'er the Green" (1860), "Little Jenny Dow" (1862), "Jenny June" (1863).

Little Marion, the daughter who came to Stephen and Jane on April 18, 1851, has told of her father's devotion. In the *Pittsburgh Press* of September 12, 1900, she made the following statement in an interview:

I was his pet. He took me everywhere with him, and I was the only one allowed to invade the sanctity of his den where he wrote his songs. I could not quite understand his sudden change from my gay, almost childlike companion of the street, to the thoughtful, preoccupied, almost stern man in the study. He could not bear the slightest noise or interruption in his work. I soon learned to respect his "composing moods" and not to interrupt him while at work.

He took us constantly to the theaters, but his love for good music and his execration of indifferent music made it often very uncomfortable for the rest of us. It was not uncommon for him to jump up and bolt right out of the theatre if some unusually vile break in the orchestra or vocalization disgusted him.

It may be wondered how Jane, Stephen's wife, viewed these unconventional departures.

When I visited with the aged Mrs. Welch (the former Marion Foster) I discussed her father with her. The little old lady was eighty-two when I first met her, and her memory was vague on many points. Of one thing she was certain, and she kept returning to it several times during the conversation. She told me repeatedly that her father always wanted her to have a good time. It pleased him when she and her mother went to parties—when Marion had dancing lessons. Stephen wanted them to be gay and happy.

Mrs. Welch also told me that her father would spend his days closeted in his room, writing music, or else he would rush out to the music store. All of which may of course be put down merely as the fond recollections of an old lady, but the insistence and the reiteration of her account surely indicates a vivid memory of a kindly spirit.

3

In addition to the newspaper notice, there is another document that may be considered a contemporary account of Stephen's marriage. This is a letter written on the day of the wedding by Agnes McDowell, to her sister, Marion Scully. The original of this letter is now in the possession of Mrs. Scully's grandson, Mr. Charles Manning of Pittsburgh.

Jane is really married, and can it be possible? It seems so strange to me that she is married and gone, I cannot realize it still. And the wedding over—Jane and Stephen. He seemed pretty much frightened, Steve, quite pale. They each had to repeat some part of the ceremony after Mr. Lyman, which made it, I think, rather embarrassing.

I was bridesmaid and Morrison, groomsman.

We had a bride's cake which was nice, two or three kinds of wine and ice cream and that was all, sufficient, too. All of Jane's dresses fit her beautifully and her other garments were made quite neatly. Sarah gave her a very pretty French work night cap.

I do wish you had been here. I think you would have enjoyed the wine.

We had a most delightful serenade last night, a parcel of plebians were serenaders. They did not know the house exactly and they went up to Mrs. Townsend's, played at least an hour and a half and then they found our house out. I really think they must have played for two hours, most horrible music, at our house.

There is no cholera here at all. I send you some bride's cake to dream on.

This letter fails to mention where Stephen and Jane went for their wedding trip, and there are no other records to show what the honeymoon may have been. It is possible that they visited Federal Hill, the Rowan home at Bardstown, Kentucky, for one of the several traditions connected with that place tells that Stephen brought his bride there shortly after they were married. This story has not been established by documentary evidence. The most exhaustive study that has been made of Stephen's relation to Federal Hill is that of Young E. Allison.[3] In his delightful account he states that Stephen visited at Federal Hill with his bride on their honeymoon. Yet, in an earlier page of his pamphlet, Mr. Allison shows that young John Rowan, who had succeeded to the estates upon his father's death in 1843, was appointed by President Polk as minister to the Two Sicilies. Upon the accession of Fillmore to the presidency Rowan resigned. This would have been in 1850, for Fillmore succeeded Zachary Taylor upon the latter's death in July of that year. Allison states that after his resignation Rowan spent some time in Europe and returned to Federal Hill in 1852. It would appear then that if Stephen and Jane did visit Bardstown on their wedding trip they did so in the absence of the head of the house and his family.[a]

How elaborate a honeymoon Stephen's finances would allow is not apparent, either. Although his account book, started in 1855, shows how much his songs had yielded him by 1857, we cannot know how much his Firth, Pond & Company and Benteen royalties had brought him by the time he was married. Probably not very much, for the best-selling songs were yet to be published.

[3] *The Old Kentucky Home, Its Song and the Story:* Bardstown, Ky., My Old Kentucky Home Commission, 1923.

[a] See *Preface to Fourth Printing.* A recently discovered letter shows that Stephen and Jane went to Baltimore and New York on their honeymoon.

We do know that on March 1, 1850, he borrowed a hundred dollars from William, but that date was more than four months before his wedding. Incidentally, an item in Stephen's account book shows that five and a half years later (October 1, 1855) the interest on that loan had accrued to $33.50. That would be simple interest at the rate of six per cent. On October 12 of that year Stephen paid William $64.

It may be that Stephen and Jane enjoyed a honeymoon of over six weeks' duration. They were married July 22 in 1850. On September 8, one day less than seven weeks later, Morrison, who was keeping the accounts for the Foster household at Allegheny, noted in his account book:

Today, Stephen and Jane came to live with us.

4

It was indeed a complete household to which Stephen took his bride. There were his father and mother, Henry and his wife, as well as Morrison, who though he travelled considerably looked after the business details of the house. William Foster, senior, had his office as Soldier's Agent, and on October 22, 1850, he made application for a land warrant for himself, based on his commission from the government in the War of 1812. This was granted February 11 of the following year. It was in 1850 also that Stephen's father presented for the last time his claim against the government for moneys and personal credit advanced while he was Deputy Commissioner of Purchases— a claim that by this time had mounted to $5,218.60. We have already found that Congress turned a deaf ear to what Foster considered a just case.[4]

In 1851 Foster, senior, became an invalid and was con-

[4] See pages 8-9.

fined to his room for the four years until his death. Stephen as well as Morrison and Henry helped him discharge his duties as Soldier's Agent. The sons called on those who were awarded bonuses and pensions in the form of land warrants, and secured both their affidavits and receipts.

The only child of Stephen and Jane, Marion, was born April 18, 1851, while they were still living with the family on the East Common. Before Marion was born, Stephen and Jane paid $5 board each week. After the baby came, the amount was increased, and Morrison recorded in his account book—"Board paid to July 14, 1852, for Stephen, Jane and nurse, $6 per wk." It may be that the little newcomer, as well as the other members of the household, made it difficult for Stephen to work at home, for a page in his manuscript book contains a pencilled note, "Rented Office July 28/51."

This manuscript book, which is undoubtedly the most important item in the Foster Hall Collection, and which we shall have occasion to examine in detail later, may indicate that Stephen decided to be very businesslike after Marion was born. Entries in the book started soon after her birth; the heading of the first page reads, "Allegheny city, June 26, 1851." It may be that the added responsibilities of parenthood roused Stephen to renting an office for a studio, and to providing a workmanlike method for pursuing his chosen profession. He could at least satisfy his wife by adopting the outward habits of a business-man.

Several other items in the first pages of the manuscript book are interesting, and may be shown before we leave it for the moment. On the inside of the front cover is another pencil notation—"July 22/51, owe Susan 2 weeks." Susan was the baby's nurse. Two entries show transactions with a "Mrs. McD," possibly Stephen's mother-in-law:—"Paid up Mrs. McD. Aug. 18/51" and "Paid up Mrs. McD. Aug. 31/51."

Another entry on the inside cover consists of remedies for common ailments:

Tonsils
2 grains sulphate zinc
4 oz rose water

Fever—Ferrocitrate quinine
5 drops cap [?]
Bush [?]

5

While we know nothing of Stephen's wedding trip, we do have records of another journey that he and Jane took early in their married life. Morrison gives an account of this trip in his biography.[5]

At the close of February 1852, brother Dunning McNair Foster came to Pittsburgh with his steamboat, the James Millingar, to load a cargo for New Orleans. Stephen and his wife, Mr. and Mrs. Andrew L. Robinson [Susan Pentland], Miss Jessie Lightner [later to become Morrison's wife], Mrs. William Robinson and her daughter, Miss Mary Ann, embarked with him on a pleasure trip to New Orleans. Miss Louisa Walker and her two brothers joined them at Cincinnati. There was a good deal of musical ability in the party, and they made the trip pleasant, not only for themselves but for the other passengers as well.

On this voyage Stephen observed a good many incidents of Southern life, which he afterwards utilized as points for poetical simile in songs. On the return trip, brother Dunning found it would be more profitable to reship his freight and passengers at Cincinnati and return from there to New Orleans. They were transferred to Captain Charles W. Batchelor's magnificent new boat, the peerless Allegheny, and arrived in Pittsburgh on her. I had met them at Cincinnati, and we were so well treated on the Allegheny that everybody on the boat joined in a complimentary card of thanks to Captain Batchelor. In those days the captains and other officers of the steamboats on the Western rivers regarded the passengers as their guests, and treated them accordingly. These officers necessarily had to be gentlemen, or otherwise they could not continue long in the trade.

[5] *Op. cit.*

Marion Foster, Stephen's Daughter, at About Twelve Years of Age

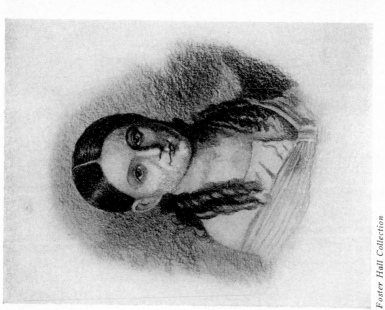

Susan Pentland

Morrison omitted one member of the party from his list, and a very important one, for it was none other than Richard Cowan, according to Mrs. Rose, Stephen's unsuccessful rival for the hand of Jane McDowell. Cowan provides what is nearest to a contemporary record of this New Orleans trip, for a letter written to Morrison just a year later, February 8, 1853, while Cowan was in the House of Representatives at Harrisburg, contains this reference:

I was out visiting to-night, and some of the musical members of the family sang "Old Folks at Home" and the Duet from Romeo and Juliet [Stephen's song, "Wilt Thou Be Gone, Love?" published, as was "Old Folks at Home" in 1851]—these songs were favorites of our party last winter on our trip to New Orleans, and I was vividly reminded of our delightful journey & when we reached the warm latitudes we used to sit on deck to enjoy the moonlight and the sight of the negroes burning the brush and cotton stalks at the plantations. Tell Miss Jessie [Lightner] that the duet was well sung to-night, but the second was very different from hers. Indeed I used to think that Steve must have written that piece of music for Miss Jessie and Mrs. R. [Robinson]—they sang it so well.

Years later, Susan Pentland Robinson gave to a reporter of the *Pittsburgh Press* her account of the trip to New Orleans. The story appeared in the September 12, 1900, issue of that newspaper.

Shortly after Foster's marriage, he and his wife, accompanied by Mrs. Robinson and a party of friends, went to New Orleans by boat to attend the Mardi Gras festival. This was Foster's first visit South, yet the words and melodies he had written before that time breathed the southern atmosphere and were photographically realistic in local color. His reference to "Old Uncle Ned," whose "fingers were long like the cane in the brake," struck every Southerner so happily that it was almost impossible to convince them that the writer had never seen a cane-brake. . . .

Mrs. Robinson recalls many amusing incidents of the journey, Foster being a genial and lovable companion either at home or abroad.

The poet was an inveterate smoker. During this trip, he had afforded great amusement to his fellow passengers by refusing to believe Mrs. Robinson's big and rather homely Irish nurse was not a man in disguise. The nurse and poet had many witty altercations until one day the composer was confined to his stateroom by a swelling of the throat that almost ended his life. His friends were in consternation until the nurse, hearing of this condition, rushed into the room, and, sizing up the situation at a glance, dashed downstairs; and, taking a dish of boiling potatoes, ran back to his side and held the steaming tubers to his mouth until the swelling caused by the excessive use of tobacco, had subsided. Ever after, Foster and the big, good-natured Irishwoman were fast friends.

6

A paragraph omitted from the above quotation has reference to Federal Hill at Bardstown.

Possibly "My Old Kentucky Home," written after his return from this trip, was the only song that he really wrote from a personal recollection of the place. It has reference to Federal Hill, the home of Judge John Rowan, who was a relative of the composer, and was United States Senator from Kentucky in 1828. The stately old southern mansion of ante-bellum days caught the poetic fancy of the composer and lingered with him until he had written this most beautiful melody. The house was situated near Bardstown, Ky. and was visited by Foster on this trip.

Although a discussion of the claims that Kentucky may have to a place in Foster's career may rightfully belong later in our narrative of his song-writing, this is probably the most appropriate place to examine the evidence in support of such claims.

The traditions associated with Foster and Federal Hill are many, and they vary according to who may be telling the story. It was in 1922 that a number of Kentuckians through subscription purchased the Rowan home for $65,000 and presented it to the State of Kentucky. In the same year the Kentucky General Assembly accepted the gift for the State and provided for its maintenance. It is now open as a museum, and ranks with the Mammoth Cave as

one of the show places of Kentucky. All over the state the
highways are marked with suggestions to visit "My Old
Kentucky Home."

Although those in charge of the shrine are more conservative in their claims, the various leaflets and road-maps
issued to advertise the place state that "the name became
popularly attached to it because of the fact that it was in
this house that Stephen Collins Foster composed and wrote
in 1852 his song 'My Old Kentucky Home.'" The memorial tablet in the front hall of the mansion makes a similar
claim. This tablet was presented by the City of Pittsburgh.

The caretakers and residents of Bardstown generally are
willing to admit that Foster did not actually compose the
song at Federal Hill, but state rather that he received his
inspiration for it on one of his visits to his cousins. The
general impression is that Stephen came there in 1852.

In company with Fletcher Hodges, jr., of Foster Hall,
Indianapolis, I visited Bardstown in the Spring of 1933.
During this trip, which took us to a number of towns and
cities in Kentucky, we made an earnest attempt to find
documentary evidence which would help to establish the
definite date of any visit by Stephen. Unfortunately our
exertions produced nothing more definite than reminiscences
of those who had known old-time residents of Bardstown.
There seemed to be no letters, no diaries, nor any current
newspaper references of the day which would show that
Stephen was at any given time visiting Federal Hill. One
kind lady, Mrs. John Thomas of Bloomfield, Kentucky, allowed us to examine all the old Bardstown newspapers in
her collection. Many of these were from the 1850's. In
Lexington we called on a noted Foster enthusiast, John
Wilson Townsend, who told us that he had examined the
almost complete files (lacking only two issues) of the Bardstown newspapers for the year 1852, as well as newspapers
in the Frankfort State Library, from Bardstown, Lexington, Lebanon and Henderson for the years 1851-1855 in-

clusive, and that in none of them did he find any news connecting Stephen Foster, "My Old Kentucky Home," and Federal Hill.

None of this disproves the belief that Stephen did actually visit the Rowans, but it does show that Kentuckians have not taken the pains to establish the authenticity of the claims they make for their shrine. We do know, of course, that Charlotte Foster and Ann Eliza visited Bardstown in 1828,[6] and we have learned that Charlotte at that time rejected the suit of the young John Rowan, but there is nothing so definite as Charlotte's earlier letters to tell us specifically of Stephen's connection with the place.

Young E. Allison [7] summarizes the various legends that have sprung into being.

The original story, whatever it was, was told to those who forgot some details and substituted others. The original is long lost in the "restorations."

They have had the composer accompanied by a gifted sister, who, the inflexible record shows, died years before the song was written. They have seated him at the prim old spindle-legged mahogany desk in the hall at Federal Hill and had him "dash it off" in the frenzy of inspiration. Or they have followed him to the rocks of the old "spring house," whither they have sent him, pencil in hand, and counted the frowns of agony with which he laboriously set down now a strain of melody and again a phrase of words. They have heard him "trying it out" with the "deep booming bass voice" of him who had never more than a weak but sweet light baritone. Every writer of it has himself for the hero and has described it as he would himself have acted it before the grand audience of posterity. These various stories cling about Federal Hill, the outgrowth of the human desire for contact with the vague figures of the past.

There are several touches which Allison might have added to his story. When we visit Federal Hill we are shown the bed that Stephen slept in. Some will show you the window where Stephen looked out on the grave of old Judge Rowan. When he saw the Negroes weeping over

[6] See pages 35 to 37.
[7] *My Old Kentucky Home, Its Song and the Story,* op. cit.

"Marse Rowan's" remains, he wrote "Massa's in de Cold Ground." The faithful Negroes must have been weeping a long, long time, for Judge Rowan died in 1843.

There is also the incident of the visit of Queen Marie of Roumania, several years ago. Her call at Federal Hill was a very formal affair, calling for engraved invitations, engraved place cards for the luncheon and many pompous speeches. There was at that time, and there is still, a piano at Federal Hill that, I am told, was presented to the museum a few years ago by a lady in Louisville. It is a beautiful old middle-century square instrument, with mother-of-pearl keys. The piano is true to the period, but it was most decidedly not at the Rowan home in Stephen's day.

During the speeches on the occasion of Queen Marie's visit, one silver-tongued orator started on his eulogy and received a sudden inspiration in the course of his oration. "This," he cried, "is the very piano upon which Stephen C. Foster wrote 'My Old Kentucky Home'"; and the fact that he was at that moment looking squarely into the eyes of the donor of the piano did not disconcert him in the slightest degree. The Queen was so delighted at this authentic touch of color that she thereupon had her picture taken beside the piano—which lightened the task of her press agents with the editors of rotogravure supplements.

There is still another legend that Young E. Allison failed to include—the one which pictures Stephen, in dire need of funds, approaching Federal Hill. Under his arm, or perhaps clasped in his hands, is the manuscript of "My Old Kentucky Home." He hopes to sell it to Judge Rowan— who had died in 1843, nine years earlier. After walking around the house several times Stephen finally goes to the door, but by the time the Judge welcomes him inside, the composer has changed his mind and offers his cousin the song as a gift.

7

Lest it seem that I am making too light of things that others take seriously, I would state right now that it is indeed a pity that all of the legends cannot be true. Federal Hill is a beautiful spot, a fine old mansion built in the days of the Revolution. It is just the sort of setting in which "My Old Kentucky Home" should have been written, and it would be pleasant to feel that this house with its wide lawns, its shade trees and the groves in which Charlotte Foster was courted by young John Rowan, had indeed been the inspiration for one of Stephen's loveliest songs.

Yet it is the duty of the historian, and the honest biographer, to distinguish between fact and fancy. As far as I can discover, the earliest mention of Federal Hill in connection with Stephen's song was made in the last decade of the nineteenth century, for, commencing in 1893, there appeared in various newspapers, among them the *Louisville Journal,* a number of news stories connecting Federal Hill with Stephen Foster and "My Old Kentucky Home." It is important too to note that Susan Pentland's statement that Foster visited Bardstown at the time of the Southern trip in 1852 was made in 1900, forty-eight years later.

That trip was undertaken in the Winter. Federal Hill was the Summer home of the Rowans, and the family generally spent the Winter at their residence in Louisville. It is possible of course that when the party passed through Louisville, some or all of them went down to Bardstown for a few days with the Rowans. Yet if that was actually the case, the steamboat "James Millingar" must have waited for the party, for according to Morrison's account, this boat of Dunning's brought them back as far as Cincinnati, where they changed to the "peerless 'Allegheny.' " [8]

[8] Upon considering all the evidence it seems more plausible that whatever visits Stephen Foster may have made to Federal Hill occurred in the 1840's, possibly during his residence in Cincinnati.

Important also is the fact that Morrison Foster's biography of Stephen, published in 1896, contains a picture of Federal Hill, and mention of the Rowans as relatives of William B. Foster. The caption of the picture reads "The Old Kentucky Home," but there is not, on any page in the *text* of Morrison's book, any reference to Stephen at Federal Hill, or any suggestion of a connection between that house and the song "My Old Kentucky Home."

There is in existence a letter written to Morrison Foster by Gilbert L. Eberhart of Beaver Falls, Pennsylvania. It is dated August 29, 1900.

In the Sept. number of The Ladies Home Journal under the head of an article entitled "Romances of Some Southern Homes," I find the following statements:

"Judge John Rowan, a famous lawyer in his day, and at one time a United States Senator from Kentucky, was the builder and owner of Federal Hill, a beautiful old homestead near Bardstown which was the scene and inspiration of Stephen Collins Foster's famous song, 'My Old Kentucky Home.'

"Stephen Collins Foster was a relative and protege of Judge Rowan and made his home at Federal Hill most of the time."

I write to you simply to learn how much of the said quotation, if any, is true. . . .

Morrison's complete reply to this letter is probably not in existence, but in the upper right-hand corner of Mr. Eberhart's letter is a pencilled notation in Morrison's handwriting.

Ans. Oct. 3
He was not a protege of Judge Rowan but only an occasional visitor at Federal Hill. Judge Rowan was his father's cousin.

To my knowledge, this is the only evidence supplied by any member of Foster's immediate family to show that Stephen actually visited Federal Hill. It may be noted that Morrison's statement was made in 1900.

And finally, the song itself. "My Old Kentucky Home" was copyrighted by Firth, Pond & Co., January 31, 1853, more than a year after "Old Folks at Home" was issued. When it was written cannot be determined exactly, but surely it was some time after July, 1851. The words of the song appear on pages 50 and 51 of Foster's manuscript book, immediately following the several pages devoted to "Massa's in de Cold Ground." "Laura Lee," which Stephen noted as sent to the publishers July 19 (1851), appears in its final form on page 11. It was probably early in 1852 that "My Old Kentucky Home" was written.

But the most interesting and significant feature of the song as it first appears in Stephen's work book is the title that was given the verses originally—"Poor Uncle Tom, Good Night." Here is the way the chorus was to go:

Oh good night, good night, good night
Poor Uncle Tom
Grieve not for your old Kentucky home
You'r bound for a better land
Old Uncle Tom.

This most decidedly does not fit the music now sung to the refrain—"Weep no more my lady."

On the following page we find the verses of the song pretty much as they were finally published. The title is again "Poor Uncle Tom, Good Night." The first line reads:

De sun shines bright in de old Kentucky home

and the others are those we know to-day, except for the last line of each verse, which is

Den poor Uncle Tom, good night.

Uncle Tom, then, was the original hero of the song, and not "my old Kentucky home." It was in 1851 that Harriet Beecher Stowe first published *Uncle Tom's Cabin* and there may have been some suggestion for Stephen's song from that. The Fosters, however, were Democrats, and hated the Abolitionists, so it is doubtful that Stephen would have had any particular fondness for Mrs. Stowe's book. He might, nevertheless, have realized its popularity.

What bearing this may have on the Bardstown legends is interesting to ponder. It does not appear from the manuscript book that Stephen started out at first to write a lyric about Federal Hill, although he may have thought of that later when he changed the name of his song.

Anyway, far be it from this biographer's purpose to explode altogether pretty myths that after all is said and done hurt nobody and give many people something pleasant to think about. No one has suffered because he was told that Washington threw a coin across the Potomac, and no one will be in any way the loser if he views the bed in which Foster slept at Bardstown, even though Stephen may have found those in Allegheny softer.

And if those in charge of "My Old Kentucky Home" are stimulating interest in the songs of Stephen Foster, and none can deny that they are, they are accomplishing a noble purpose.

VII

"OLD FOLKS AT HOME"

I

STEPHEN started to work in earnest when he returned from Cincinnati and married Jane. He would show that the creative temperament could be industrious as well as poetic and dreamy. He had a definite market for his product, and like any manufacturer with an ample stock of raw materials at hand, he would make them into finished goods to supply the demand for his trade-mark.

During the first six months of 1850 eleven songs and pieces were published, some of which must have been written before Stephen left Cincinnati. One of them was the "Soirée Polka" that Peters, in Baltimore, copyrighted February 12. It was dedicated to Mary M. Dallas, the daughter of Judge Dallas, an old family friend of the Fosters'. Six of the songs were issued by Benteen—"Oh! Lemuel!" (January 7), "Camptown Races" and "Dolly Day" (February 19), "Angelina Baker" (March 18), "Ah! May the Red Rose Live Alway" (April 12), and "Molly! Do You Love Me?" (May 6). Four were published by Firth, Pond & Co. "Mary Loves the Flowers" (January 16), "Nelly Bly" (February 8), "Way Down in Ca-i-ro" (April 17), and "The Voice of By Gone Days" (June 28).

It may be noted that of these eleven works, two were songs that have proved of lasting worth. One of them was the rollicking "Camptown Races," originally published as "Gwine to Run All Night," and the other the whimsically

The Suwannee River

charming "Nelly Bly." "De Camptown Races" ranks with
"Oh! Susanna" as foolishness of a high order. It is interesting to compare this song with "The Capital Ship," a
nonsense song that college boys delight to sing. The refrain of "The Capital Ship"—"then blow, ye winds,
heigh-ho! a roving I will go"—is almost identical in its
melody to that of Foster's song—"Gwine to run all night,
Gwine to run all day." There is also a melodic similarity
in this refrain to that of the Negro spiritual, "Couldn't
Hear Nobody Pray."

This parallel provides interesting speculation as to how
much Stephen Foster may be responsible for some of the
so-called Negro folk-songs. Certain it is that many of these
spirituals are more affected by what the Negro heard in
this country than by what he may have brought with him
from Africa. It is also a fact that thousands have sung
"De Camptown Races" without knowing at all who wrote
it, and not particularly caring. It is largely for this reason
that Foster's songs may be called folk-songs—they have
become far more important in the minds of the people who
sing them than the man who composed them.

The same fact applies to "Nelly Bly." The great majority of those who have helped her "bring de broom
along" seldom think of her as created by the man who
wrote "Old Folks at Home."

On February 23, 1850, Stephen wrote a letter to E. P.
Christy, the minstrel performer whose name became a
generic word for minstrel shows. Christy was in his prime
at this period, and Stephen's association with him as a song-
writer did much to spread the fame of Foster's songs. This
letter seems to form the first record of correspondence between Christy and Stephen, and for that reason it is a most
important document. The original is now in the Library
of Congress.

Pittsburgh, Feb. 23, 1850

DEAR SIR:

Herewith I send you copies of two of my late songs "Gwine to run all night," and "Dolly Day." I regret that the title-page had been ordered, and probably cut before I was informed of your desire that your name should not be used in connection with other bands. I have accordingly ordered my publisher in Baltimore to have a new title page cut bearing the name of your band alone like that used by Messrs. Firth, Pond & Co. N. Y. as I wish to unite with you in every effort to encourage a taste for this style of music so cried down by opera mongers. I hope to be in New York in the Spring when I will probably have an opportunity to gratify the desire which I have to hear your band. Please inform me how you are pleased with the accompanying songs.

Very respectfully yours,

STEPHEN C. FOSTER.

E. P. Christy Esq

We have already found that some of the title-pages of Foster's early songs had contained reference to Christy. Holt's edition of "Oh! Susanna" had been issued in 1848 as "Music of the Original Christy Minstrels," even though Peters' editions of Foster's songs, the printings authorized by the composer, had been issued as "Songs of the Sable Harmonists." This may no doubt be explained by the assumption that Peters was closely associated with the Sable Harmonists, and that Holt, in New York, was issuing music that was sung by the Christy troupe.

The title-pages of the ten songs issued by Benteen and by Firth, Pond during the first six months of 1850 show the situation that is explained to Christy by Foster's letter.[1] Stephen mentioned the Firth, Pond & Company title-pages as models for those that would be used in the future by Benteen. His letter was dated February 23. The title-page used by Firth, Pond for "Nelly Bly" (Feb. 8, 1850) was the same as that used for the 1849 songs:

[1] The sentimental songs—"Ah! May the Red Rose," "Molly, Do You Love Me?", "The Voice of By Gone Days," and "Mary Loves the Flowers" are omitted from the list, as they were not minstrel songs, and were published merely as songs or ballads by Stephen C. Foster, without reference to who performed them.

FOSTERS
ETHIOPIAN MELODIES
as sung by the
CHRISTY MINSTRELS
Written & Composed by
S. C. FOSTER
Author of
UNKLE [sic] NED.   OH! SUSANNA &c.

The Benteen title-pages for songs copyrighted before February 23 were as follows. For "Oh! Lemuel!" (Jan. 7):

OH! LEMUEL!
Go Down to de Cotton Field
Ethiopian Song
as sung by the
CHRISTY MINSTRELS
Also by the
CAMPBELL'S MINSTRELS &c, &c.
Written & Composed By
Stephen C. Foster

For the two songs copyrighted February 19 there was this collective title-page:

FOSTER'S
PLANTATION MELODIES
as sung by the
Christy & Campbell Minstrels
and
NEW ORLEANS SERENADERS
No. 1 Oh. Lemuel!   No. 2. Dolly Day
3 Gwine To Run All Night   4.
Written Composed & Arranged
by
STEPHEN C. FOSTER

Evidently Christy did not relish being classed with the Campbell Minstrels, "&c. &c." and later with the New Orleans Serenaders, particularly when the name of the latter troupe stood by itself, in capital letters. On the next Benteen edition the plate was corrected as Stephen had promised. "Angelina Baker" was issued March 18 and although the same plate was used for the title-page on both the new and the old songs, the names of the other bands were dropped.

FOSTER'S
PLANTATION MELODIES
as sung by the
CHRISTY MINSTRELS

No. 1. Oh Lemuel.   No. 2. Dolly Day
"   3. Gwine To Run All Night   4. Angelina Baker
Written Composed & Arranged By
STEPHEN C. FOSTER

Ironically enough, Firth, Pond & Company, who had provided the model title-page in regard to Christy, forgot or neglected the minstrel altogether when they issued the next song they had from Stephen. This was copyrighted April 17.

WAY DOWN IN CA-I-RO
Written & Composed
by
STEPHEN C. FOSTER
Author of NELLY WAS A LADY, DOLCY JONES, &c.

No mention of any performer was included on the outside of the song, but underneath the title on the first page of music was this information:

Written and Composed for
James F. Taunt of the Empire Minstrels
by Stephen C. Foster

2

During the twelve months after his marriage Stephen continued to be industrious. Starting with August 21, 1850, to the following July (1851), nine works were copyrighted and published by Benteen—"The Spirit of My Song" (Aug. 21, 1850), "Turn Not Away" and the "Village Bells

Polka" (October 15, 1850), "Give the Stranger Happy Cheer" and "Melinda May" (Jan. 6, 1851), "Mother, Thou'rt Faithful to Me" (Mar. 18, 1851), "Sweetly She Sleeps, My Alice Fair" (Mar. 18, 1851), and two gems of thought that deserve mention all by themselves. They have been mentioned before in these pages, but the story in full is worth recounting.

On October 15, 1850, Benteen copyrighted a song with this title-page:

I WOULD NOT DIE IN SPRING TIME
Ballad
Composed & Arranged
for the
PIANO FORTE
By
MILTON MOORE

Here is a gently sentimental song with verses no worse than other popular songs of a similar type written in mid-century.[2]

> I would not die in Spring time
> When all is bright around,
> And fair young flowers are peeping
> From out the silent ground,
> When life is on the water
> And joy upon the shore;
> For winter, gloomy winter
> Then reigns o'er us no more.

The second verse disclaims any desire to die in Summer, and the third

> When breezes leave the mountain,
> Its balmy sweets all o'er—
> To breathe around the fountain
> And fan our bowers no more.
> When Summer flowers are dying
> Within the lonely glen,
> And Autumn winds are sighing—
> I would not perish then.

---

[2] It is not known who wrote the words, and it may be noted that "Milton Moore" is credited with authorship of only the music.

Only one season remains for the inescapable ritual of death, so the song concludes:

> But let me die in Winter
> When night hangs dark above,
> And cold the snow is lying
> On bosoms that we love—
> Ah! may the wind at midnight,
> That bloweth from the sea,
> Chant mildly, softly, sweetly
> A requiem for me.

About nine months later (July 12, 1851) Benteen copyrighted another song:

I WOULD NOT DIE IN SUMMER TIME
An answer to the New and Beautiful
SONG
I WOULD NOT DIE IN SPRING TIME
Written and Composed
By
STEPHEN C. FOSTER

In this lyric the poet dwells upon the beauties of Summer, and ends with this desire:

> I would not die in Summer time,
> And lie within the tomb,
> When blushing fruits are in their prime,
> And fields are in their bloom;
> For I would reap the yellow grain
> And bind it in the sheaves;
> Then die when Autumn winds complain
> Among the blighted leaves.

In the bibliography of Foster first editions compiled by Walter R. Whittlesey and O. G. Sonneck in 1915,[3] only the second song, "I Would Not Die in Summer Time" is described in detail. The first is mentioned merely as included in Morrison's biography,[4] where it does indeed appear, on

[3] *Catalogue of First Editions of Stephen C. Foster:* Washington, Library of Congress, 1915.
[4] *Op. cit.*

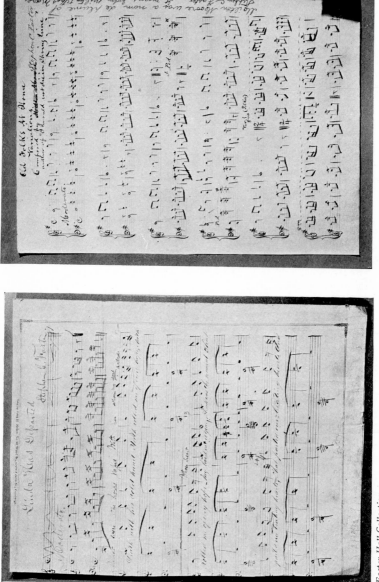

Manuscripts of "Linda Has Departed" and "Old Folks at Home Variations"

page 81. Explanation lies in a manuscript now in the collection of Foster Hall—"Old Folks at Home Variations," composed by Milton Moore, author of "I Would Not Die in Spring Time." The manuscript is in Stephen's own hand, and after it was written some one drew a line through the name "Milton Moore," and wrote beside it, "Stephen C. Foster." Later Morrison wrote in the margin: "Milton Moore was a nom de plume of Stephen C. Foster—it means John Milton & Thos. Moore."

So Foster, under his own name, provided an "answer" to the song he had written under a *nom de plume.* It would be interesting to know the real authorship of a song that appeared also in 1851—"I Would Not Die in Winter, music by J. H. Milton." Stephen can well be suspected of that too, and it is surprising that Autumn was neglected and a complete quartet left unfinished. And we have already learned how the wag of Baltimore, John Hill Hewitt, responded to "Moore," Foster, and "Milton," with "I Would Not Die At All," published in 1852. Hewitt was not one to let a chance like that go by.

3

During the same twelve months (July, 1850, to July, 1851), those following Stephen's marriage, Firth, Pond & Company issued five songs by Foster—"Lily Ray" (Dec. 9, 1850), "Wilt Thou Be Gone, Love?" (a duet from Shakespeare's "Romeo and Juliet," Mar. 12, 1851), "Farewell Old Cottage" (Mar. 22, 1851), "Once I Loved Thee, Mary Dear" (April 4, 1851) and "Ring de Banjo" (April 29, 1851). This made fourteen works issued during that period, and it may be noted that although Firth, Pond & Company were to become Stephen's principal publishers during his most flourishing years, he gave a larger number of songs to Benteen in the first months of his contracts with the two firms.

On June 12, 1851, Stephen wrote another letter to E. P. Christy.

Allegheny City, June 12, 1851

DEAR SIR:

I have just received a letter from Messrs. Firth, Pond & Co. stating that they have copy-righted a new song of mine ("Oh! boys, carry me 'long") but will not be able to issue it for some little time yet, owing to other engagements. [The song was actually entered for copyright July 25, over a month after the date of this letter.] This will give me time to send you the m.s. and allow you the privilege of singing it for at least two weeks, and probably a month before it is issued, or before any other band gets it (unless they catch it up from you). If you will send me 10$ immediately for this privilege I pledge myself, as a gentleman of the old school, to give you the m.s. I have written to F. P. & Co. not to publish till they hear from me again. This song is certain to become popular, as I have taken great pains with it.[5] If you accept my proposition I will make it a point to notify you hereafter when I have a new song and send you the m.s. on the same terms, reserving to myself in all cases the exclusive privilege of publishing. Thus it will become notorious that your band brings out all the new songs. You can state in the papers that the song was composed expressly for you. I make this proposition because I am sure of the song's popularity.

Very Respectfully Yours,

E. P. Christy Esq   S. C. FOSTER.
New York

P.S. Please direct your answer to Allegheny City, Penna.

Christy's reply was prompt indeed, for a week later (June 20, 1851) Stephen again wrote him:

Your favor of the 12th inst., inclosing ten dollars for the first privilege of singing "Oh! boys, carry me 'long" is received. Accept my thanks. Herewith, I send you the m.s. according to agreement. I am not certain that you use a piano in your band; but I have arranged an accompaniment for that instrument at a venture. If you have a tenor voice in the company that can sing up to "g" with ease (which is very probable) it will be better to sing the song in the key of "g." Thus you will not carry the bass voice quite so low. I hope you will preserve the harmony in the chorus just as I have written it,

---

[5] It will be recalled that "Oh! Boys" and "Hard Times Come Again No More" were the two songs that Stephen told Morrison were based on snatches of melody Foster heard at the Negro church to which Olivia Pise took him in his boyhood. See page 83.

and practise the song well before you bring it out. It is especially necessary that the person who sings the verses should know all the words perfectly, as the least hesitation in the singing will damn any song—but this you of course know as well as myself. Remember it should be sung in a pathetic, not a comic style. You will find the last three verses on another page of this letter. I regret that it is too late to have the name of your band on the title page, but I will endeavor to place it (alone) on future songs, and will cheerfully do anything else in my humble way to advance your interest.

Very Respectfully Yours,

S. C. FOSTER.

E. P. Christy, Esq.

I have not as yet done anything at the "night funeral &c" but will probably make something out of it one of these days.[6]

It would be interesting to know if the "night funeral" was another idea Stephen had gained from the fellow worshippers of Olivia Pise.

This correspondence shows that Stephen's relations with Christy were coming to be transacted on a business basis. From a list of moneys received from songs compiled in 1857, a document we shall examine in detail later, we find that Christy paid Foster ten dollars apiece not only for "Oh, Boys," but also for "Massa's in de Cold Ground" (July 7, 1852), "Old Dog Tray" (?1853), and "Ellen Bayne" (Feb. 3, 1854). For "Old Folks at Home" (Oct. 1, 1851) and for "Farewell My Lilly Dear" (Dec. 13, 1851) Christy paid higher—$15. We shall hear more of this later.

All of these songs were issued by Firth, Pond & Company. "Oh! Boys" bore no information about performers on the title-page, it was published merely as a "plantation melody" by Stephen C. Foster. "Farewell My Lilly Dear,"[7] "Massa's in de Cold Ground," and "Old Dog Tray" were announced on the covers as sung by the Christy Minstrels. "Ellen Bayne" was issued as No. 24 of "Foster's Melodies," "sung by Edwin P. Christy." The min-

[6] These two letters, with the manuscript of "Oh! Boys," are now in the collection of the Henry E. Huntington Library, San Marino, California.

[7] "Farewell My Lilly Dear" bore only Foster's initials—"S. C. F."

strel was apparently anxious not to share Ellen with others of his troupe.

As for "Old Folks at Home," we shall learn presently how prominently Christy's name was exhibited on its title-page.

4

Stephen dated the first page of his manuscript book "Allegheny City, June 26, 1851." Its approximately two hundred pages include the words of all but two of the songs he wrote between that time and the Summer of 1860—not only the final versions of his poems, but all of his experiments with words, meter and rhyme, and the evolution of his ideas. These pages show that as far as the verses were concerned Stephen was a careful workman; as a poet he was probably more self-critical than he was as a musician.

The first song in the manuscript book is "Laura Lee." Altogether the working out of these verses occupies eight pages. First comes a poem that is totally unlike the one that was finally published.

> When vows of love were truthful
> I loved thee Laura Lee
> Ah then thy heart was youthful
> Thy voice was glad and free
> Then life was in its morning
> With raptures running wild
> Then with each days returning
> A new born spring time smiled.   Etc. etc.

This is quite different from the final version, which reads:

> Why has thy merry face
> Gone from my side
> Leaving each cherished place
> Cheerless and void?
> Why has the happy dream,
> Blended with thee,
> Passed like a flitting beam,
> Sweet Laura Lee?

The difference in meter between these two versions may disprove the belief that Foster always composed the music to his songs before he wrote the words. It is obvious that music for the second of these poems could never be a setting for the first.

"Laura Lee" stands on the first four pages of Stephen's work-book, and again on pages 8, 9, 10 and 11. On page 12 appears a note—"Sent Laura Lee July 19." The song was copyrighted by Benteen August 7, 1851. Between the pages devoted to "Laura Lee" are two interesting items. On pages 5 and 6 appears Stephen's translation of a German song, "In the Eye Abides the Heart," poem by Franz von Kobell, with music by Franz Abt. When this was issued by Firth, Pond & Co., October 10, 1851, the printed copy stated that the translation was by "Stephen C. Foster" and the music arranged by "H. K." This was undoubtedly Henry Kleber, a fact which shows that Stephen was closely associated with Kleber during these years. The "Village Bells Polka," published in October of the preceding year (1850), was dedicated to Kleber.

The other item between the drafts of "Laura Lee" appears on page 7. It consists of the words of a song, "My Hopes Have Departed Forever." It will be recalled that in Henrietta Foster's letter to William (April 30, 1836),[8] she wrote: "I have learned a beautiful new song since I saw you, My hopes have departed forever, is the name of it." The verses in Stephen's manuscript book are indeed a wail of despair, and express the height of self-pity.

> My hopes have departed forever,
>   My vision of true love is o'er:
> My heart shall awaken, ah! never;
>   There's joy for my bosom no more.
> The roses that crowned me are blighted,
>   The garland I cherished is dead,
> The faith once confidingly plighted
>   Is broke, and my loved one has fled.

[8] See page 54.

And two more verses of similar lamenting.

When Firth, Pond & Company issued this song, August 4, 1851, the title-page bore the information that it was "written and composed BY A LADY." The work is not included in the Whittlesey-Sonneck catalogue or in Morrison Foster's biography.[9] Yet there it stands in Stephen's manuscript book, and in Foster's own account of royalties received from Firth, Pond & Company to January, 1857, we find the item—"My hopes have departed forever—25.04."

Search for another song by the same title, one which would have been published before this piece, has failed to uncover any which Henrietta might have sung in 1836. This is unfortunate, for comparison would reveal whether Stephen composed an original song, or whether he merely arranged a song he had heard Henrietta sing in his boyhood.

While Foster sometimes became sentimental to the point of mawkishness, he rarely permitted himself such a descent into the depths of the saccharine as he took in "My Hopes Have Departed." Moreover, the music to the song does not possess the characteristics of a Foster melody. It is true that many others of Foster's songs do not show his individuality either, but this one in particular smacks rather of some of the composers of the 'thirties and 'forties, men like John C. Baker and William Clifton, whose "The Last Link is Broken" is a parallel to this song that Stephen published. Maybe Foster had his tongue in his cheek when he sent it to Firth, Pond & Company. At any rate, he received royalties on the song.

5

After the last pages of "Laura Lee" the next two sheets of the manuscript book are devoted to sketches of a poem that I have not found in any of Foster's published songs,

[9] *Op. cit.*

some verses about a child and its mother. Then, on the
next following page, 14, we find the heading "Way down
upon de old plantation," and the verse:

> Way down upon de Pedee ribber
> Far far away
> Dere's where my heart is turning ebber
> Dere's wha my brudders play

That was the first draft. Immediately under it we find

> Swanee
> Way down upon de ~~Pedee~~ ribber
> Far, far away
> Dere's where my heart is turning ebber
> Dere's where de old folks stay
> All up and down de whole creation
> Sadly I roam
> Still longing for de old plantation
> And for de old folks at home

Morrison's biography of Stephen [10] tells a story that has
the ring of authenticity, even though it is not exact in detail.

One day in 1851, Stephen came into my office, on the bank of the
Monongahela, Pittsburgh, and said to me, "What is a good name of
two syllables for a Southern river? I want to use it in this new
song of 'Old Folks at Home.'" I asked him how Yazoo would
do. "Oh," said he, "that has been used before." I then suggested
Pedee. "Oh, pshaw," he replied, "I won't have that." I then took
down an atlas from the top of my desk and opened the map of the
United States. We both looked over it and my finger stopped at the
"Swanee," a little river in Florida emptying into the Gulf of Mexico.
"That's it, that's it exactly," exclaimed he delighted, as he wrote
the name down; and the song was finished, commencing "Way Down
Upon de Swanee Ribber." He left the office, as was his custom,
abruptly, without saying another word, and I resumed my work.

We know, already, from Stephen's work-book, that
"Pedee" was probably not Morrison's suggestion, but rather
Stephen's first idea, one with which he was dissatisfied.

[10] *Op. cit.*

Stephen's work on "Old Folks at Home" was apparently interrupted. After the first draft on page 14, the next five pages are devoted to "Willie My Brave," a song dedicated to Mrs. A. L. Robinson (Susan Pentland) and published by Firth, Pond & Company, October 21, 1851. Then follow four pages of a political poem, evidently written for some current campaign, with a chorus that could be sung to "De Camptown Races."

> Going to run again?
> Johnston your insane
> I'll bet my money on the Bigler boys
> For the whigs have had their reign.

Then, on page 24, we find more sketches for "Old Folks at Home," short lines and a quatrain which Stephen set down in pencil as they occurred to him.

> Oh take me to my kind old mudder
>
> Long time ago I left my fadder
> Why tell me why
> Oh take me to my kind old mudder
> Dere let me lib and die
>
> Long time ago I left my fadder
>
> Den ebry day my heart grew sadder

On the next page, 25, stand the words of the song in their final form, almost identical with the published version. I give them here as they were written in the manuscript book, with little punctuation, showing the final changes that Foster made in them.

> Way down upon de Swanee ribber
> Far, far away
> Dere's wha my heart is turning ebber
> Dere's wha de old folks stay
> All up and down de whole creation
> Sadly, I roam
> Still longing for de old plantation
> And for de old folks at home

Chorus—All de world am sad and dreary
    Ebry where I roam
Oh! darkeys how my heart grows weary
    Far from de old folks at home

All round de little farm I wandered
    When I was young
Den many happy days I squandered
    Many de songs I sung

~~Ah how I rambled with my brudder~~

When I was playing wid my brudder
    Happy—~~Joyous~~ was I
Oh take me to my kind old mudder
    Dere let me lib and die

One little hut among de bushes
    All dat I love
Still sadly to my memory rushes
    No matter where I rove

This brought Stephen to the bottom of his page, so turning to the foot of the facing left-hand page, he finished his song.

    When will I see de bees a humming
        All round de comb
    When will I hear de banjo tumming
        Down in my good old home

6

Thus was written what has proved to be one of the world's most famous songs. I doubt if any other song, even "Home, Sweet Home" or "Annie Laurie" has been printed as many times as Stephen's "Old Folks at Home," and included in as many song collections. We shall learn presently how immediate its fame was, but we, in the present which was Foster's future, can judge better than his contemporaries the worth of what he had created. We have seen that time has increased the song's appeal to fundamental emotions, that its simple, homely sentiments embody longings that are shared by rich and poor, by the weak as well as the strong. Even its crude, inconsistent Negro dialect fails either to mar the sincerity of the thought behind the words, or to localize the home we all long for.

It may be that this is a great song because it is Foster himself. He was writing for a market, trying to compose a sentimental song in Negro dialect that would be sung by black-faced singers in minstrel shows. But that did not keep him from writing into "Old Folks at Home" what was strongest in his nature—his love for his own home. Consciously or not, it makes little difference, Stephen breathed into these verses and the music that went with them, something of his own heart and soul.

Of the music to the song little need be said. It defies and disarms all who would criticize or analyze it. The breath of simplicity, it is written in a form that would prove the height of monotony in anything but a masterpiece. There are five repetitions of the opening phrase in each verse and chorus—identical each time they appear. The second phrase of each melodic period comes twice in each verse, and the second period of the "verse" section appears once more as the last part of the chorus. The only part of the melody that offers contrast is that sung to the first two lines of the chorus.

With any ordinary tune such an analysis would indeed be enough to damn it completely, yet in "Old Folks at Home" each repetition makes the same phrase more beautiful, until when we hear it once more at the end its effect is compelling. The mere fact, too, that there are so many repetitions of the central idea makes the contrast of the refrain just so much more effective.

It has sometimes been claimed that Henry Kleber helped Stephen with "Old Folks at Home," that he suggested some changes in the music which were adopted by Stephen. Of this we cannot be sure. "Old Folks at Home" is so simple both in its melody and in the three chords (tonic, dominant and subdominant) which form its accompaniment, that it does not appear that a trained musician had much hand in its editing. It would be easier to believe that Kleber had suggested such features of Stephen's songs as the coda of "Come Where My Love Lies Dreaming," or other elaborations in later works, than that he altered the form or melody of "Old Folks at Home." If Kleber is actually responsible for any part of "Old Folks at Home" his memory should be revered for his taste and judgment in leaving it as simple as he found it.

One need but listen to the countless distortions of Foster's song on the radio, in the motion picture theatres, and in numerous potpourris to realize that it should never be taken from its simple setting—that reharmonization fails to richen it, and merely makes a gaudy chromo out of a simple, truthful pen and ink drawing. If ever there were unsuccessful attempts to gild the lily, they may be found in the elaborations of "Old Folks at Home."

7

The records of the Library of Congress show that a title-page of "Old Folks at Home" was entered for copyright by Firth, Pond & Company, August 26, 1851, and a copy of the song itself deposited October 1, five weeks later. Here is that title-page, note carefully its contents.

OLD FOLKS AT HOME
Ethiopian Melody
as sung by
Christy's Minstrels
Written and Composed by
E. P. CHRISTY

Morrison has a paragraph on this in his book.[11]

[11] *Op. cit.*

Just at that time he [Stephen] received a letter from E. P. Christy, of New York, who was conducting very popular Negro Melody concerts, asking him if he would write a song for Christy which the latter might sing before it was published. Stephen showed me the letter and asked me what he should do. I said to him, "Don't let him do it unless he pays you."

This much of the account is verified by the letters Stephen wrote Christy, June 12 and 20, asking and receiving $10 for the privilege of singing "Oh! Boys" before it was published. Morrison continues:

At his [Stephen's] request I drew up a form of agreement for Christy to sign, stipulating to pay Stephen five hundred dollars for the privilege he asked. This was forwarded to Christy and return mail brought it back duly signed by the latter. The song happened to be "Old Folks at Home." It was in this manner that Christy's name came to appear on the first edition of the "Old Folks at Home." Stephen sent the manuscript to his publishers, Firth, Pond & Co., who paid him and his heirs the royalty. The publishers furnished Christy an advance copy of the song before publication.

Less than a year later, May 25, 1852, Stephen wrote the following letter:

E. P. CHRISTY, ESQ.

DEAR SIR:

As I once intimated to you, I had the intention of omitting my name on my Ethiopian songs, owing to the prejudice against them by some, which might injure my reputation as a writer of another style of music, but I find that by my efforts I have done a great deal to build up a taste for the Ethiopian songs among refined people by making the words suitable to their taste, instead of the trashy and really offensive words which belong to some songs of that order. Therefore I have concluded to reinstate my name on my songs and to pursue the Ethiopian business without fear or shame and lend all my energies to making the business live, at the same time that I will wish to establish my name as the best Ethiopian song-writer. But I am not encouraged in undertaking this so long as "The Old Folks at Home" stares me in the face with another's name on it. As it was at my own solicitation that you allowed your name to be placed on the song, I hope that the above reasons will be sufficient explanation for

Title-pages of First Editions in Foster Hall Collection

my desire to place my own name on it as author and composer, while at the same time I wish to leave the name of your band on the title page. This is a little matter of pride in myself which it will certainly be to your interest to encourage. On the receipt of your free consent to this proposition, I will if you wish, willingly refund you the money which you paid me on that song, though it may have been sent me for other considerations than the one in question, and I promise in addition to write you an opening chorus in my best style, free of charge, and in any other way in my power to advance your interests hereafter. I find I cannot write at all unless I write for public approbation and get credit for what I write. As we may probably have a good deal of business with each other in our lives, it is best to proceed on a sure basis of confidence and good understanding, therefore I hope you will appreciate an author's feelings in the case and deal with me with your usual fairness. Please answer immediately.

Very respectfully yours,

STEPHEN C. FOSTER.

If Christy replied to this letter, his answer seems to have disappeared. We shall see later how long it was before Foster's name appeared on the song, and the complications that Christy's supposed authorship caused in the matter of copyright renewal, long after Stephen had passed away.

There are several reasons for questioning the accuracy of Morrison Foster's account of the transaction between Stephen and Christy. It may have been that writing over forty years later (his book was published in 1896) his memory of the incident was not clear, but that belief seems unlikely. He must have remembered such an important episode quite accurately. It seems more probable that Stephen exaggerated to Morrison the amount that Christy was to pay him, to satisfy his brother's insistence that Stephen protect his own interests.

It is hard to believe that Christy paid Stephen Foster five hundred dollars, though even that amount would seem small payment for such a privilege. Nor is it probable that Stephen had on hand this sum to repay Christy, as he offered in his letter asking to be released from the agreement. We may note also from Stephen's letter that it was his idea, not Christy's, that the minstrel's name appear on the song as its composer. Had that statement not appeared in Foster's own handwriting it would not be easy to believe that Stephen would not want his name on "Old Folks" when it had appeared on other "Ethiopian" songs in the past— songs which were far less "refined" in their sentiments than was the "Swanee River."

The original correspondence with Christy provides for the payment of ten dollars for allowing Christy to sing the songs before published, and for having his name printed *as a performer of the songs* on the title-page. We have already noted, in writing about Foster's accounts of royalties received (dated 1857),[12] that Stephen received from Christy ten dollars each for "Oh! Boys," "Massa's in de Cold Ground," "Old Dog Tray," and "Ellen Bayne," and *fifteen* dollars each for "Old Folks at Home" and "Farewell My Lilly Dear." This last song was written just after "Old Folks," its words occupy the three following pages in the manuscript book, even though it was not published for two months after "Old Folks" was issued (December 13, 1851).

"Old Folks at Home" was issued as "written and composed" by Christy. "Farewell My Lilly Dear" was published with this title-page:

FAREWELL MY LILLY DEAR
A
Plantation Melody
As sung by
CHRISTY'S MINSTRELS
Written & Composed by
S. C. F.

It is possible that the added five dollars was in one case paid for allowing Christy's name to appear as composer, and in the other for having only Foster's initials as the au-

[12] See page 187.

thor, rather than his full name. This possibility by no means constitutes proof that Christy paid fifteen rather than five hundred dollars for the privilege, but it does seem more likely that Stephen would have fifteen dollars to return to Christy, than that he could draw five hundred from his bank account. We may note also that Stephen wrote, "I will, *if you wish,* refund the money. . . ." Had it actually been five hundred dollars that was involved, it hardly seems as though even the man who must return the money would have suggested that he who was to get it would not want it.

Another point is worthy of notice. "Oh! Boys" was the first song for which Christy paid Foster. The amount for that song was $10. The next two songs to be written and published were "Old Folks" and "Farewell My Lilly Dear." For these Christy paid $15. After these transactions the fee dropped to $10, for songs written and published later. If the $15 payments had been merely for the privilege of singing the songs before published, and for printing Christy's name on the title-pages *as a performer,* why did the amount drop back to $10 on the later songs? It would appear that added privileges were granted for the extra five dollars.

There is more evidence. A number of years after Foster's death an associate of his during his years in New York wrote an article in a March, 1877, issue of the *New York Clipper.* We shall have occasion later to quote more extensively from this essay, but there is one paragraph that has reference to Foster's relations with Christy.

One night, while sitting in my apartments, then at 311 Henry Street, my wife asked Stephen if he knew "The Old Folks at Home."

"I should think I ought to," he replied, "for I got $2,000 . . . from Firth, Pond & Co. for it."

"Why," said I, "how could that be? Was not E. P. Christy the author and composer?"

"Oh, no," he replied laughing, "Christy paid me $15 . . . for allowing his name to appear as the author and composer. I did so on condition that after a certain time his name should be superseded by my own. One hundred thousand copies of the first edition were soon sold, for which I received a royalty of two cents per copy. . . ."

The reminiscences of this writer, John Mahon, are easily confirmed by consulting the New York directories of the period for the addresses of places he mentions. It appears from such a check that he is far more accurate and reliable than the irresponsible journalists who flooded the magazine market with "recollections" of Foster during the years following his death. Also we shall find that the statement that Stephen received $2,000 in royalties from Firth, Pond & Company for "Old Folks at Home" is reasonably accurate, though a bit higher than the actual amount.

Almost twenty-three years after "Old Folks at Home" was published the following item appeared in the August, 1874, issue of *The Song Journal,* a musical magazine published in Detroit:

Christy, whose minstrels in New York twenty-five years ago were renowned throughout the United States, was regarded as the author of most of the popular songs which were used by his troupe. A collection of manuscript music numbering about one hundred pieces, which once belonged to Mr. Christy, is now on exhibition in New York. With the music there are many letters from the composers of the pieces, naming the price they hoped for which was generally ten dollars. Most of these letters were from Stephen C. Foster, of Pittsburgh, and they reveal the fact that he wrote his songs and sold them to Christy for ten dollars apiece, and that afterwards a contract was made by which, for five dollars additional compensation, Christy was to have the songs and the credit of composing them.

This fits our theory exactly, and even though the rest of the article falls into such exaggerations as stating that after this agreement all of Foster's songs bore Christy's name as composer, and that the minstrel made "hundreds for their sale," it appears that the first part of the account tells exactly what happened in the case of "Old Folks at Home."

Even though Christy bought from Stephen his most treasured possession, the credit for composing his own song, the
minstrel did indeed spread the fame of "Old Folks at
Home." When the "Christy Minstrels" went to England
(apparently without E. P. Christy, who retired in 1854)
they made the song almost as famous in that country as it
was in America. Thousands of copies were sold in England, and Englishmen too sang of the Swanee River that
Stephen Foster had never seen. Letters written by soldiers
in the Crimean War said that in the trenches the two favorite songs of the troops were the Scotch "Annie Laurie"
and the American "Old Folks at Home."

The fame of "Old Folks at Home," and of Stephen
as a composer, belongs in our next chapter. Both the song
and its composer achieved quick recognition, yet what an
irony it was that Foster's first published song, issued in
1844, should have borne his name incorrectly, and that his
finest, and most famous work should have omitted it altogether.

VIII

FAME

I

UNCLE STRUTHERS' prophecy that Stephen would some day be "something famous" came to pass in the early 1850's. On September 4, 1852, Firth, Pond & Company advertised in *The Musical World and New York Musical Times:*

As specimens of our popular pieces we will mention
THE OLD FOLKS AT HOME
that most beautiful American melody, nearly *Forty Thousand Copies* of which have already been sold! also
NELLY BLY
the popular Ethiopian melody

In the September 11 issue of the *World* appeared this news item:

A Successful Song

The "Old Folks at Home" published by Firth, Pond & Co. is one of the most successful songs that has ever appeared in any country. The publishers keep two presses running on it, and sometimes three; yet, they cannot supply the demand. The sale has already reached over forty thousand copies, and at the present rate will soon come up to a hundred thousand. When the reader takes into consideration the fact, that, fully one half of all the sheet music published proves to be a total failure—that three thousand copies of an instrumental piece, and five thousand copies of a song, is considered a *great sale,* he can form some idea of the surpassing popularity of the "Old Folks at Home."

Not the least of the many tributes to the fame of the song was the number of imitations that sprang from the pens of lesser talents. George F. Root, the song-writer who later became famous as the composer of "The Battle Cry of Freedom" and "Tramp, Tramp, Tramp, the Boys Are Marching" was frank to admit that the success of Foster's songs led him to try his own hand at song-writing. He did not, however, state in his reminiscences that among his earliest efforts was a song, "The Old Folks Are Gone," published in 1852 by William Hall & Son of New York. Hall was a former partner of Firth. Here are the words of Root's song, which he issued under the *nom de plume* he used on his early works—G. Friedrich Wurzel (the German for "root"):

> Far, far in many lands I've wander'd,
>   Sadly and lone,
> My heart was ever turning southward,
>   To all the dear ones at home;
> Here after all my weary roaming,
>   At early dawn,
> I've come and find the cot still standing,
>   But, oh, the OLD FOLKS are gone.

> *Chorus*—Here I wander sad and lonely,
>   In the dear old home,
> Those that I Lov'd so well and fondly,
>   All, all the Old Folks are gone.

In the third stanza he even went so far as to include the Swanee River:

> Where Swanee's peaceful waters laving,
>   The green turf o'er their breast—

Two editions of Root's song were issued in 1852. One published merely as a "song & chorus" by G. Friedrich Wurzel, and the other as an *authorized edition*—"Christy's Old Folks Are Gone, as sung by E. P. Christy at Christy's Opera House, N. Y., words and music by G. Friedrich Wurzel." Christy's signature was reproduced on the title-page of this "authorized" edition. In both versions the words are the same, but the music is quite different.

There was also a song "Young Folks at Home," words by Frank Spencer, music by Hattie Livingston, published in 1852 by Gould & Berry as "written & composed expressly for Wood's Minstrels, Minstrel's Hall, 444 Broadway." One of the copies of this song is marked "thirteenth edition."

The September 4, 1852, issue of *The Musical World* presents some interesting comments on Stephen's songs and its imitators.

REVIEW OF MUSIC

Inferior

1. Wurzel, G. Friedrich "The Old Folks are Gone." Song and chorus. 25 cts. Hall & Son, Broadway. See below, Nos. 8 and 20.

. . . .

Tolerable

8. Livingston, Miss Hattie. "Young Folks at Home." Song and chorus. 25 cts. Gould & Berry, New York. (See below, No. 20)

. . . .

The following are recommended for purchase.

20. Christy, E. P. "Old Folks at Home." 25 cts. Firth, Pond & Co.

A song deserving—we think—of its unexampled popularity. Its melody is fresh, and—even artistically considered—has its good points. It begins promptly upon the first *ictus* of the measure, and glides into a very light and taking rhythm, while the chorus opening upon the dominant (instead of the tonic) is a decidedly good point. This *scheme* of a song, indeed, both rhythmically and otherwise, is too good not to have its imitations, and we have therefore the two songs (noticed above) Nos. 1 and 3 [this should have read 8] very closely copied in every respect except the freshness and genuine *musicalness* of the original.

There were other imitations, all published in 1852.

" 'Young Folks from Home,' companion to 'Old Folks at Home,' written & composed expressly for & sung by Christy's Minstrels by H. Craven Griffiths." [1]

---

[1] It is interesting to observe that the second phrase in both "verse" and "chorus" of this song is almost identical to the second phrase of Foster's "Old Black Joe," published in 1860. The similarity does not extend further than this single phrase.

"Young Folks at Home, Dedicated to Messrs. Holmes, Foster,[2] Craig & Ballard of the Pittsburgh Quartette by the Publisher." [J. C. Beckel, Philadelphia—no composer's name appears on the printed copy.]

"The Young Folks at Home, by L. P. Dutton."

Nor should we omit a gem issued twenty years later (1872) in Boston—" 'The Old Home Ain't What It Used To Be,' companion song to the 'Old Folks at Home' as sung by the Original Georgia Minstrels." This was composed by C. A. White, and published by White, Smith & Perry.

2

In these years Stephen's publishers were quick to capitalize his increasing fame, even though they were not supposed to advertise "Old Folks at Home" as written by him. Nevertheless Firth, Pond & Company inserted this advertisement in the January 15, 1853, and subsequent issues of *The Musical World:*

We have just published

"My Old Kentucky Home, Good Night"

Music and words by the author of "The Old Folks at Home," which we can recommend as in every respect, a most beautiful song.

Seven weeks later in the same magazine (March 5) the firm corrected this error in a special advertisement, and omitted "Old Folks" when referring to Foster.

"My Old Kentucky Home, Good Night"

This beautiful plantation melody, sung with great success by Christy's Minstrels, is this day published by the undersigned. The words and music are by Stephen C. Foster, the well known author of "Nelly Bly," "Massa's in de cold ground," etc. Price 25 cents.

[2] The identity of this Foster is not apparent. There is no reason to believe that it is Stephen.

It was apparently noised about by this time that Foster was the actual composer of "Old Folks at Home," for in the February 19, 1853, issue of *The Musical World* this item appeared under "Answers to correspondents":

> Harry:—S. C. Foster is the author of the "Old Folks at Home."
> E. P. Christy probably bought the song and the right to be considered its author at the same time, and the publishers of course put his name to it, thinking he was the composer; but such things always "come out" sooner or later.

Nevertheless, Christy continued to appear as the composer on the many successive editions of the song.

As the months passed Firth, Pond & Company continued to feature Stephen in their advertising. On June 17, 1854, they announced (*Musical World & Times*):

> Jeanie with the Light Brown Hair. Ballad
> Words and music by S. C. Foster, 38

Mr. Foster's popularity as THE SONG WRITER OF AMERICA is too firmly established to require particular mention of any of his compositions. The above song fully sustains his reputation.

In the September 9, 1854 issue of the same magazine, the publishers continued their praise of Foster, advertising "Jeanie" as "embellished with a beautiful vignette."

> The publishers recommend this as one of the most beautiful of Mr. Foster's melodies. No song writer of the present day can approach Foster in the originality, beauty and simplicity of his melodies, and "Jeanie" is not an exception.

Firth, Pond & Company were not loath to boast about the number of copies they had sold of Foster's songs, even though we shall find later that their claims were considerably in excess of the amounts paid the composer in royalties. In the *Musical World* of November 11, 1854, they advertised:

OUR CATALOGUE OF SHEET MUSIC IS

one of the largest and *by far the most popular in the country.*

Within the past twelve months we have added to it many publications, both vocal and instrumental, which have reached *an unprecedented sale,* and entirely beyond the publications of any other house.

We have printed and sold of

"OLD FOLKS AT HOME," more than 130,000 copies.
"MY OLD KENTUCKY HOME," by Foster, 90,000 copies.
"MASSA'S IN THE COLD GROUND," by Foster, 74,000 copies.
"OLD DOG TRAY," in 6 months, by Foster, 48,000 copies.

And of Foster's new songs
"OLD MEMORIES," "ELLEN BAYNE," and "WILLIE, WE
HAVE MISSED YOU";
(The last recently issued)
Large Editions Are Daily Printed and Sold.

It will be noted that "by Foster" does not appear after "Old Folks at Home."

The publishers found it profitable to offer bargain combinations in Stephen's songs. On May 27, 1854, they advertised in the *Musical World & Times:*

FOSTER'S MELODIES

In order to encourage the already great
and
Still Increasing Demand
for the compositions of
STEPHEN C. FOSTER, ESQ.
we have concluded to make this
Liberal Offer
to purchasers.

Any person on sending us one dollar, will receive, by mail,
Free of Postage
any four of the following five of Mr. Foster's latest, and as we think
Very Best Songs

which would cost in the aggregate, when bought at retail, nearly double that amount, as will be seen by the prices annexed:

No. 22	Old Memories	price 25 cents
23	Little Ella	25
24	Ellen Bayne	38
25	Willie We Have Missed You	38
26	Jeanie with the Light Brown Hair	38

The latter three above-named are embellished with beautiful
Lithographic Vignette Titles

In case the purchasers are already in possession of one or more of these pieces, they may name as substitute, any of the other songs on our extensive catalogue. The music can be sent by mail without the slightest injury in its appearance.

In connection with the "beautiful Lithographic Vignette Titles" an anecdote is told which is interesting when we remember that Morrison wrote that Stephen was talented in drawing and in water-colors.[3] This little story cannot be taken too seriously, for it was told by George Birdseye, who in his several articles on Foster quite obviously let his journalistic instinct for a good narrative and for color get the better of his accuracy in remembering incidents. This quotation is from an article by Birdseye in the *New York Musical Gazette,* March, 1867.

When a boy, he [Stephen] was a moderately fair draughtsman; but the only attempt he made in after life to show his talents in that direction was unappreciated. When "Willie we have missed you," that fond outpouring of longing and welcome was in the printer's hands, its author was struck by a brilliant idea for a title-page illustration. After some considerable labor, not unaccompanied with pleasure, he produced what he considered an excellent representation of the scene of Willie's return. A new sensation tickling his heart-strings, he hastened to the engraver, and handing him his effort, waited with conscious pride the praise he felt sure it would call forth. The artist looked at it for a moment, then turned to him with an inquiring glance: "Ah, another comic song, Mr. Foster?" This was too much, and in an instant the design was snatched from his hand and lay in fragments on the floor. "And never after that,"

[3] See page 107.

added he, when relating the incident, "did I essay to show my versatility of talent." (See illustration facing page 196.)

It would be interesting to know if this engraver was the same as the one who also worked for Firth, Pond & Company, and who once engraved the title-page of Gottschalk's "The Last Hope" as "The Latest Hops."

Whatever may have become of Stephen's sketch, the first edition of "Willie, We Have Missed You" bore on its title page a "lithographic vignette" of Willie being greeted by his wife, or sweetheart. We may assume, however, that the lady is his wife, for a rocking horse and a drum are prominently displayed in the illustration. In the 1850's conventions were rigidly observed in depicting home scenes.

3

After "Laura Lee," copyrighted by Benteen, August 7, 1851, Stephen, with one exception, gave all his songs to Firth, Pond & Company, until he started to do business with other publishers in 1860. The exception was "Comrades, Fill No Glass for Me," issued November 23, 1855, by Benteen's successors, Miller & Beacham. Foster's industry during these years is shown by the number of songs published.

1850—	9 songs, 1 instrumental piece issued by		Benteen
	5 songs	" "	Firth, Pond
	1 instrumental piece	" "	Peters
1851—	10 songs	" "	Firth, Pond
	6 songs	" "	Benteen
1852—	4 songs	" "	Firth, Pond
1853—	5 songs, 3 instrumental pieces	" "	Firth, Pond
1854—	4 songs, 5 instrumental pieces [4]	" "	Firth, Pond
1855—	4 songs	" "	Firth, Pond
	1 song	" "	Miller & Beacham

[4] Five new instrumental pieces by Foster were included in the contents of the "Social Orchestra."

Here were sixteen songs and pieces published in 1850, some of which were written in Cincinnati, and forty-two published in the five years from 1851 to 1855. Among them were some of Stephen's finest songs, those which indicate that these years were creatively his most fertile.

After "Old Folks at Home," "Willie My Brave" and "Farewell My Lilly Dear," the last of the 1851 songs was "Eulalie" (Firth, Pond & Company, December 6), a setting of words by H. S. Cornwell. It is possible to learn how Stephen wrote the words of practically all of his songs through almost this entire decade, for with only two exceptions,[5] starting with "My Hopes Have Departed" (Aug. 4, 1851) and "Laura Lee" (Aug. 7), all of the songs to which Foster wrote the words—those written before he went to New York in the Summer of 1860—are included in the manuscript book. Some that were issued after 1860 are there too.

The first song published in 1852 (July 7) was "Massa's in de Cold Ground," which ranks with those Foster songs most deserving of immortality. Stephen worked hard over this song, and tried many ideas before it finally suited him. The accompanying illustration shows the two facing pages on which the first sketches of the song appear. The musical phrases have in them the germs of the final version, but Foster improved these ideas before they were finally incorporated in the song.

After these two pages (34 and 35) Stephen interrupted his work on "Massa" with drafts of two other songs— "Maggie by My Side" and "The Hour for Thee and Me"— and then returned to "Massa's in de Cold Ground" on page 44. Then he devoted five pages to working it out satisfactorily. Many ideas were tried and discarded, until finally the verses were written approximately as they finally appeared in the printed copies. Yet even the final written version differs in some details from the published edition,

---

[5] "Comrades, Fill No Glass for Me" and "My Loved One and My Own."

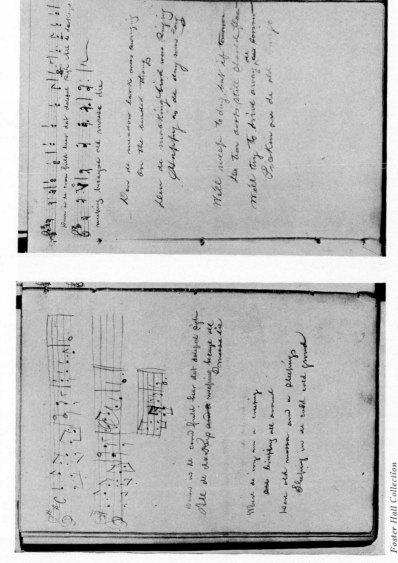

First Pages of "Massa's in de Cold Ground"
From Stephen Foster's Manuscript Book

and it may be that Stephen made these changes when he wrote the words and music together on the copy that was handed to the publisher.

As for the other two songs, "Maggie" was originally to have been "Fanny by My Side." What was to have been a Negro dialect song—

> Roll on ye breakers
> O'er de troubled tide
> Fair wedder all de day
> With Fanny by my side.

eventually became—

> Roll on ye dark waves,
> O'er the troubled tide:
> I heed not your anger,
> Maggie's by my side.

Which we all agree is better.

The *Pittsburgh Press,* June, 1895, printed the reminiscences of one who told an anecdote about this song.

I remember well the occasion that prompted him to write that beautiful song, "Maggie by My Side." We all attended a party given in honor of a young lady from Baltimore, who was the guest of one of the young ladies of our circle. Foster met her there and a warm friendship sprang up between them. I do not recall her last name, but her given name was Maggie, and shortly after he met her, Foster wrote that song.

Whatever the truth of that story, Stephen dedicated the song to a Pittsburgh girl, Eliza T. Denniston.

The other song of this trio, "The Hour for Thee and Me," occupies but a single page of the manuscript book and appears only in its final version. "Massa" was copyrighted July 7, 1852, and matters with Christy had apparently been settled satisfactorily, for while this song was issued "as sung by Christy's Minstrels," it was announced on the title-page as "written and composed by Stephen C. Foster." Although it appears from the manuscript book that "Massa" was finished after the others, it was copyrighted first. "The Hour for Thee and Me" was issued two days later (July 9) and "Maggie" did not appear until October 14. "I Cannot Sing To-night," a song with words by George F. Banister, was copyrighted August 11.

4

An entry in Morrison Foster's account book shows that on October 5, 1852, Stephen and Jane were still living with the Foster family in the house on the East Common. In September Morrison had gone to Louisville to bring Charlotte's remains from the graveyard there to the family plot in the Allegheny Cemetery in Pittsburgh. The expenses of this removal were paid by Morrison and Stephen, but later their father reimbursed them.

"My Old Kentucky Home" was copyrighted by Firth, Pond & Company, January 31, 1853, and we have already learned that on January 15 the publishers had advertised the song as "just published," and probably without thinking of Christy had announced that it was written by the "author of 'Old Folks at Home.'" We have also read how Stephen, in his manuscript book, had first called the song "Poor Uncle Tom, Good Night." [6] The two pages devoted to its words come almost immediately after the final version of "Massa's in de Cold Ground."

Stephen probably took a trip to New York early in 1853 or late in 1852, for the January 29 issue of *The Musical World and New York Musical Times* contained this item:

Pittsburgh,—
We were recently visited by a celebrated Pittsburgher, namely, Stephen C. Foster, Esq., the author of most of the popular Ethiopian melodies now afloat—such for example, as Nelly Bly; Oh! boys carry me 'long; Uncle Ned; The Old Folks at Home, and many others.

[6] See page 176.

It may have been this statement that caused "Harry" to write a letter to the *World* asking the question about the authorship of "Old Folks at Home" that was answered in the February 19 issue of the magazine.[7] The paragraph continues:

Mr. Foster possesses more than ordinary abilities as a composer; and we hope he will soon realize enough from his Ethiopian melodies to enable him to afford to drop them and turn his attention to the production of a higher kind of music. Much of his music is now excellent, but being wedded to negro idioms it is, of course, discarded, by many who would otherwise gladly welcome it to their pianos. We were glad to learn from Mr. F. that he intends to devote himself principally hereafter to the production of "White men's" music. Firth, Pond & Co. have just published Mr. Foster's last song—My Old Kentucky Home, Good Night—which he thinks will be more popular than any of his previous compositions.

This is interesting when we remember Stephen's letter to Christy written the preceding May 25 (1852),[8] in which he stated that he had "concluded to . . . pursue the Ethiopian business without fear or shame and . . . to establish my name as the best Ethiopian song-writer." If George Birdseye can be trusted, we may learn of Stephen's own opinion of "Old Folks at Home." In the article in the *New York Musical Gazette* (March, 1867) from which we have already quoted, Birdseye wrote as follows:

In "Old Folks at Home" Foster hoped, and even expected, to rival "Home Sweet Home," which he always considered was written contrary to the rules of pure melody. He could never account for its popularity, and the enthusiasm and emotion with which it was received on every occasion. Perhaps had he not made the words of his song local, by the mention of the "Swanee River" there might have been a chance of its equaling, or at least approaching, the song it was intended to eclipse, for it is a touching and beautiful composition. But few have dared to follow where Foster failed, and "Home Sweet Home" still stands secure, the home song of the world.

[7] See page 206. [8] See pages 196-197.

On that point we who have been privileged to judge a half century after Birdseye wrote those words, may have our own ideas on Stephen's "failure" to write "the home song of the world." And this "home song" was one of the "Ethiopian" ditties that critics hoped Foster would abandon!

5

Time has had the privilege of correcting critics of the 1850's on several points regarding Stephen's melodies. It is true that some were wise enough to know a good thing when they heard it. We have already read the review of "Old Folks" in the *Musical World* (Sept. 4, 1852),[9] in which the critic was a bit patronizing, but admitted that it was "a song deserving . . . of its unexampled popularity." Then there was the writer in the *Albany State Register,* quoted in the July 24, 1852, issue of *Dwight's Journal of Music,* who wrote:

> We confess to a fondness for negro minstrelsy. There is something in the . . . melodious "Uncle Ned" that goes directly to the heart, and makes Italian trills seem tame. . . . As for poor "Uncle Ned," so sadly denuded of his wool, God bless that fine old colored gentleman, who, we have been so often assured has
>
> "Gone where the good niggers go."

Probably it was the same author who wrote in the *Register* about "Old Folks at Home"; comments that were reprinted in the October 2, 1852, issue of *Dwight's Journal of Music.*

> "OLD FOLKS AT HOME," the *last* negro melody, is on everybody's tongue, and consequently in everybody's mouth. Pianos and guitars groan with it, night and day; sentimental young ladies sing it; sentimental young gentlemen warble it in midnight serenades; volatile young "bucks" hum it in the midst of their business and pleasures; boatmen roar it out stentorially at all times; all the bands play it; amateur flute blowers agonize over it at every spare moment; the street organs grind it out at every hour; the "singing stars" carol

[9] See page 204.

it on the theatrical boards, and at concerts; the chamber maid sweeps
and dusts to the measured cadence of *Old Folks at Home;* the
butcher's boy treats you to a strain or two of it as he hands in the
steaks for dinner; the milk-man mixes it up strangely with the harsh
ding-dong accompaniment of his tireless bell; there is not a "live
darkey," young or old, but can whistle, sing, dance and play it, and
throw in "Ben Bolt" by way of good seasoning; indeed at every
hour, at every turn, we are forcibly impressed with the interesting
fact, that—

> "Way down upon de Swanee ribber
> Far, far away
> Dere's whar my heart is turnin ebber
> Dere's whar de old folks stay";

While the pathetic—we may add, the soul-stirring—chorus breaks
upon the sympathetic ear in the following strain:

> "All de world am sad and dreary,
> Ebry where I roam,
> Oh! darkeys, how my heart grows weary,
> Far from de old folks at home."

Probably the most vicious attack on Stephen's songs and
others of their type appeared in *Dwight's Journal of Music,*
November 19, 1853, and was no doubt penned by that New
England highbrow, John Sullivan Dwight, himself.

We wish to say that such tunes (Old Folks at Home), although
whistled and sung by everybody, are erroneously supposed to have
taken a deep hold of the popular mind; that the charm is only skin
deep; that they are hummed and whistled *without musical emotion,*
whistled "for lack of thought"; that they persecute and haunt the
morbidly sensitive nerves of deeply musical persons, so that they too
hum and whistle them involuntarily, hating them even while they
hum them; that such melodies become catching, idle habits, and are
not popular in the sense of musically inspiring, but that such and
such a melody *breaks out* every now and then, like a morbid irritation
of the skin.

In a previous issue of the *Journal,* September 17, the
magazine's New York correspondent had written this scath-

ing comment in reporting the concerts of the sensational orchestra conductor, Louis Antoine Jullien:

. . . the great Jullien continues to draw nightly throngs to Castle Garden, giving each night an overture, a movement from a symphony, an operatic fantasia, a plenty of astonishing quadrilles and polkas, two or three solos from the best artists, and two or three songs by Anna Zerr, who (shame to say) stooped to pick up one night and sang "Old Folks at Home" for the b'hoys; one would as soon think of picking up an apple-core in the street.

Anna Zerr was reprimanded by another paper [10] for trying to please the public, although in this case the writer was a bit more gentle and delicate in his reproof.

Mlle. Anna Zerr and Mlle. Behrend also add great interest to each programme [at Jullien's concerts] by their vocal performances. It may seem unfair to particularize what we don't like, when we do not particularize what pleases us, but as *everything* pleases us except one, we will mention the exception. We don't like Mlle. Zerr's singing of "Old Folks at Home." True, she sings it only on an *encore,* but we think she sings it in bad taste; and we think, moreover, that it is bad taste for her to sing it at all.

The Musical World and New York Musical Times, which had been kindly to "Old Folks at Home," but which hoped that Foster would "turn his attention to the production of a higher kind of music," published an interesting correspondence.

In the issue of September 24, 1853:

THE NEGRO MELODY QUESTION

The following two sides of the question came to us simultaneously by mail.

Charleston, S. C.

By reference to the *Evening News* . . . of Saturday 13th inst. you will see an extract from the second article on Musical Sentiments, by Augusta Browne [herself a song-writer, sister of Mrs. Hemans], deprecatory of Ethiopian songs as so generally introduced into parlors. . . . I trust that you will lose no opportunity of crying down

10 *Musical Review and Choral Advocate* (New York), October, 1853.

this evil. . . . Such . . . melodious trash . . . [is] in a fair way
to cast all sentimental music in the shade. It is your province to
reform the taste for music.

Point Coupee, La.

I see Miss Augusta Browne sneers at negro melodies. Let her
compose one which, like *Old Folks at Home,* shall be sung, played,
and whistled from Maine to California, in four months after it is
published, and I will concede her right to ridicule them if she likes.
I don't like the *negro words* myself, and wish you would put Morris
[G. P.], S. C. Foster, and Maeder up to a partnership, Foster to
compose the airs, Morris to write the songs, and Maeder to harmonize them.

The *World's* issue of October 29, 1853, contained a letter that provides some material for thought, particularly
as it came from the far South.

Quakerville, Gulf of Mexico
12th day of the 10th month, 1853

Our negro melodies (like our negro minstrels) are black things
whitewashed, or white things blackwashed. They are imitations—
counterfeits—not nature. You may blacken the face of one or a
dozen white men, write a song, compose a melody, call it negro words
and negro tunes and negro singers, and you have just as much of
literal truth—just as much of human nature, as the majority of
so-called negro songs and melodies exhibits. Friend *Christy's* "Old
Folks at Home"—so highly applauded by your paper—may be true
to the supposed nature of a white man painted black in a condition
of servitude, but neither the character of the melody nor the expression and the sentiments of the song and words are true to the
nature of the expressed feelings of the African as a servant, "way
down on the Swanee river" nor in any other location south and
West of the Potomac that I have met with in a thirty years residence.

I have visited servants in villages, cities—in their huts on plantations and in lecture rooms—I have gathered them at night around
a large reflecting telescope to "draw down the moon and stars," that
the "colored folks" might see a little more of God's wonderful works
around them; and I testify . . . in all soberness and honesty that
the African in this wide region of thirty years' survey and observa-
tion, is a cheerful, whistling, song-singing, loud-laughing, tobacco-
chewing, variety of the human family.

Of all the negro songs, Friend Stephen's "O boys, carry me long,"

&c. is the "cap-sheaf." An old negro singing his funeral ode as his fellow-servants carry him to the grave. After "bosse" the old dog, and the old white starving horse thank him for his dying tenderness —just before being put into his grave—the kind, considerate, and, we may hope, by this time dead negro—for I am unwilling to believe Stephen intends to bury him alive, though he has already as good as done it in this song—happens to see his master weeping hard by, and sobs out: "Massa don't you cry!" The sentiment is absurd, untruthful and ridiculous; but the melody, had it been used to appropriate thoughts, might have been worthy the author of "Old Uncle Ned."

Farewell,

JACOB LITTLE.

Before leaving the contemporary critics of Foster's songs one more story must be told, the tale of the Sunday School convention where the children were made to sing "Old Folks at Home" to Sunday School words. Strange enough to us to-day, it was not the Sunday School doggerel that was blamed for desecrating a fine melody, it was the tune itself that was attacked for daring to show its face at such a lily-white gathering. The author of this "communication" to the *Musical Review and Choral Advocate* (May, 1853) was Thomas Hastings, a composer of hymn-tunes and as a music educator and editor an associate of Lowell Mason, and of George F. Root, who, we have found, was himself trying to crash the gate of plantation melodies by writing some of them under a *nom de plume*.

COMMUNICATION FROM MR. HASTINGS

I was quite sorry to see in your last number, Mr. Editor, that our Sunday-school committee had brought upon themselves so severe a rebuke as you gave them, and still more so, to feel the conviction that it had been richly merited. Not being myself very conversant with Ethiopian minstrelsy, the sorry trick of adaptation had escaped my notice, till an incident brought it to mind. A superintendent gave the music into the hands of a lady who had charge of about a hundred infant scholars. She saw the trick and remonstrated. "But," says the superintendent, "the children will never know it!" "Come and see," was her reply. She sang a line or two, and then said, "Children, have you ever heard anything like that before?" "Old folks at home! Old folks at home!" shouted the little urchins with such merry glances and gesticulations as showed them upon the very point of "Cutting up," when the experiment ended and the piece was abandoned.

It is marvellous to me that so many good men will insist on perpetrating such mischief—just as if children could not discriminate; as if it would do no injury to vitiate their taste, or tamper with their susceptibilities. If there were no good tunes or hymns in circulation, there might be some apology for the abuse. Every committeeman might then take his turn in fishing up something from the lowest dregs of music and poetry, and the poor children be allowed to suffer. But the state of the case is directly opposite. There is an abundance of available materials, and every committee, therefore, is bound to make a good selection.

The matter you refer to is nothing of a novel character. We are not referring to a first offense of the kind. It is an old trick, which many seem determined to "play off" every time they have an opportunity. No matter what is said against it; any thing will do for children: merry dances, street ballads, bacchanalian songs, and negro melodies, often tricked with parodies which, by a double power of association, bring wicked and irreverent thoughts to mind! No matter, they are for children. And thus their minds are filled with poisonous trash, to forget which in after life would be to them a blessing.

It is high time for good men to bear witness against such abuses. I fear they will not yet be abandoned. Christy has more melodies; and then "Yankee Doodle," "Frog and Mouse," and "Jim Crow," I believe, have not yet been appropriated.

Yours, &c.
TH. HASTINGS.

6

If Stephen did actually visit New York early in 1853 he was back in Allegheny by February 14, for on that day he wrote a letter to *The Musical World and Times* which he dated "Pittsburgh." This letter is interesting, because it throws some light on Foster's knowledge of music. To understand the point he was trying to make, we must consult the January 8 issue of the *World*, where in the weekly installment of "Musical Studies for the Million" the "fundamental laws of harmony" are set forth. The third of these "laws" is stated as follows:

The leading note, or 7th of the scale, may not be doubled, and must resolve upward to the 8th.

Stephen's letter of February 14 was printed in the issue of February 26, prefaced by an editor's note.

We append the following very clever letter to our Study this week. We hope to hear from the writer as often as *such* a spirit moves him.

Why the italics for "such"? Was there any "spirit" in which the *Musical World* would not be glad to hear from Foster? Was this perchance a sly dig at the "Ethiopian" style which the editor hoped Stephen would abandon? The letter itself followed the editor's introduction.

Pittsburgh, Feb. 14, 1853

R. STORRS WILLIS, ESQ.: DEAR SIR:—In your "Musical Study" of the 8th ult., you say that the seventh of the scale must resolve upwards to the eighth. Is this not too briefly stated? Many persons might not give due emphasis to the phrase "seventh of the *scale,*" and thus erroneously take the term "seventh" in its common acceptation, namely, with regard to the chord in which it stands, which would, in most cases, resolve itself downwards, being almost necessarily a *minor* seventh, as the *large* seventh is, I believe, rarely, if ever, used in harmony except as a transition note, or when heralded, or—more technically—when *prepared.*

To this the editor appended a footnote—"The remark of our friend will now prevent any mistake of the kind.— ED."

This first part of Stephen's letter shows that he knew something about the theory of music, but that his acquaintance with the subject was of the most elementary sort. In the first place, the author of the article on harmony had been perfectly clear in pointing out that it was the seventh *of the scale* he was talking about, and not the interval of the minor seventh that occurs in all but two of the seventh chords in the major mode. Stephen admitted that the author had made this distinction, and the matter was clear in his own mind, but the suggestion that it would not be equally clear to others indicates, I think, that Stephen had become acquainted with the rudimentary rules of harmony and not much more. It shows that Stephen was having, or had suffered, considerable difficulty in mastering these basic principles, for the mere fact that he made the suggestion indicates to me, at least, that he was pretty much a novice. Certainly his songs, though adequately and appropriately harmonized, show that Stephen's harmonic resources were most meagre; that he was not altogether at ease in his musical table manners.

Stephen continues his letter in playful vein, with a fanciful suggestion that shows he gave such matters considerable thought, even though he was treading on ground where he was not too sure of his footing.

By the way, botanists have divided the vegetable kingdom into genders, and I observe that Mr. Fry, taking the French cue, has given even to words, a distinction suggestive of matrimony. Might we not have a musical gender? Thus, for instance, in the tones of a four-fold chord, take the sturdy *prime* and the valorous *fifth,*—which, when sounded together, to the exclusion of the others, suggests trumpets, and "the big wars that make ambition virtue,"—and they might stand for the masculine, while the conciliating *third,* and the complaining, though gentle (minor) *seventh,* as they seem to lean for support on the sterner notes, might represent the feminine notes of the harmonic family. Then we might very appropriately lay down musical rules in this style. "The males, though noisy and boisterous, may be doubled or reinforced with propriety, while the females (bless their dear hearts) can *speak for themselves*—a rule which you have already given, though in different words. In support of this idea, is the fact that the *seventh* has a natural *penchant* for the *third,* or sister tone of the succeeding chord, where it usually resolves itself in order to unfold its sorrowful story; a proverbial weakness of the sex, confiding their secrets to each other.

In that last sentence Stephen himself failed to distinguish between the seventh of the scale and the one he was referring to—"the gentle (minor) seventh." His letter concludes with a pleasant bit of whimsy.

It will probably not weaken my hypothesis to admit that the aforesaid *seventh* can sometimes be used to great advantage in creating *discord,* but it would be ungallant to dwell on this branch of the argument.

Respectfully, yours, etc.

S. C. FOSTER.

A Pittsburgh musician, J. William Pope, gave to the *Pittsburgh Press* some recollections, which if they are reliable give us information on Foster's musicianship. These reminiscences were published in the *Press,* June 23, 1895.

In 1849, I was proprietor and manager of a minstrel company of the old school. We were playing at the historic old Lafayette Hall, when one day Stephen Foster brought me the original manuscript for "Nelly Was a Lady," also the score. My company gave the song its first rendition in public, at Lafayette Hall, and we sang it every night there for three weeks. It was a success from the start, and the people went fairly wild over it.

Inasmuch as "Nelly Was a Lady" was first published in 1849, Pope was correct as to the date. Although Stephen was living in Cincinnati in that year he could easily have called on Pope during one of his visits to Pittsburgh, perhaps in June, when he came home for Susan Pentland's wedding. Pope's account continues:

I knew Foster well, and we were great friends. He showed me the manuscript of many of his melodies before they were sent to the publishers. Foster's ear was correct as to melody, but he sometimes made amusing mistakes in trying to produce the harmonies. On one occasion, I heard him singing a song in one key and playing it on the piano in another. I presume his mind was so wrapped up in the melody he was singing, that he paid no attention to the accompaniment. He was certainly a genius for producing melodies. . . .

Another reminiscence of Foster was published anonymously in the *Pittsburgh Press* (July, 1895). This also
told of Stephen's methods in composing.

> Foster's mind seemed to be full of melodies and I never saw him
> sit down to a piano that he did not play or sing something we had
> never heard before. He was continually evolving new songs and
> new melodies, some of them strange, yet peculiarly sweet and pathe-
> tic. Often when we were spending an evening with friends, he
> would suddenly dart to the piano, unmindful of all about him, and
> seemingly unconscious of his surroundings, and pick out on the key-
> board the notes of some new melody that seemed to be passing through
> his brain. He would play it over until he had somewhat familiar-
> ized himself with the air, then jot the notes down on paper, later on
> to reproduce it and make up an accompaniment. His friends and
> acquaintances were never offended at this conduct, as they never
> went out with him that they did not expect by the close of the eve-
> ning to hear some new song from his lips. He was a maker of
> melodies, and we all recognized his talents in that direction.

In his biography of Foster,[11] Harold Vincent Milligan
tells of the concerts given in Pittsburgh during these years.
We may know from this account what music Foster could
have heard if he attended these affairs. Jenny Lind came
to Pittsburgh in 1850 and gave a concert in Masonic Hall.
Even though the shouting and whistling of rowdies marred
her performance, and a rock thrown by one of them came
into the singer's dressing room, she forgot her vow never
to visit Pittsburgh again and gave another concert there
November 13, 1851.

William Vincent Wallace, the celebrated English composer of "Maritana" who spent many years in the United
States, appeared at Masonic Hall in 1852. One of the
"grand variations" that he presented on his program was
based on "Oh! Susanna." Milligan also mentions a "Mendelssohn Quintette Club . . . organized about 1850,"
which "gave concerts for many seasons . . . of the works
of Mozart, Schubert, Cherubini, Beethoven." This group

[11] *Op. cit.*

may have been the same as that organized in Boston 1849, and not a club resident in Pittsburgh. The Boston organization made tours each season to all the principal cities of the country.

Milligan tells of an affair in which Kleber, of whom we have already heard, was involved. It appears that a critic, Augustus Schaad, had reproved Kleber in his newspaper for his "presumptious [sic] appearance" and self-admiration" when Kleber appeared in 1851 as an assisting artist at a concert given by a Madame Bornstein. The next day Kleber was ready with a cowhide when he met Schaad on the street. The critic fled and locked himself in a conveniently near-by office. When he dared to come out again, Kleber's brother renewed the fight. Much was made of the affair in the newspapers, and Kleber was fined $100 when Schaad had him arrested.

There was music in abundance for Stephen to hear, even though it was sometimes marked by riots and street fights.

7

The first of Foster's works published in 1853 was the "Old Folks Quadrilles," copyrighted March 11 by Firth, Pond & Company. This curious piano piece, with its "right and left," "forward two," and other directions for dancing, introduces "Old Folks at Home," "Oh! Boys, Carry Me 'Long," "Nelly Bly," "Farewell My Lilly Dear" and "Cane Brake Jig." Had any composer after Foster's death perpetrated this outrage, we would indeed have attacked him for defaming the composer's memory by desecrating some of his loveliest melodies. In this case, Stephen, according to the title-page, was solely responsible for the treatment he gave his own tunes.

After this "Quadrille" the next item to be published was "Annie My Own Love" (May 12). The words to this "Annie" were the work of Charles P. Shiras, one of the

former "Knights of the S.T." of whom Stephen penned the
verse:

> First, there's Charley the elder, the Sunday-School teacher,
> Who laughs with a groan,
> In an unearthly tone,
> Without moving a bone
> Or a feature.

Evidently Shiras was something of a poet himself, and
it was later claimed that he had written the words for a
number of Foster's songs. Morrison Foster denied this
assertion in a letter he wrote to S. Reed Johnston of Pittsburgh, February 14, 1886.

I thank you for your favor of 12th inclosing a newspaper article
cut from the Rochester Pa. Herald, originally published in the
Chicago News. The author of the article evidently knows nothing
personally about what he writes. . . .

I had personal cognizance of every song he [Stephen] ever wrote
at home; I mean, in Allegheny County. His regular practise was to
compose the music first, and then write the words afterwards to
suit the music. [We have already found that this was probably not
always the case.] [12] In writing the words, his practise was to write
a verse or two at a time, submitting them to me verse by verse for
my opinion, or to his mother, who possessed a fine poetic fancy. At
rare intervals he wrote music to the words of others, but he always
preferred to write his own words, in order to harmonize them with
the previously written music.

Charles P. Shiras was an intimate friend of ours. We all esteemed
him highly and admired his genius. He and his mother lived on Hem-
lock St., Allegheny City, in a two story house. . . .

Shiras' style of poetry was too heavy and sombre for Stephen's
muse. The only words of Shiras' published to which Stephen ever
wrote music were a song called "Annie, my own Love." It was
published about a year before Shiras' death, and Shiras' name is
printed on the title page as the author of the words. Shiras had
half the royalty on this song, but it did not have a very large sale.[13]

It was a subject of regret with Stephen, as well as myself, that

[12] See page 189.
[13] For a little less than a four year period Foster's share of these royalties
amounted to only $19.12.

Shiras (notwithstanding his undoubted genius) could not write suitable words for Stephen's music. Stephen would cheerfully have given publicity to them through his music for the purpose of aiding Shiras, who, though possessing some little unremunerative real estate, was dependent entirely upon his literary labours for his support, and needed money. . . .

The incident about Stephen's buying a piano for $100 and placing it in Mrs. Shiras' back parlor, is all a myth. There was no piano in Mrs. Shiras' home. Stephen had his own piano at home, which he bought from H. Kleber & Bro. and on it he practised and composed.

In regard to Stephen's piano, we shall learn later that in the years from 1857 to 1859 Stephen rented a piano from Charlotte Blume, listed in the Pittsburgh directories of those years as a piano "manufacturer."

Morrison continued his letter with a word about Stephen's trying out his songs.

He needed no one to sing for him. He had a beautiful, though not robustious [sic], baritone voice. No one could sing his songs so well, and with such pathetic tenderness as he, and his rendering of them would bring tears to listeners' eyes. For the practicing and perfecting of his choruses, he depended upon Susan Pentland, now Mrs. Andrew L. Robinson, Jessie Lightner, my late beloved wife, on Mrs. Julia Mitchell, and myself.

A personal glimpse of Stephen at about this time is afforded by some recollections published in the *Pittsburgh Press* of August 11, 1895. These were printed anonymously, merely as the words of "a prominent Pittsburgher."

I remember Foster well, and knew him personally. In fact, we had many pleasant hours together. I used to sing a little myself, and was frequently out with Foster at parties here and there, where other young people, myself included, joined in singing some new songs of his composition. . . .

Foster was just a little inclined to be moody and thoughtful. He was very modest, too, about his achievements as a composer and writer of songs unless the subject was pressed upon him in such a manner that he could not well avoid it, and then he would drop it as quickly as he got an opportunity. He was not at all conceited, and I have often thought his bearing amid the praise that was constantly showered upon him by his friends was something remarkable. It would have turned the head of any other man than Foster. He was always kind, always genial; never wanted for friends, and never had an enemy. Everybody who knew him liked him, and his temperament, tastes and general disposition were such that I could not imagine him writing anything else than the sweet plaintive lines that have made his name famous. True, he wrote some campaign songs, and several humorous negro melodies, but none are of the offensive style that is characteristic of much of the so-called popular music of the present day.

Morrison Foster tells something of his brother's personality.[14]

He was very simple in his tastes, and no matter how well his income justified it, he shrank from everything like display. The simplest forms of food satisfied him. Indeed, he never appeared to care for what was set before him on the table. If it appeased hunger it was all he cared for. His companions were seldom ever musicians. Outside of his own studies and performances he seemed to prefer to get away from music and musical topics. But he was very fond of the society of cultured people and men of genius in walks entirely different from his own.

There are numerous references to Stephen's love for reading in various reminiscences of his family and friends, and it may be that we have direct evidence of the kind of literature he read. On the inside back cover of his manuscript book, turned upside down, Stephen wrote a list of books and authors, with amounts written after each name. Two possibilities are suggested by this list. One, that it comprised books he had purchased, with an estimate of what they had cost, and the other that before he went to New York in 1860 he planned to sell his collection of books, and was figuring what they should bring.

Here is the list, and the reader may judge Stephen's taste for himself:

[14] In his biography, *op. cit.*

Bleak House ....$ .60
(Illegible) 1.50
Harp[er's?] 1.00
Littell [probably *Littell's Living Age,* which contained
    an article about Foster in its issue of May, 1859] .75
Webster 2.00
Scott .... .50
Cowper .... .25
Weber .... .35
Maryott .... .40
(Illegible) .... .30
Hutten .... .60
Meadow .... .25

                            $8.50

There are also on the last pages of the manuscript book some crude sketches which show that Stephen did have some ability in drawing, as Morrison claimed. These were probably made in 1860, but they may be shown here. First we see the lettering for the title-page of an imaginary song—"Over the Calm Lake Gliding, song dedicated to Amelia by Stephen C. Foster." Then follows a series of cartoons in which Stephen imagines himself involved in a triangle with "Amelia," whoever she might be. First we see Stephen and Amelia going to the "7 sisters," then the baby left at home with its nurse. Mr. Young, probably "Amelia's" husband, is seen inquiring about his wife. With the nurse he starts in pursuit, and the final picture shows a "Policeman after Stephen and Amelia."

With what glee a Freudian psychoanalyst could analyze those sketches. He would have Stephen actually involved in an affair of the heart, or else showing by his drawings a frustration of inhibited desires. I fear that there was nothing so exciting as that. Stephen, I am sure, was merely amusing himself and his friends.

8

The others of Stephen's works published in 1853 were the "Holiday Schottisch" (July 2), a trivial and awkward piano piece, and the songs "Old Dog Tray," "Old Memories" (December 5) and "Little Ella" (December 13). While there is no copyright deposit in the Library of Congress to establish the day and month "Old Dog Tray" was published, it was probably written before the other two songs, for in the manuscript book its four pages precede the four devoted to "Old Memories" and the three occupied by "Little Ella."

There is a pleasant anecdote about "Old Dog Tray," told by Morrison Foster in his biography.[15]

An old friend of ours, Col. Matthew I. Stewart, gave Stephen a handsome setter dog, which for a time was his constant companion. We lived upon the East Common of Allegheny, a wide open space, now improved into a beautiful park. Stephen often watched this dog with much pleasure, playing with the children on the Common. When he wrote "Old Dog Tray," he put into verse and song the sentiments elicited by remembrances of this faithful dog.

Mrs. Rose, Stephen's granddaughter, tells that Stephen owned another dog later.[16] This was a homeless mongrel he picked up in the street. Stephen named him "Calamity" because of the mournful quality of his howl.

Mrs. Rose also tells another anecdote connected with Stephen's song.

The daughter of Mrs. John Mitchell [17] told me of the writing of "Old Dog Tray." They were neighbors at the time, and Foster had dropped in as was his custom, to go over some of his writings with her mother. He played over a few of the bars of "Old Dog Tray" and jotted them down on paper. He left in a little while, and she did not see him again for three months, as he had been called to New

[15] *Op. cit.*
[16] In the article "My Grandmother's Memories," *op. cit.*
[17] The former Julia Lightner, sister of Jessie Lightner, who married Morrison Foster.

York on business with his publishers. When he returned, and came in again with more music, Mrs. Mitchell said to him, "What about that song you wrote when last here?" "O, I don't know, I didn't think much of it." "But it was very pretty, I saved it. I have it here in the table drawer. Try it again." He sat down to the piano and tried it over. Mrs. Mitchell with sympathetic understanding, slipped out of the room. Returning some time later, she knew by the high color of his cheeks and the burning intensity of his eyes that the song was made. "Listen," he said, and turning again to the piano, he played and sang the music and *words* almost exactly as they stand to-day, "The morn of life is passed, and evening comes at last."

This story does not quite correspond in its details with the facts that can be gathered from contemporary evidence. Two important events occurred in 1853 which bring light on Stephen's whereabouts at various times of that year. On May 5 he signed a new contract with Firth, Pond & Company, which may have been the business with his publishers that called him to New York. The other occurrence was the separation of Stephen and Jane.

Exactly when this took place is not certain, but on June 21, 1853, Stephen's sister, Henrietta, wrote to Morrison from her home in Youngstown:

How sorry I feel for dear Stephy, though when I read your letter, I was not at all surprised at the news it contained. I last winter felt that a separation was inevitable. Though I never wrote a word of the kind to Stephy, for I thought he had trouble enough already. Tell him to come out and stay a while with me, we have a delightful house, well shaded by trees, and I know it must be pleasanter here than in Pittsburgh this hot weather. You did not tell me what he had done with little Marion, I feel quite anxious about her, dear little lamb, who is she with? Give much love to Stephy for me, and tell him to feel assured that he has the prayers and sincere sympathy of his sister Etty, dear boy. May God lead him in the ways of peace, and fill his heart with that love which alone is satisfying, and which *never* disappoints.

In July Stephen was in New York, evidently living alone, and on the 8th of that month he wrote Morrison:

My Dear Brother:

Your letter of the 6th is received. The vest arrived safely, I am glad you sent it. I wish you could send me Mess. F. P. & Co's note for $125 which I gave you. In my anxiety to pay you I rather stinted myself expecting to be able to live modestly at home, but circumstances have increased my expenses as you know since that time. They have just rendered my account which is over five hundred dollars, and that for the dullest season in the year, so you see my prospects are good but I dare not claim any money until these notes are all paid, though full amt. of my a/c current is passed to my credit, and bal. due to be claimed after that time. If you will let me have the note I will take the first occasion to pay you. I am not living expensively, and I hope it will not be long before I can pay you back the amt. I made it payable to your order, so, if you send it, don't forget to indorse it.

I am getting along first rate, with plenty of work to keep me busy. Hippodrome no humbug—races there very exciting. Taylor's new saloon *great*. Sontag in opera with Salvi Steffarroni &c. next week. Crystal Palace in a week. Fourth of July here good for nervous sick people I dare say, cleared myself out of town, went over to Staten Island and saw Vin Smith. Gilliad and wife at Niagara— home next week.

I am about bringing out a couple of good songs.

Love to all

Your affectionate brother
STEPHEN.

Vin Smith was Lavinia Smith, Mrs. J. Edgar Thomson, wife of the engineer who with Brother William built a section of the Pennsylvania Railroad and who later became its president. Lavinia herself was a sister of William's second wife. "Gilliad" was her brother, the Gilead Smith to whom Stephen had sent the copy of "Nelly Was a Lady." [18] Stephen later dedicated a song to Mrs. Thomson, "Molly Dear, Good Night," in 1861.

Stephen stayed in New York for considerably more than a year. On March 3, 1854, Dunning concluded a letter to Morrison with this paragraph:

[18] See pages 152-153.

Have you heard anything from Stephen lately? It is a subject of much anxiety to me notwithstanding his foolish and unaccountable course. . . . I hope he will continue to make a comfortable living for himself.

By October of 1854 Stephen was evidently quite recently back in Allegheny, for on the 19th his mother, visiting William in Philadelphia, wrote thus to Morrison:

Tell Stephen I hope to find him at home when I come, to help me make it more like one, which I verily think I shall greatly treasure when I get back to it. . . . Give my love to Stephen and tell him I wrote a letter to him after I came here and directed it to New York, it was writen [sic] on Wednesday night.

Stephen came home, but whether Jane joined him at the house of his father and mother is not known. It may be that they were not re-united until they started keeping house together, and themselves rented William's house in the late Summer of 1855, after the death of Stephen's father and mother.

9

An anecdote told by Morrison [19] may shed some light on the situation; not that it is altogether accurate in its facts, but because it enables us to read between the lines and draw our own conclusions.

After his marriage, Stephen received very flattering offers from the publishers in New York, and strong inducements to make that city his home. He removed there and had every favorable prospect that a young man could hope for. . . .

He went to house-keeping and liked New York very much. But after a year the old fondness for home and mother began to be too strong for him to overcome. One day he suddenly proposed to his wife that they return to Pittsburgh. He brought a dealer to the house, sold out everything in the way of furniture, and within twenty-four hours was on the road to the home of his father in Allegheny. He arrived late at night and was not expected. When he rang the bell his mother was awakened and knew his footsteps on the porch.

[19] In the biography of Stephen, *op. cit.*

She arose immediately and went down herself to let him in. As she passed through the hall she called out, "Is that my dear son come back again?" Her voice so affected him that when she opened the door she found him sitting on the little porch-bench weeping like a child.

Morrison's account does not tally with the letters from Dunning Foster and from his mother that were in his possession when he wrote that account. It is obvious that Morrison was anxious to cover up the matter of Stephen and Jane separating. We have learned that Eliza, the mother, was in Philadelphia when Stephen came home in October, 1854. His mother's greeting, as described by Morrison, must have occurred on another, possibly earlier, occasion.

But what Morrison may have revealed is emphasized in the paragraph in his book that follows the account of Stephen's mother's greeting.

His love for his mother amounted to adoration. She was to him an angelic creature. . . . Stephen never went away from home to stay, again, as long as his mother and father lived.

In my opinion, it is quite likely that there was "too much family" in Stephen's early married life. When the young couple returned from their honeymoon in 1851 it was to live with five of Jane's newly acquired in-laws, and I think that many of the young brides among my readers will agree that such a situation seldom works. Eliza Foster was a saintly creature, of that I am sure, but Stephen was her youngest and he himself loved her so dearly that it is quite conceivable that Jane may not have had all the room in Stephen's heart she felt she was entitled to.

Then too, we can sense an antagonism in Henrietta's letter, when she wrote "I last winter felt that a separation was inevitable." Need we draw too much on our imaginations to picture the situations that probably arose when Henrietta paid the family a visit during that "last winter."

It is interesting to note, too, that although the sister sympathized with Stephen, Dunning, his brother, spoke of Stephen's "foolish and unaccountable course." We will remember that in 1849 Dunning described Jane McDowell as "a very sensible and interesting young lady." [20] This is not the first, nor by any means the last time that families have aligned themselves thus—the men-folk taking the part of their women in-laws, and the sisters rushing to the defence of their brothers, the ill-treated husbands.

I may be totally wrong in my deductions, but I feel very strongly that family complications formed the principal cause of Stephen's first separation from his wife. I am also of the opinion that two subsequent events, bringing a double loss that seemed, and in fact was, a great tragedy to Stephen, proved after all the only solution of his domestic difficulties.

Eliza Foster died suddenly January 18, 1855, and Stephen was heart-broken. The death of his father, an invalid since 1851, came six months later, July 27. It is said that the old man was so feeble, and had failed so much during these years, that the family never told him of Eliza's death. Just before he himself died a neighbor who came to see him inadvertently let him know what had happened. The shock was too much for him.

It was a double sorrow for Stephen, for no matter how much his father had failed to understand his youngest son in his youth, they were without doubt companionable, and there was surely considerable affection between them. And we know that Stephen adored his mother.

No matter how great the loss of his beloved father and mother, the fact remains that we find Stephen and Jane keeping house after these parents were gone. The evidence that Stephen paid rent to William ($31.25 a quarter) indicates that they lived in the same house the family had occupied; but Henry and his wife had gone elsewhere to live,

[20] See page 157.

and Jane could at least be mistress in her own house. And from that time she and Stephen lived together as long as he could support her.

10

The new contract which Stephen signed with Firth, Pond & Company, May 5, 1853, is probably not in existence to-day, but from a later agreement made with the firm (December 21, 1854) it is apparent that the 1853 contract increased Foster's interest in future songs to ten per cent royalty on the retail price of all copies sold, from the eight per cent (two cents on songs which sold at twenty-five cents) that he was receiving on previous songs. It is evident also, as we shall presently discover, that this 1853 agreement provided that Stephen should publish exclusively with Firth, Pond & Company. In regard to this clause, we have already learned that Foster's last song with another publisher was "Laura Lee," which Benteen copyrighted August 7, 1851, and that he dealt with no firms other than Firth, Pond until he gave "Comrades, Fill No Glass for Me" to Miller & Beacham, successors to Benteen, November 23, 1855.

During the months that Stephen spent in New York he no doubt came in touch with Christy and other minstrels. We heard from his letter to Morrison, July 8, 1853, that "he had plenty of work to keep [him] busy," and that there were many entertainment attractions in town—"Salvi Steffarroni &c.," "Taylor's new saloon," and the Crystal Palace, which was to open "in a week." It was late in August of that year that Jullien, the most magnificent of charlatans, made his début with his orchestra at Castle Garden, and Stephen may have been present on one of the occasions when Anna Zerr, as soloist, "stooped to pick up, . . . and sang 'Old Folks at Home' for the b'hoys."

In the October 8, 1853, issue of the *Musical World* we find this notice:

ETHIOPIAN MINSTRELSY

is on the increase. We now have, in New York, six companies of Minstrels in full blast.

In the November 12 issue of the same magazine we may find Christy's advertisement.

CHRISTY'S AMERICAN OPERA HOUSE

No. 472 Broadway, above Grand st.
Open Every Night

The Original and ONLY far famed

CHRISTY MINSTRELS

Organized in 1842
The first and only oldest established Company in Existence
The model Troupe of the World

Under the direction and personal supervision of Edwin P. Christy, Sole Proprietor and Manager. Admission, 25 cts.

Doors open at 6½ o'clock—Commence at 7½ o'clock

It was at this time that Foster published his "Social Orchestra," and the interest it aroused among the readers of musical journals attests to Stephen's increasing fame. In the November 12, 1853, issue of the *Musical World*, Firth, Pond & Company inserted this advertisement:

Will be published on the 1st November

THE SOCIAL ORCHESTRA

a collection of the most popular operatic
and other melodies, arranged as

SOLOS, DUETS, TRIOS, AND QUARTETTES

for Flutes, Violins, and Violoncelio [sic] (or pianoforte)
and particularly adapted to
Evenings at Home, Serenades, &c.

It is arranged by
STEPHEN C. FOSTER
The well known composer

Price $1.00

There were evidently delays in getting this work ready. In the November 26 issue of the *World* this brief item appeared under "Answers to Correspondents":

> H. B. Bethany:—Foster's Social Orchestra will be published in about two weeks, when we will send it to you.

The book was not issued for several months. In the February 4, 1854, issue of the *Musical World* another subscriber made inquiry, a correspondent who seemed to have had his doubts about Foster's ability as an arranger.

> Windsor, Bentie Co. N. C.
>
> MON CHER EDITEUR:
> Is Foster's Social Orchestra out yet? What instruments is it arranged for? What number of pieces does it contain? How is it off for consecutive fifths and octaves?
>
> W. L. H.

To which the editor replied:

> Foster's Social Orchestra will be out in a few days. When a copy is sent us we will post you up about it.

It was evidently only a few days later that the work was actually published, for the February 11 issue of the *World* informed still another correspondent, "Social Orchestra is now out." The book was entered for copyright by Firth, Pond & Company, January 26, 1854.

II

The "Social Orchestra" is a notable volume. Its eighty-three pages of music present various instrumental arrangements of popular airs of the day, melodies from well-known operas, arrangements of Foster's own songs, and several new instrumental works composed by himself—notably the "Village Festival," a series of quadrilles.[21] Nor are the arrangements particularly bad; they are playable, if by no

---

[21] The new instrumental pieces by Foster were "Anadolia," "Irene," "Jennie's Own Schottisch," "Village Festival Quadrilles," and "Village Festival Jig."

means the work of a master of instrumental combinations.
In the preface the publishers spoke a word for the qualifications of the compiler.

Having long noticed the want of such a work, they [the publishers]
have determined to issue one that will meet with general approval,
and have accordingly confided the task of selecting and arranging
the melodies to a gentleman of acknowledged musical taste, and composer of some of the most popular airs ever written in this or any
other country, as will be seen by reference to the name on the title
page.

The critical review that appeared in the February 25
issue of the *Musical World* was in the main commendatory.

It is a great gratification to us to meet with a work like this, which
aims at improving the taste of the community for social music; and
no work is better adapted for such a purpose than one which gives
opportunities of combining instruments. . . . The "Social Orchestra"
then, is a great desideratum to instrumental performers, who will
find in it a good and tasteful store of instrumental music for from
one to four instruments. We approve the plan of the author in
writing for such instruments as are more commonly the object of
practice among amateurs—the violin, the flute and the violoncello.

.   .   .   .

We have, however, a few suggestions to make. . . .
We regret that Mr. Foster has omitted to arrange some pieces
for the *tenor* [the viola]. . . . We do not entirely approve of the
management of the second violin, written as it is from beginning to
end in doubled chords, which renders the part tedious. . . . It is also
rather a pity, we think, that the author never indicates any *position*
of the violin, in passages difficult of performance. . . .
Despite these omissions, however, the work of Mr. Foster well
deserves the favor of the public. We trust that this is not the only
work of the kind which he will find the public calling for at his
hands.

The "Social Orchestra" was a popular household book
for many years. As late as 1888 we find his heirs receiving
royalties from its sale. That, however, was on renewal of
copyright. Stephen himself was evidently paid cash for his
work on the book, and had no royalty interest in it. The

1857 list of moneys received for his works shows that he received $150 for the "Social Orchestra."

In addition to this instrumental work, Foster published four songs in 1854, all of them issued probably before he returned to his home in Allegheny in October. The first of the songs was "Ellen Bayne" (Feb. 3), of which the working out of the words occupies five consecutive pages of the manuscript book. It is interesting to note that in all versions of the several stanzas in the manuscript sketches, the name is spelled "Bane," not "Bayne," as it appears on the first and subsequent editions of the printed copies.

It is often said that this song of Foster's is the source of the famous "John Brown's Body," which later became the music for Julia Ward Howe's "Battle Hymn of the Republic." This, I think, is highly improbable. It is true that there is a certain similarity between the two melodies, particularly in the cadence that marks the close of each quatrain of the stanza, and the end of the "chorus." Yet the origin of the "John Brown" tune is quite satisfactorily traced to William Steffe of South Carolina, who composed it as a Sunday School hymn, to the words "Say, brothers, will you meet us." It is apparent that Steffe's song was probably written after Stephen Foster published "Ellen Bayne" (its existence has not been established before 1856), yet it does not seem likely that Steffe consciously stole Foster's melody. He may have heard it, and it may have been in his subconscious mind when he composed his own song, but that would not convict him of plagiarism when he paralleled only a few notes of Stephen's tune.

12

The next of Stephen's 1854 songs was that choice gem of sentiment, "Willie We Have Missed You," which proved in the composer's own day one of his popular songs. It was copyrighted March 4, and on the following September

2, when "Willie" had been at large for less than six months, the publishers advertised in the *World*:

Third thousand now ready of Foster's beautiful ballad

WILLIE WE HAVE MISSED YOU   38 [cents]

This truthful and charming "Musical Home Picture" should be in the hands of every lover of music in the entire country.

The beautiful vignette title is alone worth more than the price asked for the music.

We have already heard the anecdote about that "beautiful vignette title." [22]

The six pages devoted to this song in the manuscript book show that Stephen, as was his usual custom, tried several ideas before he was finally satisfied. The original first stanza was to have read:

> The little ones were up
> Till 'twas ten oclock and past
> Then their eyes began to twinkle
> And they've gone to sleep at last
> But they listened for your voice
> Till they thought you'd never come
> Oh, Willie we have missed you
> Welcome, welcome home.

These lines later became part of the second stanza, and the first verse in the final version reads:

> Oh! Willie is it you, dear,
> Safe, safe at home?
> They did not tell me true, dear;
> They said you would not come.
> I heard you at the gate,
> And it made my heart rejoice;
> For I knew that welcome foot-step
> And that dear, familiar voice,
> Making music on my ear
> In the lonely midnight gloom:
> Oh! Willie, we have missed you;
> Welcome, welcome home!

[22] See page 208.

And if those words, coupled with a pretty tune, had failed to be popular in the sentimental 1850's, we might well ask, what would have succeeded?

Then came "Jeanie"—"Jeanie with the Light Brown Hair." This was copyrighted June 5, and as its three pages in the manuscript book follow immediately those devoted to "Willie," we may assume that it was written just after the earlier song. It will be remarked that Stephen, when he published this song, had been separated from Jane for at least a year. If he was thinking of her when he wrote it, and that is altogether probable as the name in the first draft of the manuscript is "Jennie," it may be that he really missed her. We may observe also that "Willie" is a song that describes a homecoming, and even though Stephen did not go back to Allegheny until the Fall, it is not unlikely that his thoughts were constantly of his family and his home.

Another fact is interesting, whatever it may suggest. The melodies for the opening lines of "Willie We Have Missed You" and "Jeanie with the Light Brown Hair" are almost identical. This is not the only instance in which Foster repeated himself; the opening phrases of "Oh! Lemuel!" (Jan. 7, 1850) and of "Old Dog Tray" (1853) are almost the same, but those songs were written at times three years apart, while "Jeanie" and "Willie" were almost twins.

"Jeanie" is really a beautiful creature. She is one of Stephen's very few successful love songs. Generally it was a lesser Stephen Foster that sang when he spoke of this kind of affection. His sentiment seemed more sincere, and more a part of himself, when he wrote of home. But in "Jeanie with the Light Brown Hair" the truly lovely melody is wedded to words that seem to express a genuine longing, and tend partially to contradict our theory about Stephen's love for his wife—particularly at the time he was separated from her in 1854. Listen to the last stanza.

I sigh for Jeanie, but her light form strayed
   Far from the fond hearts round her native glade;
Her smiles have vanished and her sweet songs flown,
   Flitting like the dreams that have cheered us and gone.
Now the nodding wild flowers may wither on the shore
   While her gentle fingers will cull them no more:
Oh! I sigh for Jeanie with the light brown hair,
   Floating like a vapor on the soft summer air.

13

The last of the 1854 songs was "Come with Thy Sweet Voice Again," September 19. Between this and "Jeanie" there are a number of curious items in the manuscript book. As "Jeanie" was published in June and the next song not until September, these entries of works that were never printed may indicate that Stephen's muse did not burn too brightly during the last months of his stay in New York, even though one of his best songs, "Hard Times Come Again No More," may have been written during this period.

"Jeanie" ends on page 84. On page 85 we find a couplet headed "Hoboken."

Where wranglers bid you to their scenes of strife
In wrong conception of your plan of life.

On the same page, but written with a different pencil, appears:

One hour of pain will flood the measure
That years would fail to fill with pleasure.

The next page is devoted to a single stanza of a poem Stephen commenced earlier in the books, one which may be a tribute to John Kelly, the schoolmaster of his boyhood.

Old partner of our youthful mirth
Thy fruits are scattered o'er the earth

And while they bloom scarce mellowed yet
The sun that warmed them soon must set
But when the final beam is spent
Thou shalt not lack a monument
To stand mid pride's unmeaning toys
A landmark of departed joys.

The following three pages are occupied with love verses, starting "How shall I woo thee?" Then comes a stanza in which Foster again uses the word "pleasure" for rhyming.

"WHEN THE BOWL GOES ROUND" [23]

No life so dull but hath some hours of pleasure
No heart so poor but hath some hidden treasure
  No hearth so bright
But finds its $\begin{cases} \text{night} \\ \text{blight} \end{cases}$
When the bowl goes round
When the bowl goes round

This is one of Stephen's earliest attempts at a temperance song. After it comes a single page devoted to a poem called "Parting," and then four pages of a song, "Molly Dear," in which Stephen not only writes out the words, but also inserts sketches of the melody he intended to use. This snatch of music has some of Foster's characteristics, even though the line for "Joy is sitting on thy brow, Molly," presents some Scotch-Irish traits that are not often found in his tunes.

Then come two pages of "Come with thy Sweet Voice Again," followed by seven pages of a poem that was to have commenced

There's many a "robin," a "big-bellied Ben,"
Who eats more victuals than three score men

and which finally turned out to be

[23] This is not the same verse as that used in a posthumously published song of the same title, issued in 1870. The words of that song were written by George Cooper and the melody adapted from another song by Foster, "Jenny June."

"THE ROBIN AND THE BUTTERFLY"

A Robin is perched in a sycamore tree
Feeding her little ones timorously, *etc., etc.*

After this Stephen devoted two more pages to "Come with Thy Sweet Voice," and put the poem in its final form.

14

It was on November 11, 1854, that Firth, Pond advertised that they had sold more than 130,000 copies of "Old Folks at Home," 90,000 of "My Old Kentucky Home," and 74,000 of "Massa's in de Cold Ground." On December 21, after Stephen had returned to Allegheny, he signed another contract with the publishers, one that is in existence to-day.

At the Library of Congress in Washington there are two copies of this agreement. Both are in Foster's handwriting, and strangely enough, both were acquired from the same source, William A. Pond & Company, successors to a portion of the Firth, Pond & Company catalog. Since Foster wrote both copies in his own hand, it might readily be assumed that he dictated his own terms, possibly with the help of an able lawyer. By this time he was no doubt in a position to do so, for his most popular songs had achieved tremendous vogue.

This 1854 contract refers to the two previous agreements between Foster and the firm (Dec. 3, 1849, and May 5, 1853) and declares their terms "from this date null and void." Although, as we have found, copies of these previous contracts have never come to light, this new agreement shows what their terms may have been. It is apparent, too, that each new contract was more advantageous to Stephen.

Altogether, the 1854 contract contains eighteen articles.

The first article relates to future songs, and calls for a ten per cent royalty on the retail price of all vocal compositions not yet published, "excepting all arrangements exclusively for voice and guitar." These "guitar arrangements" were highly popular in those days.

The second article provides for a ten per cent royalty on "each and every copy with vocal arrangement, excepting all arrangements exclusively for voice and guitar, which the party of the first part (Firth, Pond & Company) may hereafter publish of the songs named as follows." Then comes an enumeration of twelve songs. It is important to note the dates of their original publications, as well as the retail prices.

	Originally Copyrighted	Retail Price
Farewell My Lilly Dear	Dec. 13, 1851	25 cts
Massa's in de Cold Ground	July 7, 1852	25 cts
My Old Kentucky Home	Jan. 31, 1853	25 cts
Annie My Own Love	May 12, 1853	25 cts
Old Memories	Dec. 5, 1853	25 cts
Little Ella	Dec. 13, 1853	25 cts
Old Dog Tray	(?) 1853	25 cts
Ellen Bayne	Feb. 3, 1854	38 cts
Willie We Have Missed You	Mar. 4, 1854	38 cts
Jeanie with the Light Brown Hair	Jun. 5, 1854	38 cts
Come with thy Sweet Voice Again	Sep. 19, 1854	25 cts
Hard Times Come Again No More	Jan. 17, 1855	25 cts

The last item indicates that although "Hard Times Come Again No More" was not copyrighted until the following January 17, it was in the hands of the publisher at the time this contract was drawn up. In the manuscript book its words are found on the three pages which follow musical sketches for a "duet," immediately after "Come with Thy Sweet Voice Again."

Article Third contains another list of songs. On these the publisher agrees to pay eight per cent royalty, subject to the same exception for guitar arrangements.

	Originally Copyrighted	*Retail Price*
Dolcy Jones	Nov. 14, 1849	25 cts
Mary Loves the Flowers	Jan. 16, 1850	25 cts
Nelly Bly	Feb. 8, 1850	25 cts
Way Down in Ca-i-ro	Apr. 17, 1850	25 cts
The Voice of By Gone Days	Jun. 28, 1850	25 cts
Lily Ray	Dec. 9, 1850	25 cts
Wilt Thou Be Gone, Love?	Mar. 12, 1851	38 cts
Farewell Old Cottage	Mar. 22, 1851	25 cts
Once I Loved Thee, Mary Dear	Apr. 4, 1851	25 cts
Ring de Banjo	Apr. 29, 1851	25 cts
Oh! Boys, Carry Me 'Long	July 25, 1851	25 cts
My Hopes Have Departed Forever	Aug. 4, 1851	25 cts
Old Folks at Home	Oct. 1, 1851	25 cts
Willie My Brave	Oct. 21, 1851	25 cts
Eulalie	Dec. 6, 1851	25 cts
The Hour for Thee and Me	July 9, 1852	25 cts
I Cannot Sing To-night	Aug. 11, 1852	25 cts
Maggie by My Side	Oct. 14, 1852	25 cts

There are several significant facts about these two lists. They include all of the Foster songs published by Firth, Pond & Company to the date of the contract, except "Nelly Was a Lady" and "My Brudder Gum." The assumption is that Stephen had no royalty interest in these songs, but that he had sold all his rights in them for fifty copies of each.[24]

It will be noted that the songs enumerated in Article Third, allowing but *eight* per cent royalty, consist of songs published from November 14, 1849, to October 14, 1852. Except for three songs—"Farewell My Lilly Dear," "Massa's in de Cold Ground," and "My Old Kentucky Home"—all of the songs in Article Second, allowing *ten* per cent royalty, were published after May 5, 1853, the date of Foster's second contract with Firth, Pond & Company.

We may assume that the first contract, signed in 1849,

[24] See pages 152-153.

allowed a two cent royalty. This was offered in the publisher's letter of Sept. 12, 1849.[25] Inasmuch as two cents
is eight per cent of 25 cents (the retail price of all but one
of the songs enumerated in Article Third) it seems logical
to assume that the second contract, signed May 5, 1853, increased Foster's royalty from eight to ten per cent (2½
cents on the 25 cent songs), especially since the songs
enumerated in Article Second (the ten per cent list) were
for the most part issued during the term of the second contract—between May 5, 1853, and December 21, 1854. It
would therefore appear that the present contract (1854)
continues the arrangements provided for in the previous
contracts, with the individual songs yielding the royalty
agreed upon by the contracts under which they were published.

This leaves three songs to be explained, copyrighted
prior to the second (1853) contract—"Farewell My Lilly
Dear" (Dec. 13, 1851); "Massa's in de Cold Ground"
(July 7, 1852); and "My Old Kentucky Home" (Jan. 31,
1853). Perhaps Stephen had been an able enough sales-
man to persuade his publishers to put these in the higher
royalty group, even though they had been published while
the two cent (eight per cent) agreement was still in force.
Pity that his best seller, "Old Folks at Home," was not put
there too.

15

Articles Fourth, Fifth and Sixth of the contract provide
for royalties of one and a half cents per copy on the guitar
arrangements of future songs and of previous songs enumerated in Articles Third and Fourth, as well as on future
"exclusively instrumental compositions" by Foster. Articles
Seventh and Eighth cover other instrumental arrangements
of the songs made by Foster himself or by others. On future arrangements the composer is to receive one and a half

[25] See page 152.

cents per copy; on a group of enumerated arrangements previously published, one cent. Article Ninth specifies two arrangements, and one piano piece ("Holiday Schottisch") on which Foster is to receive a one and a half cent royalty.

Article Tenth provides for quarterly statements, payment to be made "to the party of the second part [Foster] at any time, on demand being made by the party of the second part after the rendering of said statement by the party of the first part [Firth, Pond & Co.] . . . the whole amount . . . or any part of said amount which the party of the second part may demand." Article Eleventh provides a penalty to be paid by the publisher if he fails to observe the requirements of Article Tenth.

Article Twelfth allows the publisher to take out copyrights in his name, and the publisher agrees to fight infringements—one half of the resulting indemnities going to the composer and the other half to the publisher. Article Thirteenth gives the publisher the "sole and exclusive right of proprietorship over the music published according to this contract."

It will be remembered that the letter of September 12, 1849,[26] from Firth, Pond & Company allowed Foster a two-cent royalty *after the expenses of publication are paid.* Article Fourteenth of this 1854 contract provides that the publisher "shall defray all the expenses and attend to all business matters connected with the publication of the music published according to this contract."

Articles Fifteenth and Sixteenth, respectively, cover the matter of giving others the right to reprint Foster music, and of declaring previous contracts null and void. The Sixteenth article also states that "all contracts heretofore made . . . binding the party of the second part [Foster] to make the party of the first part [Firth, Pond & Company] the *sole and exclusive* publishers of all the composi-

[26] See page 152.

tions and arrangements of the party of the second part are from this day null and void."

It is apparent, then, that one of the previous contracts had provided that Foster was to publish exclusively with Firth, Pond & Company. The 1849 agreement could obviously not have contained this provision, for in 1850 Foster had nine songs and one instrumental piece published by Benteen in Baltimore, and six songs in 1851. It was probably the 1853 contract that demanded exclusive publishing rights, since for a number of years after 1852 all of Foster's songs were issued by Firth, Pond & Company. In fact, we have already noted that although the 1854 contract releases him from publishing exclusively with this firm, Stephen published only one song with another publisher until the time of his next contract with Firth, Pond & Company—February 9, 1858. That song, we have learned, was "Comrades, Fill No Glass for Me," issued by Miller & Beacham, successors to Benteen, Nov. 23, 1855.

It is interesting to note, too, that an advertisement in which Firth, Pond & Company stated that "arrangements have been made for the EXCLUSIVE PUBLICATION of all of the new compositions" of Foster and others appeared in the November 11, 1854, issue of the *Musical World,* scarcely more than a month before Stephen was released from such an "arrangement."

The last two articles of the 1854 contract provide that any manuscript must be relinquished by the publisher, if he shall "delay during more than a reasonable length of time to publish it"; and that the publisher "derives no right from this contract to publish any future composition of the party of the second part without the future consent of the party of the second part [Foster]."

A few months after the contract was signed, a supplement was added—April 5, 1855, to become effective January 1, 1856. One of its terms provides that one half of the money due from any royalty statement shall be paid in cash, on demand, and the other half by a promissory note. In another clause the publisher agrees to "publish and issue at all times a sufficient number of copies of said music to supply the demand." One wonders in learning of these provisions whether the royalties due each quarter were of such size that they embarrassed the publisher for ready cash, and also whether he had failed to print copies fast enough to fill the demand.

16

These years mark the height of Stephen's career, and we know from the 1854 contract that he was in a strong position with his publishers. From the letter he wrote to Morrison from New York, July 8, 1853,[27] we learned that his earnings for one quarter (three months) was "over five hundred dollars . . . for the dullest season in the year," and that, we shall find, was higher than the average he earned over a period of seven or eight years—1850-1857.

The five songs Foster published in 1855 number two of his best—"Hard Times Come Again No More," already mentioned as published January 17, and "Come Where My Love Lies Dreaming" (June 28). This gentle song, and "Jeanie with the Light Brown Hair," provide the outstanding exceptions to the fact that Stephen did not write good love songs. And it may be observed that like "Jeanie" its mood is more tender than impassioned.

It was in January, on the 18th, that Stephen's mother died, and it may be that some of the tenderness of the song reflects his grief at losing this devoted friend. That, however, is but surmise, as Stephen rarely needed actual grief to become plaintive in his music. Yet there is a sincerity in the gentleness of "Come Where My Love Lies Dream-

27 See page 231.

ing" that is not found in some of Foster's purely sentimental songs.

The words occupy three pages of the manuscript book, immediately following those devoted to "Hard Times." One of the sketches presents a stanza that was not used in the final version.

> Come ere the beams of morning
> Steal from the drowsy hours the dew
> Ere blushing day retiring
> Her golden dream pursue

The song was published as a "quartette," for mixed voices, and it was Stephen's first idea that it should be issued as such, for we find the word "Quartette" written beside the title on the first page devoted to the verses in the manuscript book.

This is one of Foster's few attempts at a "composed-through" song, one in which there would not be merely several stanzas sung to the same "verse" part, and then a chorus or refrain after each stanza. In "Come Where My Love Lies Dreaming," as in the earlier duet "Wilt Thou be Gone, Love?", the composer tries a more ambitious form, with different musical phrases for varying moods of the poem. He was not altogether successful, for lovely as it is the song lacks unity. It is a little too long, and because of the abrupt changes from one section to another it lends itself easily to shortening by the omission of certain passages.

If Henry Kleber had a hand in any of Foster's songs, it is entirely credible that he helped Stephen with "Come Where My Love Lies Dreaming." [28] Kleber may have urged him to try a more involved form than he had attempted in most of his earlier songs, and Kleber may have composed himself the little "coda" at the end, where the

[28] Kleber's daughter, Mrs. Ida Kleber Todd, now living in Pittsburgh, states that her father did have a hand in revising the song and that he suggested its coda.

top voice is brought to a high A, in operatic style. In my opinion, this addition of a coda is totally out of place in this type of song.

"Come Where My Love Lies Dreaming," more than any others of Stephen's works, shows the tragedy of Foster as a musician. This is a melody worthy of Schubert, and it shows that Stephen had a natural gift that was distinctly akin to Schubert's. In this song we find an ill-equipped creator of beautiful melodies, groping with a smooth, luscious theme that cries out for its logical development, but hampered by a pen that will not flow consistently. We are allowed but a glimpse of what Stephen Foster might have achieved if he had been brought up in the environment that Schubert grew in. And we may remember too, that Schubert himself was none too well trained technically.[29]

The other 1855 songs were "Some Folks," copyrighted on the same day as "Come Where My Love Lies Dream-

[29] Henry Watterson, in his autobiography (*Marse Henry*, New York, 1919), quotes a statement by the Louisville song-writer, Will S. Hays, to the effect that Foster obtained his melodies from the scrap-book of an old German musician who had died. Watterson writes that he considered this merely "the spleen of a rival composer" but that when many years later he heard a concert in Vienna featuring the works of Schubert, particularly selections from "Rosemonde" [sic] he found many reminders of "Old Folks at Home."

In a later chapter of his book, Watterson gives considerable space to an answer to this charge, written by Young E. Allison. In his letter to Watterson Allison said: "While you may have heard something in Schubert's compositions that suggested something in Foster's most famous song, still I venture to say it was only a suggestion, such as often arises from the works of composers of a similar type. Schubert and Foster were both young sentimentalists and dreamers who must have had similar dreams that found expression in their similar progressions."

Allison might have gone further and added that it was extremely unlikely that Foster ever heard any part of the "Rosamunde" score. This incidental music to the play by von Chezy was not often performed outside of Vienna during Foster's lifetime. According to *Grove's Dictionary of Music and Musicians* it was first played in England in 1866.

In spite of Allison's denial, Watterson reiterated his assertion by stating: ". . . That the melody of 'Old Folks at Home' may be found in Schubert's 'Rosemonde' [sic] admits not of contradiction for there it is, and this would seem to be in some sort corroborative evidence of the truth of Hays' story."

There is in the "Rosamunde" score a slight rythmic suggestion of "Old Folks at Home," but the melodic intervals are so different that any claim that the two melodies are at all alike is thoroughly absurd.

ing" (June 28), "The Village Maiden" (Sept. 17), and "Comrades, Fill No Glass for Me," which was copyrighted by Miller & Beacham of Baltimore, successors to F. D. Benteen, November 23.

"Some Folks" has four pages in the manuscript book—a mirthful song, not in Negro dialect. "The Village Maiden" was an earlier idea of Foster's; he made the first draft of the words on page 54 of his work book, soon after he wrote "My Old Kentucky Home," and before "Old Dog Tray." He returned to his early idea on page 120, where on a single page he again wrote the verses with very little change from his original draft.

"Comrades, Fill No Glass for Me" is apparently not in the manuscript book. This song has been cited frequently in showing that Stephen, although he later became a victim of the drink habit himself, was aware of its dangers, and that even in 1855 he was fighting the hold it was later to take on him. I feel that such a belief draws a little too heavily on the imagination. Stephen was no doubt drinking some by 1855, but I believe convivially rather than in the manner of a confirmed drunkard. It is unlikely that at this time his desire for alcohol had grown powerful enough for him to write from his own experience a temperance song as a warning to others. It would seem rather that he was merely writing a song which he knew would strike a responsive chord in the so-called temperance circles.

In the next year, 1856, Stephen published only one song. This was another of his really good sentimental songs, tender and wistful—"Gentle Annie," copyrighted by Firth, Pond & Company, April 24. Stephen took pains with "Annie," he spent five pages of his manuscript book on getting her verses in final form. Musically the song seems related to that other "Annie" song, "Annie Laurie." There is the same spirit, and the same type of tender melody.

"Gentle Annie" is seldom heard to-day, perhaps because she is so similar to her famous rival from Scotland.[30]

17

In May of 1855, a few months after Stephen's mother died, Morrison Foster was sent on a commission by Major George Crosman, whose son was later to marry Henrietta Foster's daughter, Mary Wick. Morrison was sent with a load of supplies for the United States Army from Philadelphia to St. Louis. In his notebook he stated that he "paid Stephen on a/c house expenses, $10.00." This makes it apparent that the running of the household had passed from Morrison to Stephen.

It was on July 27 that William B. Foster, the father, died, and after this Stephen evidently took over the house altogether, for we find in his own account book items of rent owed to Brother William. On November 1, "William B. Foster, jr., by rent 3 mos. $31.25," and on April 1, 1856, "Wm. B. Foster, jr., by rent 5 months $52.08." Also an item under Stephen's ledger entries for William—"For spout on house—.75."

Dunning Foster died in Cincinnati, March 31, 1856, and Henry, Morrison and Stephen brought his remains to Pittsburgh, where they are buried in the family plot in the Allegheny Cemetery near Lawrenceville. In a little more than a year Stephen had lost three members of his family—his mother, his father, and the brother he had lived with in Cincinnati. On the following October 22 (1856) Brother William became for the second time a widower through the loss of his wife, Elizabeth.

Yet in spite of these griefs, there were merry times in Allegheny for Stephen during these years when his career

---

[30] It has already been noted that "Gentle Annie" is said to have been inspired by the death of a little girl with whose parents Stephen stayed all night after an accident in which she was killed. See page 130.

was at the height of its success. There is record of a "Phil-harmonic Society" in Allegheny which existed in these years and to which Stephen belonged. This group gave many so-called "old time concerts." Many anecdotes are told of jolly, boisterous gatherings, and of the serenading expe-ditions in which the young blades of Allegheny and Pitts-burgh paid vocal tribute to their friends.

One of these stories was told anonymously by a Pitts-burgher in a July, 1895, issue of the *Pittsburgh Press*.

During the first few months of my residence in Pittsburgh, I boarded at the Iron City Hotel, long since removed. . . . Foster often went there to see me in the evening, and we would go out together. One night, we planned to serenade some young people at the residence of Judge Irwin, on Stockton Avenue, Allegheny. About a dozen young men, Foster among the number, met me at the hotel, and we went to the Irwin residence. We sang several popular songs in concert, and Foster rendered two or three of his favorite ballads, "Old Dog Tray" among the number. Presently we heard a dis-turbance on the second floor of the house, and noticed a form at one of the windows. A moment later a jar was cautiously lowered to the ground by means of a string. We caught it, examined the con-tents and found it was filled with pickles. That ended our serenade. We returned to the hotel to discuss the incident. What did the judge's family mean by giving us a bottle of pickles? Did they wish to insult us? We could not understand it. We learned later, how-ever, that the members of the family scoured the kitchen and pantry to find something good to give us, but there wasn't a solitary thing in the house they considered fit for us. Finally they found a jar of pickles and gave that to us in the manner I have described. It ap-pears that the Judge had the reputation for making the best pickles in this part of the State, and, as we discovered afterward, he could not have paid us a higher compliment. We had preserved the pickles and afterward ate them with a relish.

Mrs. Rose, Stephen's granddaughter, tells [31] of another incident of these years, one which shows that Stephen was possibly inclined to conviviality some little time before he went to New York in 1860.

[31] In the article "My Grandmother's Memories," *op. cit.*

Popular in his youth, loved by all his friends for his magnetic personality as well as his genius, naturally he had many carefree boon companions.

When he and my grandmother in their early married life, lived . . . in old Allegheny City . . . one of these life-long friends lived next door on Union Ave. He and Stephen were both members of a small company of musicians, each playing the banjo or guitar, who met frequently for rehearsal.

One summer evening, the rehearsal seemed to prolong itself into unseemly proportions. When they were assisting one another home in the wee, small hours of the morning, they passed the old Allegheny Market House. Feeling the necessity for a peace offering of some kind for their respective and presumably unconciliatory wives, they argued the matter pro and con on the market house corner, finally deciding that a live goose would be about the right thing.

The farmers in those days drove into market at night, ready for the morning trade. . . . The first intimation that my grandmother had of the whereabouts of her convivial spouse was the uproar made by the terrified goose, when he arrived at the front door with it clutched tightly to his breast. "Oh, Jinny," he called, "see the nice goose I have for you, honey." The fate of the bird is not recorded, but my grandmother's comment at the time ran something to the effect that it would be a matter of fine distinction to know "t'other from which."

18

The most interesting organization that Stephen had a part in was the Buchanan Glee Club, organized August 6, 1856. The book of minutes of this club is still in existence, now preserved at Foster Hall in Indianapolis.

The Foster brothers had a keen interest in the presidential campaign of that year. In June the new Republican Party had been formed, and John C. Frémont chosen as its candidate. The Fosters were always ardent Democrats, and this year the standard bearer of that party was James Buchanan, the brother-in-law of their own sister, Ann Eliza.

The book of minutes starts thus on its first page:

Allegheny City, Aug. 6th/56

At a meeting of the Democrats of Allegheny City favorable to the formination [sic] of a Buchanan Glee Club the following officers were elected to serve during the campaign

President .... Wm. Bleakley [Blakely]
Vice President .... Thos. M. Smith
Secretary .... Geo. C. McKinley
Tresuer [sic] .... Morrison Foster
Musical Director .... Stephen C. Foster

From the Pittsburgh Directory of 1859/60 we learn that Thomas N. Smith was a "caulker" and that Geo. C. McKinley followed the trade of "trunk maker." At the next meeting, August 13:

The meeting was called to order by the President, after which the Constitution was called for and read by Morrison Foster. It was moved and seconded that it be adopted which it was unanimously.

Then followed the text of this "constitution," which provided for the formation of a glee club to act in conjunction with the Buchanan and Breckinridge Club of Allegheny City "in furthering the success of the Nominees of the Democratic Party." Then came the usual articles, providing for officers, including the "tresuer" as well as a musical director, and an "instrumental leader." We learn that Stephen, as musical director, "shall have control and direction over all the musical performences [our trunk-maker was none too familiar with the dictionary] of the Glee Club and shall assign to the Performers the parts they shall severally take." "The Instrumental Leader shall have charge and direction of the instrumental performers subject however to the control of the Musical Director."

Other articles state that the meetings would be held at the Excelsior Hotel, and that any Democrat was eligible to membership. Article 5th classifies the members.

Sec. 1st The members of the Glee Club shall be divided into two Classes. viz Performers and non Performers.

Sec. 2nd The performers shall be selected by the musical Director from the body of the members, at his discretion.

Sec. 3d The singing and instrumental performences [sic] shall be executed only by such members as shall be selected as performers, according to section 2d of this article.

Sec. 4th The non-performers shall attend the meetings and assist the President in preserving order wherever the Club may happen to be.

The necessity for this last clause is apparent from the recollections of one of the members, William Hamilton, who with Stephen and Thomas M. Smith, the "caulker" vice-president, formed the committee to select "Instrumental Performers." Years later, when Hamilton was Superintendent of Allegheny Parks, he gave these memories to a reporter of the *Pittsburgh Press*.[32]

I first met Steve, as we always called him, in 1855. He was such a genial young man, so kind-hearted and genteel in his manner, that I liked him from the start and we became firm friends. Both of us loved music, and hardly a week passed that we did not have some concert, musical or serenade on hand. During the summer and fall of the campaign in which Buchanan was elected president of the United States, in 1856, I saw much of Foster, and my recollections of this period are most vivid, perhaps, on account of the exciting times we had. It was a very hot campaign, as all older citizens will remember. I was a Democrat then, and so was Foster, and together we organized a Glee Club for the purpose of booming the campaign in Allegheny. Among the members of the club were Stephen C. Foster, Morrison Foster, Thomas Smith and myself. There were other vocalists, but their names have escaped my memory. Then we had a bodyguard of sometimes 50, sometimes 100 men, who joined in the chorus of the songs. We would march through the streets singing campaign songs, and had many interesting conflicts with the Whigs and other political clubs.

The excitement during that campaign was intense all over the country, and more enthusiasm was shown in Pittsburgh and Allegheny, perhaps, than in other cities of their size in the country. The feeling between the adherents of the different political bodies was not altogether as amicable as it might have been, and the various

[32] Issue of July 11, 1895.

clubs sometimes met in the streets with disastrous results. The Pittsburgh Volunteer Fire Department was an organization much feared in those days, and there were few scraps between political organizations in which the firemen were not interested in some way. Perhaps the most noteworthy incident showing the fighting propensities of the members of the Volunteer Fire Department was one which occurred during the campaign of which I speak. In those days there were no street cars between the old city and East Liberty, or what is now the East End district, and the only way for one to get there was either to walk or take a carriage. We went out there several times during the campaign with our Glee Club and body guard, usually marching out Penn Avenue the entire distance.

On our way home from one of these trips to East Liberty, we stopped at a residence this side of the forks of the road, Lawrenceville [incidentally, this spot was near Stephen's birthplace], to serenade a family with which some of us were acquainted. We sang a Foster song on this occasion, and I had the solo part. Some stranger joined the crowd, and persisted in singing the solo part with me, although he was not familiar with it. He annoyed me, and I motioned to a member of the body guard to tell him to sing only the chorus. The guardsman misunderstood me. He thought the fellow had insulted me in some way, and promptly gave him a blow on the left ear, knocking him down. The fellow got up, only to be knocked down again. Directly across the street from the residence we were serenading was the headquarters of one of the largest companies of the Pittsburgh Volunteer Fire Department. The firemen saw there had been some difficulty, but waited for no explanations. They joined the crowd and began to strike right and left. In a twinkling, our peaceful body of serenaders was transformed into a howling mob. Foster, his brother, myself and other vocalists hastened out of the crowd. We were all too small for our ages and had no business around where any fighting was going on. We always left that to our body guard, and they protected us most effectually in that case. None of us was hurt, and few of the members of the guard suffered, but the firemen were completely routed and driven back into their headquarters. They had tackled the wrong crowd that time.

The book of minutes of the glee club shows the signatures of forty-two subscribing members, from whom it was Morrison's duty to collect dues and contributions. After some of the names there appears a pencilled check. If those checks by any chance indicated which members had paid their dues, it must be recorded that the name "S. C. Foster" was not followed by a check, nor was that of James Buchanan, Jr., Stephen's nephew, and nephew of the presidential candidate in whose behalf the club was formed.

There are records of meetings to September 17, most of them called to consider invitations to the club to appear in various sections of the city. One of them may establish the approximate date of the mêlée William Hamilton described, for we read

Thursday night, Sept. 4/56

Invitation accepted from D. McClintock to attend a meeting at East Liberty.

Another entry had reference to the vice-presidential candidate, the man who four years later was to run for president against Abraham Lincoln.

Tuesday evening, Sept. 9, 1856

Invitation received from Allegheny Comm. of arrangements to join the procession to attend the Mass meeting in Pittsburgh to-morrow . . . accepted and it was resolved that we meet at the end of the . . . bridge at 8 o'clock A.M. and proceed in a body to Market Square.

On motion it was resolved also that we meet at the same place at 7 o'clock P.M. for the purpose of serenading John C. Breckinridge.

19

Stephen wrote campaign songs for the glee club to sing, and two of them have been preserved—"The Abolition Show" and "The White House Chair." Altogether ten pages of the manuscript book were given over to the words of these two songs, and various ideas tried out to be either adopted or discarded.

"The White House Chair" had its own music, composed by Stephen. It was not published until years later, when it was printed in the *Pittsburgh Dispatch,* September, 1885.

Morrison Foster entered it for copyright September 4, 1885.

> Let all our hearts for Union be
> For the North and South are one;
> They've worked together manfully,
> And together they will still work on.

Chorus

> Then come, ye men from every State,
> Our creed is broad and fair;
> Buchanan is our candidate,
> And we'll put him in the White House chair.

> We'll have no dark, designing band,
> To rule with secret sway;
> We'll give to all a helping hand,
> And be open as the light of day.

Chorus

> We'll not outlaw the land that holds
> The bones of Washington,
> Where Jackson fought and Marion bled,
> And the battles of the brave were won.

In its original version the "Abolition Show" was "The Great Baby Show." In its final form the words were printed in the *Pittsburgh Post,* September, 1856, with the note that the air was "Villikins and his Dinah." On the following March 11, 1857, Stephen wrote a letter to Brother William in Philadelphia:

My Dear Brother:
Herewith I send you the words of the show song in full, with one verse of the music.
We are all quite well.

> Your affec. brother
> S. C. Foster.

Here is Stephen's enclosure, as it was written in his own hand. The words I have put in italics are given as they appeared in the manuscript copy Stephen sent to William.

Those in brackets show how the newspaper version differed from the manuscript.

THE ABOLITION SHOW

[September 17, 1856]

On the Seventeenth day of September, you know,
Took place in our city the great *baby* [Frémont] show;
They shut up the factories and let *out the schools* [the schools out],
For *the Seventeenth day was the day of all fools* [the children will
    all vote for Frémont, no doubt].

    Sing tu ral lal lu ral, etc.

They made a procession of wagons and boats,
Of racoons and oxen (they *all have their* [also have] votes)
Sledge hammers, triangles and carpenter's tools,
One thousand and eight hundred horses and mules.

    Sing tu ral lal lu ral, etc.

They had gemmen ob color to join in their games
And jokers and Clowns of all ages and names
They had pop guns and tin pans and all kinds of toys
And a very fine party *of women and boys* [all made up of boys].

    Sing tu ral lal lu ral, etc.

They had young men on horse back, so nice and so gay
Aged Seventeen years on this Seventeenth day,
And the ladies all thought they were bold cavaliers
These bright looking lads aged seventeen years.

    Sing tu ral lal lu ral, etc.

They had grim border-ruffians, I'll bring to your mind,
And they've plenty more left of the very same kind,
They drank from a flask and played cards on the way,
And the children looked on, on this Seventeenth day.

    Sing tu ral lal lu ral, etc.

They had Ohio Yankees of Western Reserve
Who live upon cheese, ginger cakes and preserve,

Abolition's their doctrine, their rod, and their staff
And they'll fight for a sixpence an hour and a half.
       [This verse was not included in the printed version.]

   Sing tu ral lal lu ral, etc.

Now *was* [is] it not kind in these good simple *clowns* [souls]
To amuse all the children *in both of our towns* [with antics so droll]
To shut up their *work shops* [houses] and spend so much money
To black up their faces, get tight and be funny.

   Sing tu ral lal lu ral, etc.

They called it a council of *free men* [voters] you know,
But *I told you before* [I'll tell you the truth] 'twas a great baby
       show,
But when they had met they had nothing to say
But "Poor Bleeding Kansas" and "Ten Cents a Day."

   Sing tu ral lal lu ral, etc.

   Then followed two more verses, which Stephen explained
were written by "Mit," as the family called Morrison.

Then their ship Constitution was hauled through the street
With sixteen small guns she was armed compleet
But the *brave* [old] ship of State by which Democrats stand
Carries thirty one guns with old Buck in command.

   Sing tu ral lal lu ral, etc.

In the year '45 when the fire laid waste
Old Buck gave us five hundred dollars in haste
They then took his money and *lauded his* [blest his great] name
But he's now "Ten Cent Jimmy," their banners proclaim.

   Sing tu ral lal lu ral, etc.

   And those were the days, which some cynics feel we have
not altogether left even in our own enlightened age, when
slogans won political campaigns. "Old Buck" proved more
potent in putting Buchanan in the "White House Chair,"
than "Ten Cent Jimmy" in keeping him out of it.

———————

Thus ends a long, and perhaps rambling account of Stephen in the years when recognition came to him, a period which, I fear, marks the climax of our story. All but a few of his best songs are written by now, and we approach the last few years, when we must look with sympathy and understanding on the declining fortunes of one who gave us so freely of himself.

IX

FINANCES

I

IT IS apparent from Stephen's records that he often spent more money than he earned. We have already read his letter of July 8, 1853, written to Morrison, in which he tells his brother of drawing ahead on his account with his publishers. This practice became a chronic habit, as may be learned from the account book [1] which Foster kept from 1855 to the middle of 1860.

On January 1, 1857, Stephen's credit with Firth, Pond & Company for "commissions on music" (presumably for the preceding quarter) amounted to $267.72. Here is a list of the moneys he received from the publishers during the preceding and following months, drawn through drafts which Foster presented for collection at his own bank in Pittsburgh.

1856

Dec. 11	$ 50.
Dec. 22	65.
Dec. 31	100.

1857

Jan. 5	60.
Jan. 14	75.
Feb. 2	60.
Feb. 19	65.
Mch. 3	65.
Mch. 14	100.

$640.

[1] Now in the Foster Hall collection at Indianapolis.

In a little over three months, then, Stephen drew from his publishers $640, $372.28 more than the earnings credited for the three-month period of the preceding quarter ($267.72). The manner in which the composer balanced his account is important to our story. He sold to his publishers for cash his entire future interest in all of his songs they had published to date.

At the Library of Congress there is a curious document in Foster's handwriting—a list of moneys received from songs. As will be seen later, the fact that this sheet of paper came to the Library of Congress from the successors to Firth, Pond & Company is significant to us in determining its purpose. The list is dated January 27, 1857, and it gives the total amounts received from each of the songs published with Firth, Pond & Company to that date, except those in which Foster apparently had no royalty interest— "Nelly Was a Lady" and "My Brudder Gum." To show how long each of the songs had been published, I am inserting in brackets the date of copyright by each title.

There are two columns of figures in the list, explained thus by Foster:

The first column is the amt. I have already recd. on the songs, the second column is the computed future value to me.

The list is given in full, with Stephen's abbreviations of titles, on the next page.

It is evident, because of the even amount and the lack of a valuation for the future, that Foster was paid $150 outright for the "Social Orchestra," and that he had no royalty interest in its sale.

The total of amounts earned from Firth, Pond & Company—from November 14, 1849, to the date of this list, January 27, 1857—was as follows:

For royalties..........................$9,436.96
For "Social Orchestra" and "Arranging".. 160.
                                         ─────────
                                         $9,596.96

		$ ¢	$ ¢
Old Folks, and all arrangements	[Oct. 1, 1851]	1647.46	100
Kentucky Home do do	[Jan. 31, 1853]	1372.06	100
Dog Tray " "	[? 1853]	1080.25	150
Massa's in, &c " "	[July 7, 1852]	906.76	50
Nelly Bly " "	[Feb. 8, 1850]	564.37	20
Farewell Lilly " "	[Dec. 13, 1851]	551.12	50
Ellen Bayne " "	[Feb. 3, 1854]	642.34	350
Oh boys " "	[July 25, 1851]	394.70	25
Willie we have missed "	[Mar. 4, 1854]	497.77	497.77
Maggie by my side "	[Oct. 14, 1852]	278.01	75
Hard Times " "	[Jan. 17, 1855]	283.84	200
Eulalie " "	[Dec. 6, 1851]	203.14	50
Jeanie with light &c "	[June 5, 1854]	217.80	350
Willie my brave " "	[Oct. 21, 1851]	91.15	20
Old Memories " "	[Dec. 5, 1853]	62.52	15
Some folks " "	[June 28, 1855]	59.91	25
Come where my love lies dreaming	[June 28, 1855]	59.88	100
Little Ella " "	[Dec. 13, 1853]	50.72	10
Come with thy sweet voice	[Sep. 19, 1854]	54.33	25
Way down in Cairo	[Apr. 17, 1850]	44.72	5
Ring de banjo	[Apr. 29, 1851]	35.24	1
Village Maiden	[Sep. 17, 1855]	36.08	15
Crystal Schottisch [this is apparently not an original work by Foster]		44.06	20
Farewell Old Cottage	[Mar. 22, 1851]	30.58	5
Wilt thou be gone love	[Mar. 12, 1851]	22.20	10
My hopes have departed	[Aug. 4, 1851]	25.04	5
Gentle Annie	[Apr. 24, 1856]	39.08	500
Dolcy Jones	[Nov. 14, 1849]	21.46	1
Annie my own love	[May 12, 1853]	19.12	1
Lilly [sic] Ray	[Dec. 9, 1850]	18.08	1
Voice of bygone days	[June 28, 1850]	17.54	1
Holiday Schottisch	[July 2, 1853]	17.37	5
I cannot sing tonight	[Aug. 11, 1852]	16.98	1
The hour for thee and me	[July 9, 1852]	14.30	1
Mary loves the flowers	[Jan. 16, 1850]	8.98	1
Once I Loved thee Mary	[Apr. 4, 1851]	8.00	1
Social Orchestra		150.	$2,786.77
For arranging		10.	

2

Before discussing the purpose of this document in Stephen's handwriting, there are two other points that should be set forth. First, the footnote at the bottom of the list, to which we referred in telling of Foster's relations with E. P. Christy, the minstrel performer.[2]

In the amts. recd. I have included $15 on each of the two songs "Old Folks" and "Farewell Lilly," from E. P. Christy, also $10 on each of the songs "Dog Tray," "Oh boys," "Massa's in" & "Ellen Bayne."

The other point to be observed is the comparison that may be made between the amounts on Stephen's list, and the claims in the publishers' advertisements. From the list it appears that in five and a half years "Old Folks at Home" had earned the composer $1,647.46 in royalties (including the $15 from Christy). On the regular sheet music editions of this song Foster according to his contract received two cents a copy; on the guitar arrangements, one and a half cents; on instrumental arrangements by himself and on those made by others, including "variations" and "quadrilles," one cent.

We have learned that in November, 1854, more than two years before Stephen compiled his list, the publishers claimed they had sold 130,000 copies of the song.[3] Had these all been copies of the minimum class (various instrumental arrangements) the royalties would have amounted to $1,300, and if they had all been guitar arrangements, Stephen's share would have been $1,900, over $250 more than he actually received. Boasting by publishers is apparently a time-honored custom.

And now for the original purpose of the paper. This Foster royalty list has been a familiar document to Foster students for a number of years. H. V. Milligan referred

[2] See pages 187, 197-200.   [3] See page 207.

to it in his biography of Foster, published in 1920,[4] and I myself printed it as an illustration in my own volume, *Our American Music* (1931). The parallel figures, one column representing amounts received and the other Foster's estimate of future values, have been puzzling, and I had always assumed that in 1857, Stephen, like many of us, started the New Year by figuring for his own amusement what his assets would be worth to him in the future. Such was not the case, the estimates were for a far more practical purpose, one that has become evident since Foster's account book was acquired by Foster Hall.

This account book contains a similar list of royalties received, *without the estimates of future values.* With a few slight differences the amounts received from individual songs are identical. Stephen's book, as we have found, contained also various ledger accounts to show his business and financial transactions with those he dealt with. One such record covers his dealings with Firth, Pond & Company, from which we have already learned that by March 14 Stephen was drawn ahead on his publishers by $372.28.

Under date of March 14, Foster made this entry on the debit side of his ledger account with Firth, Pond & Company:

To Copyrights in full till date............$1,872.28

On the credit side of the ledger we find these amounts recorded:

March 19.....................By draft $ 300
May 30......By their notes, 3, 6, & 9 mos. 1,200

On the list of "amounts received for songs" *in the account book,* the following item appears directly under the last of the Firth, Pond & Company songs:

From F. P. for bal. of claim............$1,872.28

[4] *Op. cit.*

What could be more logical to suppose than that the list dated January 27, 1857, acquired by the Library of Congress from the successors of Firth, Pond & Company, should represent the estimate on which Stephen based the amount he asked that firm to pay him for his future copyright interest? It will be noted that Foster estimated his future interest as worth $2,786.77, and that the publishers actually paid approximately two-thirds of the composer's asking price—$1,872.28.* The assumption that Foster sold his entire interest in these songs is further supported by the fact that the names of none of them appear in any future records in Stephen's account book.

Thus Stephen, in 1857, started anew his relations with Firth, Pond & Company with a clean slate and with credit at the bank. On March 19, we have found, he drew $300 on Firth, Pond & Company, and on May 30 received the firm's notes for $1,200. Thus his account was balanced. The moneys previously drawn ($640) and the cash and notes ($1,500) amounted to $2,140, as did the sum of the January 1 royalties—$267.72—and the amount agreed upon for copyright sale—$1,872.28.

The account book also shows what Stephen did with the money. On May 27, three days before the notes were dated, he discounted the three four-hundred-dollar notes at the Pittsburgh Trust Company. The twelve hundred dollars was put to his credit at this bank, from whence Stephen drew it out in small amounts over a period lasting until December 29 of the same year (1857). On that date he had a balance left of $256, and as the last of the notes was due on about that date from Firth, Pond & Company, the bank was apparently willing to let Foster draw his balance.

* It may further be noted that this amount is $372.28 more than $1,500. $372.28 was the amount to which Foster was overdrawn at the time.

3

There is more information in these pages of Stephen's account book. Added to the Firth, Pond & Company list are the songs published by F. D. Benteen of Baltimore, with the royalties they had earned. As in the Firth, Pond list, I have inserted the dates of copyright.

Camptown Races	[Feb. 19, 1850]	$101.25
Oh! Lemuel	[Jan. 7, 1850]	100.00
Dolly Day	[Feb. 19, 1850]	33.75
Molly Do You Love Me	[May 6, 1850]	32.50
Angelina Baker	[Mar. 18, 1850]	16.87
Sweetly She Sleeps	[Mar. 18, 1851]	5.62
Mother thou'rt faithful to me	[Mar. 18, 1851]	6.87
Give the stranger happy cheer	[Jan. 6, 1851]	7.50
I would not die in Springtime	[Oct. 15, 1850]	78.12
I would not die in Summer time	[July 12, 1851]	11.26
Laura Lee	[Aug. 7, 1851]	13.12
Spirit of my Song	[Aug. 21, 1850]	5.00
Ah! may the red rose live alway	[Apr. 12, 1850]	8.12
Melinda May	[Jan. 6, 1851]	24.37
Village Bells Polka	[Oct. 15, 1850]	10.00
Turn Not Away	[Oct. 15, 1850]	7.50

[$461.85]

[I have inserted the total—it does not appear for these items in the account book.]

Under this list of amounts received from Benteen for individual songs (just as an item "for bal. of claim" appeared under the Firth, Pond list) we find an entry:

From F. D. B. for bal. of claim............$200.

So Stephen wiped the slate with Benteen too, and took two hundred dollars for all his rights in the sixteen songs that had earned him $461.85 since 1850.

Added to the amounts received from Firth, Pond & Company and Benteen, we find another item in the account book list—"From Fisher & Bro. 110." Fisher & Bro. was a concern that issued little books with the words only of popular songs. The $110 was probably paid for permission to use the words of some of Foster's well-known songs.

These entries enable us to arrive at an average for Stephen's income during the preceding years. Omitting the lump sums paid for copyright interests in 1857, we may total the payments received from the time of publication of the earliest song on the lists ("Dolcy Jones" by Firth, Pond & Company, November 14, 1849) and the time Foster compiled his figures, January, 1857.

From Firth, Pond & Co. for royalties (including $70 paid by Christy)	$ 9,436.96
From F. D. Benteen for royalties	461.85
	—————$ 9,898.81
From outright sale of the "Social Orchestra," and for "arranging"	210.
[This is $50 higher than the amount on the Library of Congress list (page 267), for the record in the account book gives $60. for "arranging," rather than the $10 in the L. of C. list.]	
From Fisher & Bro., for right to use words of songs	110.
Total amount received in approximately 7 years and two months	$10,218.81
Average monthly income during these years	118.82
Average yearly income during these years...	1,425.84

It is probable that Foster's income was considerably larger after "Old Folks at Home" was issued than it had been before, and that in the years from 1851 to 1855 he received considerably more than fourteen hundred dollars a year. The letter to Morrison in 1853 showed that Stephen's earnings for a single quarter amounted to $500. We have learned, too, that the average had dropped by 1857, for on January 1 of that year his earnings for the

preceding quarter had been but $267.72, an average rate
per annum of $1,070.88.

4

On January 16, 1857, Stephen, in Pittsburgh, wrote a
letter to his friend William Hamilton, then a clerk on the
steamboat "Ida May."

DEAR BILLY:

Your letter from Point Pleasant has been received and I am glad
to know the whereabouts of the great, American ballad singer.
When can you promise to appear again before a Pittsburgh audience?
Masonic Hall can be had now.

I have also had an engagement tendered me, but I declined.
Kleber is going to give a concert and he has offered me the post of
first Anvil player in the "Anvil Chorus" from a new opera. I was
unwilling to go through the course of training and dieting requisite
for the undertaking, and consequently declined. I understand he has
sent to Europe for a "First Anvil."

It is interesting to note that the first American performance of "Il Trovatore," the opera in which the "Anvil
Chorus" occurs, was given in New York, May 2, 1855. It
was presented in Philadelphia, January 14, 1856. Stephen,
then, was discussing something relatively new when he joked
about Kleber's concert.

The letter continues with family news.

We have had another little political brush in the election of Mayor,
but there was very little excitement. I have not yet received the
Cincinnati Gazette and suppose that puff has not appeared. I will
send you by this mail a copy of "Jeanie with the light brown hair"
if I can find a copy. Mit [Morrison] is now living with us. James
Buchanan [Stephen's nephew, also a nephew of the President-Elect]
returned yesterday from a long visit home. Mrs. F. and Miss Maggie
[probably Stephen's wife and daughter, Marion] are quite well.
Your account of your appearance on the stage rather got them.

I am much obliged to you for that dog, "Rat-trap" as we called
him on account of his well-known ferocity towards those animals.
He continued to devour shoes, stockings, spools, the Cat, and every-

thing else that he could find lying around loose. At last we held a council of war, and thought that we would put him in the yard, then we thought we wouldn't. . . . We put him in the cellar . . . He howled all the time and would have howled until now if I had not let him out. I was afraid the neighbors would inform on us for keeping a nuisance. Solitary confinement did not agree with him. He lost his appetite. Then I gave him some garlic as you had instructed me. . . . He got to Mit's room, . . . scattered his . . . shirts over the floor . . . and played hob generally. This performance seemed to bring him to his appetite, for the same evening he stole a whole beefsteak off the kitchen table and swallowed it all, raw. We concluded this was too much to stand even from "Friendships offering" so I made up my mind to trade him off. John Little had a friend in Chicago who wanted *just such a dog* so he gave me a very fine Scotch terrier eighteen months old for him. "Trap" is enjoying the lake breezes. *I am very much obliged to you for that dog.*

James Buchanan has just come in to see me, so here I will wind up.

Your Friend,

S. C. FOSTER.

From this letter it is evident that Stephen and his wife were still keeping house, possibly in the same house owned by William on the East Common in Allegheny. Stephen told Hamilton that Morrison was living with them, and in Stephen's account book we find that Morrison was paying Stephen four dollars a week for board and washing. Among the entries for transactions with Morrison are "Mch 6, 2 weeks," and "Mch. 30, 3½ weeks." On April 30 Stephen credited Morrison with three dollars, which Morrison had paid him for "concert tickets."

It appears that about the middle of April, probably the 13th, Stephen and his family gave up housekeeping and went to board with a John Mish. According to Stephen's account book, board for the family was paid at the rate of approximately twelve dollars per week, four dollars apiece for each member of the family.

Through the Pittsburgh Directory we may know exactly where the Fosters lived, for in the issue of 1859-60 we learn that John Mish was the proprietor of the "Eagle

Hotel, 274 Liberty." Stephen's account book has a complete record of his dealings with Mish, and I give the account in full—it shows something of Stephen's financial status in these years.

1857

John Mish	Dr.	John Mish	Cr.
Apr. 27 To Cash $ 22.		Apl. 27 By Boarding 2 weeks $ 22.	
June 1 " " 40.		June 8 " " 57.26	
" 8 " " 17.26			
$79.26		$79.26	
July 21 To Cash 72.		July 20 By boarding 6 weeks 72.	
Aug. 12 " " 40.		Dec. 1 " boarding, &c 172.	
Nov. 3 " " 35.		" " " Old a/c Aug. 12 40.	
" 20 " " 40.			
Dec. 1 " Old a/c			
Aug. 12 1.58			
" Bal. [owed] 95.42			
$284.		$284.	
Dec. 14 To Cash 95.42		Dec. 1 By bal. as per his bill 95.42	
" 29 " " in		" 29 " boarding 48.	
full 48.			
$143.42		$143.42	

My readers will appreciate, I trust, that the foregoing figures represent far more to our narrative of Stephen Foster than a mere exercise in copying the record of his financial dealings with his boarding-house or hotel keeper. There is a human record here that shows Foster's habits, if we know also his ability to meet his obligations.

Comparison with his account at the Pittsburgh Trust Company, and with his dealings with Firth, Pond & Company reveal some interesting facts.

On March 19 Stephen drew $300 from his publishers. This money evidently lasted long enough for him to pay his first two weeks' board promptly, April 27. After that he may have been short of cash, for he waited until he owed Mish $57.26 before he paid him any more money. On May 27 he discounted the $1,200 in notes from Firth, Pond & Company at the Pittsburgh Trust Company and drew $75 in cash, so on June 1 he paid Mish $40 and the remaining $17.26 a week later, when he had drawn another $50.

Presumably Stephen had ample resources for the rest of the year with the credit from the discounted notes at the bank. Nevertheless he took his time in paying his board bill. On July 20 he withdrew $100 from the bank, and on July 21 we may note that he handed Mish the $72 that had accrued as a debt for six weeks' board since June 8. From that time the record shows that Stephen's payments were irregular. When he drew another hundred from the bank August 12 he gave Mish forty dollars, and then paid him nothing more until he handed him thirty-five dollars November 3, and another forty November 20. On December 1 Stephen still owed $95.42 which he paid two weeks later, December 14. Then, as we have already learned, the song-writer drew his entire balance from the Pittsburgh Trust Company on December 29, amounting to $256. Of this amount he paid Mish $48 for the past four weeks' board.

Thus he started the New Year fresh as far as his board bill was concerned, but he continued to pay for his family's board at infrequent intervals during the little over four months more they lived with John Mish at his Eagle Hotel. Here is the rest of the ledger account as kept by Stephen.

1858

John Mish		Dr.	John Mish	Cr.
Mch. 5 To Cash		$75.	Apr. 8 By boarding	$170.
Apr. 8 " "		50.		
Apr. 8 Note 14 days		45.		
		$170.		$170.

Whether Stephen met his note promptly at the end of "14 days" we cannot tell. On March 5 he drew on Firth, Pond & Company for a hundred dollars. Seventy-five of this amount evidently went to Mish. There is no record of Foster's receiving any further cash until August 10, when he drew over four hundred dollars from his publishers; all of which, as we shall learn, was in advance of actual earnings.

5

When Stephen gave up housekeeping it was apparently necessary for him to rent a piano, for on December 7, 1857, he paid to Charlotte Blume,[5] according to the Directory a piano "manufacturer," twelve dollars for (three months) "piano hire" and one dollar for "carriage of same." Stephen continued to rent a piano from Charlotte Blume until September 3, 1859, when we find him charged with an unpaid balance of $36.75 (of which one dollar was for "carriage of piano"). On January 1, 1860, he gave the lady his note for the amount he owed her.

It would be interesting to learn where Stephen had this rented piano. It was probably not at the various places he lived in during these years, for the family moved frequently, and there are only two charges for piano moving— one of them when he first rented the instrument and the other when it went back to its owner in September of 1859. It may be that Stephen again had an "office," or a studio, just as he had rented one in 1851. The Pittsburgh Directory of 1859-60 lists "Foster, Stephen C, music composer, 112 and 114 Smithfield." The location, as well as the double number of the building, suggests that this is a business address, rather than a residence.

The letter to William Hamilton (Jan. 16, 1857) [6] spoke of John Little, the man who had traded a Scotch terrier

[5] The Blumes, Frederick and Charlotte, had a music store in Pittsburgh as early as 1840.
[6] Pages 273-274.

for the dog Hamilton had given Stephen. In Stephen's account book we find a ledger account with "J. M. Little," dated July 23, 1857, showing an amount "By Bal. Due Him—$20.50." The Pittsburgh Directory yields the information that "Little, John M." was a merchant tailor at 54 St. Clair. On the following January 1 (1858), we find record of an account with Samuel Gray, showing "By Bal. due him—$42." Again the Directory shows that "Gray, Samuel" was also a "merchant tailor," at an address almost the same as that of Little's establishment, "52 St. Clair." It may not be altogether fair to observe that there is no record of payment to either party in Foster's account book, yet the fact remains that he seems to have kept that book faithfully until he went to New York in the Summer of 1860.

When Stephen and his wife quit housekeeping in the Spring of 1857 and went to board with John Mish, it is evident that Morrison remained for a while in the Pittsburgh district. He too may have boarded at this "Eagle Hotel." At any rate he was in the neighborhood until December, when he went to Philadelphia to help Brother William, whose health was failing.

All this time Stephen was living on the money he had received from the sale of copyrights to Firth, Pond & Company and to Benteen. His income from royalties was practically nothing. In 1857 he published only one song, "I See Her Still in My Dreams," copyrighted by Firth, Pond & Company, June 8. Except for a single page of "Lula is Gone," a song issued in 1858, the manuscript book shows that there were no other songs that Stephen worked on between the time of writing the political songs in 1856 and his work on "I See Her Still in My Dreams." On July 1, Stephen was credited with royalties on "I See Her Still" to the amount of $8.75 and on July 11 he received the firm's check for that amount. On January 1, 1858, "commissions on music" amounting to $31.25 were charged to the publishers in Stephen's account book, as well as an item "To Balance on song—$25." As for moneys received from the publishers, Stephen drew on them for $75 January 1st, in addition to $25 in cash received from them on the same date. On February 25 he received a "loan" of $50 from the firm, with an item credited to them "Discount on same—$7.50."

On the opposite side of the ledger Stephen charged Firth, Pond & Company "Travelling expenses—43.75" entered under the same date as that of the "loan"—February 25. Apparently Stephen made a trip to New York in February at his publisher's expense, and it is evident that the purpose of that journey was to draw a new contract with Firth, Pond & Company. A copy of that document is in the Library of Congress, dated February 9, 1858.

6

This new contract contained some provisions that sought to clarify Foster's complex financial dealings with his publishers. Its first three articles stated that the composer would receive ten per cent royalty on copies of all his *future* songs, and one cent on instrumental arrangements of songs. Accounts were to be rendered quarterly, with full settlement on demand.

The fourth article is interesting, particularly when we compare its provisions with the account book items we have just examined.

In consideration of the sum of twenty five dollars paid this day by the party of the first part [Firth, Pond] to the party of the second part [Foster], the party of the second part hereby relinquishes all his claim in any music heretofore published by the party of the first part.

We already know that the only "music heretofore published" by Firth, Pond & Company in which Stephen had any royalty interest was the song "I See Her Still in My Dreams," and we have further learned that his only earnings from the publisher for several months had been entered thus in his ledger record in his account book:

> July 1, 1857 To Commissions on music.... $ 8.75
> Jan. 1, 1858 To Commissions on music.... 31.25

Then followed the item, also under date of January 1:

> To Balance on Song .... $25.

All of which made a total of $65, which agrees perfectly with an entry inserted at the end of the list of moneys received from songs, in the account book (directly under the item, "From Fisher & Bro.—110)—"I see her still in my dreams—65."

So Stephen again started with no royalty interest in previous songs when he signed his new contract in February of 1858.

Article Fifth of this agreement contains a curious provision for advance royalties, one which indicates that the publishers were trying to find some way of controlling Foster's habit of drawing ahead on his future earnings.

> On receiving for publication from the party of the second part the manuscript of each new or unpublished vocal composition of the party of the second part the party of the first part agrees to advance to the party of the second part the sum of one hundred dollars, or such sum as, together with the balance due according to the first, second and third articles of this agreement, shall amount to not less than one hundred dollars on each vocal composition so received, and the number of vocal compositions as aforesaid on which money shall be advanced as aforesaid shall not exceed twelve per year dating from the date of this agreement, and the sums advanced as aforesaid shall be considered as payment in part for the amounts due according to the first, second, and third articles of this agreement.

The Sixth Article binds Foster to publish exclusively with Firth, Pond & Company until August 9, 1860—for a period covering two and a half years from date of contract.

In regard to the advance royalty provisions in Article
Fifth, it is important to our story to follow Stephen's payments from Firth, Pond & Company in comparison with
his royalty earnings. Although it takes us ahead of our
narrative for the moment, it will be well to draw up a com-
parative table, to which we may refer in discussing the coming events of these years. (See pages 282 and 283.) Before each statement of royalties earned I have inserted the
names of the new songs published during the preceding
three months.

These figures provide a background which will be helpful in understanding what is to happen in the next few
years.

7

It was on April 8, 1858, that Stephen settled his account
with John Mish by giving him fifty dollars in cash and a
fourteen-day note for forty-five dollars to settle his board
bill. It appears that Stephen left the Eagle Hotel at about
this time, and that he may have taken his family to live in
a house that he rented from William and James Murdock.
Under date of July 18 we find an entry under a ledger account with the Murdocks—"By Rent 5 quarters [months?]
$40." On August 11 Stephen entered in his Murdock ac-
count—"To cash paid formerly—$8," and under the same
date "To cash paid this day $10." This left twenty-two
dollars of the rent to Murdock apparently unpaid.

It further appears that about August 9 the Fosters went
to live with a "Mrs. Johnston," for on September 6 we
find that Stephen owes such a person "By Board 4 weeks."
The Pittsburgh Directory lists "Johnston, William, of
Johnston's Hotel, East Liberty Station." Possibly Mrs.
Johnston managed the affairs of her husband's "hotel."

If the assumption is correct that the Fosters lived in a
house rented from the Murdocks, and that Stephen actually

1858

Lula is Gone (April 19)			
July 1 By royalties	$ 56.55	Amount drawn in preceding quarter	$ 644.25
Linger in Blissful Repose (July 13)			
Where Has Lula Gone? (Sept. 7)			
Oct. 1 By royalties	120.88	Amount drawn in preceding quarter.	325.25
My Loved One and My Own, or Eva (Nov. 24)			
Sadly to Mine Heart Appealing (Dec. 28)			

1859

Jan. 1 By royalties	58.50	Amount drawn in preceding quarter	262.15
Total royalties for preceding 9 months	$235.93	Drawn during 1858 from Firth, Pond & Co.	1,231.65
		Drawn ahead, Jan. 1, 1859	995.72
Linda Has Departed (Mar. 1)			
Apr. 1 By royalties	165.01	Amount drawn in preceding quarter	324.60
Parthenia to Ingomar (Apr. 4)			
For Thee, Love, for Thee (June 10)			
July 1 By royalties	38.97	Amount drawn in preceding quarter	271.24
		(It was during this period, May 16, that Firth, Pond refused payment on one of Foster's drafts.)	
Fairy Belle (Aug. 19)			
Oct. 1 By royalties	84.38	Amount drawn in preceding quarter	80.25
Thou Art the Queen of My Song (Dec. 21)			

1860

Jan. 1 By royalties   3.50

Total royalties for preceding year $291.86

Amount drawn in preceding quarters   100.

Drawn during 1859 from Firth, Pond & Co.   776.09

Balance from Jan. 1, 1859   995.72

   $1,771.81

   1,479.95

Drawn ahead, Jan. 1, 1860

The Wife (Feb. 9)

None Shall Weep a Tear for Me (Feb. 9)

Poor Drooping Maiden (Feb. 9)

Apr. 1 By royalties   97.45

Amount drawn in preceding quarter   92.60

Under the Willow She's Sleeping (May 3)

The Glendy Burk (May 29)

Cora Dean (probably between May 29 and July 1)

July 1 By royalties   109.75

Amount drawn in preceding quarter   31.29

Total royalties for preceding 6 months $207.20

Drawn during first six months of 1860 from Firth, Pond & Co.   123.89

Balance Jan. 1, 1860   1,479.95

   $1,603.84

   1,396.64

Drawn ahead, July 1, 1860

did mean "months" instead of "quarters" in his account book record, it would then appear that the family occupied the house for four months, from April 8 to August 8 or 9. Yet this supposition may be entirely wrong. If Stephen wrote correctly when he referred to "5 quarters," the rental may have been for an office or studio, rather than for a house in which his family lived. However, the dates of the Murdock transaction dovetail into the period between the Fosters' residence with John Mish at the Eagle Hotel and their going to "Mrs. Johnston" early in August.

A letter from Henrietta's daughter, "Lidie" (Eliza) Wick, written from Warren, Ohio, to her Uncle Morrison in Pittsburgh, shows that Stephen had planned to move at this time. The letter is dated May 27, 1858, seven weeks after "Lidie's" Uncle Stephen had settled his account with John Mish.

> Have any of you heard from Uncle Steve lately? I wonder if he is moved yet? He said perhaps they would make us a visit before they went away. . . .

At Mrs. Johnston's Stephen was regular in paying his board bill. He was charged less for his family than at the Eagle Hotel, nine dollars per week rather than twelve, and after paying the full amount due at the end of the first four weeks, he continued to pay at the end of every three weeks all that he owed for the preceding period, thus:

Sept. 6	$ 36
Sept. 27	25
Oct. 18	29
Nov. 8	27
	$117 [7]

From his Firth, Pond & Company account we find that Foster drew on his publishers a few days *after* each payment to his landlady:

[7] On page 158 of Foster's manuscript book (one of the pages devoted to "Where Has Lula Gone?") is a pencilled note—"Johnston a/c $117."

Sept. 8 .... $100
Sept. 29   60
Oct. 25   65
Nov. 9   80

In this year (1858) Stephen published five songs. Even though none of them is up to the standard of his best works, he was at least increasing the quantity of his output over the two preceding years—when he had issued but one song in 1856 and one in 1857. Of the 1858 songs, three of the four to which Stephen himself wrote the words are in the manuscript book, and we find that on two of them he took great pains to work the poems into the final versions that would satisfy him. To "Lula is Gone" (Apr. 19) he devoted nine pages, to "Linger in Blissful Repose" (July 13) only one, and to "Where Has Lula Gone?" (Sept. 7) eight pages. The fact that "Lula" had gone, and the attempt to discover her whereabouts, seemed deserving of more attention than the poet's merely admonishing an unnamed "love" to "Linger in blissful repose, Free from all sorrowing care." The manuscript of the music to "Where Has Lula Gone?" is still in existence, in the Library of Congress at Washington.

The words of "My Loved One and My Own, or Eva" (Nov. 24), published as "written and composed by Stephen C. Foster" are apparently not in the manuscript book. The poem of the other 1858 song "Sadly to Mine Heart Appealing" (Dec. 28) was written by Eliza S. Carey. It was this song, we will remember, which Robert Peebles Nevin stated was written in 1839, when Stephen was only thirteen.[8] While that is possible, and Stephen, in 1858, may have taken from his files a song that would have antedated the "Tioga Waltz," it does not seem likely that "Sadly to Mine Heart Appealing" was such an early work, even though it is decidedly inferior to others of Foster's songs. It would be easier to believe, if Stephen actually composed

[8] See page 99.

such a song in his youth, that not having published it, he wrote an entirely new song to the same poem in 1858.

The postscript of a letter Stephen wrote to Morrison in Philadelphia, October 22, 1858, may shed some light on the song.

> If you have the book containing scotch melodies I wish you would send it to me, I will return it to you. I have sent to F. P. & co. the song "Sadly to mine heart appealing" (Lines suggested on hearing an old Scottish melody) and would like to select an old tune for the introductory Symphony. If you have not the book probably you can tell me where to find one.

The manuscript of this song (music and words) is in the Foster Hall Collection in Indianapolis. This is the copy that Stephen sent to the publisher; according to his letter it was already in the hands of Firth, Pond & Company by October 22. The eight measures for the "introductory symphony" and the four measures for the concluding "symphony" are blank in the manuscript. Morrison apparently sent Stephen the book of Scotch melodies, for in the published version of the song, the last four measures of the "introductory symphony", and the last measures of the concluding "symphony" are based on "Robin Adair."

"Sadly to Mine Heart Appealing" was dedicated to Mrs. Harry Woods, the former Rachel Keller, to whose sister Mary Stephen had inscribed "There's a Good Time Coming" (1846), and to whose memory, after her death in 1846, he dedicated "Where is Thy Spirit, Mary?", a song published posthumously in 1895. We have also learned that according to tradition it was on Mrs. Woods' piano in Hazelwood that Stephen first played "Old Folks at Home." [9]

8

The main portion of Stephen's letter to Morrison, October 22, 1858, contained news of William Blakely, the

[9] See pages 129-130.

friend of Stephen and Morrison who had been president
of the Buchanan Glee Club.

DEAR MIT:

I recd the medicine you sent me for Bill Blakely and took it over
to him. I also left with him all the directions contained in both your
letters. Bill looks worse than when I last saw him, and he told me
that he had been sinking for the past two weeks more than formerly.
He says that your medicine is much better than that by the same
name which he has been using. I will call on Cupid and get the
shaving fixings.

If you are not in any particular hurry for Benton's books I would
like to read a little in them before sending them to you.

Please give my love to Brother William and ask him whether he
would like to have me send him the Assembly books that Pa had.
We are all well.

Your Affec. bro.

S. C. FOSTER.

In a little over two weeks, November 11, Stephen again
wrote Morrison:

Our old friend, Bill Blakely died this morning. There is a very
favorable notice of him in this evening's "Chronicle." I posted
O'Neil on the matter. When I saw him last he said he wondered
whether he would ever see you again.

The opening paragraph of the foregoing letter contained
news of Stephen himself. We have already learned that
according to his account book he made his last payment for
board to Mrs. Johnston on the 8th of November. It is
therefore important to note again the date of this letter—
November 11.

DEAR MIT:

Mary Wick [Henrietta's daughter], Jane, Marion and I start
to-morrow for Cincinnati on Billy Hamilton's boat, the "Ida May."
We all went to see Miss Davenport last night at the "old" theatre.
We will stirr [sic] old John McClelland up in Cincinnati, make
the children sing and bring in Billy's bass voice. The trip will be
a recreation and variety for me. Siss [Susan Pentland Robinson]
gets along very well since her mother's death. We had a nice duck

supper with her the other evening. She had plenty of jokes about Andy, as usual. [Her husband, Andrew Robinson.]

Hamilton told of this trip when he was interviewed by the *Pittsburgh Press* in 1895. His recollections were printed in that newspaper's issue of July 16.

I think it was in 1858 [that] . . . I was clerk of the steamer Ida May, plying between this city and Cincinnati, and one day invited Stephen and his wife to take a trip to Cincinnati with me. They accepted my invitation, and we had a very enjoyable time. On the way down the river, Foster wrote and composed the song, "Ingomar to Parthenia," which was afterward published and enjoyed quite a season of popularity in concert circles. He had written some of the melody before, but most of it was composed on that occasion.

It is, however, to an incident that occurred in Cincinnati that I have particular reference. During our brief stay there, we called on several friends and one evening Foster and I went to the office of the "Commercial Gazette," on Third Street, to see Cons Miller, river editor of that journal, with whom we were both well acquainted. After a pleasant chat, we bade him good-by and started back to the boat to make preparations for our return to Pittsburgh. On our way down Broadway, we heard music, and discovered a party of serenaders in the yard of a residence, directly opposite the home of George K. Shoenberger, a brother of the late John Shoenberger,[10] the iron manufacturer of this city. Serenading was a popular form of amusement for young men in those days, and many serenading parties were formed. We stopped and listened. The melody was strangely familiar.

"Why, they are singing my song, 'Come Where My Love Lies Dreaming,' " exclaimed Foster.

"It is a bungling effort they are making, too," I replied. "Let us go over and help them out."

We had some time to spare, and Foster accepted my proposition. We crossed the street and joined the party. They had not yet finished the song and we chimed in. Naturally they regarded us as intruders, and when the song was finished demanded what right we had to interfere with them in their enjoyment. I asked them if they knew the composer of the song they had just sung. They replied that they knew Stephen C. Foster composed the song, but they were not

---

[10] George and John M. Shoenberger were owners of the Juniata Iron Works, a company which Morrison Foster represented in Cleveland for a number of years.

personally acquainted with him. I then introduced Foster, but the young men refused to believe he was the composer of the song, and declared we were impostors.

The situation began to grow alarming, and we were in danger of having a lively set-to with the young serenaders, when a happy thought struck me. I asked the leader of the party if he knew Cons Miller, of the "Commercial Gazette." He said he did, and I proposed that we all go over to the Gazette office and see Miller. The young men agreed to this, and in a few minutes Miller established our identity in the eyes of the serenaders beyond any question. Nothing was too good for us after that, and although we would have willingly excused ourselves and retired to the steamer, the young men would not hear of it, and we spent the balance of the evening in their company serenading in the residence quarter of the city. We enjoyed the occasion, however, and had many a laugh over it afterward.

In this case there is no record to show whether a peace offering to Jane, presumably waiting on the steamboat, was either required or offered.

Mary Wick and her Uncle Stephen were close friends. Mary's daughter, Henrietta Crosman, has told me that Mary would often play Stephen's songs for him on the piano, while he whistled the melody. Miss Crosman's son by her first marriage, Sedley Brown, relates several anecdotes of Stephen Foster, told him by his grandmother, Mary Wick Crosman. One of these stories upholds Morrison's statement that Stephen was possessed of his full share of physical courage.

It seems that Stephen was one day walking with Mary, his niece, when two ruffians made an insulting remark as they passed. Stephen took Mary to a near-by drugstore and told her to wait for him. He then went back to the two toughs and gave them both a beating. After this he walked to the police station, paid a fine for disorderly conduct, and then returned to the drugstore for Mary. He told her nothing of what had happened, and it was many months before she learned from someone else where Stephen had gone or what he had done when he left her.

9

There is no record to show how long the visit to Cincinnati lasted. Hamilton spoke of the "brief stay" there, so the entire trip probably occupied only a week or so. It is not possible to learn where Stephen and his family went to live immediately upon their return. We do know, however, that for several months in 1859 they boarded with a Mrs. A. Miller, a lady whose daughter is still living in Pittsburgh at the time this account is written (1933). The chronology of Stephen's account with Mrs. Miller is confusing, as it appears in his account book. The dates of amounts due do not always run in sequence, and it is not clear when the family first went to live with the lady. The first item of $1 due "for boarding" requires an explanation that is not contained in the record. It is apparent that while board for the family was at first charged at the rate of $9.50 per week, the amount was raised to $10.50, May 10. Perhaps Mrs. Miller raised the board for little Marion from $2.50 to $3.50 when she found that the child had passed her eighth birthday on April 18.

The reader will gain the clearest account of Stephen's method of paying Mrs. Miller from the complete ledger record as it appears in Stephen's account book.

1859

Apr. 4 To Cash	$35.	Feb. 6 By Boarding	$ 1.
May 16 " "	50.	Apr. 5 " "	9.50
		12 " "	9.50
		19 " "	9.50
		26 " "	9.50
		May 3 " "	9.50
		10 " "	10.50
		17 " "	10.50
$69.50[!!!]			$69.50

Something clearly had happened to Stephen's bookkeeping ability in this instance. Perhaps he made a fresh start when he continued the record under his first attempt at a balance.

May 16 To Cash in all	$85	May 14 By Boarding	$107.
July 23 " " " "	10.		
Aug. 19 " " " "	20.		
Sep. 15 " " " "	15.		

We may hope that Dunning's books had not been kept in this fashion in the years Stephen was in Cincinnati. Probably they were not, for this evidence of carelessness in Stephen's records appears to be something that was developing in these years. His accounts with Firth, Pond & Company were kept with a fairly high degree of accuracy, yet there, too, were occasional slips which made such adjustments as those noted under "error their a/c," or "error in a/c," necessary for striking a balance.

By his 1858 contract with his publishers Stephen was allowed an advance royalty of one hundred dollars for each song he gave them to publish. Our table showing the financial dealings with the firm indicates that by January 1859 he had drawn over twelve hundred dollars and had given Firth, Pond & Company only five songs, works that during the year had earned royalties of only $235.93.[11]

In addition to being drawn ahead far beyond his earnings, Stephen was spending part of his income on the discount charges on the drafts he presented at the bank—seven per cent of the face value of the drafts. On May 16 Foster presented a draft which Firth, Pond & Company refused to pay, but Stephen was charged with the discount fee just the same. After this refusal Stephen drew on his publishers less generously, and he was forced somehow to get along on a reduced income. While in 1858 (in nine months) he drew $1,231.65, the table shows that in the whole twelve months of 1859 he only drew $776.09. It is

[11] See pages 282-283.

small wonder that Stephen's accounts with Mrs. Miller were confused and irregular. They were kept at the time he was having difficulties with his income from Firth, Pond & Company.

Although Foster published five new songs in 1859 the royalties on these and on the five songs of 1858 were unsatisfactory. Starting with the April 1 statement, $165.01, the quarterly accounting of sales showed an almost vertical decline—$38.97 July 1; $84.38 October 1; and only $3.50 on January 1, 1860. Even though Stephen had drawn less during the past few months than was his habit, the first of the New Year found him in his publisher's debt by $1,-479.95.

Like those published during the previous year, the 1859 songs were none too good. To three of them Stephen wrote only the music, the words were by William Henry McCarthy—"Linda Has Departed" (Mar. 1), "Parthenia to Ingomar" (Apr. 4) and "For Thee, Love, for Thee" (June 10).

Hamilton was evidently mistaken when he remembered that Stephen both *"wrote* and composed" "Parthenia to Ingomar" on the "Ida May," for it is apparent that he could merely have been composing a musical setting to McCarthy's words. It is interesting to note, however, that five pages of the manuscript book are devoted to the words of "For Thee, Love, for Thee." Evidently Stephen spent considerable time and thought in revising McCarthy's poem. The manuscript of "Linda Has Departed" is now in the Foster Hall Collection. Over the first page of music there is no mention of the author of the words, but due credit was given to McCarthy on the title-page of the printed copy.

We know, too, that McCarthy was to share equally with Stephen in the royalties from these three songs, for Stephen's account book contains a page which records his dealings with his collaborator. Incidentally, the amounts

credited to McCarthy agree with the amounts earned by the
songs shown on Stephen's royalty lists. Note carefully how
our composer discharged his debts to his librettist.

1859

Feb.	10 To Cash	$ 5.	Apr.	1 By Commissions	$24.98
"	28 " "	2.	July	1 " "	10.57
Mch.	1 " "	1.			
Apr.	26 Amts pd formerly	2.			
May	16 " " "	1.			
"	" Half Buggy Hire	1.			
"	20 Cash	.50			
June	28 Cash	1.			
Bal.		22.05			
		$35.55			$35.55

The record is continued, showing a feeble, though novel,
attempt to discharge part of the "Bal $22.05."

July	15 To hat	$1.50	Bal.		$22.05
Dec.	10 Cash	.50	Oct.	1 By Commissions	1.25
Dec.	17 "	2.00			

The two 1859 songs to which Stephen wrote the words,
"Fairy Belle" (Aug. 19) and "Thou Art the Queen of My
Song" (Dec. 21), like the others of this period, are un-
worthy of his talent. They cannot equal in any way, musically or in the words, the truly great songs Foster had
written but a few years before, even though these later
works may be no worse than the lesser songs of his earlier
years. And yet Stephen took pains with "Thou Art the
Queen of My Song"; nine pages of the manuscript book
are given over to working out the. verses.

10

Before leaving the year 1859 there are two more letters
for us to read. Both were written by Stephen to Morrison,

who stayed in Philadelphia with William until he returned to Pittsburgh in September. The first letter refers to a song that may have been "Fairy Belle."

Pittsburgh, June 13, 1859

MY DEAR BROTHER MIT,

Yesterday my neighbor who has the Daguerreotype establishment invited me to have my picture taken. I think it is rather good and I send it to you, my dear brother.

Did you receive my letter intended for Mr. Bateman? and did you forward it?

I sent off a first-rate song the other day to Firth, Pond & Co. When I receive a printed copy I will send it to you.

Your affectionate Bro.
STEPHEN.

The second letter was dated August 15. It refers to rental owed Morrison for the use of a farm he owned at Baden.

DEAR MIT:

I went to Baden on Saturday, and took Jane with me. I saw Mr. Deerdorf who said that the crops had been bad and dull payments, &c., &c. In short, he had not the money. He had not recd "the scratch of a pen" from you for a long time, that you had not demanded the money when it was due, &c. I asked him when he would be ready with the money, he said, about the 1st of October. I told him to leave it with Henry. We took dinner and tea at Mr. Aderson's. He was not at home, but the girls were. Mrs. Berry (the youngest daughter) is very pretty and entertaining, being a combination of Mary Wick, Mary McClelland, Mrs. Mitchell, Mrs. Woods, &c.

With much love to all
Your affec. bro.
S. C. FOSTER.

The year 1860 opened in its first few months with two events, one happy and the other sad. Each of them seemed to lend its own suggestion of foreboding for Stephen. The first event, the happy one, was the marriage of Morrison to Jessie Lightner, February 23, 1860. Morrison had moved to Cleveland, and while the older brother's marriage was a happy occasion to Stephen as well as to Morrison, it did, as it should, give Morrison other responsibilities and interests than the welfare of his brothers and sisters. His younger brother was going to need him in the next few years more than he had ever needed him before. Yet we shall see that Morrison stood by to help as best he could.

The other event was the death of Brother William, March 4, 1860. William's help had not, of course, been as necessary in recent years when the Fosters were grown, as it had been when they were children. He had done his part in their youth, and when he had a family of his own and had gone to Philadelphia, his brothers and sisters did not have the need to turn to him for aid as they had in former years. His passing was therefore a sorrow, rather than a tragedy, to Stephen.

It is not to be doubted that Stephen was sorely pressed for funds in the early months of 1860. Although his royalties increased materially over the record for the preceding year ($97.45 in April, and in July $109.75) the January 1 statement, covering the preceding three months, had amounted to but $3.50. He was drawn ahead almost fifteen hundred dollars, and it was no doubt difficult for him to persuade his publishers to honor even the two drafts totalling $123.89 which he presented during the first six months of the year. One of these was for $80 (January 9) and the other for $25 (April 5). The balance to form the total consisted of discount charges and an "error in a/c." These drafts represent the only income received during this period that is recorded in Stephen's account book.

All of this tends to lend authenticity to the anecdotes regarding Stephen's impoverished condition during the time that preceded his going to New York later in the year. It is generally supposed that his wife became a telegrapher, and in this way helped to provide some of the money necessary to the support of the family. It is not established, however, whether this step was taken while Stephen and his wife were still living in Pittsburgh. It is said that Andrew Carnegie, then superintendent of the Pittsburgh division of the Pennsylvania Railroad,[12] gave Jane Foster an appointment as telegrapher at the Greensburg station of the railroad, a few miles from Pittsburgh. Gossip also has it that the bachelor Carnegie was not altogether platonic in his attitude toward Stephen's wife, yet those who advance such a suggestion are emphatic in stating that Jane was quick to discourage whatever advances the little Scotchman may have made to her.

Whether or not Andrew Carnegie did actually appoint Jane to her position, we know of course that there were several Foster connections with the Pennsylvania Railroad. Brother William was vice-president of the company until his death in March, and the associate engineer with whom William had built the railroad across the Allegheny Mountains, J. Edgar Thomson, was president. His wife, Lavinia Smith, was a friend of Stephen's, and not only his friend, but also the sister of Brother William's late wife, Elizabeth. We may assume that Jane did not particularly need the young Carnegie's favor to keep whatever job she may have had.

There is one anecdote, unconfirmed by any sort of documentary evidence, which suggests that Jane became a telegrapher before she went to New York with Stephen. If this story is true, it could not have occurred in the very last years of Stephen's life, for he did not live in Pittsburgh again after 1860.

A resident of Pittsburgh states that his aunt was a pupil and assistant to Jane at Greensburg. He further claims that his aunt was sixteen or seventeen at the time, and that as she was born in 1843, she would therefore have been Jane's assistant in 1859 or 1860. He relates that his aunt told him that she and Jane Foster worked on the night

---

[12] Carnegie was promoted to this position December 1, 1859.

shift, and that often Stephen would come out on the midnight train, sometimes a bit the worse for wear. Stephen
would be talkative, and insist on distracting Jane from her
work.

After this had occurred a few times, Jane would send
her assistant to the station platform when she heard the
train coming, to see if Stephen was aboard. If he was,
the assistant would run back to the telegrapher's room in
time to lock the door before Stephen got there. Then, according to the story, Stephen would sit down on the door
sill and play the violin he carried with him until his wife
and her assistant were ready to come out at the close of
their working hours.

One more anecdote belongs here, one which shows something of Stephen's generous nature. It is taken from an
article by Col. John A. Joyce,[13] printed in the *Washington
Post*, September 9, 1900.

I had the pleasure and honor of knowing personally Stephen C.
Foster, the great song composer.

In the spring of 1860 at my home in Mount Sterling, Ky., . . .
I had a sudden fever and desire to take a course in bookkeeping at
Duff's celebrated Commercial College at Pittsburgh.

Equipped with a good suit of clothes and a hundred dollars, I
took the fine steamboat Allegheny at Maysville, Ky., and after a few
days of puffing and paddling . . . we arrived on time at the Smoky
City. . . .

After spending a few days between the college, the hotel and social resorts about town . . . I imagined that my mission in life was
. . . the theatrical stage, where as a minstrel song and dance man
and Shakespearean poetical "prodigy," I would fire the town. . . .

I went to a printer and had struck off a thousand small hand bills
for a "Musical Entertainment" and posted up large bills through the
city—having secured for one night the Lafayette Theater.

A few nights before the performance, I met the musical genius,
Foster, in the tavern where I was staying, and he seemed particularly
friendly, perhaps for the reason that I was announced to sing a number of his "Darky Songs," and on account of my youth. He intro-

13 "Stephen Collins Foster, A Musician and Poet."

duced me to some of his "boon companions," who indulged in social cheer till after the noon of the night. And while Foster did not indulge very much himself in Bacchanalian eccentricities, we youngsters made up for his conservative conduct.

He played on the banjo and piano and sang for us many of his noted melodies, and occasionally he played the flute with a sweetness I never heard before or since.

He had a sweet, low barytone voice, and when playing the piano swayed backward and forward with his rhythmic numbers, like the sighing surges of a summer sea. . . . Foster was about thirty-three years of age when I met him, but with the settled melancholy look that occasionally swept over his charming face, like a passing cloud over a field of wild flowers, he seemed older.

The night for my entertainment finally arrived, with Duff's College boys and the tavern "rounders" occupying some of the best seats in the theater, and the gallery gods were in loud evidence.

Foster and a few of his friends occupied the front bench, and were, from the start, lavish in their applause, leading off with hands and feet when I made a hit with one of his own songs, or danced a shuffle or a jig to the music of a small string band that volunteered for my benefit.

The more I danced, sang, and spouted, the wilder grew that impromptu audience, and after an hour and a half, from sheer exhaustion, I bowed myself out through the wings, rang down the curtain, and left the house for the tavern, not even stopping to share the few dollars that the ticket-seller had in his box. . . .

II

Whether or not Jane was a telegrapher before she and Stephen left Pittsburgh, we know that in April of 1860 she and Marion were with Stephen in Warren, Ohio, the town in which Henrietta Thornton, Stephen's sister, lived. Here is a letter Stephen wrote at that time to Morrison. It reveals his financial condition as well as news of his health.

Warren, O., Apl. 27, 1860

DEAR MIT:

Please send me by return mail $12—I have received from F. P. & Co. a letter stating that they cannot advance me any more money till I send them the songs now due them (about two as I make the calculation) as our present agreement is about expiring. They show a disposition to renew agreement, but, very properly require payment in music before any new arrangement. I have entered into an agreement with a new house for part of my music, but, as the terms are not entirely fixed, I cannot well draw on them just now.

I expect to be in Cleveland very soon on my way to New York, and will be able to settle with you. I require this amount for little washing bills, &c. which are, you know, the most perplexing. Please send the amt. immediately on receipt of this.

Jane and Marion are well, also Etty's family. I am very well, but had, as I supposed a slight touch of ague yesterday. I think to-day that it was only a false alarm.

I have written two songs since I have been in Warren and have two under way, but do not feel inclined to send them off half made up.

Much love to Jessie.

Your affec. bro.

STEPHEN.

Morrison sent the twelve dollars immediately in the form of a check. A month later Stephen again wrote him.

Warren, O., May 31, 1860

DEAR MIT:

Herewith I send you a draft on Firth Pond & Co. for $50—which I wish you would hold for ten days, and if you can conveniently, please send me the amount by return mail. There will be no trouble about payment of draft. I have only one song to finish in the time mentioned. I desire to pay Mr. Shoenberger (the landlord) at the end of the month as I engaged to do, and have told him that I would pay him when I would hear from Cleveland.

I received a very cheering letter yesterday from F. P. & Co. and feel in good spirits generally.

Jesse Thornton [Henrietta's husband] arrived yesterday looking very well. We all did our best to give him a hearty welcome and you never saw such a happy family. He informs me that Jessie (yours) was in Cleveland, therefore I infer that you have been in Pittsburgh since I saw you.

I expect to start for New York before very long and hope to see you both.

Your affectionate brother

S. C. FOSTER.

Mr. Shoenberger, "the landlord" to whom Stephen refers, was the proprietor of the Austin House in Warren, so it is apparent that Stephen and his family stayed there while they were in that town. Mr. H. T. Richards, grandson of Edward Shoenberger, states that Stephen wrote "one of his songs" at the Gaskill House. A picture of Jane Foster and a book of Byron's poems, both left by Stephen at the Gaskill House, are still in the possession of the Richards family.

Whether Morrison sent Stephen the fifty dollars, or whether the draft was presented and payment accepted or refused is not known. There is no record of it in Stephen's account book. The original draft was among Morrison's papers when he died.

Stephen was evidently working hard, in something of a rush to deliver to Firth, Pond & Company enough songs to warrant their advancing him further funds. In the first six months of 1860, six songs were published. Three were issued February 9—"None Shall Weep a Tear for Me" (words by R. H. Wilde), "Poor Drooping Maiden," and "The Wife," the last a temperance song. On May 3, when Stephen and his family were in Warren, "Under the Willow She's Sleeping" was copyrighted. This was dedicated to a Mrs. W. H. Whitney. On May 29 the publishers issued another of Stephen's lively songs, "The Glendy Burk," by no means an equal of "Oh! Susanna" or "De Camptown Races," but a song with at least a reminder of the youthful Stephen who wrote fascinating nonsense.

It is important to note that "The Glendy Burk" is written in Negro dialect, and that Stephen's songs in recent years had numbered very few of this variety. It is true that the dialect of "The Glendy Burk" is less extreme than it was in Foster's earlier "Ethiopian" songs, yet it makes us feel as though Stephen had gone down to the wharves for another glimpse of the Negro deckhands and stevedores,

Draft on Firth, Pond and Company which Stephen Foster sent to Morrison

and had written a song for them as of yore. And he chose
for his theme a steamboat, the "Glendy Burk," which plied
the waters of the Ohio River.

It is interesting to know that about a year before this
an article had appeared in the *New York Evening Post*,
"Who Writes Our Songs?",[14] in which the author wrote
in part:

> Ethiopian minstrelsy, as it is called, has . . . culminated, and is
> now in its decline. Appreciating this fact, Mr. Foster has lately
> somewhat changed his style, and abandoning the use of negro jargon,
> he now writes songs better adapted for general use.

The last of the six songs published in the first half of
1860 was "Cora Dean." There is no copyright entry in the
Library of Congress to establish the day and month this
song was copyrighted, yet it was surely published before
August as it appears on a list of songs that were issued
prior to that time. Its words appear in Foster's manuscript
book just before and after the pages devoted to "The
Glendy Burk."

Stephen probably left his manuscript book, by this time
completely filled, behind him when he went to New York,
and it may be safe to assume that the songs in its last pages
were written in Pittsburgh, or possibly in Warren.[15] It
would be important if we could be sure of this, for then we
would know where Stephen wrote "Old Black Joe," a song
in which he regains for the moment all of his power to
write melodies that live.

Two pages of the work book are given to "Old Black
Joe." The verses are written only once; except for minor
changes, they appear in this single version just as they are
found in the printed copy which was copyrighted by Firth,
Pond & Company, November 8 (1860). It may be that

---

[14] Reprinted in *Littell's Living Age*, May 14, 1859.
[15] An entry in the manuscript book indicates that Foster had the book with
him in Warren, August 1860.

"Old Black Joe" is a truly great song for the same reason that "Old Folks at Home" is a masterpiece. Stephen put himself into the song, sincerely and without any attempt at manufacturing an idea. The "old days" may have seemed gone to Stephen, and while he still had courage, and spoke bravely to Morrison of his prospects for the future, yet he knew want and privation intimately, and the present could not have seemed as bright as the past. Then too, if he was thinking, as Mrs. Rose suggests, of the old Negro servant at the McDowell home,[16] he had real memories to cling to.

It is important to observe that the words of "Old Black Joe" are not in Negro dialect. Stephen had no need of that device in this song, for he was no longer writing for Christy's minstrels. He could sing again from his own deepest feelings, this time with his own voice and speech.

> Gone are the days when my heart was young and gay,
> Gone are my friends from the cotton fields away,
> Gone from the earth to a better land I know,
> I hear their gentle voices calling, "Old Black Joe."
>
> I'm coming, I'm coming, for my head is bending low:
> I hear those gentle voices calling, "Old Black Joe."

12

As a published song, "Old Black Joe" takes us ahead of our story; we are concerned for the moment only with those works which were published before August 1860. It was about this time, somewhere in the Summer of that year, that Stephen again drew up in his account book a list of what his songs had earned. This, of course, included only the sixteen songs in which he still had a royalty interest, those published since Stephen had made his contract with Firth, Pond & Company, dated February 9, 1858.

[16] See pages 159-160.

Lula is Gone	[April 19, 1858]	$182.07
Linger in Blissful Repose	[July 13, 1858]	49.76
Where Has Lula Gone	[Sept. 7, 1858]	86.85
My Loved One and My Own, or Eva	[Nov. 24, 1858]	54.15
Sadly to Mine Heart	[Dec. 28, 1858]	43.44
Linda Has Departed	[Mar. 1, 1859]	33.65
Parthenia	[April 4, 1859]	46.30
For Thee Love	[June 10, 1859]	21.15
Fairy Belle	[Aug. 19, 1859]	111.38
Thou Art the Queen	[Dec. 21, 1859]	12.50
None Shall Weep	[Feb. 9, 1860]	13.75
Poor Drooping Maiden	[Feb. 9, 1860]	13.75
The Wife	[Feb. 9, 1860]	13.75
Glendy Burk	[May 29, 1860]	21.25
Under the Willows	[May 3, 1860]	13.75
Cora Dean	[? 1860]	13.75

$731.25 [17]

We have already learned how far in excess of these earnings was the total of amounts actually received from the publisher, and how by July 1 of 1860 Stephen was drawn ahead $1,396.64.[18] We have learned also that Stephen in the Spring of this year was corresponding with Firth, Pond & Company, hopeful of working out some new arrangement to take the place of the 1858 contract that would expire August 9. After this date Stephen would no longer be required to publish exclusively with Firth, Pond & Company, and in his letter to Morrison of April 27 he told his brother of "an agreement with a new house for part of [his] music." We shall find later that this new house was either Daughaday & Hammond of Philadelphia, publishers of *Clark's School Visitor,* who paid Stephen $400 for six songs, or Lee & Walker, music publishers of the same city.

It is certain too, that some new agreement was reached

[17] Please note that this total figure differs slightly from the sum of royalties received from these sixteen songs as added from the entries in Stephen's ledger account with Firth, Pond & Co.—$734.99. In future calculations in these pages the latter total will be used.
[18] See page 283.

with Firth, Pond & Company, even though it may not have been an $800 salary for twelve songs a year, as suggested by John Mahon in his recollections of Foster.[19]

Before making any new contract with Firth, Pond & Company it was obvious that old accounts must be settled, and it does not require undue imagination to guess how this was accomplished. Just as he had cleaned off old scores in 1857, and again a year later, Stephen on August 9, 1860, assigned to Firth, Pond & Company all future interest in the sixteen songs they had published under the present contract for one hundred dollars each. With this sixteen hundred dollars he was able to clear his drawing account, and to have at his publishers a credit of $203.36, which he no doubt needed when he went to New York to live. At about the same time he may also have received all or some of the $400 which the Philadelphia publishers paid him.

Exactly when Stephen went to New York we cannot know. Apparently it was some time after August 10, 1860, for an entry under that date in the manuscript book reads: "Was in Warren at the Gaskell House." Nor do we know why he left Pittsburgh. Morrison said it was to be near his publishers, and there are some who suggest that Stephen was lonely in Pittsburgh now that all of his brothers and sisters, except Henry, had moved away or were dead. Whatever the reasons, it was the worst possible move Stephen could have made. New York was not the place for him. Perhaps there was no spot where he could have been happier, or where he might have avoided his sad fate, but certainly the cosmopolitan surroundings of New York, unfriendly to strangers who could not adjust themselves to its environment and withstand its pitfalls, did not offer an atmosphere in which Stephen could either flourish or exist. He was one who needed the surroundings of his youth, and the relatives and friends who knew

[19] In an article in the *New York Clipper* of March 1877. See page 321, also pages 199-200.

how to handle him. And moreover, if, as has been suggested, the "ague" from which he suffered at times was in fact a symptom of tuberculosis, Stephen went to a climate that would prove almost fatal, and would weaken his resistance to the habit of drink that was growing on him.

————

And now, before leaving this chapter called "Finances," we may draw a summary of all the moneys that we know Stephen received from the time of his first contract with Firth, Pond & Company in 1849, to his arrival in New York in 1860. Through this table we may at least know how much Stephen received, and judge for ourselves whether he was paid adequately for the profit that others might gain from his works. We must remember that standards of value differ to-day from those in the 1850's, and that Stephen's income may be multiplied several times in comparing it with that of a song-writer living in our generation.

Firth, Pond & Co., royalties to January, 1857 (including $70 from Christy)	$9,436.96
F. D. Benteen, royalties to January, 1857	461.85
Firth, Pond, for Social Orchestra	150.00
Firth, Pond, for arranging	60.00
Fisher & Bro., for words of songs	110.00
Firth, Pond, for copyrights in full, Mch. 14, 1857	1,872.28
Benteen, for copyrights in full, no date	200.00
Firth, Pond, for "I See Her Still in My Dreams," 1857-8	65.00
Firth, Pond, royalties, 1858-60	734.99
Firth, Pond, for sale of copyrights, Aug. 9, 1860	1,600.00
From Daughaday and Hammond (or Lee & Walker), 1860-2	400.00

Total amounts known to have been paid Foster during his productive years—1849-60 ....$15,091.08

Average per year (11 years) $1,371.92

X

NEW YORK

I

IT IS not a grateful task to write the final chapter of
Stephen's life. Ironically enough, it is this last, dismal
period that has been made the most of by those who have
written about Stephen Foster. The very fact that there
are few records and contemporary documents to establish
events and dates during these years has allowed legend and
tradition to run rampant, and such tawdry stage properties
as shabby clothes, a glazed cap, brown wrapping paper for
writing songs, and the inescapable wine cup have provided
journalists with items that have grown in their hands until
they have become synonyms for the name of Stephen Foster.

Be it recorded to his everlasting credit that Harold V.
Milligan, in his biography of Foster,[1] handled this phase of
his subject's career like a gentleman and a scholar. There
was nothing of the whitewash brush in his account of his
hero's tragic end, yet there was nothing either of the lurid
merely for the sake of sensation, or what newspapermen
would call good copy. What facts were known were met
squarely and without quibbling, and legends were treated
as such and their gross exaggerations bitterly attacked.

It was natural that Morrison Foster, Stephen's own
brother, should have omitted from his life of Stephen [2] all
reference to the weakness that proved his undoing. It is
easy to understand also his feelings when he protested
against others making capital of such matters, and wrote

[1] *Stephen Collins Foster, A Biography,* New York, 1920. G. Schirmer.
[2] *Op. cit.*

to an editor who had published a particularly lurid article about Stephen:

I can see no possible good to be attained by publishing it. If my brother had been distinguished as an orator, an actor, appearing before the public in person, references to the only failing he ever had might perhaps be relevant, but the public knew not *him* but only of him, his poetry and music being the only visible sign that such a being really existed at all; reference to certain peculiarities is not only out of place, but is a cruel tearing open of old wounds, which the grave should close forever.

Yet the honest biographer, who aims to give his readers a complete record of his hero's career, cannot escape his duty, even though he may be permitted to approach his task with sympathy and understanding—which, after all, is also his duty.

Up to this time in our story we have been able to document almost all of the events in Stephen Foster's life. Family letters, the manuscript book, Stephen's own accounts and records, and items in musical journals and newspapers have given current testimony to the facts of the song-writer's career. With August of 1860, and Stephen's coming to New York, all records virtually cease, and we are left with an absence of contemporary evidence that is as baffling as the wealth of documents up to this period was almost unbelievably fruitful.

Our procedure, then, must be one of first presenting the few known facts, and after that examining the traditions, seeking to determine which of them are true and which are exaggerated, if not altogether false. In this way we may be able to unfold something of the story of Stephen's last years, which we will find, in spite of its dismal and sordid aspects, is only an intensely human tragedy. We will not forget what we have already learned of Stephen's early life, and the pitiful lack of preparation he had for the career he had chosen.

2

The most important documents of these years, in showing Stephen's condition, financial and otherwise, before the time of his death, are excerpts from four letters written to Morrison by Jane Foster, Stephen's wife. The first three of these letters are dated from Lewistown, Pennsylvania, where Jane stayed with her sister Agnes, who had married a Dr. Cummings. These letters show that while Jane was not living with Stephen, they were not estranged, even though it is probable that the separation was more or less permanent, principally because Stephen was not earning enough to support her. It may be that Jane was again, or perhaps for the first time, engaged as a telegrapher, even though there are no letters from Greensburg, where she was supposed to have been employed in the local station of the Pennsylvania Railroad.[3] It is said that the husband of Jane's other sister, Marion, a banker named John D. Scully, had helped Stephen's wife by making it possible for her to get her training as a telegrapher. Little Marion Foster visited the Scullys frequently during these years.

Here are the excerpts from the three letters Jane wrote from Lewistown. They reveal much.

September 30th, 1861

DEAR MIT:

I have been spending a couple of months here, and I am now beginning to feel very uneasy about Steve, and he has not at present the money to send me. I concluded to ask you to lend me ten dollars as I wish to go back to him immediately, and indeed it is very necessary that I should be with him. You will oblige me very much if you can send it, do so as soon as possible. I would not ask you, Mit, for I know you have your own family to take care of.

Jane's next letter to Morrison, written less than a week later, shows that Morrison was quick to respond to the call for help.

[3] See pages 295-296.

Oct. 5th, 1861

I received your letter yesterday, enclosing ten dollars and I assure you that I am very much obliged indeed. When I arrive in New York, I will deliver your message to Steve. Marion is well and sends her love to you. She goes to school every day; she is very attentive to her studies and is a most excellent child in every respect.

It may be that Jane was with Stephen for the Winter and Spring of that year (1861-2). At any rate she had recently been with him when she wrote Morrison, June 30, 1862:

I received a few days ago your very kind letter. You have my best and warmest thanks for your kindness. Marion is no worse, but she is still very delicate. I left Steve in New York; he was well, and publishes once in a long while with Pond. The clothing you sent him he was very much obliged to you & he told me that he would write and thank you.

The fourth and last letter from Jane does not show the place it was written from, nor does it give the day of the month. All we know is that it was addressed to Morrison, and that it was written in October of 1863, about three months before Stephen met his tragic end. The letter contained this paragraph:

You do not know, dear Mit, how much relieved I felt about Steve when I read your letter. If you can persuade him to return to Cleveland with you, I am sure that all will soon be well with him again.

These four letters are almost all we have in the way of contemporary documents, but they do outline something of the story, and they are helpful in establishing the reliability of the several reminiscences of Stephen's years in New York which were published after his death. They show, these letters, that Jane never really deserted Stephen as she has sometimes been accused of doing. They seem to prove that though it was not possible for her to live with him, and even though she herself may not have made his life at home particularly easy or comfortable, she by no means abandoned Stephen, nor gave him up altogether.

3

And now for the recollections and reminiscences. There are many of them. First, and perhaps most important, are the memories of Jane Foster herself, as told to her granddaughter, Mrs. Rose.[4] Mrs. Rose writes frankly of Stephen's failing and seeks to explain its cause.

After moving to New York, they were at once drawn into musical circles. People entertained musically to a large extent in those days. There were balls, singing clubs, minstrels, concerts, etc., with invitations often to the Fosters. Wine flowed freely—like water. This is where Stephen C. Foster met the crushing defeat of his life. He was highly strung, temperamental, frail of physique. He sank rapidly where a physically stronger man might have survived. He suffered much and died for his fault.

Mrs. Rose retells an anecdote of her grandmother's about one of the parties Jane and Stephen attended.

Although impatient and highly nervous as most people are who do creative work . . . on the day of a great New Year's Ball in New York, when my grandmother found her costume unfinished, he [Stephen] patiently sat all day and clumsily sewed spangles on her dress inwardly cursing (as Grandma could see) the needles which pricked his fingers. It was to be a Masque Ball. Grandma was dressed as a fairy Queen, but grandfather would not reveal to her his costume. All evening at the ball Grandma hunted him, but could not find him. Being young and a good dancer, she had no lack of partners, but her husband was missing. At midnight they unmasked, when down from the stage came Foster; he had been playing first violin in the orchestra. With the aid of false whiskers and "plumpers" he had been entirely unrecognizable.

Mrs. Rose recounts another story, one which shows something of Stephen's kindly nature. This occurred, according to Jane, shortly after she and Stephen first went to New

4 In the article, "My Grandmother's Memories," op. cit.

York, and were living at a boarding house. The incident
occurred at the dinner table.

According to custom, the whole meal except dessert was on the
table. The pièce-de-résistance being of course, the fowl, or roast,
or steak. In this particular boarding-house, the star boarder for a
number of years had been a tall, gaunt Episcopal minister, very
courteous, gentle and humble in his mien. He occupied the end seat
at table, and did the carving. So thoughtful and generous to others
was this kindly man, that after he had bountifully helped the rest
at table, it generally fell to his lot to enjoy the neck of the fowl or a
tough end of steak. After this had gone on for several weeks, so
enraged was my grandfather at the penuriousness of the boarding
house mistress, who by cutting corners so closely, allowed this sort
of thing to continue, that he refused to stay any longer and witness
the daily sacrifice of this *too* Christian gentleman.

It is probable that Stephen and Jane, with little Marion,
boarded during most of the time they lived together in New
York. We shall find later that the location of at least one
of these boarding places may be partially verified. According to what Mrs. Rose has told me, however, there was at
least a period when the Fosters kept house in New York.
It may have been during this time that an episode occurred
which was told me verbally; when Stephen, in the habit
of being away from home for several days at a time, finally
returned to his wife and child. It was late at night, and
Jane and whoever was staying with her heard a picking at
the lock of one of the front windows. They were intensely
frightened, thinking a burglar was trying to gain entrance.
The intruder proved to be the unfortunate Stephen, mis-
taking the window for a door.

Mrs. Rose, in her memories of what her grandmother
told her, recounts a pathetic story which may be substanti-
ated by Jane's letter to Morrison, thanking him for the
clothes he had given Stephen.

In the latter days of his life, when he had become quite careless
in his garb, and indifferent to the world's opinion, his brother Morrison often tried to inject new ambition into his world-weary heart.

"Steve," he said one day, "why do you go around looking so careless and unkempt? If I went around like that, I would be afraid of being insulted." Raising his head, and looking wearily at his brother, he replied, "Mitty, don't worry so about me. No gentleman will insult me, and no other can."

4

One of the first of the more lurid articles containing reminiscences of Foster was that written by George W. Birdseye, previously quoted in these pages.[5] In various forms this article appeared in many magazines and some of its apparent exaggerations have contributed to the various legends surrounding Stephen's career. Birdseye's writings on Foster seem first to have been printed in two installments of the *New York Musical Gazette* (January, 1867, and March, 1867) and simultaneously in the *Western Musical World*. Twelve years later, January, 1879, the article was reprinted in abbreviated form in *Potter's American Monthly*.

Morrison evidently did not believe that Birdseye had even known Stephen, for on the margin of a clipping of one of Birdseye's articles among Morrison's papers is this pencilled comment: "This fellow is evidently a fraud. M. F." Yet it is apparent that Birdseye was at least acquainted with Stephen, for what appears to be the only letter in existence that Stephen wrote in these years was addressed to Birdseye.[6]

N. Y., Feb. 11, 1863

DEAR SIR:

I will arrange Mr. Cooper's melody when my hand gets well.

Very Respectfully Yours,

S. C. FOSTER.

G. W. Birdseye, Esq.

[5] See page 208.
[6] From a manuscript, in Stephen's handwriting, now at Foster Hall, it is apparent also that Stephen set to music a poem by Birdseye, "Down by the Gate." Foster's setting was evidently not published.

This is rather a formal note to one who claimed to be on such intimate terms with Stephen. If the first-hand account of his friendship with Foster is as inaccurate as the other facts regarding the song-writer in his article, much that Birdseye tells can be discounted. These "reminiscences" show, however, where many of the traditions regarding Stephen have come from.

So that the reader may judge for himself the accuracy of Birdseye's narrative, I give in full those passages which relate to his personal knowledge of Foster. This version of the article is the one that appeared in the *Western Musical World,* issue of January, 1867.

It was my pleasure, a somewhat sad one it must be confessed, to be personally acquainted with Stephen C. Foster during the last year of his brief existence. It was in the latter part of the year 1862 that I saw him for the first time; and his appearance was so very different from what I had anticipated, that I was, to say the least, disappointed. The occasion is still fresh in my memory. "I was introduced to Foster, the composer, last night," said a friend to me; "would you like to know him?" I had for a long time desired such an opportunity, and signified as much; while the songs I had loved from my very babyhood, almost all associated with Foster's name, bubbled up from my heart, and murmured in my ear, and I already imagined myself before a hale, merry old man, with long white hair, his head bald at the top, and a kindly smile ever upon his lips—the man for whom I had long felt a sort of reverence. Talking of him and his melodies, we walked some distance down the Bowery, and turned into Hester Street. On the north-west corner of Christie and Hester streets stands an old tumble-down Dutch grocery, and into this we entered. I followed my friend into the dingy bar-room at the back of the store, and a moment afterward was introduced to Stephen C. Foster. Let me briefly describe him as he then appeared to me. A figure slight, and a little below the medium stature, appareled in clothing so well worn as to betoken "the seedy gentleman who had seen better days"; his face long and closely shaven; the mouth of Silenus; soft brown eyes, somewhat dimmed by dissipation, shaded by

"Downfalling eyelids, full of dreams and slumber";

a rather high forehead, disfigured by the peak of an old glazed cap that hung closely to his head, scarcely allowing his short-cut brown hair to be seen. His appearance was at once so youthful and so aged, that it was difficult to determine at a casual glance if he were twenty years old or fifty. An anxious, startled expression hovered over his face that was painful to witness. It was hard for me to force myself to believe that that poor, wretched-looking object was at that moment the most popular song-composer in the world; but it was Foster indeed! He seemed as embarrassed as a child in the presence of a stranger, and this diffidence never entirely wore off. As I afterward discovered, he would walk, talk, eat and drink with you, and yet always seem distant, maintaining an awkward dignity, if I may so term it. Whether it was a natural bashfulness, or a voluntary reserve, I cannot say, but those who knew him most intimately were never familiar. His conversation, made up mostly of musical reminiscences, was profitable as well as interesting; and at his kind and pressing invitation, I took many an opportunity to visit him. He slept in an old lodging-house in the Bowery as a general thing; but that dark grocery bar-room was for a long time his sole head-quarters, and many an exquisite melody has had its birth in that uncongenial place. In his latter years he seldom wrote, unless he found himself without means to indulge his insatiable appetite for liquor. At such a time I have seen him take a sheet of brown wrapping-paper from the counter, and, seating himself at a little drinking-table, or more probably a bean-box, rapidly dot down a few bars of some sweet air that had been haunting him perhaps for many days, meantime whistling over and over again, modifying it until he felt satisfied. Then would follow simple, liquid words, appropriate in sentiment —then a few more bars of melody—then more words, and thus music and words would develop themselves together, and form literally "one harmonious whole." He was not one to haggle about the price when selling his songs; and it was not seldom, in consequence, that a publisher would take advantage of his miserable condition, paying him a paltry sum for what other composers would demand and receive fair compensation. It may be that such small transactions were deemed to be all for his good, in order not to minister to his well known passion for drink, and not for any pecuniary profit to his publishers; it is at least charitable to believe so. Some petty meannesses, however, he could not forget. He entered the store of one of his Broadway publishers, one evening, and asked him personally for a few copies of one of his songs ("Why have my loved ones gone?" if I remember rightly),[7] as he had opportunity to dispose of them. They were refused him, and he left the store with the tears rolling down his cheeks, for he was very sensitive, and weeping came to him far more easily than smiling.

Birdseye then tells of Foster's early years, and his writing for minstrel performers. He also spoke of the serenading parties in Pittsburgh and Allegheny.

Stephen's voice was then clear and beautiful in tone, and of course he became quite a leading spirit in serenading expeditions; and in these his own songs were always the favorites. He sometimes said that he believed that it was in these parties, and the feelings of social good-fellowship generated by them, that the germs of his love for strong drink were first planted, to be the bane of his whole future existence.

This is followed by a somewhat garbled account of the first singing of "Oh! Susanna," and its publication by Peters, and then a statement that "Hard Times Come Again No More" sprang from a "Methodist" camp meeting. In regard to this song, Birdseye continues:

. . . on more than one occasion, in that self-same grocery barroom, I have heard him sing that good old song of his, with a pathos that a state of semi-inebriation often lends the voice; while his pockets were in the peculiarly appropriate condition of emptiness not unusual to them, and the forlorn-looking habitués of the place joined dismally in the chorus.

In his second article Birdseye tells some of the circumstances of Stephen's death, an account which does not tally with known facts. In the foregoing narrative it is apparent that the author is going the limit, and making the most of the picturesque phases of his story, particularly of those phases which are drab and ugly. It is evident, too, that he does not let cold facts interfere with his journalistic instinct. Yet, while exaggeration is no doubt part of Birdseye's method, the story he tells is not altogether made of whole cloth. There are undeniably elements of truth in it, even

[7] This song was copyrighted by Horace Waters, August 5, 1861.

though he has made it difficult for the later historian to distinguish between fact and fancy.

5

Robert Peebles Nevin had the following to say about Stephen's habit of drink.[8]

His disposition was naturally amiable, although, from the tax imposed by close application to study upon his nervous system, he was liable to fits of fretfulness and scepticism that, only occasional and transient as they were, told nevertheless with disturbing effect upon his temper. In the same unfortunate direction was the tendency of a habit grown insidiously upon him—a habit against the damning control of which (as no one better than the writer of this article knows) he wrestled with an earnestness indescribable, resorting to all the remedial expedients which professional skill or his own experience could suggest, but never entirely delivering himself from its inexorable mastery.

When Milligan gathered the data for his biography of Foster,[9] it was his good fortune to find George Cooper, then an old man, but one who in his younger days had been one of Stephen's companions in New York.[10] It was Cooper who was closest to Stephen at the time of his death, and it was he who collaborated with Foster as the author of the words of many of his last songs.

Cooper also spoke of the grocery store at Hester and Christie Streets, for, like Birdseye, he said that he met Foster there. Milligan writes in his book:

George Cooper tells of meeting Stephen Foster in the back-room of a disreputable grocery on the corner of Hester and Christie Streets. According to the custom of that time, the front of the shop was devoted to the sale of groceries, but back of the partition was a small room which was used as a saloon, and here Stephen spent much of his time. Mr. Cooper describes him as a man utterly care-

---

[8] In "Stephen C. Foster and Negro Minstrelsy," *The Atlantic Monthly,* November, 1867.

[9] *Op. cit.*

[10] Cooper lived until September, 1927.

less of his appearance, having apparently lost the incentive power of self-respect. He lived at 15 Bowery, in a cheap lodging-house where he paid 25 cents a night. He told Mr. Cooper that he had had a regular income of $1,500 a year from his songs [we know this to be approximately correct], and Mr. Cooper is under the impression that, although in destitution himself, he was at this time supporting his wife and daughter in Pittsburgh. He was very fond of the poetry of Edgar Allan Poe, and recited long extracts from it with thrilling effect.

Young Mr. Cooper was something of a poet, and the two formed a partnership. The first of the songs of which Cooper wrote the words was published in 1863 [11] and in less than a year they wrote and published eighteen. [There were twenty-three on which Cooper and Foster collaborated—1 copyrighted in 1862, 14 in 1863, and the rest after Foster's death: 5 in 1864, 1 in 1866, 1 in 1869 and an adaptation in 1870.] These songs they sold for whatever they could get for them, which was never much. The song "Willie Has Gone to the War" was written one morning, and after it was finished, Stephen rolled it up and tucking it under his arm, said, "Well, where shall we put this one?" Cooper says that he remembers it was a cold, raw, winter day, snow falling drearily, and the pavements covered with slush. Stephen's shoes had holes in them and he had no overcoat, but he seemed oblivious to discomfort and misery. As the author and composer proceeded up Broadway, they passed Wood's Music Hall, and the proprietor, standing in the lobby, hailed them as they passed with the question, "What have you got there, Steve?" The song was sold then and there, Wood paying $10 cash, $15 more to be paid at the box-office that evening.

This incident may be partially verified by the fact that "Willie Has Gone to the War" was published by William A. Pond & Company (successors to Firth, Pond & Company) as "Composed for and Sung by Wood's Minstrels, 514 Broadway, New York." Cooper said the song was composed in the Winter; it was entered for copyright July 1, 1863, which may indicate that the Cooper-Foster songs were sung in the music halls for some time before they were published. This theory may explain also some

---

[11] This may not be accurate—"There Are Plenty of Fish in the Sea," the first known Foster song to which Cooper wrote the words, was marked "Copyright, 1862."

of the confusion that is apparent in the numbering of the various song titles on the covers of the sheet music, and the order in which the corresponding songs were actually copyrighted.

Milligan continues his account of Stephen's association with George Cooper.

Stephen called Cooper "the left wing of the song factory," and most of their songs were written and sold in very much the same manner as "Willie Has Gone to the War." They sold all of their songs for cash, receiving no royalties on any of them. This was not important to Cooper, who was a youth of about twenty, and song-writing was something of a pastime for him, but to Stephen, entirely dependent upon his songs for livelihood, it meant destitution. His clothes were poor and sadly worn, a fact to which he seemed totally indifferent. Cooper says that on several occasions friends gave him clothes, but usually Stephen appeared again after a few days in his ragged suit and glazed cap. This cap seems to have been an out-standing feature of his appearance in these last days, as it is mentioned by several biographers. . . .

Although he drank constantly, Cooper says that Stephen was never intoxicated. He was indifferent to food, often making a meal of apples or turnips from the grocery shop, peeling them with a large pocket-knife. The "rum" he drank was concocted by the barkeeper from French spirits and brown sugar, and was kept in a keg.

He wrote with great facility and without the aid of a piano. If no music-paper was handy, he would take whatever paper he could find, and ruling the lines on it, proceed without hesitation to write. He seemed never at a loss for a melody, and the simple accompaniment caused him no trouble. These first drafts were taken out and sold to a publisher or theatre manager, practically without correction. To this habit is evidently due the "brown wrapping paper" legend, as Cooper says that he would use brown wrapping paper if he couldn't find anything else.

Milligan states that Cooper enlisted in the 22nd New York Regiment in 1862, and served in the Civil War, in-cluding the Gettysburg campaign, until his return to New York when the regiment disbanded, July 24, 1863. Inas-much as a number of the songs Stephen wrote with Cooper were published before July, 1863, it would appear that they worked together before Cooper enlisted.

It was Cooper, incidentally, who was later to achieve fame as the author of a song to which Henry Tucker composed the music—"Sweet Genevieve."

6

It is said that when Susan Pentland Robinson visited New York with her husband and son, Stephen called on her. Susan's son, John W. Robinson, told Milligan of his recollections of this visit. The Robinsons stayed at the St. Nicholas Hotel, 513 Broadway. John Robinson believed that the trip to New York occurred before the outbreak of the Civil War, late in 1860 or early in 1861, so it was probably soon after Stephen himself had come to the city.

According to the account, Susan's husband hunted up Stephen and brought him to the hotel for dinner. Afterwards they all went to Laura Keene's Theatre. Stephen was bright and entertaining, and seemingly in the best of health. No mention is made in the account of Jane or Marion. John Robinson, when he talked to Milligan, was under the impression that Stephen was making his living as a music-teacher. That, however, seems hardly possible.

Reference has already been made to an article of reminiscences written by John Mahon.[12] We will remember that it was Mahon who reported a conversation with Foster, in which the composer told him that he himself had written "Old Folks at Home," and that Christy had paid him $15 for allowing his name to appear as composer of the song.

This article by Mahon contains much information on Stephen during the years in New York, and because much of its data may be confirmed from contemporary sources, it probably offers the most reliable account of Stephen's last years in existence.

[12] In an article from the *New York Clipper* (March, 1877). See pages 199-200.

Mahon tells of meeting Foster in 1861, at "Windust's Restaurant in Park Row." The New York Directory of 1860/61 shows that Edward Windust had an "eating-house" at 11 Park Row. Mahon describes Stephen as "a short man, who was very neatly dressed in a blue swallow-tailed coat, high silk hat, and-so-forth (the and-so-forth I forget)."

I must say I found him most social and conversational. I took him to my residence and introduced him to my family, and nearly all of his latest songs were composed upon my piano. At that time he boarded at No. 83 Greene Street, with his wife and little daughter Marian, who was about eight years old. The boarding-house was kept by a Mr. & Mrs. Stewart.

Mahon is obviously a bit mistaken as to Marion's age, but not seriously so. The little girl's tenth birthday was April 18, 1861. The boarding place may be confirmed, but not with the spelling that Mahon has given, nor at the exact address. The address and the name, however, are close enough to indicate that Mahon's memory was essentially accurate. The 1859/60 New York Directory lists

Stuart—boardingh 113 Greene

The Directories for '61/'62 and '62/'63 contain no similar listings, but in the issue of '63/'64 there appears

Stuart Louisa boardingh 97 Greene

It is probable, then, that Stephen and his family went to Mrs. Stuart early during their stay in New York, and it may be that this was the place in which the boarding-house anecdote told by Mrs. Rose occurred.[13]

In his account of the conversation regarding "Old Folks at Home," [14] Mahon states that it occurred at his own apartments, "311 Henry Street." The New York Directories contain the following listings for Mahon:

---

[13] See pages 310-311.   [14] See pages 199-200.

1859/60	Mahon John	reporter	h[ouse]	256	Broome
1860/61	no listing				
1861/62	Mahon John	reporter	h	311	Henry
1862/63	Mahon John	reporter	h	22	Willett
1863/64	Mahon John	reporter	h	22	Willett
1864/65	Mahon John	reporter	h	135	Clinton [15]

After telling Mahon and his wife about "Old Folks at Home" and the royalties he had received on the song, Stephen is reported to have said:

Subsequently I sold out my royalties, and have now a contract to furnish Pond with twelve songs a year, for which I receive $800 per annum, payable monthly at $66.66, and I have permission to furnish six songs per annum to Lee & Walker of Philadelphia for $400, so my income is now $1200 per annum.

We shall find in a moment how accurately that statement may be checked from known data, but first we should learn what Mahon has to say about Stephen's subsequent dealings with publishers.

I now have come to a turn in the tide of poor Foster's life. I believe I have already stated that he wrote and composed most of his latest songs at my rooms, in Henry Street. One of these, and a most beautiful one, "Our Bright Summer Days Are Gone," he took to Pond, who refused it for some reason or other and it made him feel very despondent; for about this time Lee & Walker had ceased employing him in consequence of hard times. I was then "under the weather" myself, and I remember one evening when we were both pretty "hard up" indeed, neither of us had a cent, and I had a family besides, suddenly he sat down to the piano.

"John," he said, "I haven't time to write a new song, but I think I can write 'Our Bright Summer Days Are Gone' from memory."

"Take this round to Daly," he said, "and take what he will give you."

Mr. John J. Daly, now of 944 Eighth Avenue, was then my publisher, and was at 419 Grand Street. I took the song to Mr. Daly.

---

[15] Additional confirmation of the accuracy of Mahon's article may be found in his statement that in January, 1864, he was a patient in Bellevue Hospital, at the same time Foster died there. The register of Bellevue Hospital shows that John Mahon, "newspaper writer," was admitted January 7, 1864, and discharged the following May 16.

He was proud to get a song from Foster. He tried it over and it
was really beautiful. He offered a sum, which, though not a tithe
of what Foster got in his better days, was still considered very handsome; and this "stone which the builders (Pond & Co.) rejected" became very popular.

This story becomes credible when we know that not only
was John J. Daly at 419 Grand Street in these years, but
also that "Our Bright Summer Days Are Gone," entered
for copyright June 4, 1861, was the first of Stephen's songs
to be published by him. Why Firth, Pond & Company may
have rejected the song is not clear. It is by no means a
remarkable song, but it is no worse than many others of the
Firth, Pond publications, by Foster or by other composers.

7

Mahon's statement about Stephen's contracts is interesting. We have no record to verify the agreement with
Firth, Pond & Company, calling for a salary of $800 per
year, for which Foster was to compose twelve songs annually. All we know is the number of songs the firm apparently published.

After August 9, 1860, when the existing contract expired
and Stephen settled his accounts with the publishers assign-
ing his royalty interest in all previous works, Firth, Pond &
Company issued the following songs:

1860

Copyrighted Nov. 8—Old Black Joe
Copyrighted Nov. 15—Down Among the Canebrakes
Copyrighted Nov. 15—Virginia Belle

1861

Copyrighted Mar. 9—Don't Bet Your Money on de Shanghai
Copyrighted Apr. 6—Molly Dear, Good Night
Copyrighted May 9—Our Willie Dear is Dying
Copyrighted Oct. 16—Farewell Sweet Mother

1862

Copyrighted Apr. 29—That's What's the Matter
Copyrighted Sep. 10—I'll Be Home Tomorrow

Sometime during 1863 the firm of Firth, Pond & Company dissolved. Pond maintained the business at 547 Broadway as William A. Pond & Co., and Firth established himself as Firth, Son & Company at 563 Broadway. The previous Foster copyrights were divided among the two firms in a manner noted in the next chapter. During the remaining year of his life Foster published the following songs with the two houses:

1863

William A. Pond & Co.	Firth, Son & Co.
July 1—Willie Has Gone to the War	Apr. 17—Jenny June May 27—A Soldier in de Colored Brigade

Published Posthumously

William A. Pond & Co.	Firth, Son & Co.

1864

Mar. 10—Beautiful Dreamer	None

1865

Jan. 31—My Angel Boy, I Cannot See Thee Die Mar. 23—The Voices That Are Gone	None

1869

Apr. 10—Kiss Me Dear Mother	None

Whatever the agreement, or whatever may have happened to mar the relations between Foster and the firm that had been his principal publishers, it is evident that there were far less than twelve songs issued by Firth, Pond & Company during even the first year Stephen was in New York.

It is possible to find indirect evidence on the contract

with Lee & Walker of Philadelphia, which Mahon said called for a salary of $400 per year, and for which Stephen was to compose six songs. In his letter to Morrison,[16] April 27, 1860, Stephen wrote:

> . . . I have entered into an agreement with a new house for part of my music, but, as the terms are not entirely fixed, I cannot well draw on them just now. . . .

A clue to this "agreement" is furnished by an item that appeared in *Clark's School Visitor* after Foster's death, in the April, 1864, issue of this magazine.

STEPHEN C. FOSTER

This great American song-writer and composer is no more. He died in January, in New York. . . .

Our readers well remember his contributions to the *Visitor* in 1860-61. They have never been told, however, that for the six beautiful songs written for us by Mr. Foster, our publishers paid the sum of $400, or $66-2/3 apiece for the manuscripts. We mention this merely to show that we are not neglectful to procure the very best articles for every department of our paper.

The biographer of Foster may well be thankful for the *Visitor's* desire to receive full credit for its lavish expenditure; for the sum of $400 and the six songs establish a connection between the *Visitor* and Mahon's account.

Unfortunately only four issues of the *Visitor* containing Foster songs have come to light.

> Issue of October, 1860—Beautiful Child of Song [17]
> Issue of December, 1860—The Little Ballad Girl
> Issue of May, 1861—Lizzie Dies To-night
> Issue of May, 1862—The Merry, Merry Month of May

The third song, "Lizzie Dies To-night," was later issued in sheet music form by Horace Waters in New York, and

---

[16] See page 299.

[17] The month of issue, October, is an assumption. The page from the issue of the *Visitor* containing the song does not bear a date, but the copyright entry at the Library of Congress is dated October 6, 1860.

the fourth, "The Merry, Merry Month of May," was reprinted in 1862 by Oliver Ditson & Company of Boston. The fact that the other two songs from the *Visitor* were also reprinted by other publishers in sheet music form provides the clue to the connection between the $400 transaction and the Lee & Walker episode that Mahon spoke of. The two remaining songs published in the *Visitor* may be traced through reprints as follows:

JENNY'S COMING O'ER THE GREEN

"Ballad written and composed for Clark's School Visitor." Issued in sheet music form by Lee & Walker, and copyrighted by that firm July 21, 1860.

This would seem to indicate that Lee & Walker had some arrangement with the publishers of the *Visitor* (Daughaday & Hammond of Philadelphia) for reprinting in sheet music form the songs by Foster which were originally published in the magazine. The date of copyright of "Jenny's Coming O'er the Green," we have noted, was July 21, 1860. In his account of the sale of "Our Bright Summer Days Are Gone" to Daly, Mahon stated that "about this time Lee & Walker had ceased employing him [Stephen] because of hard times." The break with Lee & Walker must have occurred some time before June 4, 1861, for that was the date on which Daly entered "Bright Summer Days" for copyright.

"Jenny's Coming O'er the Green" was subsequently issued by Horace Waters, and it may be that this firm took over the publishing rights to the song. The history of Lee & Walker does not furnish much light on the situation. The firm was established in 1848 by Julius Lee and William Walker, both of whom had previously been employed by George Willig, the publisher of Stephen Foster's "Open Thy Lattice, Love." The firm of Lee & Walker continued in existence until 1875 or 1876, when its catalog was sold to Oliver Ditson in Boston.

It may be that the hard times at the outbreak of the Civil War made it impossible for Lee & Walker to continue their arrangements to reprint the songs of Foster that appeared in the *Visitor*. At any rate, here is the form in which the remaining song from the magazine was published as sheet music:

MINE IS THE MOURNING HEART

"A duett . . . written and composed expressly for Clark's School Visitor & dedicated to Rev. Alexander Clark"

Copyright Feb. 1, 1861, by Daughaday & Hammond, and issued in sheet music form by Root & Cady, Chicago.[18]

8

Stephen was prolific after he came to New York. He turned out more songs than he had ever published before; more than half of his works were issued after July of 1860. According to present knowledge, one hundred and five new songs were issued during these years—six in the last half of 1860, fifteen in 1861, seventeen in 1862, forty-six in 1863, and twenty-one published after Stephen's death.[19] There was also a number of adaptations of earlier songs, such as "While the Bowl Goes Round" to the same music that was used for "Jenny June." Mr. Lilly of Foster Hall has coined a term for such items which has already passed

[18] In his article in the *New York Clipper* (*op. cit.*), Mahon speaks of a duet called "The Mourning Heart" as one of the songs "composed for Lee & Walker." This seems to be added confirmation that there was some connection between Lee & Walker and Daughaday & Hammond.

[19] Omitted from this number are works posthumously published which are known to have been composed a number of years before Foster's death, viz.:

"The Tioga Waltz," composed about 1841, published in 1896.

"Where is Thy Spirit, Mary?", presumably composed in 1847, published in 1895.

"Long Ago Day" and "This Rose Will Remind You," apparently composed before 1851, published in 1931.

"The White House Chair," composed in 1856, published in 1885.

into the lexicon of Foster collectors—"Derivata Fosteriana."

There were both a cause and an effect of Stephen's musical fecundity in his last years. Most important, he needed cash, and there were plenty of publishers who were anxious to get anything he would write, so long as it bore his name, especially as they did not have to pay much for it. That was the cause. The effect was that Stephen wrote very little that was worth preserving after he came to New York.

It has already been noted that several songs published after Stephen left Pittsburgh are found in the manuscript book, which may indicate that they were written before he came to New York. Here is a list of the songs, showing the pages of the book on which they appear.

Pages in Mss. Book	Title of Song	Date of Copyright
202-203	Virginia Belle	Nov. 15, 1860
204-205	Old Black Joe	Nov. 8, 1860
206-207	Down Among the Cane Brakes	Nov. 15, 1860
208-209-210-211	Molly Dear, Good Night	Apr. 6, 1861
212-213 223-226	The Merry, Merry Month of May	? 1862
216-218	Our Bright Summer Days Are Gone	June 4, 1861
220	Our Willie Dear Is Dying	May 9, 1861

It is interesting to note that "Our Bright Summer Days Are Gone," the song Stephen sold to Daly, may have originally been written in Pittsburgh.

After Stephen broke with Firth, Pond & Company, he issued few more songs with either that firm or its successors. We have already noted the exact number of works he either gave them, or they accepted.[20] He began from that time to publish songs with a miscellany of publishing houses, whose very obscurity to the music lover of to-day has made

[20] See pages 322-323.

the hunting and collecting of Foster first editions both an exasperating and fascinating pastime. Thanks to the pioneer work of W. R. Whittlesey and O. G. Sonneck,[21] and the subsequent research of Foster Hall in Indianapolis, we have what seems to be a complete record of what Stephen wrote, and where it was published.

The full list of Foster's works during this period would merely serve to block our narrative at this point. The names of the songs may all be found chronologically listed in the appendix, but the quantity that Stephen composed and the publishers he dealt with belong to our story. With John J. Daly Stephen published sixteen; twelve were issued while he was living, four after his death. Starting with "Why Have My Loved Ones Gone?", August 5, 1861, Stephen published forty-seven songs with Horace Waters of New York, five of them issued after the composer's death.

The firm of Horace Waters & Company is still in existence, but only as piano merchants, not as music publishers. Horace Waters the elder, the founder of the firm, first came to New York in 1849 as an agent for a Boston piano manufacturer. In 1858 he started to publish hymn-books, the first of them "The Sabbath School Bell," which was so successful that it enabled Waters to pay off the many debts that still troubled him, even though he had been discharged from bankruptcy three years before. From that time until 1867, when he sold his sheet music catalog to one of his clerks, C. M. Tremaine, his publishing business was indeed prosperous.

Waters was intensely religious, one of the original members of the Prohibition Party, and an ardent anti-slavery man. C. M. Tremaine and his brother, William, were singers. With some other relatives they formed the Tremaine Family, which became a highly popular concert at-

[21] Published in *Catalogue of First Editions of Stephen C. Foster*, Library of Congress, 1915.

traction in those days. Later William Tremaine and his son Henry formed the Æolian Company, and the son of Charles Tremaine, himself named Charles Milton, is now the director of the National Bureau for the Advancement of Music. Stephen dedicated "Why Have My Loved Ones Gone?" to the Tremaine Family—the first song of his that Waters published.

Many of the Foster songs published by Waters were hymns and Sunday School songs. They were issued chiefly in the collections that Waters printed. On April 14, 1863, the "Golden Harp" appeared, a little oblong song book containing ten new songs by Stephen. Later in the same year came the "Athenæum Collection," to which Foster contributed ten new songs. How successful these books were may not be known to-day. Copies are exceedingly scarce, however, and are considered rare treasures by collectors of Foster items, solely because they contain so many of the songs in their first edition.

9

These hymns by Stephen are almost worthless musically. Written probably to order, they are obviously pot-boilers which the composer tossed off hastily, thinking chiefly of the few dollars they would bring him. And most of the other songs he wrote in these last years are of the same quality—particularly the Civil War songs. When the War broke out, Stephen, formerly a Democrat and not an Abolitionist, kept his sympathies for the Union cause, even though his political principles were against the Administration of the Republicans.[22]

Consequently he wrote many songs for the Northern side, some of them composed to words by others. One was a setting of James Sloane Gibbons' "We Are Coming

[22] In 1863, Stephen composed the music for a poem by his sister Henrietta—"Sound the Rally," verses written for the Ohio Democratic campaign for governor. Stephen's music is apparently not in existence to-day.

Father Abraam, 300,000 More," verses which were in error attributed to William Cullen Bryant, and for which several other composers wrote music. Another Foster song was called "We've a Million in the Field," and there were a number of the sentimental type—"Was My Brother in the Battle?", "When This Dreadful War is Ended," and others of their kind.

There were other publishers than Daly and Waters whom Stephen dealt with. S. T. Gordon issued eleven Foster songs; P. A. Wundermann, two published after Foster's death; D. S. Holmes of Brooklyn, two, one of them posthumously; C. M. Tremaine, two issued after Foster's death (these were probably originally sold to Waters); J. Marsh of Philadelphia, one (posthumously published). Also issued after Stephen's death were two songs that appeared in magazines, one in *Holloway's Musical Monthly* and the other in *Demorest's Magazine*. There was also printed in *Demorest's Illustrated Monthly* a song published in 1865 —"Our Darling Kate, words and melody by John Mahon, Music arranged for the piano by the late Stephen Foster."

Mahon referred to this song in his article in the *New York Clipper*.[23]

> Perhaps the last music he ever wrote was the piano accompaniments to a piece of mine called "Our Darling Kate," which was written (words and music) for the late Miss Kate Newton. The circumstances under which he requested me to let him arrange the accompaniment were very painful indeed. He was suffering from sheer want at the time; and although I offered him money for what he wanted (a bed at the New England Hotel, where he was seized with the illness which proved unexpectedly fatal), he refused it unless I would let him arrange the song, which I gladly did. Madam Demorest, the celebrated *modiste,* paid me a handsome sum for it, and published it in her magazine for March, 1865.

This episode, like most of Mahon's statements, is confirmed by documentary evidence. It is apparent that

[23] *Op. cit.*

"Madam Demorest" also considered the sum she paid "handsome," for when the song appeared in the magazine it was accompanied by this paragraph:

The arrangement of this melody was the last musical effort of Stephen Collins Foster, and the value placed upon it by its owner as a relic and favorite work of the late eminent composer rendered the securing of it exclusively for the *Illustrated Monthly* a costly affair.

The collaboration with George Cooper produced little that was worthy of Stephen's talents in early years. Some of the songs to which Cooper wrote the words were sentimental ballads, and many of them were "comic" songs, which dealt chiefly with topics of contemporary interest, or else embodied such trifles as "Mr. & Mrs. Brown," or "If You've Only Got a Moustache." Stephen had himself been a better comedian when he made no attempt at sophistication but abandoned himself to the naïve foolishness of "Oh! Susanna" and "De Camptown Races."

Milligan has pointed out that Stephen seemed to have no difficulty in finding a melody when he was writing so many songs, but that he invariably fell into an accustomed pattern and became repetitious. This is where we find the great tragedy of Stephen Foster, his inability to develop his musical ideas. If he had been a trained musician, he could at least have done something to cloak the sterility of his talent when it began to wane, for he would have had the inventiveness to make something of little. If all of our great composers had been forced to conceive basic ideas as vital and compelling as the few phrases of "Old Folks at Home" or "My Old Kentucky Home" whenever they created works of lasting merit, we would have far fewer masterpieces in musical literature to-day.

After "Old Black Joe" there is only one song that suggests the melodic power of the earlier Stephen Foster—

"Beautiful Dreamer," copyrighted several weeks after the composer's death, March 10, 1864. And even this sentimentalizes in a bit more saccharine fashion than the best of the Foster songs. Its nine-eight, waltz-like rhythm does not have the dignity of "Come Where My Love Lies Dreaming," nor the melodic chastity of the earlier song. It smacks somewhat of the idiom of Irving Berlin.

"Beautiful Dreamer" was published by William A. Pond & Company as "the last song ever written by Stephen C. Foster. Composed but a few days before his death." This statement is interesting when we consult the first edition of "Willie Has Gone to the War," the song Cooper said he and Stephen sold to Wood's Minstrels. William A. Pond & Company copyrighted this "Willie" song July 1, 1863, and announced on the title-page that its music was "composed by Stephen C. Foster, *author of Beautiful Dreamer, Come Where My Love Lies Dreaming, &c. &c.*" [24]

Here is another puzzle that Foster collectors are trying to solve. We shall learn, too, that there were a number of "last" songs by Stephen Foster.

10

Among the recollections of Foster in his last years are those of Mrs. Parkhurst Duer, published as an article in *The Étude*.[25] Mrs. Duer was employed in the music store of Horace Waters, and it was there that she first met Stephen. While these reminiscences were written many years later, and the author's memory seems to be confused

[24] It is worthy of note that although "Beautiful Dreamer" was not entered for copyright until March 10, 1864, the copyright line under the first page of music in the first edition of the song reads: "Entered . . . A.D. 1662." This undoubtedly was intended to read "1862," and, if so, it may indicate that the song was not only written but that its plates were engraved before "Willie Has Gone to the War" was copyrighted July 1, 1863. The assumption would then be that "Beautiful Dreamer" was not actually issued, nor entered for copyright until 1864.

[25] "Personal Recollections of the Last Days of Foster," *The Étude*, September, 1916.

on a number of details, it appears that her story gives a reasonably faithful picture of Foster during his last days.

All that this writer knows of Stephen Foster's early days was heard from his own lips, when his troubled existence was drawing to its close. He told of the wrongs he had suffered, of the temptations thrown around him during his years of prosperity and popularity, until all he possessed was gone. With a broken heart, crushed spirit, health destroyed, nerves shattered, he broke away from old associations, and secluded himself, hoping to regain his health, and position in the world. Nobly he struggled to conquer his foe, the "wine cup," by which means, evil companions had sought his ruin. . . .

I shall never forget the day I met him. I was engaged in a large music publishing house on Broadway, New York City, leading a very busy life, although but twenty-one years of age. Every day I met teachers and composers, and was ever hoping Stephen Foster would appear. I had heard that he was living in New York but had never known anything about his life; yet his songs had created in me a feeling of reverence for the man, and I longed to see him. One day I was speaking with the clerks, when the door opened, and a poorly dressed, very dejected man came in, and leaned against the counter near the door, I noticed he looked ill and weak. No one spoke to him. A clerk laughed and said:

"Steve looks down and out."

Then they all laughed, and the poor man saw them laughing at him. I said to myself, "who can Steve be?" It seemed to me, my heart stood still. I asked, "who is that man?"

"Stephen Foster," the clerk replied. "He is only a vagabond, don't go near him."

"Yes, I will go near him, that man needs a friend," was my reply.

I was terribly shocked. Forcing back the tears, I waited for that lump in the throat which prevents speech, to clear away. I walked over to him, put out my hand, and asked, "Is this Mr. Foster?"

He took my hand and replied:

"Yes, the wreck of Stephen Collins Foster."

"Oh, no," I answered, "not a wreck, but whatever you call yourself, I feel it an honor to take by the hand, the author of *Old Folks at Home,* I am glad to know you." As I spoke, the tears came to his eyes, and he said:

"Pardon my tears, young lady, you have spoken the first kind words I have heard in a long time. God bless you." I gave him both hands, saying:

"They will not be the last." I asked him to sit at my desk awhile, and get acquainted. (He seemed pleased, but apologized for his appearance. He was assured it was not his dress, but Mr. Foster I wanted to see.) I judged him to be about forty-five years of age, but the lines of care upon his face, and the stamp of disease, gave him that appearance. We had a long conversation. (I told him of the effect his music had upon me, since my childhood, and how I had longed to know him.) He opened his heart to me, and gave me an insight of his true character, which greatly increased my admiration, but which cannot be repeated in a writing of this length. Stephen Foster was a man of culture and refinement. . . .

When this first visit was ended, Mr. Foster thanked me for my interest in him, and said it had done him a world of good to have some one to talk with. He had no one to call a friend. I asked him to let me be a friend, and perhaps in my humble way, I might be of service to him. I said if he would bring me the manuscript songs that he had not been able to write out, I would do the work for him at his dictation. He was very grateful, and from that time until he died I was permitted to be his helper. Out of respect for my efforts to aid Mr. Foster, all the men in the store treated him kindly. He was made welcome, and no one laughed at him. They were convinced he was no vagabond, and no drunkard. He was poor; disease brought poverty; he had been unable to write, and soon his personal appearance caused him to be misjudged. No hand was stretched out to rescue him in a great Christian community. I dared not question him concerning his comforts in life, or how he existed, but I was confident he needed help, yet how to aid without humiliating him was a study.

When he brought me his rude sketches, written on wrapping paper, picked up in a grocery store, and he told me he wrote them while sitting upon a box or barrel, I knew he had no home. I asked him if he had a room; he said:

"No—I do not write much, as I have no material or conveniences." He then told me that he slept in the cellar room of a little house, owned by an old couple, down in Elizabeth Street in the "Five Points," who knew who he was, and charged him nothing. He said he was comfortable, so I suppose he had a bed. Then I told him that unless he had the right kind of food, he could not be restored to health, and a kind manager of a nearby restaurant had arranged to provide him with a hearty dinner every day, and he need not pay for anything until he was able to do business, and a friend had sent him some medicine which he must take. He looked at me for a moment and that fervent "God bless you," paid for all the planning. It was an easy matter to provide other necessary comforts, to be paid for when he recovered his health. We who were near him had no hope of his recovery, but the few comforts provided lessened the suffering of a dying man. This messenger of song, God had given to the world, was not appreciated, and when overtaken by misfortune, was treated as other great souls in the past, left to die, forsaken by a nation he had blessed by his living.

One day Mr. Foster came to my desk with the sketch of a song entitled *When old friends were here*. He remarked it might be his last song, and that would be the end of "Foster." Like an inspiration came an impression to my mind, yet in a joking way I said:

"Mr. Foster, I am not a prophet, but I will tell you now, that fifty years hence monuments will be erected to Stephen Collins Foster all over this nation. You will be called the author of 'American Folk Song,' and your songs will live forever."

He laughed at the idea, but to-day the monuments are appearing, and during the past few years there has been a Foster revival throughout the United States. As Mr. Foster prepared to leave the store, it was growing dark, and as he appeared weaker than usual, I offered to go with him to the street, as I helped him into the stage, he said very earnestly "you are my only friend," and as the door closed he waved his hand, and the last words I heard were "God bless you." I am sure they were his last words on earth. . . .

The next day he did not call for his song, but the evening paper appeared with a great headline, "Stephen C. Foster, dead." "At eleven o'clock last night"—the paper stated—a policeman heard groans, in the cellar of a house he was passing, and upon entering found a man bleeding to death, from a gash in the throat. He had evidently arisen from his bed for some water, and had fallen over a broken pitcher. He was taken to Bellevue Hospital in an unconscious condition, and passed away at one o'clock. He was identified by a manuscript in his pocket with his name upon it. Relatives in Pennsylvania claimed the remains. Nothing more concerning his death was published.

II

It is obvious that there are a number of embellishments in Mrs. Duer's account, even though she herself believed she was writing accurately. The intervening years had no doubt lent color to the facts as she recalled them. As far as the song "When Old Friends Were Here" is concerned, this was actually one of Stephen's last works, and was one of those published by Waters after the composer's death, having been entered for copyright with three other songs by Foster, January 23, 1864.

Of the accuracy of the cellar room on Elizabeth Street we cannot know to-day. The grocery store and the brown wrapping paper that Mrs. Duer introduces into her narrative may lend weight to the Birdseye and Cooper testimony, or it may be that Mrs. Duer had herself read the Birdseye article in one of its early printings, and years later, when she came to write her own reminiscences, thought that she knew of these adjuncts at first hand.

In regard to Stephen's shabbiness in his last years, the photograph of Stephen and George Cooper seems a contradiction of the belief that he always appeared in worn and threadbare clothing. This picture is said to have been taken late in 1863 or early in January, 1864, shortly before Stephen's death. It may be that the frock coat was borrowed for the occasion,[26] but surely there is no evidence in this picture to show that Stephen, a vagabond, was totally a wreck, or a creature utterly abandoned. His carriage is erect, and if, as has often been said, his self-esteem was gone, Stephen was at least a good enough actor to assume the appearance of self-respect while his picture was being taken. Photographers were not as expert in those days as they are to-day in retouching photographs.

While the picture may not show Stephen as actually robust, it certainly does not indicate that he was in the last stages of any disease. Mrs. Duer's references to Foster's ill-health are important, however, for they may throw some light on the theory that Stephen suffered from tuberculosis. We shall find that there are further references to the "fever

[26] Cooper, on one occasion, told H. V. Milligan that he had given clothes to Foster.

Stephen Foster

From an ambrotype taken probably in 1859

Foster Hall Collection

Stephen Foster and George Cooper

From an ambrotype taken shortly before Foster's death

and ague" that troubled him, and while such a malady
would seem to indicate a recurring malaria, it is not impossible that they were evidence of tubercular symptoms.
Such an ailment would weaken his resistance to his crav-
ing for drink, and increase his dependence on alcoholic
stimulant.

It is in her account of Stephen's death that Mrs. Duer
leaves facts entirely behind her. The events of Foster's last
days may be documented by contemporary evidence, and
she was obviously writing from a somewhat confused memory in relating this part of the story. It is not possible that
she could have put Stephen on the bus, or stage, one evening
and read of his death the next night, for three days elapsed
between Stephen's accident and his death. Nor is it likely
that there were "great headlines in the newspapers." My
own search of newspaper files has not revealed any account
headed "Stephen C. Foster Dead," or one which tells of a
policeman hearing groans in the cellar of a house he was
passing "at eleven o'clock last night." The *New York Evening Post* printed an obituary article of considerable length,
but not until several days after Foster's funeral, in the issue
of January 26, 1864. This was largely biographical, with
no details of what had caused Stephen's death. The Pittsburgh newspapers ran accounts of the funeral services, and
news of his passing reached musical journals abroad as well
as in America. But I have found no article such as Mrs.
Duer describes.

12

It is in their accounts of Stephen's death that the various
narratives become most garbled. Morrison Foster, in his
biography of Stephen,[27] told the story simply and plainly,
and probably accurately as far as he cared to tell it.

In January 1864, while at the American Hotel, he was taken with
an ague and fever. After two or three days he arose, and while wash-

[27] *Op. cit.*

ing himself fainted and fell across the wash basin, which broke and cut a gash in his neck and face. He lay there insensible and bleeding until discovered by the chambermaid who was bringing the towels he had asked for to the room. She called for assistance and he was placed in bed again. On recovering his senses he asked that he be sent to a hospital. Accordingly he was taken to Bellevue Hospital. He was so much weakened by fever and loss of blood that he did not rally. On the 13th of January he died peacefully and quietly. Under request of his family his body was immediately taken to an undertaker's, by direction of Col. William A. Pond, and placed in an iron coffin. On arrival of his brother, Henry Baldwin Foster, and myself, his remains were taken to Pittsburgh, accompanied by his wife. The Pennsylvania Railroad Company carried the party free of charge, and the Adams Express Company declined to receive pay for transporting his body.

What is probably the most inaccurate account of Foster's accident and death that I have examined is that presented by C. A. Browne, in the book, "The Story of Our National Ballads." This is so patently incorrect that it is the duty of Foster's biographer to contradict its statements with actual evidence. The author has stated in private correspondence that the information was derived largely from letters of the late Harry Houdini, the famous magician.[28] Browne first recounts an anecdote that is supposed to have occurred a few months earlier, and which may be true.

Brickett Clarke, a newspaper man, who knew Foster well, recalls a unique experience which happened about the middle of June, 1863, at the time of the Wheeling Convention, in which forty counties of Virginia repudiated secession and applied for admission to the Union. The day following the event Clarke was seated with Stephen Foster and Daniel Decatur Emmett in the old Collamore House in New York, talking over war topics in general, when they saw through the window, a brigade on its way to the front, led by a band playing "I Wish I Were in Dixie."

"That is your song," said Foster.

"Yes," admitted Emmett.

[28] Most of this information was included in a letter by Houdini which appeared in *The Étude,* November 1916.

Presently another regiment went by, and the band was playing "Old Folks at Home."

"That's yours," rejoined Emmett.

There is no reason to quarrel with any one who tells that pretty story, but then the author comes to the account of Stephen's death.

For a time Clarke and Foster shared a room on the south side of Hester Street, New York City. On Mr. Clarke's return to his room one night (so the story goes) he found a letter telling him to come immediately to the American Hotel, as Foster was hurt. Hurrying there, he found the composer unconscious. In his weakened condition he had slipped, and in falling struck his head against the stove, fracturing his skull over the right temple. Clarke carried Foster to a four-wheeler and then took him to Bellevue Hospital. In the excitement of rushing out to send a wire to Dr. McDowell, Foster's father-in-law, he neglected to inform the hospital authorities that Foster was the composer and author, and this is why the record of the hospital states that "A Stephen Foster, 39 years of age, born in Pennsylvania, a laborer, was admitted to this hospital on January 8th, 1864, the diagnosis being injuries, accidentally received." The nature of the injuries was not stated. Clarke was faithful in visiting the sick man two or three times a day, until, on the morning of the thirteenth of January, he arrived to find that poor Stephen had passed away.

Where this transcript of the "record of the hospital" came from I do not know. The date of admittance is wrong, and Stephen was not entered as a "laborer." Here is what the hospital register actually said about Foster's stay in the hospital, entries copied from the 1864 volume of that register, still preserved at Bellevue Hospital.

First appear the initials "P.W.P.C.A." Mr. Louis Rothman, the present registrar of Bellevue, is not certain of exactly what these letters indicate. He thinks that they may show that the patient was brought in some sort of public conveyance. "P.W.P." might have meant "police patrol wagon." In those days there were no ambulances; these were an outgrowth of the Civil War. Initials appear before the names of all those who were unable to come to the hospital themselves, and some of these cases were initialed "pr." or marked by the full word "private," which would seem to indicate a private rather than a public vehicle as the means of being brought to the hospital.

The next item in Foster's entry was the date of admission—"Jan. 10, 1864," not January 8, as Browne stated. Then came the name, misspelled—"Forster Stephen." After this, under the proper columns, Age "39" (which was of course incorrect—he was in his thirty-eighth year), Nativity, "Penna," and under the column headed "Time," the initials "NB." Mr. Rothman states that this meant "native born." The next column is headed "Occupation," under which we find written "Composer." This seems to put the "laborer" tradition forever at rest!

Under the heading of "Condition" there is an initial "M." It is not clear what this would indicate; Mr. Rothman believes that civil condition, rather than physical, was meant. The last five columns, with their entries, read: "Ward. No.—11," "Disease—Injuries accidentally received," "Result—Died," "Date—Jan. 13, 1864," "Remarks—Friends—Cor. Inq." These last entries denote that the body was claimed by friends and that a coroner's inquest was held.

There is another item to discredit the account in Browne's book. Dr. McDowell, Stephen's father-in-law, died before Stephen was married, and it was not Clarke who sent a telegram, either to Dr. McDowell or any one else connected with Stephen. The actual correspondence relating to Stephen's accident and death is preserved at Foster Hall in Indianapolis. The tragic story is told briefly.

First comes a letter, dated "New York City, January 12th, 1864."

Morrison Foster, Esq.,
Your brother Stephen I am sorry to inform you is lying in Bellevue Hospital in this city very sick. He desires me to ask you to send

him some pecuniary assistance as his means are very low. If possible, he would like to see you in person.

Yours very truly,
G. COOPER.

176½ Bowery, New York City.

Then a telegram which probably reached Morrison before he received the letter.

Cleveland, Jany 14, 1864, By Telegraph from New York.

To MORRISON FOSTER,
Stephen is dead. Come on.

GEO. COOPER.

13

There are two more documents issued from Bellevue Hospital, the two little papers mentioned in the opening page of this volume. One of them was the inventory of Stephen's personal belongings.

Ward 11, Stephen Foster, Died January 13.
Coat, pants, vest, hat, shoes, overcoat, January 10, 1864.

The other was the receipt for the amount Morrison paid for Stephen's care.

Recd of Mr. Foster ten shillings [29] charge for Stephen C. Foster while in Hospital—Jany 16, 1864. Wm. E. White, Warden, Bellevue Hospital

These two papers are now preserved at Foster Hall, together with the pitiful little purse with its thirty-eight cents, three pennies and thirty-five cents in scrip, and the little piece of paper with its five pencilled words—

Dear friends and gentle hearts.

Because we know that it was George Cooper who notified Morrison of Stephen's illness and death, the account this friend gave of Stephen's accident and his last days is im-

[29] The figures $1.25 appear in pencil on this receipt.

portant, and probably more reliable than anything that has been told or written of the manner in which Stephen came to his sad end. The story was told verbally by Cooper to Harold V. Milligan, and printed by Milligan in his life of Foster.[30]

Early one winter morning I received a message saying that my friend had met with an accident; I dressed hurriedly and went to 15 Bowery, the old lodging-house where Stephen lived, and found him lying on the floor in the hall, blood oozing from a cut in his throat and with a bad bruise on his forehead. Steve never wore any night-clothes and he lay there on the floor, naked, and suffering horribly. He had wonderful big brown eyes and they looked up at me with an appeal I can never forget. He whispered, "I'm done for," and begged for a drink, but before I could get it for him, the doctor who had been sent for arrived and forebade it. He started to sew up the gash in Steve's throat, and I was horrified to observe that he was using black thread. "Haven't you any white thread," I asked, and he said no, he had picked up the first thing he could find. I decided the doctor was not much good and I went down stairs and got Steve a big drink of rum, which I gave him and which seemed to help him a lot. We put his clothes on him and took him to the hospital. In addition to the cut on his throat and the bruise on his forehead, he was suffering from a bad burn on his thigh, caused by the overturning of a spirit lamp used to boil water. This had happened several days before, and he had said nothing about it, nor done anything for it. All the time we were caring for him, he seemed terribly weak and his eyelids kept fluttering. I shall never forget it.

I went back again to the hospital to see him, and he said nothing had been done for him, and he couldn't eat the food they brought him. When I went back again the next day they said "Your friend is dead." His body had been sent down into the morgue, among the nameless dead. I went down to look for it. There was an old man sitting there, smoking a pipe. I told him what I wanted and he said "Go look for him." I went around peering into the coffins, until I found Steve's body. It was taken care of by Winterbottom, the undertaker in Broome Street, and removed from Bellevue. The next day his brother Morrison, and Steve's widow, arrived. They stayed at the St. Nicholas Hotel. When Mrs. Foster entered the room where Steve's body was lying, she fell on her knees before it, and remained for a long time.

[30] *Op. cit.*

Telegram Announcing Foster's Death

Stephen Foster's Pocketbook, with Slip of Paper Found in
His Clothes at the Time of His Death

There remains but one more discrepancy to be discussed, one which may never be satisfactorily explained. Morrison wrote that Stephen met with his accident at the "American Hotel," and Cooper states that the lodging house where Stephen lived was at 15 Bowery. The first time that an "American Hotel" is listed in the New York Directories was in the issue of 1864/65, where we find it located at "1 Eighth." In those years this address would have been at the corner of Broadway, a location far too expensive for Stephen's slender purse.

Mr. Joseph Muller, the collector of musical *Americana* and Foster enthusiast, has discussed this matter with those who are close to the Bowery and familiar with its history. Mr. Muller believes that it is possible that the lodging house at 15 Bowery (opposite Pell Street) may have been known as the *North* American Hotel. This is possible, yet the supposition cannot be verified by the directories— there is no such hotel listed.

It will be remembered, however, that John Mahon spoke of Foster's procuring a bed at the "New England Hotel," where "he was seized with the illness that proved unexpectedly fatal." [31] An article in the *New York Times,* August 31, 1891, discusses the demolition, a few weeks earlier, of the historic "New England Hotel." According to this account the building, erected sometime after 1828, was originally called the *North American* Hotel, and was located at the corner of Bayard Street and the Bowery. In 1855 it became the "Moss Hotel" and in the early 1860's a new proprietor, P. V. Husted, changed the name to the New England Hotel. These facts may help to reconcile Morrison's account of Foster's death with those of Cooper and the others who claimed that Stephen lived at 15 Bowery. That address is only a few doors below the corner of Bayard Street.

[31] See page 330.

14

One may wonder what passed through Jane Foster's mind and heart as she knelt by Stephen's coffin. Such speculation is out of our province, for that was a matter that lay solely between Jane and Stephen. Yet, whatever Stephen may have done to make it impossible for them to live together, no matter how improvident he may have been, or how slavishly he became the victim of rum, there is nothing in the records to show that he ever, in all his life, committed a disgraceful act. There is no trace of anything contemptible; meanness and pettiness were as far from his nature as dissonance was absent from his music.

Bigness he may have lacked, but tenderness and sweetness he had in abundance. He was in truth a dear friend and gentle heart, so gentle that all who knew him and told of their recollections have never failed to speak of his shy friendliness, and his generous, kindly ways. Weak he apparently was, yet though he stepped aside from what the moralists are pleased to call the straight and narrow path, the cause of such straying was one of sociability, the love of companionship. Pity Stephen Foster if we must, but no honest man can despise him. If those noted for virtue were all as gentle-hearted as this man who never really had his rightful chance, the world would be a better place.

There is little more of the story. That which had been Stephen Foster, that part of him which was weary and wanted rest, was taken to Pittsburgh, where touching and suitable honors were paid to him who had been one of the city's most enduring gifts to posterity. Services were held in Pittsburgh's Trinity Church, January 21st, with the Rector, the Reverend C. E. Swope, officiating, assisted by Dr. Page of Christ Church, Allegheny. The music was in charge of Stephen's old friend, Henry Kleber, who sang an air from the oratorio "Joseph and His Brethren," to the words:

Vital spark of heavenly flame,
Quit, oh, quit this mortal frame.

Many of those at the church services followed the procession to the cemetery. At the gate they were met by the Citizen's Brass Band, and as the remains of Stephen were lowered into the grave, these friends played "Come Where My Love Lies Dreaming" and "Old Folks at Home."

Stephen was laid to rest beside the grave of his father. A simple headstone was placed above him which reads:

STEPHEN C. FOSTER
of Pittsburgh, Pa
BORN
July 4, 1826
DIED
January 13, 1864

The stone is crumbling to-day, but that which was immortal of Stephen Foster sings on; simply, as he would have wished it to sing, but unceasingly on—through the years, and perhaps through the ages.

XI

IN AFTER YEARS

I

ON FEBRUARY 5, 1864, less than a month after Stephen died, George Cooper wrote to Morrison Foster:

New York

My Dear Sir:

I received yours to-day. From time to time I have called upon Frank Leslie in relation to the daguerreotype of your brother, and the last time I saw him (3 inst) he stated that it was in the hands of the engraver, and was to be published. I received the sketch which you so kindly sent me, and with this I send you a number of "The Round Table" a journal that stands very high in Musical and Literary matters, and which contains the best article I have seen on your brother's genius.

I shall immediately collect your brother's songs and have them bound and forwarded to you. It has been suggested through the press of this city that a monument should be erected to Stephen's memory by contributions from musical men and others all over the country, and I am in hopes something will be done in the premises.

If you ever write to Mrs. Foster I wish you would tell her that I have not forgotten my promise to send her some of her husband's late compositions but am only waiting until two or three of his last songs which are in the hands of the publishers are printed.

I am, Dear Sir,

Yours Very Truly,

G. Cooper.

No monument was erected so soon after Stephen's death; that was to come many years later.

Soon after Stephen had passed, the "last songs" began to appear. The fact that there were so many of them shows that even though he had not been writing songs equal in quality to the best of those he had issued in former years, his reputation was still an asset to a publisher.

Horace Waters was the first to make capital of the "last song" idea. On January 23 he copyrighted four songs by Foster—"If You've Only Got a Moustache," "Mr. & Mrs. Brown," "When Old Friends Were Here," and "Wilt Thou Be True?" These, however, were issued under the same collective title-page of *Foster's Melodies* that Waters had been using for Stephen's songs in sheet-music form. A month later, February 23, Waters copyrighted "She Was All the World to Me," and issued it as "the last song of the late Stephen C. Foster, who died January 13th, 1864." The title-page was printed in black and white, with a heavy black border. On the back cover of the music sheet was a descriptive list of Foster's songs published by Waters, and excerpts from some of the eulogies that had appeared in the newspapers.

William A. Pond & Company was next with "Beautiful Dreamer," copyrighted March 10. We have already noted that when "Willie Has Gone to the War" was issued some nine months earlier (it was copyrighted July 1, 1863) the title-page stated that it was written by the composer of "Beautiful Dreamer." Yet when the latter song was published as "the last song ever written by Stephen C. Foster" it was announced on the title-page that the work was "composed but a few days previous to his death."

On May 7 P. A. Wundermann, a New York publisher, copyrighted a song "Give This to Mother," which he issued as "Stephen C. Foster's last musical idea." Above the first page of music appeared this explanatory note:

Upon one of the Battle fields near Washington, a dying patriotic drummer boy pulled off a locket from his neck; saying to one of his comrades in his last expiring moments: "Give this to Mother."

It is mysterious that the last words of this drummer boy, should form also a subject for the last musical composition of Stephen C.

Foster, the well celebrated composer of a thousand [!] popular American songs.

Three days after he handed us *this his last composition,* for which he promised to write a biographical sketch of the subject of this song, death summoned him to his last account.

We therefore where [sic] obliged to fill up this space, with the present sad remarks.

The melody of "Give This to Mother" is so similar to one of Stephen's hymns that had appeared in the *Golden Harp*—"Tears Bring Thoughts of Heaven"—that the staff of Foster Hall was at first tempted to list the song as a *derivata,* rather than as a new Foster work. The similarity does not continue through the entire melody, however, and if "Give This to Mother" was actually a new song by Stephen, it would not have been the first time that he quoted from himself musically.

The same problem is found in the political song, "Little Mac! Little Mac! You're the Very Man." This was published as a "campaign song by Stephen C. Foster" sometime in 1864 by J. Marsh of Philadelphia, but there is no copyright entry in the Library of Congress to establish the day and month. Of course Stephen, as a Democrat, would no doubt have been happy to write a song in behalf of McClellan, one which ran:

> Little Mac, little Mac, you're the very man,
>   Go down to Washington as soon as you can—
> Lincoln's got to get away and make room for you,
>   We must beat Lincoln and Johnson too.
>
> *Chorus:* Hurrah, Hurrah, Hurrah!
>   Sound the rally thro' the whole United States,
>   Little Mac and Pendleton are our candidates.
>
> Democrats, Democrats, do it up brown,
>   Lincoln and his Niggerheads won't go down.
> Greeley and Sumner and all that crew,
>   We must beat Lincoln and Johnson too.
>
> *Chorus:* Hurrah, *etc.*

This song was copyrighted in the name of Marion Foster. Stephen's daughter was thirteen years old in April of 1864, and it may be that she had some part in the song. At any rate Stephen could not have written the words, for he died on January 13, and Lincoln and Johnson were not nominated until June 8, 1864, while McClellan was not named as the Democratic candidate until August 29. The opening phrase of the music is similar to "Nelly Bly," but the relationship does not extend much further.

There were other songs, too, issued after Stephen's death, and a complete list of them is given chronologically in Appendix I.

2

It is apparent from correspondence between Morrison and Stephen's publishers that the vogue of "Old Folks at Home" had not been maintained from the time of its first popularity. Sometime between 1870 and 1872 an event occurred which may be in part responsible for our own familiarity with the song to-day. In the Autumn of 1870 the famous Swedish prima-donna, Christine Nilsson, paid her first visit to America, and gave concerts in this country almost continuously until the Spring of 1872. She paid a second visit to the United States in the 1873-4 season, and until the time of her retirement from the stage in 1888 she came here frequently.

The Song Journal of January, 1872, contained an item of great interest to us.

THE OLD FOLKS AT HOME

It is said that Miss Nilsson first heard the "Old Folks at Home," sung at the house of Parke Godwin, in New York, soon after her arrival in this country and that she was so much struck by its plaintive melody and touching words, finding a response as they did in her own heart, that she immediately set herself to learning both, and rarely fails to sing them in some portion of each concert.

Her exquisite utterance of the melody will give renewed interest to a song which, in the last quarter of a century, has had an almost unparalleled success. . . .

In 1873, Oliver Ditson & Co., the firm which had acquired those of Foster's songs which had gone to Firth, Son & Company when Firth, Pond & Company had dissolved, issued a special title-page for songs "sung by Mlle. Nilsson," decorated with a full-length portrait of the singer. One of these songs was "Old Folks at Home," still issued, twenty-two years after it was first published, with the information that "words and music" were by E. P. Christy.

In those years copyrights were good for an initial period of twenty-eight years, and renewals were allowed for an additional term of fourteen years. The renewals, however, must be taken out in the name of the author, or of his heirs. Stephen of course had died without any royalty interest in his songs, so there was nothing of such nature that he himself could will to his wife and daughter.

The copyrights on many of Foster's songs had changed hands since they were first published. When Firth, Pond & Company dissolved, William A. Pond & Company retained most of the Foster songs, but Firth, Son & Company were given some of them, namely:

> Old Folks at Home
> Massa's in de Cold Ground
> Nelly Bly
> Gentle Annie
> Ellen Bayne

There were several others, too, but these were the ones on which there was a continued sale for a number of years.

Firth remained in business independently for only a short time, and then sold out to Oliver Ditson & Company in Boston. In 1864 Ditson had acquired the catalog of Miller & Beacham of Baltimore, who had succeeded F. D. Benteen. Ditson had in addition purchased the catalogs of Lee & Walker, P. A. Wundermann, J. L. Peters (suc-

cessor to W. C. Peters), and John J. Daly, so that when
the Foster copyrights expired, the most valuable of them
were controlled by two firms—Oliver Ditson & Company
and William A. Pond & Company.

On March 29, 1879, Oliver Ditson & Company addressed a brief letter to "Mrs. S. C. Foster, Pittsburgh,
Pa." The note expressed the hope that its message would
reach Mrs. Foster, as the firm had something of importance
to communicate—something to her advantage. Another
letter, dated April 22, 1879, explained this matter of importance. The Ditson firm had been trying to locate
Stephen's widow for some time, but had not succeeded before because Jane had married again, and was now Mrs.
Matthew D. Wiley.

In the letter of April 22 the Ditson firm stated that it
had been publishing "Old Folks at Home" as successors
to Firth, Pond & Company (actually successors to Firth,
Son & Co.) and that the copyright on the song would run
out in July of that year (1879). The firm proposed on
renewal for fourteen years to pay Foster's widow a royalty
of three cents a copy, or should she prefer "a bird in
hand," one hundred dollars in full. It may be observed to
Ditson's credit that the letter advised Jane to take the
royalty. The lump sum was named to show that the firm
was "not trifling."

This letter contained another bit of information, a statement that the "song was dying out when Nilsson revived
it."

3

Evidently Mrs. Wiley (Jane) turned the Ditson letter
over to Morrison, for the firm's next letter was addressed
to him. Dated April 28, 1879, this message explained that
there was "a little cloud over the title" of "Old Folks at
Home." According to the Ditson letter, the original copy
of the song had been issued as composed by Christy and

"copyrighted by him." Morrison immediately replied that he knew of this situation, and that there was no flaw in the copyright. He then proceeded to state the terms of an acceptable agreement. Morrison's letter was dated May 5, 1879:

Your favor of the 28th ult I find on my return from a journey to Ohio. On your statement of the case I am willing to assume that you are the present owners of the copy right of "Old Folks at Home." The title is all right. I was personally cognizant of all the facts concerning its first composition and copy right. My brother Stephen C. Foster wrote it and forwarded it to his publishers Firth, Pond & Co. who took out the first copy right that was ever issued for it and for his use. He authorized F. P. & Co. to print Christy's name on it. This was in pursuance of an arrangement between him and Christy by which Christy paid him a liberal sum for this privilege. My brother retained all the ownership of the song and copy right, and Christy never asked nor thought of asking for any interest in them. Firth, Pond & Co. paid my brother for several years a royalty on the song & afterwards bought out the copy right of that and some others of his songs, for a specific sum. The oldest copy right of the song has not run out, nor does it expire (as stated in yours of 22 April to Mrs. Foster) on 1st of July, but later. The copy rights of several others of his songs besides Old folks at home, expire this year after this date, viz. "Oh, boys carry me long" "I would not die in Summer time" "Laura Lee" "Willie my brave" "Eulalie" "Farewell my Lilly dear." They can only be renewed by the author's family. You cannot do it for them.

If you will pay my brothers widow 100$, and 3 cents per copy afterwards, (commencing after the royalty would at 3¢ have reached 100$) I will advise her to assign to you the renewed copy rights of all the above including Old folks at home. The copy rights of a number of his best songs run out next year, and each year for several years yet. Please reply promptly.

The Ditson firm replied promptly indeed. The next letter, May 7, opened with the statement, "Terms accepted —check inclosed." Under date of May 10th a formal agreement was drawn up "by and between Mrs. Matthew Wiley formerly widow of Stephen C. Foster deceased, and

Mrs. Marion Foster Welsh[1] only child of said Stephen C. Foster: of Allegheny City, Penna, of the first part and Oliver Ditson & Co. of the City of Boston of the second part."

Then followed a correspondence between the publishers and Morrison that extended over a number of years, at all times friendly yet always businesslike. On one occasion the firm wrote Morrison "your brother's wife and daughter ought to be grateful for your care of their interests," and later they stated that "it is very pleasant to deal with a courteous gentleman."

The first statement on "Old Folks at Home" was rendered August 2, 1880. During the time since the original copyright had been renewed, approximately twelve months, 4,400 copies had been sold. The hundred dollars paid in advance had been earned, and thirty-two dollars more. Thereafter royalty statements were sent to Morrison semiannually, each statement accompanied by two checks, as Morrison had stipulated, one payable to Mrs. Wiley, and the other to Mrs. Welch.

The accompanying chart of "Royalties paid to the heirs of Stephen C. Foster" shows the total amounts as well as the itemized account of individual songs, and the manner in which the income varied from year to year. Altogether the Ditson songs brought Mrs. Wiley and Mrs. Welch $2,618.34. $2,234.59 of this total was gained from the three cent royalty on sales of sheet music, and $383.75 came from permissions granted publishers of song collections to include "Old Folks at Home" and others of Stephen's songs in such books.[2]

It is interesting to note that the first of these permissions was granted in 1883, at a time when the sales on the songs

---

[1] Marion Foster had married Walter Welsh. Later Marion changed the spelling of the name to Welch, although her daughter, Jessie Welsh Rose, continues the original spelling.

[2] The total received by Ditson from reprint permissions was $767.50. Of this amount, one-half was paid to the Foster heirs, and one-half belonged to the publisher.

RC

Paid to the Heirs of Stephen C. Fo:

Compiled from the Original St

OLIVER DITSON & CO.	1879	1880	1881	1882	1883	1884	1885	1886	
Old Folks at Home (song)........	...	$132.00	$157.71	$220.80	$161.52	$90.00	$144.00	$147.30	$
Old Folks at Home (arrangements)	...	...	...	...	...	...	...	9.78	
Massa's in de Cold Ground.......	...	...	9.00	15.36	18.06	15.00	15.00	12.00	
Nelly Bly	...	...	...	...	3.75	1.20	1.26	.60	
Gentle Annie	...	...	...	...	...	...	...	...	
Ellen Bayne	...	...	...	...	...	.33	1.23	.30	
Total Royalties from Ditson by Years	...	$132.00	$166.71	$236.16	$183.33	$106.53	$161.49	$169.98	$

WM. A. POND & CO.	1879	1880	1881	1882	1883	1884	1885	1886	
My Old Kentucky Home.........	...	...	...	$13.50	$31.50	$35.00	...	$85.50	$
Old Black Joe....................	...	...	...	...	...	...	...	...	
Come Where My Love...........	...	...	...	...	...	...	...	...	
Oh Boys Carry Me Long.........	...	...	...	1.50	.75	...	...	.75	
Ring de Banjo....................	...	...	...	.75	...	.75	...	...	
Wilt Thou Be Gone..............	...	...	...	2.40	1.50	2.00	...	1.50	
Old Dog Tray....................	...	...	...	1.50	3.00	1.50	...	6.00	
My Loved One, or Eva..........	...	...	...	...	...	...	...	...	
Hard Times	...	...	...	...	...	...	...	...	
Linger in Blissful.................	...	...	...	...	...	...	...	...	
Willie We Have Missed..........	...	...	...	...	...	...	...	...	
Lula is Gone.....................	...	...	...	...	...	...	...	...	
Maggie by My Side..............	...	...	...	...	...	...	...	...	
Social Orchestra	...	...	...	...	...	...	...	...	
Nelly Was a Lady................	...	...	...	...	...	...	...	...	
Linda Has Departed..............	...	...	...	...	...	...	...	...	
Farewell Sweet Mother..........	...	...	...	...	...	...	...	...	
Voice of Bygone Days............	...	...	...	...	...	...	...	...	
None Shall Weep.................	...	...	...	...	...	...	...	...	
Some Folks.......................	...	...	...	...	...	...	...	...	
Willie Has Gone..........:.......	...	...	...	...	...	...	...	...	
I'll Be Home Tomorrow..........	...	...	...	...	...	...	...	...	
I Dream of Jeanie................	...	...	...	...	...	...	...	...	
Total Royalties from Pond by Years	...	...	...	$19.65	$36.75	$39.25	...	$93.75	$
Grand Totals by Years.........	...	$132.00	$166.71	$255.81	$220.08	$145.78	$161.49	$263.73	$

ES

ing the Period of Copyright Renewal

by John Tasker Howard, 1933

8	1889	1890	1891	1892	1893	1894	1895	1896	1897	1898	Totals by Songs
.68	$113.61	$134.82	$129.24	$136.62	$106.05	$4.95	...	...	...	...	$1,923.09
.49	3.93	6.03	2.64	5.13	4.17	1.05	...	...	...	...	40.53
.00	12.30	14.70	19.64	14.87	24.81	24.09	$9.84	...	...	...	231.49
.26	1.17	1.23	.81	.69	.60	.60	.60	$.42	...	...	15.09
.52	1.80	1.38	.54	1.86	1.62	.87	.75	.48	$.90	$.45	16.68
.26	.66	1.02	.30	.30	.30	.45	.30	...	...	...	7.71
.21	$133.47	$159.18	$153.17	$159.47	$137.55	$32.01	$11.49	$.90	$.90	$.45	$2,234.59

From Reprint Permission
Granted by Ditson $ 383.75 $2,618.34

88	1889	1890	1891	1892	1893	1894	1895	1896	1897	1898	Totals by Songs
.00	$37.50	$69.00	$66.00	$57.00	$52.50	$49.50	$30.00	$15.00	...	...	$656.00
.00	63.00	48.00	36.00	54.00	75.75	45.75	37.50	30.00	...	...	444.00
.00	24.00	15.00	22.50	21.00	13.50	6.00	18.00	6.00	...	...	270.00
...	.75	...	...	...	...	.75	...	...	...	...	4.50
...	...	...	...	...	...	...	...	...	...	...	1.50
.50	3.00	1.50	1.50	.75	...	1.50	...	...	...	...	17.90
.50	7.50	3.00	...	3.00	.60	1.65	...	.75	...	...	34.50
...	...	...	...	...	...	...	...	...	...	...	.75
.50	16.50	10.50	10.50	6.75	9.45	7.80	5.25	3.75	...	...	87.00
.50	.75	.75	...	...	...	...	...	...	...	...	3.00
.25	1.50	.75	.75	...	.30	1.20	...	.75	...	...	7.50
.75	...	...	...	.75	...	...	...	...	...	...	1.50
.00	4.50	3.00	...	...	...	...	...	...	...	...	10.50
.00	...	...	...	...	...	...	...	...	...	...	25.00
.50	.75	1.50	1.50	...	.90	1.35	...	...	...	...	10.50
...	.75	...	...	...	...	...	...	...	...	...	.75
...	...	.75	...	...	...	...	...	...	...	...	.75
...	...	.75	...	...	...	...	...	...	...	...	.75
...	...	...	...	...	...	...	...	.75	...	...	.75
...	...	.75	...	...	...	.75	...	...	...	...	1.50
...	...	...	...	.75	...	...	...	...	...	...	.75
...	...	...	.75	...	...	...	...	...	...	...	.75
...	...	...	.75	...	...	...	...	...	...	...	.75
.50	$160.50	$155.25	$140.25	$144.00	$153.00	$116.25	$90.75	$57.00	...	...	$1,580.90 $1,580.90
3.71	$293.97	$314.43	$293.42	$303.47	$290.55	$148.26	$102.24	$57.90	$.90	$.45	$3,815.49

Ditson Permissions $ 383.75 $4,199.24

had about reached their peak. The fact that in July of this same year (1883), the royalties on "Old Folks at Home" dropped to almost one half of the amount paid in January of the same year, is no doubt explained by a note from the publisher to Morrison Foster, accompanying the July, 1885, statement:

We enclose check—sorry they are not larger but Nil[s]son has not been singing it lately.

And again in February of 1887:

We feel ashamed to send so small a royalty for last 6 months—but "Old Folks" has had no lift from Nilsson or Patti, for a year or two, & without their aid, the sales fall off. Let us hope some other artist will revive it.

It will be seen from the chart that the sales of sheet music copies of "Old Folks at Home" never returned to the mark set in the years from 1880 to 1883, yet the number of reprint permissions increased each year, running right up to 1893, when the renewal of copyright finally expired. The song was becoming an indispensable item in standard song collections.

When Morrison came to correspond regularly with Oliver Ditson & Company, that firm told him that some of Stephen's songs were owned by William A. Pond & Company, and Morrison accordingly communicated with them. After exchange of several letters in which there was considerable haggling over terms, he finally persuaded the New York concern to agree to three cents royalty, with one hundred dollars paid in advance. The chart shows which of the songs Pond retained, and the various amounts earned by each through the years of copyright renewal. The Pond royalties amounted to considerably less than those paid by Ditson—$1,580.90 (lacking the royalties for 1885, which are missing from the present records), yet it must be remembered that Ditson published "Old Folks at Home," a song which had always proved Stephen's best-selling work.

It is possible to determine almost to a penny the total amounts in royalties paid by publishers to Foster and later to his heirs. We do not know what Stephen was given for the earliest songs issued by Peters, or what he was paid for the songs written in the last four years of his life. But we do know that in the ten and a half years of his prime (from the date of his first contract with Firth, Pond & Company, December 3, 1849, to the expiration of his last-known contract with that firm, August 9, 1860) he received from Firth, Pond & Company and from other publishers $15,091.08.[3]

The royalties paid to Foster's heirs enable us to reach the following total:

Total of amounts known to have been paid Foster during his life-time	$15,091.08
Paid to Foster's heirs on renewal of copyrights	
Oliver Ditson & Co. for royalties $2,234.59	
Oliver Ditson & Co. for share of reprint permissions 383.75	
Wm. A. Pond & Co. for royalties 1,580.90	4,199.24
Total amounts known to have been paid to Foster and his heirs	$19,290.32

4

So much for the material rewards, stingy or adequate, however we may regard them. Now for the intangible returns, those things that bear witness to the place Stephen Foster occupies in the hearts of men.

Many years passed after Stephen's death before monuments first appeared. His native city, Pittsburgh, was probably first to honor him. The *American Art Journal* of October 25, 1890, tells of a plan to erect a statue of

[3] See page 305.

Foster in the Allegheny parks, but nothing seems to have come from the suggestion. In 1900 the newspapers were filled with items about the drive started by Thomas J. Keenan, editor of the *Pittsburgh Press*, to raise funds for a Foster memorial, and prominent citizens of the city were interviewed and their recollections of Foster printed. Pittsburgh to-day has several monuments to Stephen Foster: a statue in Highland Park by Guiseppe Moretti (the result of the 1900 campaign), a Stephen Foster School (a unit in its public school system), and the Stephen Foster Memorial Home, the house that stands on the supposed site of the White Cottage, Stephen's birthplace. This property was purchased by James H. Park, and presented to the City of Pittsburgh in 1914. It is maintained as a museum by the city. Living in the house are Stephen's daughter, Marion Foster Welch, her son, Matthew Wiley Welch, her daughter, Jessie Welsh Rose, and Mrs. Rose's husband, Alexander D. Rose.

Pittsburgh is now erecting the finest memorial of all. Born of the efforts of the Tuesday Musical Club, the Stephen Foster Memorial Association has been at work raising funds for a building which will be a suitable tribute, and plans are now (1933) complete for the erection of a hall to be located on ground donated by the University of Pittsburgh, on the Cathedral of Learning Quadrangle. There will be a room devoted to the preservation of Foster mementoes, and an auditorium to seat a thousand persons for intimate concerts and recitals.[a]

We have already learned that Kentucky has had its share in honoring Foster. In 1922 the State formally accepted the gift of a number of its citizens who had subscribed to a fund to purchase the Rowan mansion at Bardstown, and since that time the State has maintained the house and grounds as a museum—"My Old Kentucky Home." There are monuments in other parts of the

[a] See *Preface to Fourth Printing*.

Architect's Drawing of Proposed Stephen C. Foster
Memorial Building, Pittsburgh

country. In Fargo, Georgia, the source of the S[u]wanee
River is marked by a granite shaft unveiled in 1928, the
gift of Charles J. Haden. Its lettering reads:

Erected in Memory of

STEPHEN COLLINS FOSTER

At the Source of the Stream
Which he made Immortal
in Song

SUWANEE RIVER

On March 9, 1926, a bill was introduced in the House of
Representatives to authorize the coinage of 50-cent pieces
in commemoration of the one hundredth anniversary of
Foster's birth. Unfortunately, this bill failed of passage.

In the Calvary Episcopal Church at Fletcher, North
Carolina, is a plaque that memorializes Stephen Foster; in
the Cincinnati Music Hall a bust, the work of the sculptor,
Arturo Ivone; in the State Capitol at Frankfort, Kentucky,
a statue; and in the basement of the public library at Louisville a plaster replica of the Frankfort statue.

5

There is one more bust of Stephen Foster, also modelled
by Arturo Ivone. This stands just inside the entrance of
Foster Hall at Indianapolis, welcoming those who visit
what is probably a shrine unique in the list of memorials
to great men.

The man who conceived the idea of Foster Hall, the
one who has been its guiding spirit and sole contributor of
funds for maintenance, is a person who dislikes publicity
and anything in the nature of personal eulogy, yet the story
of Stephen Foster is not complete without an account of
Foster Hall and its founder.

A few years ago, in 1930, Josiah Kirby Lilly, a retired

manufacturer of Indianapolis, purchased some records for a sound-reproducing machine which had been installed in a little stone building that lay on his estate, a building originally erected a few years before to house a pipe organ. Among the records for the phonograph was an album containing a number of the songs of Stephen Foster. A lover of Foster's songs since childhood, Mr. Lilly was once more delighted with the old, familiar melodies. Musical friendships were renewed, and the name of Stephen Foster became again a living embodiment of wistful, gentle music.

One of Mr. Lilly's sons, himself a *bibliophile,* was present when the records were first played. He was asked where some of the first editions of Foster's songs might be obtained. He suggested a book-dealer in Boston as a likely source of information, a merchant who subsequently obtained for Mr. Lilly several hundred sheets of Foster's songs, among which a large number of first editions was discovered.[4]

Thus started a fascinating sport, the finding of more first editions, and the checking of each copy with available information to determine which editions were "firsts" and which were later prints. What had started as the pursuit of a private hobby soon grew to a wide correspondence with other collectors, the issuance of a "bulletin," first mimeographed and in later issues printed, announcing Lilly acquisitions, and also advertising for items which the Lilly collection lacked. This bulletin soon grew to the dimensions and importance of a magazine, with discussion of the authenticity of various editions, as well as numerous discoveries regarding Foster, made either by Mr. Lilly and his assistants or by some correspondent. The early bulletins have already become collectors' items.

The little stone house was soon named Foster Hall, and its publication the *Foster Hall Bulletin.* Gradually a staff

---

[4] The music sheets were received by Mr. Lilly January 5, 1931. This date is considered the birthday of the Foster Hall Collection.

has been assembled to help in the work of research, in cataloguing acquisitions, and in answering the many questions regarding Foster that arrive daily at the Hall. *Foster Hall Bulletin* Number 8 (issued February, 1933) contains the roster of the staff. I quote the exact wording of the *Bulletin*.

Mr. Fletcher Hodges, Jr., Harvard '28—Director, delver, sleuth, expert examiner, gravedigger and marvel of memory.

Mr. Walter R. Whittlesey, Washington, D. C.—Guide, counsellor and friend, judge, jury, attorney and preventer of errors.

Mrs. Katharine W. Copley—Research, expert examiner, recorder and keeper of the Washington archives.

Miss Dorothy J. Black—Chief of correspondence, grand keeper of the Foster Hall archives, keeper of the peace and great seal.

Josiah K. Lilly—Aider and abetter.

In the Summer of 1933, Mr. Eli Messenger joined the Foster Hall staff to describe and catalog acquisitions.

At present the collection at Foster Hall includes, in some form, all of the songs and compositions of Stephen Foster that are known to be his work. Of a large number of these, first editions are at the Hall. Of those of which the first editions have to date proved unobtainable, photostats and reproductions in the Library of Congress are included in the collection.

In addition to sheet music (which includes not only first and early editions, but modern prints as well), there is assembled a large collection of holograph letters, manuscripts, books and magazine articles regarding Foster, portraits, contemporary newspapers and magazines, broadsides, pamphlets, phonograph, piano and organ records of Foster songs, and miscellaneous "Fosteriana," all being studied, described and catalogued. The numerous references in this volume to items now at Foster Hall show something of the scope and source nature of the collection.

6

Foster Hall has much; almost everything pertaining to Stephen that can be imagined, yet what it has is but half of the story. It is not a mere museum, to which those interested may come and see what they may be interested in. Visitors are welcomed royally, but that is a small part of the Hall's purpose—the keeping of records about a man dead for seventy years.

The idea of Foster Hall came from the love that one man has for Stephen's music, for something that is still alive—a love that this individual shares with millions of his fellow men. One never forgets Stephen's music when he is at Foster Hall, the melodies are in the very spirit of the place, and so that none will fail to feel them they are actually sung and played whenever those who visit the Hall come in groups, performed either through the phonograph or organ, or sung by a quartet of singers that comes to the Hall at least once a week during each season.

The bulletins of Foster Hall have been free to all who have asked for them, and so have its other publications. Some of these have been little volumes of tribute to Foster, and one was a handsome reprint of Morrison Foster's biography of Stephen, long unobtainable and out of print. The latest project of the Hall is the reproduction of the first editions of all of Foster's songs and pieces, and the presenting of one thousand sets of these reproductions to libraries in the United States and England.

The objective of Foster Hall is expressed through its founder's own words in one of the issues of the *Bulletin.*

The objective of this effort to secure Fosteriana is to have in America, in permanent form, as complete data as possible concerning the life and work of Stephen Collins Foster, to belong to the people of these United States and to be made available in perpetuity for view or study by any one interested in the subject.

To this end the owner has provided that at his death, or sooner if

Josiah Kirby Lilly

Foster Hall

reasonable completeness be attained, arrangements be made to insure the proper placement of the Collection in order that it may be conveniently available to all citizens of our country and of other countries as well. [See *Preface to Fourth Printing.*]

The Hall is a beautiful little building, altogether in keeping with the gentle nature we have learned was Stephen Foster's. In the Spring the apple-blossoms lend a touch of white and pink that seems to bring to life "Jeanie with the Light Brown Hair," or "Nelly Bly." As one comes near the Hall he hears the organ from the open windows— "Come Where My Love Lies Dreaming," or "Old Folks at Home." And as he comes to the door and faces the bust of Stephen, he reads the inscription at the threshold—

Let no discordant note enter here.

APPENDIX I

CHRONOLOGICAL OUTLINE

(Including only events that can be verified by contemporary evidence)

1728 (circa)
Alexander Foster (Stephen's great-grandfather) settles in Little Britain Township, Lancaster County, Pennsylvania.

1779
Sept. 7   William Barclay Foster (Stephen's father) born.

1782 (circa)
James Foster (Stephen's grandfather) settles near Canonsburg, Pennsylvania (19 miles from Pittsburgh).

1788
Jan. 21   Eliza Clayland Tomlinson (Stephen's mother) born in Wilmington, Delaware.

1796
Apr. 21   William B. Foster goes to Pittsburgh.

1807
Nov. 14   William B. Foster and Eliza Tomlinson married.

1808
Nov. 2   Ann Eliza Foster born. (Died in infancy, Dec. 23, 1808.)

1809
Dec. 14   Charlotte Foster born.

1812
Jan. 12   Ann Eliza Foster born. (The second child to bear this name.)

1814
Apr. 5   William B. Foster buys tract of land, 123 acres, two miles above Pittsburgh, and establishes town of Lawrenceville.

Apr. 7   James Foster, Stephen's grandfather, dies.

Apr. 18   William B. Foster appointed Deputy Commissioner of
             Purchases (War of 1812).

May 7   William Barclay Foster, junior, born.

Dec. 15   William B. Foster loads "Enterprise" with supplies for
             the expedition to relieve Jackson at New Orleans.

1815

Jan. 5   "Enterprise" reaches New Orleans.

Jan. 8   Andrew Jackson wins Battle of New Orleans.

Circa   William B. Foster manager of turnpike transportation
             company.

Feb. 18   War Department instructs Treasury Department to
             pay William B. Foster $21,308.08.

Mar. 26   William Barclay Foster, junior, dies.

Apr. 30   William B. Foster files claim for $2,704.90 additional
             from the Government.

Circa   Young relative of William B. Foster, senior, joins fam-
             ily and is given the name of William B. Foster, junior.

Circa   Foster family moves into White Cottage at Lawrence-
             ville.

1816

Mar. 23   Henry Baldwin Foster born.

1818

Sept. 14   Henrietta Foster born.

Circa   Turnpike transportation company ceases business.

Circa   Government arsenal opened at Lawrenceville.

1821

Jan. 26   Dunning Foster born.

Nov. 2   Father has been "drawing a few tunes on the violin."
             Family apparently has a piano.

1822

Day and   Suit on transportation company bond entered against
month   William B. Foster and his bondsmen.
unknown

1823

Feb. 10   Jury returns verdict in favor of Wm. B. Foster for his
             claim against the federal government. Foster received
             $1,107.89, leaving $1,597.01 of his claim unpaid.

June 10   Morrison Foster born.

1825

Day and   William B. Foster elected to Pennsylvania State Leg-
month   islature.
unknown
                              1826

Jan. 20   Letter from Wm. B. Foster shows he was in State
              Legislature at this time.
July 4   Stephen Collins Foster born.
Circa   William B. Foster, junior, leaves home to join a party
              of engineers.

                              1827
              Boston & Albany and Pennsylvania Railroads started.

                              1828
              Baltimore & Ohio Railroad started.
Mar. 17   Charlotte's letter to William, junior, tells that "Stevy
              is still very weak."
Mar. 23   William B. Foster still in Legislature.
May   Charlotte starts for visits in Cincinnati and Louisville.
June 13   Charlotte visiting Barclays in Louisville. Reference to
              Barclays' piano shows that there is no piano in the
              Foster home at this time.
June 26   William, junior, has been promoted. Pay raised to
              $3.50 per day.
Aug. 12   William, junior, has presented family with a new
              piano.
Sept. 7   William B. Foster, senior, has declined re-election to
              Legislature, because of "arrangements with canal com-
              missioners."
Sept. 16   Charlotte visiting Rowans in Bardstown. Uneasy
              about Stephen's health.
Oct. 12   Charlotte on "Wednesday last" returned from Bards-
              town to Louisville. Writes her mother that she has
              rejected the marriage proposal of John Rowan, junior.
Autumn   Andrew Jackson elected President.
Nov. 30   Charlotte has returned to Pittsburgh.

                              1829
Feb. 3   James Foster born.
Mar. 4   Andrew Jackson inaugurated.
May   Charlotte and Ann Eliza have been visiting Cincin-
              nati, Louisville and Bardstown. Ann Eliza returns
              home, but Charlotte extends her visit. Charlotte later
              becomes engaged to William Prather.

July 29	Stephen and James have the whooping cough.
Aug. 12	Charlotte in Louisville.
Oct. 20	Charlotte dies in Louisville.

1830

Mexican President forbids all further immigration from U. S. to Texas.

Baltimore & Ohio Railroad opens its 23 miles of track.

| Circa | Foster family leaves the White Cottage at Lawrenceville. |
| May 19 | James Foster dies. |

1831

| Jan. 1 | William Lloyd Garrison prints first issue of *The Liberator*. |

1832

Andrew Jackson vetoes renewal of National Bank charter.

May 14	Stephen's mother writes that he marches around with a drum and whistles *Auld Lang Syne*.
Summer	Family (except William B. Foster, senior and junior) at Harmony, Pennsylvania.
June 16	Boys taken out of school because of sore-throats. Ann Eliza teaching them at home.
June 17	Water expected in canal in about ten days, when William B. Foster will take office as Collector of Tolls.
Autumn	Family moves into a house in Allegheny (location uncertain).

1833

Feb. 8	William B. Foster, senior, has joined the temperance society.
Mar. 4	Andrew Jackson inaugurated for second term.
Apr. 9	Ann Eliza marries Edward Buchanan.
May-July 2	Stephen takes trip to Augusta, Ky., Cincinnati, and Louisville with his mother and Henrietta.
Oct. 27	Stephen's eye has been "bitten by a spider."

1834

Major political parties become Whigs and Jacksonian Democrats.

March	William B. Foster resigns as Collector of Canal Tolls.
May 2	Family moves to a frame house on Ohio River, "¼ mile below Allegheny Town."
July 14	Stephen studying with Mr. Kelly.
Aug. 3	Boys having a vacation from school.

Circa Sept.	Verdict rendered in William B. Foster's favor in suit against defunct transportation company.
Day and month unknown	William B. Foster runs for assembly on Jackson anti-bankite slate, and is defeated with the rest of the ticket.
Dec. 7	William B. Foster presses his claim against his former bondsman in the transportation company. Family has moved to three-story brick house, 100 yards north of Allegheny Bridge.

1835

Day and month unknown	Stephen's mother (with Henrietta, Morrison and Stephen) go to live in Youngstown, while father enters partnership with Hall in a general store in Pittsburgh.

1836

Apr. 21	Sam Houston wins independence for Texas and is elected its President.
July 11	President Jackson forbids Treasury to accept anything but gold or silver specie for sales of public lands.
Oct. 20	Henrietta Foster marries Thomas L. Wick.

1837 (year of financial panic)

Jan. 14	Stephen writes letter to his father.
Feb.-Mar.	Bread riots in New York.
February	Attempt to settle affairs of Foster & Hall.
Mar. 4	Martin Van Buren, Democrat, inaugurated as President.
Spring	Family moves back to Allegheny, occupying a house belonging to William Foster, junior, on the East Common.
May 15	President calls special session of Congress, for the first Monday of September, to consider measures of relief.
June 6	William Foster, senior, writes: "Such times you never saw—the banks refuse specie, and nothing but shinplasters for change."
June 16	Stephen and Morrison going to school with Mr. Todd. Stephen has recovered from whooping cough.
July 16	Stephen, with his mother, visiting Uncle Struthers at Poland, Ohio.
July 28 (ca.)	William B. Foster goes to Erie, Pa., to enter his claim against one of the directors of the transportation company. Arrives too late.

Sept. 5   Stephen has returned from a visit to Henrietta.
Nov. or Dec. William B. Foster, junior, marries Mary Wick.

1838

Garrison organizes the Liberty Party.
Jan. 9   Mary, William's wife, dies.

1839

Jan. 31   James Buchanan, and hundreds of Pennsylvania citizens, recommend William to the Canal Commissioners.
March   William goes to Towanda, on appointment as principal engineer of canals and railroads of Eastern Pennsylvania.
July 1   William Foster, senior, and his wife go to Poland, Ohio, to board with Uncle Struthers. Morrison and Stephen board at Mr. Reno's in Youngstown, and attend "free school."
Sept.   Morrison goes to work with Mr. Evans at Pittsburgh. Stephen "enjoys himself at Uncle Struthers."

1840

Sub-Treasury system started.
Railroad mileage increased to 2,818 miles.
Jan. 15 (ca.) Stephen leaves Youngstown with Brother William, bound for Towanda.
Feb. 7   William Foster, senior, and his wife boarding at Mr. Richards' in Youngstown.
Nov. 9   Stephen at Athens Academy. Writes Brother William asking if he can study Latin or bookkeeping.
Nov. 16   William Foster, senior, and his wife in Pittsburgh, boarding at Mrs. Paul's.

1841

Mar. 4   William Henry Harrison and John Tyler, Whigs, inaugurated as President and Vice-President.
Apr. 1 ?   Exhibition in Presbyterian Church at Athens, at which Stephen's *Tioga Waltz* may have been played.
              (There is an undated letter from Stephen to William, belonging to this period, which shows that he has left Athens. It is apparent that Stephen attended the Towanda Academy either before or after he was a student at the Athens Academy.)
Apr. 4   President Harrison dies; succeeded by John Tyler.

Spring	William Foster, senior, expecting an appointment to the Treasury Department in Washington.
July 20-27	Stephen a student at Jefferson College.
Aug. 12	Stephen with his mother in Pittsburgh.
Aug. 20	Family move into Brother William's house on the East Common, Allegheny.
Aug. 28	Stephen writes Brother William that he would like to be a midshipman. Has "commenced going to School to Mr. Moody."
Sept.	Transportation company case transferred to Erie, Pa., courts. William B. Foster, after several trips, finally accepts a settlement of $2,000.
Nov. 30	William Foster, senior, in Washington. Expects to be in office to-morrow.
Dec. 15	William B. Foster leaves Washington for Allegheny, where he is elected Mayor.

1842

Feb. 16	Stephen's mother visiting Henry in Washington, where Henry has a position in the Land Office.
Mar. 14	Stephen "uncommonly studious at home, but dislikes going to school."
Mar. 30	Stephen and his father to call on Dickens to-morrow.
May 24	Thomas Wick, Henrietta's husband, dies in Youngstown.
Aug. 27	Stephen and his mother go to stay with Henrietta.
Sept. 22	William B. Foster, junior, marries Elizabeth Burnett.
Nov.	Stephen's mother returns to Allegheny, leaving him with Henrietta.
Dec. 3	Stephen back in Allegheny.

1844

	Free Soil Party, forerunners of Republicans, founded.
Dec. 7	*Open Thy Lattice, Love,* copyrighted by G. Willig, Philadelphia.

1845

	"Knights of the S.T." formed, for which Stephen wrote some of his early songs.
Feb.	Bill for annexation of Texas passes Congress; signed by President, Mar. 3.
Mar. 4	James K. Polk, Democrat, nominated as President.
May 6	Stephen writes poem, "The Five Nice Young Men."

1846

Day and month unknown	John H. Eaton presents to Congress William B. Foster's claim against the Government—now $4,820.
Mar. 16	Henry, in Washington, writes that Stephen has failed to get an appointment to West Point.
Apr. 23	War between U. S. and Mexico started by attack on Zachary Taylor on the Rio Grande. War declared May 13.
Oct. 9	*There's a Good Time Coming,* copyrighted by Peters & Field, Cincinnati.
Oct. 31	Stephen still in Allegheny; must have left for Cincinnati to become bookkeeper for his brother Dunning after this date.

1847

Day and month unknown	*Where Is Thy Spirit, Mary?* presumably composed. Published in 1895.
Jan. 5	Henrietta marries Jesse Thornton.
Feb. 23	Taylor wins victory at Buena Vista.
April 9	William Foster, junior, appointed one of three chief engineers of Pennsylvania Railroad.
June 9	Dunning Foster makes will before going to Mexican War.
Sept. 11	*Susanna* announced as sung by the "vocalists" at Andrews' Eagle Ice Cream Saloon, Pittsburgh.
Sept. 13	Winfield Scott captures Mexico City.
Oct. 18	*Lou'siana Belle,* and *What Must a Fairy's Dream Be?,* copyrighted by W. C. Peters, Cincinnati.

1848

	Railroad mileage increased to 8,000.
Jan.	Gold discovered in California.
Feb. 2	Treaty with Mexico. California and New Mexico ceded to U. S.
Feb. 25	*Oh! Susanna,* copyrighted by C. Holt, Jr., New York.
May 16	*Old Uncle Ned,* copyrighted by W. E. Millet, New York.
May 16	Peters advertises *Uncle Ned* as "this day published."
June	Stephen, in Cincinnati, helps care for Morrison, who stops there, ill with the cholera.
June	Dunning returns from Mexican War, in poor health.

July 15	Peters advertises *Stay Summer Breath* as "just published."
Sept. 6	Peters advertises *Susanna, Don't You Cry* as "recently published."
Dec. 16	*Old Uncle Ned,* copyrighted by F. D. Benteen, Baltimore.
Dec. 30	*Away Down South, Stay Summer Breath, Santa Anna's Retreat from Buena Vista, Uncle Ned,* and *Susanna,* copyrighted by W. C. Peters, Louisville.

1849

	Stephen and Dunning boarding with Mrs. Griffin, Cincinnati. Family in Allegheny boarding in various places—Mrs. Lynch, Mrs. Thompson, Mrs. Hart. Wm. Foster, senior, now a Soldier's Agent.
Jan. 13	Jane McDowell visiting in Cincinnati. Stephen visiting in Pittsburgh.
Feb.	Stephen returns to Cincinnati.
Mar. 4	Zachary Taylor and Millard Fillmore, Whigs, inaugurated as President and Vice President.
Apr. 27	Stephen, in Cincinnati, writes Morrison about his having given Gilead Smith a song (*Nelly Was a Lady*), and asks that Smith take the manuscript to Firth, Pond & Co.
May 25	Stephen, in Cincinnati, writes Millet in New York explaining how he had given copies of his songs to minstrel performers, without permission to publish them.
Day and month unknown	*Nelly Was a Lady,* copyrighted by Firth, Pond & Co., New York.
June	Stephen visiting Allegheny.
July	Stephen visits Henrietta in Warren, Ohio.
Aug. 13	Henry Foster has been removed from office.
Sept. 12	Firth, Pond & Co. agrees to pay Stephen 2 cents per copy on all future songs, and refers to 50 copies as Stephen's interest in *Nelly Was a Lady* and *My Brudder Gum.*
Oct. 1	*My Brudder Gum,* copyrighted by Firth, Pond & Co.
Oct.	Stephen back in Cincinnati.
Nov. 14	*Dolcy Jones,* copyrighted by Firth, Pond & Co.

Nov. 21	*Summer Longings,* copyrighted by W. C. Peters, Baltimore.
Dec. 3	Date of first contract with Firth, Pond & Co.

1850

Day and month unknown	William B. Foster presses for the last time his claim against the government. It has grown to $5,218.60.
Jan. 7	*Oh! Lemuel!* coprighted by F. D. Benteen, Baltimore.
Jan. 16	*Mary Loves the Flowers,* copyrighted by Firth, Pond & Co.
	Stephen returns to Allegheny permanently in January or early in February.
Feb. 8	*Nelly Bly,* copyrighted by Firth, Pond & Co.
Feb. 12	*Soirée Polka,* copyrighted by W. C. Peters, Baltimore.
Feb. 19	*Camptown Races* and *Dolly Day,* copyrighted by F. D. Benteen.
Feb. 23	Stephen sends E. P. Christy copies of *Camptown Races* and *Dolly Day.*
Mar. 1	Stephen borrowed $100 from Brother William.
Mar. 18	*Angelina Baker,* copyrighted by F. D. Benteen.
Apr. 12	*Ah! May the Red Rose Live Alway,* copyrighted by F. D. Benteen.
Apr. 17	*Way Down in Ca-i-ro,* copyrighted by Firth, Pond & Co.
Apr. 22	Foster family move into Brother William's house on East Common, Allegheny.
May 6	*Molly! Do You Love Me?* copyrighted by F. D. Benteen.
June 28	*The Voice of By Gone Days,* copyrighted by Firth, Pond & Co.
July 9	President Taylor dies; succeeded by Millard Fillmore.
July 22	Stephen and Jane McDowell married.
Aug. 21	*The Spirit of My Song,* copyrighted by F. D. Benteen.
Sept. 8	Stephen and Jane go to live with the Foster family.
Oct. 15	*I Would Not Die in Spring Time* (Milton Moore *pseud.*), *Turn Not Away* and *Village Bells Polka,* copyrighted by F. D. Benteen.
Oct. 22	William Foster, senior, applies for a land warrant.
Dec. 9	*Lily Ray,* copyrighted by Firth, Pond & Co.

1851

Jan. 6	*Give the Stranger Happy Cheer* and *Melinda May,* copyrighted by F. D. Benteen.
Feb. 11	William Foster, senior, receives his land warrant. An invalid from this year.
Mar. 12	*Wilt Thou Be Gone, Love?,* copyrighted by Firth, Pond & Co.
Mar. 18	*Sweetly She Sleeps, My Alice Fair* and *Mother, Thou'rt Faithful to Me,* copyrighted by F. D. Benteen.
Mar. 22	*Farewell Old Cottage,* copyrighted by Firth, Pond & Co.
Apr. 4	*Once I Loved Thee, Mary Dear,* copyrighted by Firth, Pond & Co.
Apr. 18	Marion Foster, Stephen's daughter, born.
Apr. 29	*Ring de Banjo,* copyrighted by Firth, Pond & Co.
June 12	Stephen offers to allow E. P. Christy to sing "Oh! Boys, Carry Me 'Long" before publication for $10.
June 20	Stephen acknowledges receipt of $10 from Christy.
June 26	Stephen starts his manuscript book.
July 12	*I Would Not Die in Summer Time,* copyrighted by F. D. Benteen.
July 19	Stephen sends manuscript of *Laura Lee* to Benteen.
July 25	*Oh! Boys, Carry Me 'Long,* copyrighted by Firth, Pond & Co.
July 28	Stephen rents office.
Aug. 4	*My Hopes Have Departed Forever,* copyrighted by Firth, Pond & Co.
Aug. 7	*Laura Lee,* copyrighted by F. D. Benteen.
Aug. 26	Title-page of *Old Folks at Home,* copyrighted by Firth, Pond & Co.
Oct. 1	*Old Folks at Home* (complete song), copyrighted by Firth, Pond & Co.
Oct. 21	*Willie My Brave,* copyrighted by Firth, Pond & Co.
Dec. 6	*Eulalie,* copyrighted by Firth, Pond & Co.
Dec. 13	*Farewell My Lilly Dear,* copyrighted by Firth, Pond & Co.

1852

Feb.	Stephen and Jane take steamboat trip to New Orleans.
May 25	Stephen writes Christy, asking that he be released from agreement to have Christy's name appear as composer of *Old Folks at Home.*

July 7	*Massa's in de Cold Ground,* copyrighted by Firth, Pond & Co.
July 9	*The Hour for Thee and Me,* copyrighted by Firth, Pond & Co.
Aug. 11	*I Cannot Sing To-night,* copyrighted by Firth, Pond & Co.
Sept. 4	Firth, Pond & Co. advertise 40,000 copies of *Old Folks at Home* sold.
Oct. 14	*Maggie by My Side,* copyrighted by Firth, Pond & Co.

1853

Jan. 15	Firth, Pond & Co. advertises *My Old Kentucky Home* as "just published."
Jan. 29	Stephen has visited *Musical World* office in New York.
Jan. 31	*My Old Kentucky Home,* copyrighted by Firth, Pond & Co.
Feb. 14	Stephen, in Pittsburgh, writes *Musical World* a letter on musical theory.
Feb. 19	*Musical World* tells an inquiring correspondent that S. C. Foster is the composer of *Old Folks at Home.*
Mar. 4	Franklin Pierce, Democrat, inaugurated as President. Government under influence of Jefferson Davis and other pro-slavery leaders.
Mar. 11	*Old Folks Quadrilles,* copyrighted by Firth, Pond & Co., including also the *Cane Brake Jig.*
May 5	New contract with Firth, Pond & Co. raises Stephen's royalty on future songs to ten per cent.
May 12	*Annie My Own Love,* copyrighted by Firth, Pond & Co.
June 21	Letter from Henrietta indicates that Stephen and Jane are separated.
July 2	*Holiday Schottisch,* copyrighted by Firth, Pond & Co.
July 8	Stephen in New York. "Circumstances have increased my expenses." Has borrowed money from Morrison. Firth, Pond & Company's last (quarterly) statement $500.
Day and month unknown	*Old Dog Tray,* copyrighted by Firth, Pond & Co.
Dec. 5	*Old Memories,* copyrighted by Firth, Pond & Co.
Dec. 13	*Little Ella,* copyrighted by Firth, Pond & Co.

1854
Stephen in New York until October.

Jan. 26   *Social Orchestra,* copyrighted by Firth, Pond & Co., containing new works by Foster, as follows:
> *Anadolia*
> *Irene*
> *Jennie's Own Schottisch*
> *Village Festival Quadrilles*
> *Village Festival Jig*

Feb. 3   *Ellen Bayne,* copyrighted by Firth, Pond & Co.

Mar. & May Stephen Douglas Kansas-Nebraska bill passed.

Mar. 3   Dunning writes Morrison, referring to Stephen's "unaccountable course."

Mar. 4   *Willie We Have Missed You,* copyrighted by Firth, Pond & Co.

June 5   *Jeanie with the Light Brown Hair,* copyrighted by Firth, Pond & Co.

July 6   New state party, to become Republican, meets at Jackson, Mich.

Sept. 2   Firth, Pond & Co. advertises "3rd thousand" of *Willie We Have Missed You.*

Sept. 19   *Come with Thy Sweet Voice Again,* copyrighted by Firth, Pond & Co.

Oct. 19   Stephen has recently returned to Allegheny.

Nov. 11   Firth, Pond advertises following sales: *Old Folks at Home,* more than 130,000; *My Old Kentucky Home,* 90,000; *Massa's in de Cold Ground,* 74,000; *Old Dog Tray,* 48,000.
            (N.B. These figures cannot be substantiated from Stephen's later royalty accounts.)

Dec. 21   New contract with Firth, Pond & Co.

1855
Jan. 17   *Hard Times Come Again No More,* copyrighted by Firth, Pond & Co.

Jan. 18   Eliza Foster, Stephen's mother, dies.

June 28   *Come Where My Love Lies Dreaming* and *Some Folks,* copyrighted by Firth, Pond & Co.

July 27   William B. Foster, Stephen's father, dies.

Sept. 17   *The Village Maiden,* copyrighted by Firth, Pond & Co.

Oct. 12   Stephen pays Brother William $64.

Nov. 1	Stephen owes Brother William, "rent 3 mos. $31.25." Stephen and Jane are keeping house where the family had lived before his father's and mother's deaths.
Nov. 23	*Comrades, Fill No Glass for Me,* copyrighted by Miller & Beacham, Baltimore.

1856

Apr. 24	*Gentle Annie,* copyrighted by Firth, Pond & Co.
Mar. 31	Dunning Foster dies in Cincinnati.
Spring	Civil War in Kansas. Missourians attack Lawrence. John Brown's raid at Pottawatomie Creek.
Apr. 1	Stephen owes Brother William five months' rent, $52.08.
June	James Buchanan nominated by Democrats; John C. Frémont by Republicans.
Aug. 6	Buchanan Glee Club organized—Stephen musical director.
Sept.	*The Abolition Show,* a poem written for the Buchanan Glee Club, printed in the *Pittsburgh Post. The White House Chair* was also written for the club.
Oct. 22	Elizabeth, William's wife, dies.

1857

Jan. 27	Stephen prepares list showing royalties received to date on Firth, Pond & Co. songs amounting to $9,436.96. He estimates that these songs should be worth $2,786.77 in future royalties.
Mar. 4	James Buchanan inaugurated as President.
Mar. 6	Dred Scott Decision.
Mar. 14	Stephen drawn ahead at Firth, Pond & Co. by $372.28. Sells his entire future interest in previous songs for $1,872.28. At about the same time he sells to F. D. Benteen all his future rights in the songs published by that firm for $200.
March	Morrison boarding with Stephen; pays $4 per week, including washing.
Starting Apr. 13	Stephen and family boarding at Eagle Hotel, John Mish, proprietor. Board $12 per week.
June 8	*I See Her Still in My Dreams,* copyrighted by Firth, Pond & Co.
December	Morrison leaves Allegheny and Pittsburgh to be with Brother William in Philadelphia.

1858

Lincoln-Douglas debates.

Railroad mileage increased to 22,500.

Feb. 9	New contract with Firth, Pond & Co. Stephen sells the firm his interest in *I See Her Still in My Dreams,* and starts again with no interest in any previous songs.
Feb. 25	Stephen has taken a trip to New York. Charges Firth, Pond & Co. $43.75 for travelling expenses.
Apr. 8	Stephen and his family leave the Eagle Hotel. May have rented a house from William and James Murdock.
Apr. 19	*Lula Is Gone,* copyrighted by Firth, Pond & Co.
July 13	*Linger in Blissful Repose,* copyrighted by Firth, Pond & Co.
Aug. 9	Stephen and his family start boarding with Mrs. Johnston. Board at $9 per week.
Sept. 7	*Where Has Lula Gone?* copyrighted by Firth, Pond & Co.
Nov. 12	Stephen, with Jane and Marion, take a trip to Cincinnati with William Hamilton on the "Ida May."
Nov. 24	*My Loved One and My Own, or Eva,* copyrighted by Firth, Pond & Co.
Dec. 28	*Sadly to Mine Heart Appealing,* copyrighted by Firth, Pond & Co.

1859

Jan. 1	Stephen drawn ahead at Firth, Pond & Co. $995.72.
Mar. 1	*Linda Has Departed,* copyrighted by Firth, Pond & Co.
Apr. 4	*Parthenia to Ingomar,* copyrighted by Firth, Pond & Co.
April-May (perhaps earlier)	Stephen and his family boarding with Mrs. A. Miller. Board at $9.50 and $10.50 per week.
May 16	Firth, Pond & Co. refuses Stephen's draft for $100.
June 10	*For Thee, Love, for Thee,* copyrighted by Firth, Pond & Co.
June 10	Henrietta pleads with Morrison and Stephen to join the church.
June 13	Stephen writes Morrison he has had his picture taken.
Aug. 15	Stephen has been to Baden, trying to collect some money due Morrison.
Aug. 19	*Fairy Belle,* copyrighted by Firth, Pond & Co.
Sept.	Morrison returns from Philadelphia.

Oct. 17   John Brown seizes arsenal at Harper's Ferry, and is captured.

Dec. 2   John Brown executed.

Dec. 21   *Thou Art the Queen of My Song,* copyrighted by Firth, Pond & Co.

1860

Jan. 1   Stephen drawn ahead at Firth, Pond & Co. $1,479.95.

Feb.   Lincoln's speech at Cooper Union, New York.

Feb. 9   *None Shall Weep a Tear for Me, Poor Drooping Maiden,* and *The Wife,* copyrighted by Firth, Pond & Co.

Feb. 23   Morrison Foster marries Jessie Lightner. Living in Cleveland.

Mar. 4   William B. Foster, junior, dies.

Apr. 27   Stephen, with Jane and Marion, at the Austin House in Warren, O. Writes Morrison asking loan of $12. Firth, Pond & Co. will not advance any more money until Stephen sends them some more songs. Firth, Pond & Co. show disposition to renew agreement, expiring August 9, 1860. "Have entered into an agreement with a new house for part of my music."

May 3   *Under the Willow She's Sleeping,* copyrighted by Firth, Pond & Co.

May   Republican convention nominates Abraham Lincoln for President.

May 29   *The Glendy Burk,* copyrighted by Firth, Pond & Co.

Day and month unknown   *Cora Dean,* copyrighted by Firth, Pond & Co.

May 31   Stephen still in Warren, O. Asks Morrison to lend him $50, and sends draft on Firth, Pond & Co. as security. "Received yesterday a very cheering letter from F. P. & Co."

June   Democrats nominate Stephen A. Douglas for President.

July 1   Stephen drawn ahead at Firth, Pond & Co. $1,396.64.

July 21   *Jenny's Coming O'er the Green,* copyrighted by Lee & Walker, Philadelphia. (Reprinted from *Clark's School Visitor.*)

Aug. 9   Expiration date of Feb. 9, 1858, contract with Firth, Pond & Co., providing that Stephen should publish exclusively with that firm.

Under this date Stephen sold all his rights in songs published under that contract (16) for $1,600, thus repaying the amount drawn ahead ($1,396.64) and gaining a credit of $203.36.

Aug. 10   Stephen apparently still in Warren. Presumably he took his wife and daughter to New York after this date.

Oct. 6   *Beautiful Child of Song,* as published in *Clark's School Visitor,* entered for copyright. The publishers of the *Visitor* later claimed that they paid Stephen $400 for six songs.

Nov. 6   Lincoln elected President.

Nov. 8   *Old Black Joe,* copyrighted by Firth, Pond & Co.

Nov. 15   *Down Among the Cane Brakes* and *Virginia Belle,* copyrighted by Firth, Pond & Co.

Dec. 11   *The Little Ballad Girl,* as published in *Clark's School Visitor,* entered for copyright.

Dec. 20   South Carolina secedes.

1861

Feb. 1   *Mine Is the Mourning Heart,* copyrighted by Daughaday & Hammond, Philadelphia (publishers of the *Visitor*). Reprinted from *Clark's School Visitor* by Root & Cady, Chicago.

Feb. 8   Confederacy formed. Jefferson Davis elected President.

Mar. 4   Lincoln inaugurated.

Mar. 9   *Don't Bet Your Money on de Shanghai,* copyrighted by Firth, Pond & Co.

Apr. 6   *Molly Dear, Good Night,* copyrighted by Firth, Pond & Co.

Apr. 12   Fort Sumter fired upon. Captured two days later.

Apr. 15   Lincoln issues call for troops.

May 9   *Our Willie Dear Is Dying,* copyrighted by Firth, Pond & Co.

May 23   *Lizzie Dies To-night,* as published in *Clark's School Visitor,* entered for copyright.

June 4   *Our Bright Summer Days Are Gone,* copyrighted by John J. Daly. (John Mahon wrote that this song was rejected by Firth, Pond & Co.)

July 18   *I'll Be a Soldier,* copyrighted by John J. Daly.

Aug. 5   *Why Have My Loved Ones Gone?* copyrighted by

Horace Waters. (The Waters copyrights are in the name of E. A. Daggett, Waters' son-in-law.)

Aug. 20   *Oh! Tell Me of My Mother,* copyrighted by John J. Daly.

Sept. 9   *Farewell Mother Dear,* copyrighted by John J. Daly.

Sept. 30   Jane, Stephen's wife, and Marion, their daughter, in Lewistown, Pa. She writes Morrison that she is uneasy about "Steve." Asks a loan of $10 so that she may join Stephen immediately.

Oct. 5   Jane acknowledges Morrison's $10. Is going to New York.

Oct. 7   *Sweet Little Maid of the Mountain,* copyrighted by John J. Daly.

Oct. 16   *Farewell Sweet Mother,* copyrighted by Firth, Pond & Co.

Nov. 5   *Little Belle Blair,* copyrighted by John J. Daly.

Dec. 3   *Nell and I,* copyrighted by John J. Daly.

Dec. 16   *A Penny for Your Thoughts,* copyrighted by Horace Waters.

1862

Day and month unknown [1]   *We've a Million in the Field,* copyrighted by S. T. Gordon.

Jan. 10   *Little Jenny Dow,* copyrighted by Horace Waters.

Day and month unknown   *I Will Be True to Thee,* copyrighted by Horace Waters.

Apr. 16   *A Dream of My Mother and My Home,* copyrighted by Horace Waters.

Day and month unknown   *Better Times Are Coming,* copyrighted by Horace Waters.

Apr. 29   *That's What's the Matter,* copyrighted by Firth, Pond & Co.

May   Robert E. Lee becomes commander of Confederate forces.

May   *The Merry, Merry Month of May,* published in *Clark's School Visitor.*

---

[1] Where the day and month of copyright entry are not known, the song is listed in the chronological place that the details of the first editions seem to show it belongs.

June 10   *Merry Little Birds Are We,* copyrighted by Horace Waters.

June 30   Stephen's wife and daughter again in Lewistown, Pa. Jane writes Morrison that "Steve" publishes once in a long while with Pond, and that he appreciates the clothing Morrison has sent him.

July 24   *Why, No One to Love?* copyrighted by S. T. Gordon.

July 26   *No Home, No Home,* copyrighted by John J. Daly.

Aug. 9   *Was My Brother in the Battle?* copyrighted by Horace Waters.

Day and month unknown   *Slumber, My Darling,* copyrighted by Horace Waters.

Sept. 5   *We Are Coming, Father Abraam,* copyrighted by S. T. Gordon.

Sept. 10   *I'll Be Home To-morrow,* copyrighted by Firth, Pond & Co.

Nov. 22   *Happy Hours at Home,* copyrighted by John J. Daly.

Dec. 31   *Gentle Lena Clare,* copyrighted by S. T. Gordon.

Day and month unknown   *There Are Plenty of Fish in the Sea,* copyrighted by Horace Waters.

1863

Jan. 1   Lincoln issues Emancipation Proclamation.

Day and month unknown   *Bring My Brother Back to Me,* and *My Boy Is Coming from the War,* copyrighted by S. T. Gordon.

Day and month unknown   *We Will Keep a Bright Lookout,* copyrighted by Horace Waters.

Jan. 14   *The Love I Bear to Thee,* copyrighted by Horace Waters.

Day and month unknown   *When This Dreadful War Is Ended,* copyrighted by Horace Waters.

Jan. 31   *Bury Me in the Morning, Mother; Little Ella's an Angel; Suffer Little Children* and *Willie's Gone to Heaven,* copyrighted by Horace Waters.

Feb. 11   Stephen, in New York, writes G. W. Birdseye: "I will arrange Mr. Cooper's melody when my hand gets well."

Feb. 14   *Nothing But a Plain Old Soldier,* copyrighted by John J. Daly.

Feb. 25 — *I'd Be a Fairy,* copyrighted by S. T. Gordon.

Mar. 3 — Draft Act becomes law.

Mar. 10 — *Oh! There's No Such Girl as Mine,* copyrighted by Horace Waters.

Apr. 14 — The *Golden Harp,* a hymn-book for Sunday Schools, containing ten new songs by Stephen Foster, copyrighted by Horace Waters:

The Angels Are Singing unto Me.
The Beautiful Shore.
Give Us This Day Our Daily Bread.
He Leadeth Me Beside Still Waters.
Leave Me with My Mother.
Oh! 'tis Glorious!
Seek and Ye Shall Find.
Tears Bring Thoughts of Heaven.
We'll All Meet Our Saviour.
We'll Still Keep Marching On.

Apr. 17 — *Jenny June,* copyrighted by Firth, Son & Co.

May 27 — *A Soldier in de Colored Brigade,* copyrighted by Firth, Son & Co.

June 27 — *Lena Our Loved One Is Gone,* copyrighted by John J. Daly.

June 29 — *Larry's Good Bye, There Was a Time* and *Katy Bell,* copyrighted by S. T. Gordon.

July 1-3 — Battle of Gettysburg.

July 1 — *Willie Has Gone to the War,* copyrighted by Wm. A. Pond & Co.

July 13-16 — Draft riots in New York.

July 24 — George Cooper returns to New York.

Aug. 8 — *Kissing in the Dark,* copyrighted by John J. Daly.

October — Jane, Stephen's wife, writes Morrison hoping that he can persuade Stephen to return to Cleveland with him. Then "All will soon be well with him again."

Nov. 13 — *The Soldier's Home,* copyrighted by S. T. Gordon.

Nov. 20 — *Oh! Why Am I So Happy, My Wife Is a Most Knowing Woman,* and *Onward and Upward,* copyrighted by Horace Waters.

Day and month unknown — *For the Dear Old Flag I Die,* copyrighted by Horace Waters.

Dec. 4 — *The Song of All Songs,* copyrighted by D. S. Holmes.

Dec. 9   *The Athenæum Collection,* a hymn-book for Church
          and Sunday School, containing ten new songs by Fos-
          ter, copyrighted by Horace Waters:
            The Bright Hills of Glory.
            Choral Harp.
            Don't Be Idle.
            Over the River.
            The Pure, the Bright, the Beautiful.
            Stand Up for the Truth.
            Tell Me of the Angels, Mother.
            We'll Tune Our Hearts.
            What Shall the Harvest Be? (Music similar to but
              not identical with *Why, No One to Love?*)
            While We Work for the Lord.

                              1864
Jan. 10   Stephen taken to Bellevue Hospital.
Jan. 12   George Cooper writes Morrison Foster of Stephen's
          illness.
Jan. 13   Stephen dies at Bellevue Hospital.
Jan. 14   George Cooper telegraphs Morrison, "Stephen is
          dead."
Jan. 21   Funeral services in Trinity Church, Pittsburgh, and
          burial in Allegheny Cemetery, Pittsburgh.
Jan. 23   *If You've Only Got a Moustache, Mr. & Mrs.
          Brown, When Old Friends Were Here* and *Wilt
          Thou Be True?* copyrighted by Horace Waters.
Feb. 23   *She Was All the World to Me,* "the last song of the
          late Stephen C. Foster," copyrighted by Horace
          Waters.
Mar.   U. S. Grant appointed Commander-in-Chief of Union
          forces.
Mar. 10   *Beautiful Dreamer,* "the last song ever written by
          Stephen C. Foster, composed but a few days before his
          death," copyrighted by William A. Pond & Co.
Mar. 10   *All Day Long,* copyrighted by J. Starr Holloway.
          Reprinted from *Holloway's Musical Monthly.*
Apr. 20   *Sitting by My Own Cabin Door,* copyrighted by John
          J. Daly.
May 7   *Give This to Mother,* "Stephen C. Foster's last mu-
          sical idea," copyrighted by P. A. Wundermann. (The
          music is similar to but not identical with *Tears Bring
          Thoughts of Heaven,* originally published in the

	Golden Harp.) The words written by S. W. Harding.
May 7	*When Dear Friends Are Gone,* copyrighted by P. A. Wundermann.
May 14	*Somebody's Coming to See Me To-night,* copyrighted by D. S. Holmes.
June 8	Lincoln and Andrew Johnson nominated by Republicans.
June	Horace Waters advertises *When Old Friends Were Here* and *She Was All the World to Me* as the last songs of Foster.
Aug. 3	*Tell Me Love of Thy Early Dreams,* copyrighted by John J. Daly.
Aug. 29	McClellan and Pendleton nominated by Democrats.
Day and month unknown	*Little Mac! Little Mac! You're the Very Man,* copyrighted by Marion Foster. Published by J. Marsh of Philadelphia. The words could not have been written by Stephen, for they refer to the Lincoln-McClellan campaign, which did not commence until the Summer of 1864. The first phrase of the music is similar to *Nelly Bly.*
Nov.	Lincoln and Johnson elected.

1865

Jan. 31	*My Angel Boy, I Cannot See Thee Die,* "composed by the late Stephen C. Foster in 1858 and now for the first time published," copyrighted by Wm. A. Pond & Co.
Mar. 4	Lincoln and Johnson inaugurated.
Mar. 23	*The Voices That Are Gone,* copyrighted by Wm. A. Pond & Co.
Apr. 2	Lee withdraws from Richmond.
Apr. 9	Lee surrenders at Appomattox.
Apr. 14	Abraham Lincoln assassinated by John Wilkes Booth.

1866

Nov. 1	*Sweet Emerald Isle That I Love So Well,* copyrighted by John J. Daly.

1867

Day and month unknown	*Heavenly Echoes,* a hymn-book, compiled by Horace Waters, published by C. M. Tremaine, containing two songs by Stephen Foster: *What Does Every Good*

Child Say? (poetry by a friend) and *Praise the Lord,* "written and composed by Stephen C. Foster." (The music is the same as *Willie's Gone to Heaven.*)

1869

February	*Dearer Than Life,* published in *Demorest's Magazine.*
Apr. 10	*Kiss Me Dear Mother,* copyrighted by Wm. A. Pond & Co.

1870

Aug. 19	*A Thousand Miles from Home,* copyrighted by John J. Daly.

1879

Mar. 29	Oliver Ditson & Co. writes Stephen's widow regarding renewal of expiring copyrights.
May 10	Contract signed with Oliver Ditson Co. by which the firm agrees to pay Stephen's widow and daughter a royalty on copyright renewals for sales of all songs acquired from Firth, Son & Co. and several other publishers of Stephen's songs.
May ?	Morrison Foster enters into correspondence with Wm. A. Pond & Co. regarding copyright renewals on Stephen's songs.
July 24	Morrison sends Wm. A. Pond & Co. signed contract by which the firm agrees to pay a royalty on copyright renewals for sales of all of Stephen's songs published by that firm.

1885

Sept. 20	*The White House Chair,* published in the *Pittsburgh Dispatch.* Originally written in 1856.

1895

Dec. 9	*Where Is Thy Spirit, Mary?* (presumably written in 1847), published by George Mercer, Jr., Pittsburgh.

1896

Morrison Foster publishes his book, *Biography, Songs and Musical Compositions of Stephen C. Foster.* In this *The Tioga Waltz* was printed for the first time.

1900

Sept. 12	First monument to be erected to Foster unveiled at Highland Park, Pittsburgh. Music at the ceremony conducted by Victor Herbert.

1903

Jan. 3   Stephen's widow, Jane (Mrs. Matthew D. Wiley) dies.

1904

May 14   Morrison Foster dies.

1914

James H. Park purchases the probable site of Stephen's birthplace and presents it to the City of Pittsburgh. Dedicated and maintained as the Stephen Foster Memorial Home.

1915

Catalogue of First Editions of Stephen C. Foster, by Walter R. Whittlesey and O. G. Sonneck, published by Library of Congress (Gov't Printing Office).

1920

Harold Vincent Milligan publishes his book, *Stephen Collins Foster, A Biography* (G. Schirmer, Inc., New York).

1922

State of Kentucky accepts as a gift from subscribers to fund the Rowan home "Federal Hill" at Bardstown, and dedicates and maintains the old mansion as "My Old Kentucky Home."

1926

Mar. 9   Bill introduced in House of Representatives to authorize 50-cent pieces commemorating 100th anniversary of Foster's birth. Failed of passage.

1931

Jan. 5   Josiah K. Lilly of Indianapolis starts a collection of Fosteriana and establishes Foster Hall for the purpose of assembling, in permanent form, as complete data as possible concerning the life and work of Stephen Foster, to belong to the people of the United States and to be made available in perpetuity for view or study by any one interested in the subject.

Sept. 29   *Long Ago Day* and *This Rose Will Remind You,* two songs sold by Stephen to T. D. (Daddy) Rice, *circa* 1851, copyrighted by D. J. Rice and published by J. Fischer & Bro., N. Y.

APPENDIX II

THE PUBLISHED WORKS OF STEPHEN C. FOSTER

(The year of publication is given in parentheses, as is the name of the poet in songs for which Stephen Foster composed only the music)

Songs

The Abolition Show. This is a political satire sung to the air "Villikins and His Dinah." It was published in the *Pittsburgh Post,* September, 1856, as "A Song." Foster's manuscripts of this song in the Foster Hall Collection bear the titles "The Abolition Show" and "The Great Baby Show." The standard title is considered to be "The Abolition Show" (1856)

Ah! May the Red Rose Live Alway (1850)

All Day Long (1864) (Clara Morton)

Angelina Baker (1850)

The Angels Are Singing unto Me (1863)

Annie My Own Love (1853) (Charles P. Shiras)

Away Down South (1848)

Beautiful Child of Song (1860)

Beautiful Dreamer (1864)

The Beautiful Shore (1863) (Mrs. O. S. Matteson)

   Better Days Are Coming. See "Better Times Are Coming."

Better Times (Days) Are Coming (1862)

The Bright Hills of Glory (1863) (Mrs. M. A. Kidder)

Bring My Brother Back to Me (1863) (George Cooper)

Bury Me in the Morning, Mother (1863)

Camptown Races. First issued as "Gwine to Run All Night." (1850)

Choral Harp (1863) (William Ross Wallace)

Come Where My Love Lies Dreaming (1855)

Come with Thy Sweet Voice Again (1854)

Comrades, Fill No Glass for Me (1855)

Cora Dean (1860)

   De Camptown Races. See "Camptown Races."

Dearer Than Life! (1869) (George Cooper)

Dolcy Jones (1849)

Dolly Day (1850)

Don't Be Idle (1863) (Mrs. M. A. Kidder)

Don't Bet Your Money on de Shanghai (1861)
Down Among the Cane Brakes (1860)
A Dream of My Mother and My Home (1862)
Ellen Bayne (1854)
Eulalie (1851) (H. S. Cornwell)
  Eva. See "My Loved One and My Own."
Fairy Belle (1859)
Farewell Mother Dear (1861)
Farewell My Lilly Dear (1851)
Farewell Old Cottage (1851)
Farewell Sweet Mother (1861)
For the Dear Old Flag I Die! (1863) (George Cooper)
For Thee, Love, for Thee (1859) (William Henry McCarthy)
Gentle Annie (1856)
Gentle Lena Clare (1862)
Give the Stranger Happy Cheer (1851)
Give This to Mother (1864) (S. W. Harding)
Give Us This Day Our Daily Bread (1863)
The Glendy Burk (1860)
  Golden Dreams & Fairy Castles! See Derivata.
  The Great Baby Show. See "The Abolition Show."
  Gwine to Run All Night. See "Camptown Races."
Happy Hours at Home (1862)
  Happy Little Ones Are We. See Derivata.
Hard Times Come Again No More (1855)
He Leadeth Me Beside Still Waters (1863) (W. R.)
  He'll Come Home. See "The Wife."
  Home, Heavenly Home. See Derivata.
The Hour for Thee and Me (1852)
I Cannot Sing To-night (1852) (George F. Banister)
  I Dream of My Mother. See "A Dream of My Mother and
    My Home."
I See Her Still in My Dreams (1857)
I'll Be a Soldier (1861)
I'll Be Home To-morrow (1862)
I Will Be True to Thee (1862)
I'd Be a Fairy (1863)
I Would Not Die in Spring Time. Issued under pseudonym, "Mil-
    ton Moore." (1850) (Anonymous)
I Would Not Die in Summer Time (1851)
If You've Only Got a Moustache (1864) (George Cooper)
  In the Eye Abides the Heart. See "Translations."
Jeanie with the Light Brown Hair (1854)
Jenny's Coming o'er the Green (1860)
Jenny June (1863) (George Cooper)
Katy Bell (1863) (George Cooper)

Kiss Me Dear Mother (1869)
Kissing in the Dark (1863) (George Cooper)
Larry's Good Bye (1863) (George Cooper)
Laura Lee (1851)
Leave Me with My Mother (1863)
Lena Our Loved One Is Gone (1863)
Lily Ray (1850)
Linda Has Departed (1859) (William Henry McCarthy)
Linger in Blissful Repose (1858)
The Little Ballad Girl (1860)
Little Belle Blair (1861)
Little Ella (1853)
Little Ella's an Angel (1863)
Little Jenny Dow (1862)
Little Mac! Little Mac! You're the Very Man (1864) (Words
    anonymous, written after Foster's death)
Lizzie Dies To-night (1861) (Mary Byron Reese)
Long Ago Day (1931)
Lou'siana Belle (1847)
The Love I Bear to Thee (1863)
Lula Is Gone (1858)
Maggie by My Side (1852)
Mary Loves the Flowers (1850)
Massa's in de Cold Ground (1852)
Melinda May (1851)
Merry Little Birds Are We (1862)
The Merry, Merry Month of May (1862)
Mine Is the Mourning Heart (1861)
Mr. & Mrs. Brown (1864) (George Cooper)
Molly Dear, Good Night (1861)
Molly! Do You Love Me? (1850)
Mother, Thou'rt Faithful to Me (1851)
    Music Everywhere, That's Why I Love It So. See Derivata.
My Angel Boy, I Cannot See Thee Die (1865) (H. Brougham)
My Boy Is Coming from the War (1863) (George Cooper)
My Brudder Gum (1849)
My Hopes Have Departed Forever (1851)
My Loved One and My Own, or Eva (1858)
My Old Kentucky Home, Good Night (1853)
My Wife Is a Most Knowing Woman (1863) (George Cooper)
Nell and I (1861)
Nelly Bly (1850)
Nelly Was a Lady (1849)
No Home, No Home (1862)
None Shall Weep a Tear for Me (1860) (Richard Henry Wilde)
Nothing But a Plain Old Soldier (1863)

Oh! Boys, Carry Me 'Long (1851)
Oh! 'tis Glorious! (1863) (Edwin H. Nevin)
Oh! Lemuel! (1850)
   Oh! Meet Me, Dear Mother. See Derivata.
Oh! Susanna (1848)
Oh! Tell Me of My Mother (1861)
Oh! There's No Such Girl As Mine (1863) (Samuel Lover)
Oh! Why Am I So Happy? (1863) (Francis D. Murtha)
Old Black Joe (1860)
Old Dog Tray (1853)
Old Folks at Home (1851)
Old Memories (1853)
Old Uncle Ned (1848)
Once I Loved Thee, Mary Dear (1851) (William Cullen Crook-
   shank)
Onward and Upward (1863) (George Cooper)
Open Thy Lattice, Love (1844) (George P. Morris)
Our Bright Summer Days Are Gone (1861)
   Our Darling Kate. See Arrangements.
Our Willie Dear Is Dying (1861)
Over the River (1863) (H. C.)
Parthenia to Ingomar (1859) (William Henry McCarthy)
A Penny for Your Thoughts (1861)
Poor Drooping Maiden (1860)
Praise the Lord (1867)
The Pure, the Bright, the Beautiful (1863) (Charles Dickens)
Ring de Banjo (1851)
Sadly to Mine Heart Appealing (1858) (Eliza Sheridan Carey)
Seek and Ye Shall Find (1863)
She Was All the World to Me (1864) (Dr. Duffy)
Sitting by My Own Cabin Door (1864)
Slumber, My Darling (1862)
A Soldier in de Colored Brigade (1863) (George Cooper)
The Soldier's Home (1863) (George Cooper)
Some Folks (1855)
Somebody's Coming to See Me To-night (1864) (George Cooper)
   A Song. See "The Abolition Show."
The Song of All Songs (1863) (Tony Pastor)
   Sorrow Shall Come Again No More. See Derivata.
The Spirit of My Song (1850) (Metta Victoria Fuller)
   Stand Up for the Flag! See Derivata.
Stand Up for the Truth (1863) (J. C.)
Stay Summer Breath (1848)
Suffer Little Children to Come unto Me (1863)
Summer Longings (1849) (Denis Florence MacCarthy)
   Susanna. See "Oh! Susanna."

Sweet Emerald Isle That I Love So Well (1866) (George Cooper)
Sweet Little Maid of the Mountain (1861)
Sweetly She Sleeps, My Alice Fair (1851) (Charles G. Eastman)
Tears Bring Thoughts of Heaven (1863)
Tell Me Love of Thy Early Dreams (1864)
Tell Me of the Angels, Mother (1863)
That's What's the Matter (1862)
There Are Plenty of Fish in the Sea (1862) (George Cooper)
There's a Good Time Coming (1846) (Charles Mackay)
  There's a Land of Bliss. See Derivata.
  There Is a Land of Love. See Derivata.
  There's No Such Girl As Mine. See "Oh! There's No Such Girl
    As Mine."
There Was a Time (1863) (J. D. Byrne)
This Rose Will Remind You (1931) (G. Mellen)
Thou Art the Queen of My Song (1859)
A Thousand Miles from Home (1870)
  'Tis My Father's Song. This is the title under which "The Little
    Ballad Girl" was republished by John Church, Jr., of Cincin-
    nati in 1865.
Turn Not Away! (1850)
  Uncle Ned. See "Old Uncle Ned."
Under the Willow She's Sleeping (1860)
The Village Maiden (1855)
Virginia Belle (1860)
The Voice of By Gone Days (1850)
The Voices That Are Gone (1865) (Robert Campbell)
Was My Brother in the Battle? (1862)
Way Down in Ca-i-ro (1850)
We Are Coming, Father Abraam, 300,000 More (1862) (James
  Sloane Gibbons)
We've a Million in the Field (1862)
We'll All Meet Our Saviour (1863)
We Will Keep a Bright Lookout (1863) (George Cooper)
We'll Still Keep Marching On (1863) (Mrs. M. A. Kidder)
We'll Tune Our Hearts (1863)
What Does Every Good Child Say? (1867) (Poetry by a Friend)
What Must a Fairy's Dream Be? (1847)
What Shall the Harvest Be? (1863) (Emily Sullivan Oakley)
When Dear Friends Are Gone (1864)
When Old Friends Were Here (1864) (Henry [George] Cooper)
  When the Bowl Goes Round. See "While the Bowl Goes Round."
When This Dreadful War Is Ended (1863) (George Cooper)
Where Has Lula Gone? (1858)
Where Is Thy Spirit, Mary? (1895)
  While (When) the Bowl Goes Round. See Derivata.

While We Work for the Lord (1863)

The White House Chair. This is a political song published in the Pittsburgh *Dispatch,* Sept. 20, 1885. Earlier publication, if any, unknown.

Why Have My Loved Ones Gone? (1861)

Why, No One to Love? (1862)

The Wife, or He'll Come Home (1860)

Willie's Gone to Heaven (1863)

Willie Has Gone to the War (1863) (George Cooper)

Willie My Brave (1851)

Willie We Have Missed You (1854)

Wilt Thou Be Gone, Love? (1851) (adapted from Shakespeare)

Wilt Thou Be True? (1864) (George Cooper)

Total Number of Songs—188

Instrumental Works

(Exclusive of Arrangements of Works by Other Composers)

Anadolia, solo for flute or violin (unaccompanied) in the *Social Orchestra* (1854)

Cane Brake Jig, for piano, included in *Old Folks Quadrilles* (1853)

The Holiday Schottisch, for piano (1853)

Irene, solo for flute or violin (unaccompanied) in the *Social Orchestra* (1854)

Jennie's Own Schottisch, a trio for 1st violin or flute, second violin and bass, in the *Social Orchestra* (1854)

Old Folks Quadrilles, for piano (1853)

    Plantation Jig. This is the title under which the *Cane Brake Jig* appears in the *Old Folks Quadrilles,* arranged as a quartet in the *Social Orchestra*

Santa Anna's Retreat from Buena Vista, quick-step for piano (1848)

Social Orchestra, see arrangements

Soirée Polka, for piano (1850)

The Tioga Waltz, for piano (1896) (Supposedly written in 1841 for three flutes)

Village Bells Polka, for piano (1850)

Village Festival Jig, No. 5 of *Village Festival Quadrilles* (1854)

Village Festival Quadrilles (including *Village Festival Jig*), a quartet for flute, first violin, second violin and bass, in the *Social Orchestra* (1854)

Total Number of Instrumental Works—12

Arrangements

1. Foster's Social Orchestra. For flute or violin—arranged as solos, duets, trios, and quartets. 1854. Firth, Pond & Co.

(* Indicates first appearance of original compositions by Foster)

Part I. Solos (for flute or violin, unaccompanied)

Agatha (F. Abt)
* Anadolia (S. C. Foster)
Bridal Waltz (Jullien)
Broadway Quickstep (Gungl)
Come Where the Fountains Play (Donizetti)
Cally Polka (?)
Commence, Ye Darkies All (W. D. Corrister)
Eulalie (S. C. Foster)
Evening Star Waltz (Lanner)
Hohnstock Polka (?)
I Love the Merry Sunshine (S. Glover)
* Irene (S. C. Foster)
Italian Melodies No. 1 (Blangini)
Italian Melodies No. 2 (Donizetti)
Italian Melodies No. 3 (Bertoni)
Italian Melodies No. 4 (Vaccai)
Italian Melodies No. 5 (Mozart)
I'd Offer Thee This Hand of Mine (L. T. Chadwick)
Love Launched a Fairy Boat (Tully)
My Old Kentucky Home, Good Night (S. C. Foster)
Nelly Was a Lady (S. C. Foster)
Nancy Till (?)
O Would I Were a Boy Again (F. Romer)
Old Dog Tray (S. C. Foster)
Old Folks at Home (with variations) (E. P. Christy ! ! ! !)
On the Banks of Guadalquiver (Lavenu)
Pearl Polka (H. Kleber)
Roll On, Silver Moon (Sloman)
Saratoga Lake Waltz (?)
Scenes That Are Brightest (W. V. Wallace)
Sontag Polka (D'Albert)
Thou Art Gone from My Gaze (G. Linley)
Twilight Song (H. W. Pond)
Wait for the Wagon (?)
Waltz (Beethoven)
Widow Machree (S. Lover)
Wild Haunts for Me (Swiss)

Will You Come to My Mountain Home (F. H. Brown)
Will You Love Me Then, as Now (?)

Part II. Melodies Arranged as Duets (for flute and violin)

Introduction to Caliph of Bagdad (Boildieu)
Duet from "Lucia de Lammermoor" (Donizetti)
The Hour for Thee and Me (S. C. Foster)
Katy Darling (Bellini)
Make Me No Gaudy Chaplet Now (Donizetti)
Massa's in the Cold Ground (S. C. Foster)
On to the Field of Glory (from Belisario)
The Old Pine Tree (C. White)
Pirate's Chorus (M. W. Balfe)
Would I Were with Thee (?)

Part III. Melodies Arranged as Trios (for first violin or flute,
second violin and bass)

Air, from "Preciosa" (von Weber)
Air (de Beriot)
Byerly's Waltz (Byerly)
Gems from "Lucia," No. 1 (Donizetti)
Gems from "Lucia," No. 2 (Donizetti)
Gems from "Lucia," No. 3 (Donizetti)
* Jennie's Own Schottisch (S. C. Foster)
March from "The Daughter of the Regiment" (Donizetti)
Maria Redowa (Donizetti)
Rainbow Schottisch (H. Kleber)
Waltz (Strauss)

Part IV. Melodies Arranged as Quartets (for flute, first and
second violins, and bass)

Coral Schottisch (H. Kleber)
Crystal Schottisch (Wm. Byerly)
French Quadrille, No. 1 (Tolbeuque)
French Quadrille, No. 2 (Bosissio)
French Quadrille, No. 3 (Bosissio)
French Quadrille, No. 4 (Tolbeuque)
French Quadrille, No. 5 (?)
Gems from "Lucia," No. 4 (Donizetti)
Gems from "Lucia," No. 5 (Donizetti)
Happy Land.
O Summer Night! (Donizetti)
Old Folks Quadrilles, No. 1, Old Folks at Home (no composer
indicated)

Old Folks Quadrilles, No. 2, Oh! Boys, Carry Me 'Long (S. C. Foster)

Old Folks Quadrilles, No. 3, Nelly Bly (S. C. Foster)

Old Folks Quadrilles, No. 4, Farewell, My Lilly Dear (S. C. Foster)

Old Folks Quadrilles, No. 5, Plantation Jig (S. C. Foster) (This is the same as the "Cane Brake Jig")

La Serenade (Schubert)

Ton-Mahrchen Waltz (Gungl)

* Village Festival—Quadrille No. 1 (S. C. Foster)

* Village Festival—Quadrille No. 2 (S. C. Foster)

* Village Festival—Quadrille No. 3 (S. C. Foster)

* Village Festival—Quadrille No. 4 (S. C. Foster)

* Village Festival—Jig, No. 5 (S. C. Foster)

Waltz (Lanner)

Where Are the Friends of My Youth? (G. Barker)

2. Our Darling Kate. *Demorest's Illustrated Monthly,* March, 1865. Words and melody by John Mahon. Arranged for the piano by Stephen C. Foster.

3. Foster's Songs with Guitar Accompaniment, Arranged by Himself.
   Camptown Races
   Come with Thy Sweet Voice Again
   Ellen Bayne
   Eulalie
   Farewell my Lilly Dear
   Gentle Annie
   Hard Times Come Again No More
   Jeanie with the Light Brown Hair
   Laura Lee
   Little Ella
   Maggie by My Side
   Massa's in de Cold Ground
   My Old Kentucky Home, Good Night
   Oh! Boys, Carry Me 'Long
   Old Dog Tray
   Old Memories
   Some Folks
   Willie My Brave
   Willie We Have Missed You

Translations

In the Eye Abides the Heart. The original poem (In den Augen liegt das Herz) was written in 1842 by Franz von Kobell.

Franz Abt set it to music in 1846. It was published in 1851 as "In the Eye Abides the Heart. Song by F. Abt. Arranged by 'H. K.' Translated by Stephen C. Foster (Firth, Pond & Co.)." "H. K." was undoubtedly Henry Kleber.

Derivata

As used by Foster Hall, the term "derivata" designates all songs, the words for which were written by others and which utilize a previously published Foster melody. Most of the "derivata" were published in hymn books, temperance songsters, political song books, etc., in large numbers.

Golden Dreams & Fairy Castles! Air is "We'll Still Keep Marching On." (1864) (Mrs. M. A. Kidder)

Happy Little Ones Are We. Air is "Merry Little Birds Are We." (1863) (Mrs. M. A. Kidder)

Home, Heavenly Home! Air is "Little Ella's an Angel." (1863) (Mrs. M. A. Kidder)

Music Everywhere, That's Why I Love It So. Air is "Jenny's Coming O'er the Green." (1863) (Mrs. M. A. Kidder)

Oh! Meet Me, Dear Mother. Air is adapted from "The Bright Hills of Glory." (1865) (Mrs. M. A. Kidder)

Sorrow Shall Come Again No More. Air is "Hard Times Come Again No More." (1858) (Rev. W. Kenney)

Stand Up for the Flag! Air is "Stand Up for the Truth." (1865) (Mrs. M. A. Kidder)

There's a Land of Bliss. Air is "Old Uncle Ned." (1853) (N. C. Brook)

There Is a Land of Love. Air is "Why Have My Loved Ones Gone?" (1863) (Mrs. M. A. Kidder)

While (When) the Bowl Goes Round. Air is "Jenny June." (1870) (George Cooper)

APPENDIX III

AUTHORS OF WORDS TO SONGS FOR WHICH STEPHEN FOSTER WROTE ONLY THE MUSIC

Anonymous
   I Would Not Die in Spring Time (1850)
   Little Mac! Little Mac! (1864)
   The Pure, the Bright, the Beautiful (1863)
Banister, George F.
   I Cannot Sing To-night (1852)
Brook, N. C.
   There's a Land of Bliss (1853), *derivata* Old Uncle Ned
Brougham, H.
   My Angel Boy (1865)
Byrne, J. D.
   There Was a Time (1863)
C., H.
   Over the River (1863)
C., J.
   Stand Up for the Truth (1863)
Campbell, Robert
   The Voices That Are Gone (1865)
Carey, Eliza Sheridan
   Sadly to Mine Heart Appealing (1858)
Cooper, George
   Bring My Brother Back to Me (1863)
   Dearer Than Life (1869)
   For the Dear Old Flag I Die (1863)
   If You've Only Got a Moustache (1864)
   Jenny June (1863)
   Katy Bell (1863)
   Kissing in the Dark (1863)
   Larry's Good Bye (1863)
   Mr. & Mrs. Brown (1864)
   My Boy Is Coming from the War (1863)
   My Wife Is a Most Knowing Woman (1863)
   Onward and Upward (1863)
   A Soldier in de Colored Brigade (1863)
   The Soldier's Home (1863)
   Somebody's Coming to See Me To-night (1864)
   Sweet Emerald Isle That I Love So Well (1866)

Cooper, George (Cont.)
  There Are Plenty of Fish in the Sea (1862)
  We Will Keep a Bright Lookout (1863)
  When This Dreadful War Is Ended (1863)
  While (When) the Bowl Goes Round (1870), *derivata* Jenny June
  Willie Has Gone to the War (1863)
  Wilt Thou Be True ? (1864)
Cooper, Henry (George)
  When Old Friends Were Here (1864)
Cornwell, H. S.
  Eulalie (1851)
Crookshank, Wm. Cullen
  Once I Loved Thee, Mary Dear (1851)
Duffy, Dr.
  She Was All the World to Me (1864)
Eastman, Charles G.
  Sweetly She Sleeps, My Alice Fair (1851)
Friend, Poetry by a
  What Does Every Good Child Say? (1867)
Fuller, Metta Victoria
  The Spirit of My Song (1850)
Gibbons, James Sloane
  We Are Coming, Father Abraam, 300,000 More (1862)
Harding, S. W.
  Give This to Mother (1864)
Kenney, Rev. W.
  Sorrow Shall Come Again No More (1858), *derivata* Hard
    Times, Come Again No More
Kidder, Mrs. M. A.
  The Bright Hills of Glory (1863)
  Don't Be Idle (1863)
  Golden Dreams & Fairy Castles (1864), *derivata* We'll Still
    Keep Marching On
  Happy Little Ones Are We (1863), *derivata* Merry Little Birds
    Are We
  Home, Heavenly Home (1863) *derivata* Little Ella's an Angel
  Music Everywhere, That's Why I Love It So (1863), *derivata*
    Jenny's Coming O'er the Green
  Oh! Meet Me, Dear Mother (1865), *derivata* The Bright Hills
    of Glory
  Stand Up for the Flag (1865), *derivata* Stand Up for the Truth
  There Is a Land of Love (1863), *derivata* Why Have My Loved
    Ones Gone?
  We'll Still Keep Marching On (1863)
MacCarthy, Denis Florence
  Summer Longings (1849)

McCarthy, William Henry
  For Thee, Love, for Thee (1859)
  Linda Has Departed (1859)
  Parthenia to Ingomar (1859)
Mackay, Charles
  There's a Good Time Coming (1846)
Matteson, Mrs. O. S.
  The Beautiful Shore (1863)
Mellen, G.
  This Rose Will Remind You (1931)
Morris, George P.
  Open Thy Lattice, Love (1844)
Morton, Clara
  All Day Long (1864)
Murtha, Francis D.
  Oh! Why Am I So Happy (1863)
Nevin, Edwin H.
  Oh! 'tis Glorious (1863)
Oakley, Emily Sullivan
  What Shall the Harvest Be? (1863)
Pastor, Tony (Harlan Page Halsey)
  The Song of All Songs (1863)
R., W.
  He Leadeth Me Beside Still Waters (1863)
Reese, Mary Byron
  Lizzie Dies To-night (1861)
Shakespeare, William (adapted from)
  Wilt Thou Be Gone, Love? (1851)
Shiras, Charles P.
  Annie My Own Love (1853)
Wallace, William Ross
  Choral Harp (1863)
Wilde, Richard Henry
  None Shall Weep a Tear for Me (1860)

ADDENDA TO FOURTH PRINTING

Dickens, Charles
  The Pure, the Bright, the Beautiful (1863)
Lover, Samuel
  Oh! There's No Such Girl As Mine (1863)

APPENDIX IV

BIBLIOGRAPHY

Compiled by Fletcher Hodges, Jr., of Foster Hall,
Indianapolis, Indiana

BOOKS AND PAMPHLETS CONCERNING STEPHEN FOSTER

Allison, Young E. *The Old Kentucky Home, Its Song and the Story.* Published under the auspices of My Old Kentucky Home Commission, Federal Hill, Bardstown, Ky., 1923.

Stephen C. Foster and American Songs. Reprinted from *The Register of the Kentucky State Historical Society* (Frankfort, Ky.), September, 1919. (The original title was "Stephen C. Foster as I Know Him.")

Foster, Morrison. *Biography, Songs and Musical Compositions of Stephen C. Foster.* Pittsburgh, 1896. Percy F. Smith Printing and Lithographing Company. (Two editions.)

My Brother Stephen. Indianapolis, 1932. Privately printed for the Foster Hall Collection by the Hollenbeck Press. (This book is a reprint of the biographical foreword in Morrison Foster's *Biography, Songs and Musical Compositions of Stephen C. Foster.*)

Hays, Matilda Orr. *A Handbook of History Containing an Authentic Genealogic Chart of Stephen Collins Foster and His Immediate Family.* Pittsburgh, Penna., 1932. For the Author.

Jillson, Willard Rouse. *The "Old Kentucky Home."* Reprint from *The Register of the Kentucky State Historical Society,* May, 1921.

MacGowan, Robert. *The Significance of Stephen Collins Foster.* Indianapolis, 1932. Privately printed for the Foster Hall Collection of Fosteriana by the Hollenbeck Press, Indianapolis, March, 1932. Reprinted from *The Pittsburgh Record,* of December, 1931-January, 1932.

Martens, Frederick H. *Stephen Collins Foster.* New York, 1925. Breitkopf Publications, Inc.

Milligan, Harold Vincent. *Stephen Collins Foster, A Biography of America's Folk-Song Composer.* New York, 1920. G. Schirmer.

Morneweck, Mrs. Evelyn Foster. *Chronicles of a Foster Family, from Which Came a Great Genius.* To be published in 1936 by Foster Hall, Indianapolis, Ind.

Pictorial Biography of Stephen Collins Foster. Lantern slides issued by Sims Visual Music Co., Quincy, Ill.

Pittsburgh's Tribute to Her Gifted Son, Stephen Collins Foster. (On the occasion of the dedication of the Old Kentucky Home, July 4, 1923.)

Smith, Earl Hobson. *Oh Stephy C. Foster.* Lexington, Ky., 1926. The Kentucky Playmakers.

Stephen Collins Foster; America's Greatest Balladist; His Birthplace in Pittsburgh. Pittsburgh, 1918.

Stephen Collins Foster—Songs and Compositions—Foster Hall Reproductions. Published by Foster Hall, Indianapolis, Ind., 1933.

Walker, T. M. *The Melodies of Stephen C. Foster.* Pittsburgh, 1909. T. M. Walker. (Four editions.)

Whittlesey, Walter R., and Sonneck, O. G. *Catalogue of First Editions of Stephen C. Foster (1826-1864).* Washington, D. C., 1915. Government Printing Office.

Wohlgemuth, E. Jay. *Within Three Chords, the Place of Cincinnati in the Life of Stephen Collins Foster.* Indianapolis, 1928. The Rough Notes Press.

Lilly Bulletin No. 1. Indianapolis, Ind., July 1, 1931.

Lilly-Foster Hall Bulletin No. 2. Indianapolis, Ind., August 22, 1931.

Foster Hall Bulletin No. 3. Indianapolis, Ind., October 13, 1931.

Foster Hall Bulletin No. 4. Indianapolis, Ind., December 19, 1931.

Foster Hall Bulletin No. 5. Indianapolis, Ind., March, 1932.

Supplement to Foster Hall Bulletin No. 5. Indianapolis, Ind., April 20, 1932.

Foster Hall Bulletin No. 6. Indianapolis, Ind., August, 1932.

Foster Hall Bulletin No. 7. Indianapolis, Ind., September, 1932.

Foster Hall Bulletin No. 8. Indianapolis, Ind., February, 1933.

Foster Hall Bulletin No. 9. Indianapolis, Ind., November, 1933.

The Centenary of the Founder of American Folk Music. Educational Monographs. Harrisburg, Pa., 1927. The Commonwealth of Pennsylvania, Department of Public Instruction.

BOOKS CONTAINING REFERENCE TO STEPHEN FOSTER

Abernethy, Julian W., Ph.D. *American Literature.* New York, 1902. Maynard, Merrill & Co.

Adams, James Truslow, *The March of Democracy.* New York, 1932. Charles Scribner's Sons.

Adams, Oscar Fay. *A Brief Handbook of American Authors.* Boston, 1884. Houghton Mifflin and Company.

A Dictionary of American Authors. Boston, 1901. Houghton Mifflin and Company.

Allen, James Lane. *The Bride of the Mistletoe.* New York, 1909. The Macmillan Company.

"American Songs and Song-Writers," in Vol. 3, *The International Library of Music.* New York, 1925. The University Society.

America's Music in Review. New York, 1929. National Bureau for the Advancement of Music.

Baker, Ellen Friel. *The Wonderful Story of Music.* New York, 1931. Thomas Y. Crowell Company.

Baltzell, W. J. *Baltzell's Dictionary of Musicians.* Boston, 1911. Oliver Ditson Company.

A Complete History of Music. Philadelphia, Pa., 1931. Theodore Presser Co.

Noted Names in Music. Boston, 1927. Oliver Ditson Company.

Banks, Rev. Louis Albert, D.D. *Immortal Songs of Camp and Field.* Cleveland, 1899. The Burrows Brothers Company.

Barton, Bruce. *A Parade of the States.* Garden City, New York, 1932. Doubleday, Doran & Company.

Bauer, Marion and Peyser, Ethel. *How Music Grew.* New York, 1925. G. P. Putnam's Sons.

Music Through the Ages. New York, 1932. G. P. Putnam's Sons.

Beach, Chandler B., A.M., editor, and Adam, Graeme Mercer, associate editor. *The Student's Reference Work.* New York and Chicago, 1908. F. E. Compton & Company.

Beers, Henry A. *An Outline Sketch of American Literature.* New York, 1887. Chautauqua Press.

Brief History of English and American Literature. New York, 1897. Eaton & Mains.

Initial Studies in American Letters. New York, 1891. Chautauqua Press.

Brenner, Henry. *Messages of Music, Mood Stories of the Great Masterpieces.* Boston, 1923. The Stratford Company.

Bristed, C. Astor? *Pieces of a Broken-Down Critic, Picked up by Himself.* Baden-Baden, 1858. Printed by Scotzniovsky.

Brown, T. Allston. *History of the American Stage.* New York, 1870. Dick & Fitzgerald.

Browne, C. A. *The Story of Our National Ballads.* New York, 1931. Thomas Y. Crowell Company.

Burton, Frederick R. *American Primitive Music.* New York, 1909. Moffat, Yard and Company.

Butler, Lorine Letcher. *My Old Kentucky Home.* Philadelphia, 1929. Dorrance & Company.

Cairns, William B., Ph.D. *A History of American Literature.* New York, 1930. Oxford University Press.

Calverton, V. F. *The Liberation of American Literature.* New York, 1932. Charles Scribner's Sons.

A Catalogue of Music for the Ampico. New York, 1925. The Ampico Corporation.

The Centenary of Kentucky. Proceedings at the celebration by the Filson Club, Wednesday, June 1, 1892, of the one hundredth anniversary of the admission of Kentucky as an independent state into the Federal Union. Louisville, Ky., 1892.

Champlin, John Denison, Jr., editor. *Cyclopedia of Music and Musicians.* New York, 1889. Charles Scribner's Sons.

Church, Samuel Harden. *A Short History of Pittsburgh, 1758-1908.* New York, 1908. The De Vinne Press.

The City of Pittsburgh and How it Grew (1790-1930). Pittsburgh, The Chamber of Commerce.

Clifford, John H., editor. *The Musiclover's Handbook.* New York, 1911. The University Society.

Cobb, Irvin S. *Kentucky.* New York, 1924. George H. Doran Company.

Cooke, James Francis. *Standard History of Music.* Philadelphia, 1910. Theodore Presser Company.

Crosby, Oliver Marvin. *Florida Facts.* New York, 1887. For the Author.

Dahlinger, Charles W. *Pittsburgh, a Sketch of Its Early Social Life.* New York, 1916. G. P. Putnam's Sons.

DeBekker, Leander Jan, editor. *Black's Dictionary of Music and Musicians.* London, 1924. A. & C. Black, Ltd.

De Voto, Bernard. *Mark Twain's America.* Boston, 1932. Little, Brown, and Company.

Dickinson, Thomas H. *The Making of American Literature.* New York, 1932. The Century Co.

Downes, Olin. *The Lure of Music.* New York, 1918. Harper & Brothers.

Egle, William Henry, M.D. *Some Pennsylvania Women During the War of the Revolution.* Harrisburg, Pa., 1898. Harrisburg Publishing Company.

Eighth Annual Meeting and Banquet of the Pennsylvania Scotch-Irish Society at the Hotel Bellevue, Philadelphia, February 26th, 1897. Philadelphia, 1898. Allen, Lane & Scott's Printing House.

Elson, Arthur. *The Book of Musical Knowledge.* Boston, 1927, 1933. Houghton Mifflin Company.

Elson, Louis C. *The History of American Music.* New York, 1904. The Macmillan Company.
   The History of American Music. New York, 1925. The Macmillan Company. (Edition revised to 1925.)
   The National Music of America and Its Sources. Boston, 1924. L. C. Page & Company.

Evans, James W., and Harding, Captain Gardiner L. *Entertaining the American Army.* New York, 1921. Association Press.

Faulkner, Anne Shaw. *What We Hear in Music*. Camden, New Jersey, 1931. R.C.A. Victor Co., Inc. (Eighth revised edition.)

Music in the Home. Chicago, 1917. Ralph Fletcher Seymour.

Finck, Henry T. *Musical Progress*. Philadelphia, 1923. Theodore Presser Co.

Fish, Carl Russell. *The Rise of the Common Man, 1830-1850*. New York, 1929. The Macmillan Company.

Fisher, William Arms. *One Hundred and Fifty Years of Music Publishing in the United States*. Boston, 1933. Oliver Ditson Company, Inc.

Fitz-Gerald, S. J. Adair. *Stories of Famous Songs*. London, 1898. John C. Nimmo.

Fleming, George T., collector. *Fleming's Views of Old Pittsburgh*. Pittsburgh, Pennsylvania, 1932. The Crescent Press.

Foster, W. T. *The Foster Family and Its Ancestors, The Norman-French*. Washington, D. C., 1916. Published by the Author.

Galsworthy, John. *Worshipful Society*. New York, 1932. Charles Scribner's Sons.

Gehrkens, Karl W. *The Fundamentals of Music*. Boston, 1924. Oliver Ditson Company.

George Gershwin's Song-book. New York, 1932. Simon and Schuster, Inc.

Goldberg, Isaac. *George Gershwin, a Study in American Music*. New York, 1931. Simon and Schuster.

Tin Pan Alley. New York, 1930. The John Day Company.

Good, Marian Bigler. *Some Musical Backgrounds of Pennsylvania*. Carrolltown, Penn., 1932. Carrolltown News Press.

Green, Janet M., compiler. Hubbard, W. L., editor. *Musical Biographies*. New York, 1908. Irving Squire.

Halleck, Reuben Post. *History of American Literature*. New York, 1911. American Book Company.

Hamilton, Clarence G. *Music Appreciation*. Boston, 1920. Oliver Ditson Company.

Haney, John Louis. *The Story of Our Literature, An Interpretation of the American Spirit*. New York, 1923. Charles Scribner's Sons.

Hansl, Eva vB., and Kaufmann, Helen L. *Minute Sketches of Great Composers*. New York, 1932. Grosset & Dunlap.

Harlow, Alvin F. *Old Bowery Days*. New York, 1931. D. Appleton and Company.

Herringshaw, Thomas William. *Herringshaw's National Library of American Biography*. Chicago, Ill., 1909. American Publishers' Association.

Heyward, DuBose. *Peter Ashley*. New York, 1932. Farrar & Rinehart.

Holland, Rupert Sargent. *Sons of Seven Cities.* Philadelphia, 1929. Macrae, Smith Company.

Horton, Judge. *Driftwood of the Stage.* Detroit, Mich., 1904. Winn & Hammond.

Howard, John Tasker. *Our American Music, Three Hundred Years of It.* New York, 1931. Thomas Y. Crowell Company.

Hubbard, W. L., editor. *History of American Music.* New York, 1908. Irving Squire.

Hughes, Rupert, M. A. *Music Lovers' Cyclopedia.* Garden City, New York, 1932. Doubleday, Doran & Company, Inc.

Hulbert, Archer Butler. *Forty-Niners, The Chronicle of the California Trail.* Boston, 1931. Little, Brown, and Company.

Hutton, Laurence. *Curiosities of the American Stage.* New York, 1891. Harper & Brothers.

Isaacson, Charles D. *Face to Face with Great Musicians.* New York, 1927. D. Appleton and Company.

Jackson, George Pullen. *White Spirituals in the Southern Uplands.* Chapel Hill, North Carolina, 1933. University of North Carolina Press.

Jacobson, Arthur C. *Genius, Some Revaluations.* New York, 1926. An Adelphi Publication—Greenberg: Publishers.

James, Marquis. *The Raven, a Biography of Sam Houston.* Indianapolis, 1929. The Bobbs-Merrill Company.

Jillson, Willard Rouse. *Edwin P. Morrow—Kentuckian.* Louisville, 1921. C. T. Dearing Printing Company.

Kentucky in American History. Louisville, Kentucky, 1933. The Courier-Journal Job Printing Co.

Tales of the Dark and Bloody Ground. Louisville, 1930. C. T. Dearing Printing Co.

Johnson, Allen, and Malone, Dumas, editors. *Dictionary of American Biography,* Vol. 6. New York, 1931. Charles Scribner's Sons.

Johnson, Helen Kendrick. *Our Familiar Songs and Those Who Made Them.* New York, 1881. Henry Holt and Company.

Johnson, Rossiter. *Campfire and Battle-Field.* New York (1896?). Knight & Brown.

Johnston, William G. *Life and Reminiscences from Birth to Manhood of William G. Johnston.* Pittsburgh, 1901. (The Knickerbocker Press, New York.)

Jones, F. O., editor. *A Handbook of American Music and Musicians.* Canaseraga, N. Y., 1886. F. O. Jones.

A Handbook of American Music and Musicians. Buffalo, 1887. C. W. Moulton and Company.

Kellogg, Clara Louise (Mme. Strakosch). *Memoirs of an American Prima Donna.* New York, 1913. G. P. Putnam's Sons.

Ketler, Isaac C. *The Pilgrims, an Epical Interpretation.* New York, 1910. Fleming H. Revell Company.

Killikelly, Sarah H. *The History of Pittsburgh, Its Rise and Progress.* Pittsburgh, Pa., 1906. B. C. & Gordon Montgomery Co.

Kingsbury, A. H. "The Old Towanda Academy. *Annual Number Four,* Bradford County Historical Society. Towanda, Pa., 1910.

Knight, Grant C. *American Literature and Culture.* New York, 1932. Ray Long & Richard R. Smith, Inc.

Kobbé, Gustav. *Famous American Songs.* New York, 1906. Thomas Y. Crowell & Co.

Koch, Theodore Wesley. *War Libraries and Allied Studies.* New York, 1918. G. E. Stechert & Co.

Kramer, Mary Eleanor. *One Thousand Literary Questions and Answers.* New York, 1917. George Sully and Company.

Krehbiel, Henry Edward. *Afro-American Folksongs.* New York, 1914. G. Schirmer, Inc.

Krohn, Ernst C. *A Century of Missouri Music.* St. Louis, 1924. Privately printed.

Kyger, John Fremont. *Florida in Verse.* Chicago, Illinois, 1925. John C. F. Kyger.

Landormy, Paul. *A History of Music.* New York, 1923. Charles Scribner's Sons.

Lawton, William Cranston. *Introduction to the Study of American Literature.* Yonkers-on-Hudson, New York, 1914. World Book Company.

Long, William J. *American Literature.* Boston, 1913. Ginn and Company.

Lowe, Orton, and Reitell, Jane. *Pennsylvania, a Story of Our Domain, Our Chronicles, Our Work.* Boston, 1927. Richard G. Badger.

McElroy, John. *Andersonville: A Story of Rebel Military Prisons.* Toledo, 1879. D. R. Locke.

McGehee, Thomasine C. *People and Music.* Boston, 1929. Allyn and Bacon.

McLoughlin, Peter P. *Father Tom, Life and Lectures of Rev. Thomas P. McLoughlin.* New York, 1919. G. P. Putnam's Sons.

Mabie, Hamilton Wright, editor. *Music and Fine Arts.* New York, 1906. The University Society, Inc.

Madigan, Thomas F. *Word Shadows of the Great.* New York, 1930. Frederick A. Stokes Company.

Mason, Daniel Gregory, editor. *The Art of Music.* New York, 1915. The National Society of Music. (References to Foster on pages 286, 318, 416, 451-2, Vol. 4; 106-7, 129, 163, Vol. 5.)

Mathews, W. S. B., associate editor. *A Hundred Years of Music in America.* Chicago, 1889. G. L. Howe.

Metcalf, Frank J. *American Writers and Compilers of Sacred Music.* New York, 1925. The Abingdon Press.

Metcalf, John Calvin, Litt.D., LL.D. *American Literature.* Richmond, Virginia, 1914. Johnson Publishing Company.

Milligan, Harold Vincent. "Stephen C. Foster." (Report included in *Papers and Proceedings of the Music Teachers' National Association at Its Thirty-ninth Annual Meeting, New Orleans, December 27-29, 1917.*) Hartford, Conn., 1918. Published by the Association.

Minnigerode, Meade. *The Fabulous Forties, 1840-1850, A Presentation of Private Life.* New York, 1924. G. P. Putnam's Sons. *Oh, Susanna! A Romance of the Old American Merchant Marine.* New York, 1922. G. P. Putnam's Sons.

Murray, Louise Welles. *A History of Old Tioga Point and Early Athens, Pennsylvania.* Athens, Penna., 1908. (Raeder Press, Wilkes-Barre, Penn.)

Music Appreciation for Little Children. Camden, New Jersey, 1920. Educational Department, Victor Talking Machine Company.

Nevin, Robert P. *Les Trois Rois.* Pittsburgh, 1888. Jos. Eichbaum & Co. (The last article in the book, "Stephen C. Foster and Negro Minstrelsy," is a reprint from the *Atlantic Monthly* of November, 1867.)

Newcomer, Alphonso G. *American Literature.* Chicago, 1906. Scott, Foresman and Company.

Nisenson, Samuel, and Parker, Alfred. *Minute Biographies.* New York, 1931. Grosset & Dunlap.

Norton, Charles Ledyard. *A Handbook of Florida.* New York, 1894. Longmans, Green & Co.

O'Neill, Capt. Francis. *Irish Minstrels and Musicians.* Chicago, 1913. The Regan Printing House.

Osgood, Henry O. *So This Is Jazz.* Boston, 1926. Little, Brown, and Company.

Pancoast, Henry S. *An Introduction to American Literature.* New York, 1930. Henry Holt and Company.

Parke, Judge John E. *Recollections of Seventy Years and Historical Gleanings of Allegheny, Pennsylvania.* Boston, 1886. Rand, Avery & Company.

Paskman, Dailey, and Spaeth, Sigmund. *"Gentlemen, Be Seated!"* Garden City, New York, 1928. Doubleday, Doran & Company, Inc.

Pastor, Tony. *George Christy, or the Fortunes of a Minstrel.* New York, 1877 and 1885. George Munro.

Patterson, Norma. *The Sun Shines Bright.* New York, 1932. Farrar & Rinehart.

Pennypacker, Samuel Whitaker. *Pennsylvania, the Keystone.* Philadelphia, 1914. Christopher Sower Company.

The Playground and Recreation Association of America, prepared by. *Community Music*. Boston, 1926. C. C. Birchard and Company.

Post, Charles Asa. *Some American Writers and Their Songs*. Cleveland, 1902. Rowfant Club.

Pratt, Waldo Selden. *The History of Music*. New York, 1907. G. Schirmer.

Pratt, Waldo Selden, editor. Boyd, Charles N., associate editor. *Grove's Dictionary of Music and Musicians*. New York, 1920. The Macmillan Company.

Pratt, Waldo Selden. *The New Encyclopedia of Music and Musicians*. New York, 1931. The Macmillan Company.

Remy, Alfred, M.A., editor. *Baker's Biographical Dictionary of Musicians*. New York, 1919. G. Schirmer.

Report of the Librarian of Congress for the Fiscal Year Ending June 30, 1932. Washington, 1932. Government Printing Office.

Reynolds, George F., and Greever, Garland. *The Facts and Backgrounds of Literature, English and American*. New York, 1920. The Century Co.

Reynolds, Harry. *Minstrel Memories*. London, 1928. Alston Rivers, Ltd.

Rice, Cale Young. *Bitter Brew*. New York, 1925. The Century Co. (Includes a poem, "Lines Written for the Dedication to Kentucky of 'The Old Kentucky Home.'")

Rice, Edward LeRoy. *Monarchs of Minstrelsy from "Daddy" Rice to Date*. New York City, 1911. Kenny Publishing Company.

Richardson, Charles F. *American Literature 1607-1885*. New York, 1889. G. P. Putnam's Sons.

Ridley, Bromfield L. *Battles and Sketches of the Army of Tennessee*. Mexico, Mo., 1906. Missouri Printing & Publishing Co.

Ritter, Frédéric Louis. *Music in America*. New York, 1883. Charles Scribner's Sons.

Music in America. New York, 1890. Charles Scribner's Sons. (New edition, with additions.)

Root, George F. *The Story of a Musical Life. An Autobiography*. Cincinnati, 1891. The John Church Co.

Rothert, Otto A. *Local History in Kentucky Literature*. A manuscript read before the Louisville Literary Club, September 27, 1915.

Rothbert, Otto A., compiler. *Young E. Allison Memorial Meeting, Henderson, Kentucky, June 24, 1933*. Reprinted from *The Filson Club History Quarterly*. Louisville, Ky., October, 1933.

Rourke, Constance. *American Humor, a Study of the National Character*. New York, 1931. Harcourt, Brace and Company.

Sargent, C. E., A.M. *Our Home, or the Key to a Nobler Life*. Springfield, Mass., 1894. King, Richardson & Co.

Scarborough, Dorothy. *On the Trail of Negro Folk-Songs.* Cambridge, Mass., 1925. Harvard University Press.

Scholes, Percy A., and Earhart, Will. *The Third Book of the Great Musicians.* New York, 1931. Oxford University Press.

Scott, Henry Brownfield, editor and compiler. *Sesqui-Centennial and Historical Souvenir of the Greater Pittsburgh, 1758-1908.* Pittsburgh, 1908.

Seldes, Gilbert. *The Seven Lively Arts.* New York, 1924. Harper & Brothers.

Seventh Annual Meeting and Banquet of the Pennsylvania Scotch-Irish Society, at the Hotel Bellevue, Philadelphia, February 13th, 1896. Philadelphia, 1897. Allen, Lane & Scott's Printing House.

Shoemaker, Henry W., compiler. *Mountain Minstrelsy of Pennsylvania.* Philadelphia, 1931. Newman F. McGirr.

Simpson, Eugene E. *America's Position in Music.* Boston, 1920. The Four Seas Company.

"America's Position in Music," in Vol. 2, *The International Library of Music.* New York, 1925. The University Society.

Smith, C. Alphonso. *What Can Literature Do for Me?* Garden City, New York, 1921, 1924. Doubleday, Page & Company.

Smith, Colonel Nicholas. *Stories of Great National Songs.* Milwaukee, 1930. Morehouse Publishing Co.

Smith, Percy F. *Memory's Milestones.* Pittsburgh, December 25, 1918. Copyright by Percy F. Smith.

Smith, Percy F., compiler. *Notable Men of Pittsburgh and Vicinity.* Pittsburgh, 1901. Pittsburgh Printing Company.

Sousa, John Philip. *Marching Along, Recollections of Men, Women and Music.* Boston, 1928. Hale, Cushman & Flint.

Spaeth, Sigmund. *The Common Sense of Music.* New York, 1924. Boni & Liveright.

Read 'em and Weep, the Songs You Forgot to Remember. New York, 1927. Doubleday, Page & Company.

Weep Some More, My Lady. Garden City, N. Y., 1927. Doubleday, Page & Company.

Stedman, Edmund Clarence. *Poets of America.* Boston, 1885. Houghton Mifflin & Company.

Stephen C. Foster. In *Golden Jubilee Cincinnati Music Hall, 1878-1928.*

Sullivan, Mark. *Our Times, III: Pre-War America.* New York, 1930. Charles Scribner's Sons.

Tapper, Thomas, Litt.D. *First Year Music History.* Boston, 1926. The Arthur P. Schmidt Co.

Taylor, Bayard. *Eldorado, or Adventures in the Path of Empire.* New York, 1850. George P. Putnam.

A Visit to India, China and Japan in the Year 1853. London, 1855. Sampson, Low, Son & Co.

Thomas, Joseph, M.D., LL.D. *Universal Pronouncing Dictionary of Biography and Mythology.* Philadelphia, 1899. J. B. Lippincott Company.

Thompson, Maurice. *Hoosier Mosaics.* New York, 1875. E. J. Hale & Son.

Tomas, G. M. *Invincible America; the National Music of United States in Peace and at War.* Havana, 1919.

The National Music of United States in Peace and at War. Havana, 1919. Printing "El Siglo XX."

Townsend, John Wilson. *Kentuckians in History and Literature.* New York and Washington, 1907. The Neale Publishing Company.

Trent, William Peterfield; Erskine, John; Sherman, Stuart P.; Van Doren, Carl (Editors). *The Cambridge History of American Literature.* New York, 1931. The Macmillan Company.

University Musical Encyclopedia. New York, 1908. The University Society.

Upton, George P. *Musical Memories.* Chicago, 1908. A. C. McClurg & Co.

The Song. Chicago, 1915. A. C. McClurg & Co.

Standard Musical Biographies. Chicago, 1910. A. C. McClurg & Co.

Upton, William Treat. *Art-Song in America, a Study in the Development of American Music.* Boston, 1930. Oliver Ditson Company.

Van Vechten, Carl. *Interpreters and Interpretations.* New York, 1917. Alfred A. Knopf.

Red. New York, 1925. Alfred A. Knopf.

Visscher, William Lightfoot. *Rattles and Rhymes.* Chicago, 1905. Bowen & Company.

Watterson, Henry. *"Marse Henry."* New York, 1919. George H. Doran.

Welles, R. M. *"The Old Athens Academy." Annual Number Five,* Bradford County Historical Society. Towanda, Pa., 1911.

White, Stewart Edward. *Gold.* Garden City, New York, 1931. Doubleday, Doran & Company, Inc.

Whitlock, Virginia Bennett. *Come and Caper.* New York, 1932. G. Schirmer, Inc.

Wier, Albert E. *What Do You Know About Music?* New York, 1930. D. Appleton and Company.

Wilm, Grace Gridley. *A History of Music.* New York, 1930. Dodd, Mead and Company.

Wilson, Samuel M. *History of Kentucky.* Chicago-Louisville, 1928. The S. J. Clarke Publishing Co.

Wilson, William Bender. *History of the Pennsylvania Railroad,* Vol. II. Philadelphia, 1899. Henry T. Coates & Co. (Contains a chapter on Wm. B. Foster, Jr.)

Winkler, John K. *Morgan the Magnificent.* New York, 1930. The Vanguard Press.

Winter, Nevin O. *Florida, the Land of Enchantment.* Boston, 1918. The Page Company.

Wittke, Carl, Ph.D. *Tambo and Bones, a History of the American Minstrel Stage.* Durham, North Carolina, 1930. Duke University Press.

Wynn, William T. *Southern Literature.* New York, 1932. Prentice-Hall, Inc.

ARTICLES ON STEPHEN FOSTER IN MAGAZINES AND NEWSPAPERS (SINCE 1864)

Adams, Lady. "The Plantation Poet." *Chamber's Journal* (London and Edinburgh), May, 1930.

Allison, Young E. "My Old Kentucky Home, the Song and the Story." *The Courier-Journal Sunday Magazine* (Louisville, Ky.), April 10, 1921.

"Stephen C. Foster as I Know Him." *The Register of the Kentucky State Historical Society* (Frankfort, Ky.), September, 1919.

"An American Song Writer." *American Art Journal* (New York), January 17, 1880.

"America's Foremost Balladist." *Literary Digest* (New York), January 1, 1910.

Appel, Richard G. "Stephen Collins Foster, 1826-1864." *The Phonograph Monthly Review,* December, 1926.

Baker, Will E. "The Romance of a Song." *Potter's American Monthly* (Philadelphia), December, 1880.

Benswanger, William E. "Pittsburgh to Hold Special Foster Celebration." *Musical America* (New York), June 26, 1926.

Birdseye, George W. "A Reminiscence of the Late Stephen C. Foster," (Part) I. *New York Musical Gazette,* January, 1867.

"A Reminiscence of the Late Stephen C. Foster" (Part II). *New York Musical Gazette,* March, 1867.

"Sketch of the Late Stephen C. Foster" (Part I). *Western Musical World,* January, 1867. Reprinted from the *New York Musical Gazette.*

"Stephen C. Foster." *Potter's American Monthly* (Philadelphia), January, 1879.

"Bowery Dwelling the Scene of Stephen Foster's Tragic Death." *Musical America* (New York), December 25, 1929.

Burtnett, J. G. "National Elements in Stephen Foster's Art." *The South Atlantic Quarterly* (Durham, N. C.), October, 1922.

"California's Half Century." *The Land of Sunshine* (Los Angeles), August, 1900.

Chappell, D. H., and Chappell, J. F. "The Real Suwanee River."
  Musical Courier (New York), March 22, 1930.
Clark, Kenneth. "A Stephen C. Foster Program." *The Playground*
  (Cooperstown, N. Y.), August, 1922.
Cowan, John L. "America's Greatest Balladist." *The Taylor-
  Trotwood Magazine* (Nashville, Tenn.), December, 1909.
"Popular Songs That Are Almost Classic." *Illustrated Sunday
  Magazine* (St. Paul, Minn.), Sept. 12, 1909.
Crosby, Agnes Foster. "The Man Who Wrote 'Old Folks at
  Home.'" *The Bookman* (New York), February, 1914.
Darkow, Dr. Martin. "Stephen C. Foster und das Amerikanische
  Volkslied." *Die Musik* (Berlin and Leipzig), IV. Jahr 1904/
  1905 Heft 16.
"The Days of 'Forty-Nine." *Out West* (Los Angeles-San Fran-
  cisco), February, 1903.
Duer, Mrs. Parkhurst. "Personal Recollections of the Last Days
  of Stephen Foster." *The Étude* (Philadelphia), September,
  1916.
Emery, Stewart. "Stephen Foster's Laurels Stay Green." *The New
  York Times Magazine* (New York), June 13, 1926.
English, Anne. "My Old Kentucky Home." *Holland's Magazine*
  (Dallas, Texas), January, 1930.
Finck, H. T. "The Position of Stephen Foster in Musical History."
  The Étude (Philadelphia), March, 1912.
Fisher, William Arms. "A Sketch of Music Publishing in the
  United States." *The Étude* (Philadelphia), October, 1923.
"Foster Memorial." *The Music Club Magazine* (Peoria, Ill.),
  January, 1930.
"Foster Memorial Planned for Pittsburgh." *Musical Courier* (New
  York), December 15, 1927.
Foster, Morrison. "Stephen C. Foster's Last Song." *The Musical
  Courier* (New York), August 20, 1884. (Reprinted from the
  Philadelphia *Times.*)
"Foster's Songs." *Brainard's Musical World* (Cleveland, O.),
  June, 1868.
Gaul, Harvey B. "The Life of Stephen Collins Foster." *The Mu-
  sical Forecast* (Pittsburgh), April, 1929.
"Stephen Foster, Who Composed 'Old Folks at Home,' Left
  Many Songs Unpublished, Says Daughter." *Musical America*
  (New York), August 28, 1920.
Gordon, Griffith L. "Old Kentucky Home: Foster Not the Au-
  thor." *Kentucky Magazine* (Lexington, Ky.), June, 1907.
Grant, Frances R. "Stephen Collins Foster, Maker of American
  Folk-Song." *Musical America* (New York), July 2, 1921.
"A Great Song-Writer and His Songs." *The Christian Union
  Herald,* October 12, 1922.

Hanley, Mrs. Elizabeth H., arranger. "Song Scenes from Stephen C. Foster." *The Playground* (Cooperstown, N. Y.), August, 1922.

Haywood, P. D. "Stephen C. Foster." *Pittsburgh Leader,* October 25, 1889. (Contains a lurid account of Foster's alleged vagabondage. An answer by Morrison Foster appears in the October 28, 1889, issue of this newspaper.)

Henderson, W. J. "American Composers." *The Mentor* (New York), February 1, 1918.

"Henry Kleber." *Musical Courier* (New York), February 27, 1897.

Hervey, D. E. "American Music and Composers." *Frank Leslie's Popular Monthly* (New York), January, 1891.

Hill, Harry. "Thirty Years in Gotham" (Chapter XL). *Sunday-Mercury* (New York), October 18, 1885.

Hodges, Fletcher, Jr. "The Hall That Pays Honor to Old Songs." *Graphic Arts Bulletin* (Indianapolis, Ind.), December, 1933.

"Horace Waters." *Musical Courier* (New York), Vol. 26, No. 17.

Holliday, Carl. "Stephen Collins Foster." *Overland* (San Francisco), July, 1930.

Hopkins, Lulu D. "Unweaving the Pattern of 'Old Folks at Home.'" *The Étude* (Philadelphia), January, 1929.

Houdini, Harry. "The Last Days of Stephen Foster." *The Étude* (Philadelphia), November, 1916.

Howard, John Tasker. "Creative Music in America." *The American Magazine of Art* (Washington, D. C.), June, 1931.

"Stephen Foster and His Publishers." *Musical Quarterly* (New York), January, 1934.

Hutton, Laurence. "The Negro on the Stage." *Harper's New Monthly Magazine* (New York), June, 1889.

"An Important Decision in a Music Copyright Suit." *American Art Journal* (New York), July 12, 1890.

"In Honor of Stephen Foster." *The Étude* (Philadelphia), December, 1923.

Ingraham, Charles A. "Stephen C. Foster's Romantic Career." *The Étude* (Philadelphia), September, 1916.

"An Intimate View of Stephen Foster." *The Étude* (Philadelphia), September, 1916.

Jillson, Willard Rouse. "The Old Kentucky Home." *The Register of the Kentucky State Historical Society* (Frankfort, Ky.), May, 1921.

"John Prosy on Musical Appreciation." *The Song Messenger of the Northwest* (Chicago), April, 1864.

Jones, F. O. "The Old Folks at Home." *Brainard's Musical World* (Cleveland and Chicago), July, 1883.

Kemp, Stephen. "Mme. Galli-Curci Tells How to Sing Foster's Most Famous Song." *The Musical Observer* (New York), April, 1925.

"Kentucky Pays Homage to Stephen C. Foster." *Musical Courier* (New York), June 16, 1921.

King, Mrs. A. T. "Some Facts About Stephen Collins Foster." *Musical Courier* (New York), August 14, 1919. (Also reprinted in issue of July 1, 1926.)

King, H. C. "The Songs of the People." *Church's Musical Visitor* (Cincinnati, O.), June, 1875. Reprinted from *The Christian Union*.

L., C. F. "Oh, Susanna." *Out West* (Los Angeles-San Francisco), September, 1904.

Lilly, Josiah K. "Fosteriana at Foster Hall." *The Colophon* (New York), Part Fifteen, October, 1933.

Long, Haniel. "Stephen Foster (Memo for 1894)." *Scribner's Magazine* (New York), October, 1933.

M'Cann, Walter Edgar. "American Ballad-Writers." *Frank Leslie's Popular Monthly* (New York), January, 1889.

MacGowan, Dr. Robert. "The Significance of Stephen Collins Foster." *The Musical Forecast* (Pittsburgh), January, 1933. (Reprinted from the *Pittsburgh Record,* December, 1931-January, 1932.)

Mahon, John. "The Last Years of Stephen C. Foster." *New York Clipper* (New York), March (17 or 24), 1877.

"The Makers of Our Popular Songs." *Munsey's Magazine* (New York), June, 1895.

Martens, Frederick H. "100 Years of 'Old Folks at Home.'" *Singing* (New York), April, 1926.

"Stephen Foster's Impress on American Music." *Singing* (New York), May, 1926.

"Massa's in de Cold Ground." *The Evening Sun* (New York), October 12, 1888. (Reminiscences of Foster's last years.)

"Material by and About Stephen Collins Foster in the St. Louis Public Library." *St. Louis Public Library Monthly Bulletin* (St. Louis), January, 1933.

"A Melodic River That Flows Around the Globe." *Musical America* (New York), June 26, 1926.

"The Minstrel Melodist." *New York Clipper* (New York), March 3, 1877.

Monroe, Broderick. "My Old Kentucky Home." *National Republic* (Washington, D. C.), November, 1928.

"A Monument for Foster." *Brainard's Musical World* (Cleveland, O.), December, 1875.

Mosgrove, George Dallas. "My Old Kentucky Home." *The Farm and Fireside,* May 1, 1906.

"The Most Pathetic Story of American Music." *Literary Digest* (New York), April 16, 1904.

"The Most Popular Song." *The Mentor* (New York), February, 1921.

Muller, G. F. "The City of Pittsburgh." *Harper's New Monthly Magazine* (New York), December, 1880.

"Music Shrine to Honor Foster." *Musical America* (New York), April 25, 1929.

" 'My Old Kentucky Home' and Other Foster Songs." *The Prairie Farmer,* January 11, 1931.

"Negro Minstrelsy—Ancient and Modern." *Putnam's Monthly,* January, 1855.

Nevin, Robert Peebles. "Stephen C. Foster and Negro Minstrelsy." *The Atlantic Monthly* (Boston), November, 1867.

O., H. O. [Osgood, H. O. ?] "A Biography of Stephen Collins Foster." *Musical Courier* (New York), June 17, 1920.

"Old Folks at Home." *Pittsburgh Leader,* February 23, 1879. (This article tells of a controversy regarding the authorship of the song. An answer by Morrison Foster appears in the February 25, 1879, issue of this newspaper.)

"An Old Time Song Writer." *Brainard's Musical* (New York), November, 1903.

Osgood, H. O. "The Unknown Foster." *Musical Courier* (New York), July 1, 1926.

Pine, Jane. "Stephen Foster—Father of American Folk Songs." *The World Review* (Chicago), May 10, 1926.

"Pittsburgh Tuesday Musical Club Plans Stephen Foster Memorial." *The Music Club Magazine* (Peoria, Ill.), February, 1929.

"Popular Songs." *The Galaxy,* February, 1868.

"Pratt's Transmigration of a Tune." *American Art Journal* (New York), April 19, 1890.

"Preserving the Stephen Foster Tradition." *The Musician* (New York), February, 1932.

"Retelling the Tragic Story of Stephen Foster's Life and Death." *Current Opinion* (New York), September, 1921.

Rieck, Waldemar. "A Melodic River That Flows Around the Globe." *Musical America* (New York), June 26, 1926.

Robinson, Ruth. "Stephen Collins Foster, Peoples Were Made Glad Because of Him." *The Étude* (Philadelphia), October, 1927.

Rose, Mrs. Jessie Welsh. "My Grandmother's Memories." Appeared simultaneously in the *Pittsburgh Post* and Louisville *Courier-Journal,* July 4, 1926. A manuscript copy, with amplifications, is in the Foster Hall Collection, Indianapolis.

Saerchinger, César. "Stephen Foster and the American Folksong." *The International, a Review of Two Worlds* (New York), February, 1914.

Scott, Margaret M. "Shrine to Stephen Collins Foster—Melody Maker." *Music Trades* (New York), February, 1932.

"Semi-Centennial of the Death of Stephen Foster." *Musical America* (New York), December 13, 1913.

Sims, Grover, collector; Tirindelli, Margherita, editor. "Pictorial Biography of Stephen Collins Foster." *Musical Courier* (New York), in two parts—March 22, 1930; March 29, 1930.

"Some Old Teachers." *Musical Courier* (New York), February, 1891. (Taken from *Pittsburgh Bulletin*.)

"Stephen C. Foster." *Pittsburgh Dispatch,* September 20, 1885. (Includes words and music of "The White House Chair.")

"A Stephen C. Foster Memorial." *American Art Journal* (New York), October 25, 1890.

"Stephen Collins Foster." *Brainard's Musical World* (Cleveland), January, 1870.

"Stephen Collins Foster." *The Étude* (Philadelphia), September, 1916.

"Stephen Collins Foster." *Musical Courier* (New York), January 11, 1923.

"Stephen Collins Foster." *The Musical Standard* (London), November, 1931.

"The Stephen Collins Foster Memorial." *Musical Digest* (New York), April, 1930.

"Stephen Collins Foster Memorial." *The New England Conservatory of Music Bulletin* (Boston), November, 1932.

"The Stephen Collins Foster Memorial Building." *The Musical Forecast* (Pittsburgh), February, 1930.

"A Stephen Collins Foster Memorial Fund." *Musical Courier* (New York), June 30, 1921.

"Stephen Foster—Centenary Sketches, 1826-1926." *Music and Youth* (Boston), June, 1926.

"Stephen Foster a Maker of Folk Songs." *The Étude* (Philadelphia), January, 1913.

"Stephen Foster vs. Franz Schubert." *The Literary Digest* (New York), September 25, 1920.

"Stephen Foster's Hundredth Birthday." *The Literary Digest* (New York), July 24, 1926.

"Stephen Foster's Versatility and Industry." *The Étude* (Philadelphia), September, 1916.

Stewart, M. Christie. "A Century of Negro Minstrelsy." *The Landmark,* November, 1931.

Stuckey, Norman. "America's Greatest Song Writer." *The Étude* (Philadelphia), October, 1929.

Sykes, Edward C. "Old Pittsburgh Homestead to be Perpetual Foster Memorial." *Musical America* (New York), January 10, 1914.

"To Honor Foster." *Musical Courier* (New York), June 30, 1921.

"Two New Stephen Foster Songs." *Fischer Edition News* (New York), July-September, 1931.

Upton, George P. "The Romance of Stephen Collins Foster." *The Étude* (Philadelphia), November, 1914.

"Vivifying the Master-Songs of Foster as Vehicles of Community Expression." *Musical America* (New York), April 9, 1921.

Watts, Harvey M. "Foster and the American Folk Song." *The Weekly Review* (New York), August 13, 1921.

"Way Down Upon the Suwanee River." *Pathfinder* (Washington, D. C.), May 27, 1933.

Weiss, Harry B. "Foster Hall and Its Collection of Fosteriana." *The American Book Collector* (Metuchen, N. J.), October, 1932.

Whitmer, T. Carl. "Stephen Foster, an American." *The Musician* (Boston), December, 1913.

"William A. Pond." *Harper's Weekly* (New York), August 22, 1885.

Wilson, K. McN. "The Stephen C. Foster Memorial Building Fund." *Musical Courier* (New York), January 4, 1930.

Z., K. "Stephen Collins Foster." *Brainard's Musical World* (Cleveland), January, 1870.

ISSUES OF PERIODICALS CONTAINING DATA ON STEPHEN FOSTER
(SINCE 1864)

The Amateur (Philadelphia), May, 1871.

Arthur's Illustrated Home Magazine, January, 1877.

Book Collecting for Love or Money (San Francisco), 1931 to the present.

Collecting for Profit (Los Angeles), 1931 to May, 1932.

The Collector's Journal (Los Angeles), July, 1932, to the present.

Demorest's Monthly Magazine (New York), 1869.

The Diapason (Chicago), July 1, 1931; October 1, 1931.

The Étude (Philadelphia), April, 1919; January, 1920; February, 1925.

Every Saturday (Boston), January to June, 1871.

The Filson Club History Quarterly (Louisville, Ky.), 1933.

Godey's Lady's Book (Philadelphia), April, 1873.

Harper's Bazaar (New York), January 28, 1871.

Harper's New Monthly Magazine (New York), June to November, 1878.

Indiana History Bulletin (Indianapolis), December, 1931.

Kunkel's Musical Review (St. Louis), July, 1899.

Mellor's Melody Magazine (Pittsburgh), 1929.
The Mentor (New York), December, 1920.
Music (Chicago), September, 1900.
Musical Courier (New York), March 27, 1889,
The Musician (Boston), September, 1906.
The Music Trades (New York), February, 1933.
The News Sheet, Official Publication of the Pennsylvania Federa-
   tion of Music Clubs (Pittsburgh), 1932, 1933.
The Phonograph Monthly Review. November, 1926, to December,
   1930.
Pittsburgh First (Pittsburgh), July 3, 1926. "Stephen C. Foster
   Centennial Number." Contains several articles dealing with
   Foster.
Pittsburgh Press (Pittsburgh), June 23; July 7, 11, 16; August 11,
   17, 1895: September 9, 12, 1900.
The Pittsburgh Record (Pittsburgh), April-May, 1933.
The Register of the Kentucky State Historical Society (Frankfort,
   Ky.), September, 1918.
The Song Journal (Detroit), January, 1872; August, 1874.
Thomas F. Madigan's Autograph Bulletin (New York), February,
   1925.
Trifet's Monthly Budget of Music (Boston), October, 1893. This
   issue is entitled "Trifet's Harmonized Melodies."
Werner's Magazine, February, 1898-December, 1900.
Western Pennsylvania Historical Magazine (Pittsburgh), October,
   1924.

A SELECTED LIST OF BOOKS CONTAINING WORKS BY STEPHEN FOSTER

(Arranged Chronologically by Date of Publication)

Songsters, Hymnals, etc.

Christy, George. *George Christy's Essence of Old Kentucky.* New
   York (no date). Dick & Fitzgerald.
Christy's Bones and Banjo Melodist. New York (no date). Dick
   & Fitzgerald.
Old Uncle Ned Songster. Philadelphia (no date). Fisher & Brother.
Chaff, Gumbo, A.M.A. *The Ethiopian Glee Book.* Boston, 1848
   and 1849. Elias Howe.
Christy, Edwin P., authorized by. *Christy's Plantation Melodies.*
   Philadelphia, 1851-1853. Fisher & Brother.
Oh, Boys, Carry Me 'Long Songster. Philadelphia, 1851. Fisher
   & Brother.
Davidson's Universal Melodist. London, 1853. G. H. Davidson.

Christy's Plantation Melodies. Philadelphia, 1854. Fisher & Brother.

Christy, George, and White, Charles, published under the authority of. *Christy's and White's Ethiopian Melodies.* Philadelphia, 1854. T. B. Peterson & Brothers.

Gentle Annie Melodist, No. 1. New York, 1858. Firth, Pond & Co.

Jenks, A. S., and Gilkey, D., compilers. *The Chorus.* Philadelphia, 1858. A. S. Jenks.

The American Dime Song Book. Philadelphia, 1859. Fisher & Brother.

Jenks, A. S., compiler. *Devotional Melodies.* Philadelphia, 1859. A. S. Jenks.

Waters, Horace, compiler. *The Sabbath School Bell No. 1.* New York, 1859. Horace Waters.

Beadle's Dime Song Books. New York, 1859-1862. Beadle and Company.

Beadle's Dime Song Books. New York, 1860-1864. Irwin P. Beadle & Co.

Waters, Horace, editor. *Sabbath School Bell No. 2.* New York, 1860. Horace Waters.

The Wide-Awake Vocalist. New York, 1860. E. A. Daggett.

The Book of Popular Songs. Philadelphia, 1861. G. G. Evans.

Waters, Horace, editor. *Day School Bell No. 1.* New York, 1861. Horace Waters.

The Love and Sentimental Songster. New York, 1862. Dick & Fitzgerald.

Waters, Horace, editor. *The Athenæum Collection of Hymns and Tunes for Church and Sunday School.* New York, 1863. Horace Waters.

Waters' Choral Harp. New York, 1863. Horace Waters.

Waters' Golden Harp. New York, 1863. Horace Waters.

Bradbury, William B., editor. *The New Golden Trio.* New York, 1866. William B. Bradbury.

The Canteen Songster. Philadelphia, 1866. Simpson & Co.

Waters, Horace, editor. *Heavenly Echoes.* New York, 1867. C. M. Tremaine.

Waters, Horace, compiler. *Zion's Refreshing Showers.* New York, 1867. C. M. Tremaine.

Perkins, W. O., editor. *The Golden Robin.* Boston, 1868. Oliver Ditson & Company.

Smith, M. F. H., compiler. *The Sparkling Stream.* New York, 1870. Charles W. Harris.

Sherwin, W. F., and Vail, S. J., editors. *Songs of Grace and Glory.* New York, 1874. Horace Waters & Son.

Perkins, W. O., editor. *The Whippoor-Will.* Boston, 1876. Oliver Ditson & Company.

Illustrated Editions of Foster Songs

My Old Kentucky Home. New York, 1887. H. M. Caldwell Co. Written and composed by Stephen Collins Foster. Illustrations by Mary Hallock Foote and Charles Copeland.

Old Folks at Home. Boston, 1887. Joseph Knight Company. Written and composed by Stephen Collins Foster. Illustrations by Charles Copeland.

The Swanee River. New York and Boston, 1887. H. M. Caldwell Co. Written and composed by Stephen Collins Foster. Illustrations by Charles Copeland.

Massa's in the Cold, Cold Ground. New York, 1888. H. M. Caldwell Co. Written and composed by Stephen Collins Foster. Illustrations by Charles Copeland.

Massa's in the Cold, Cold Ground. London (no date—about 1888-1890). John Walker & Co. Written and composed by Stephen Collins Foster. Illustrations by Charles Copeland.

My Old Kentucky Home. Boston, 1888. Ticknor and Company. Written and composed by Stephen Collins Foster. Illustrations by Mary Hallock Foote and Charles Copeland.

Old Folks at Home. Boston, 1888. Ticknor and Company. Written and composed by Stephen Collins Foster. Illustrations by Charles Copeland.

The Old Folks at Home. Boston, 1888. Charles E. Brown & Co. Written and composed by Stephen Collins Foster. Illustrated by G. W. Brenneman.

The Old Folks at Home. New York and London, 1888. White and Allen. Written and composed by Stephen Collins Foster. Illustrated by G. W. Brenneman.

The Old Plantation Melodies. New York, 1888. H. M. Caldwell Co. Written and composed by Stephen Collins Foster, Walter Kittredge and others. Illustrated by Charles Copeland and Mary Hallock Foote.

Plantation Melodies. Boston, 1888. Joseph Knight Company. Written and composed by Stephen Collins Foster. Illustrations by Charles Copeland and Mary Hallock Foote.

Massa's in the Cold, Cold Ground. Boston, 1889. Ticknor and Company. Written and composed by Stephen Collins Foster. Illustrations by Charles Copeland.

Dear Old Songs. New York, 1889. White and Allen. (Includes "Old Uncle Ned," illustrated by G. W. Brenneman.)

My Old Kentucky Home. Boston, 1889. Ticknor and Company. Written and composed by Stephen Collins Foster. Illustrations by Mary Hallock Foote and Charles Copeland.

Nelly Was a Lady. Boston, 1889. Ticknor and Company. Written and composed by Stephen Collins Foster. Illustrations by Charles Copeland.

Old Folks at Home. Boston, 1889. Ticknor and Company. Written and composed by Stephen Collins Foster. Illustrations by Charles Copeland.

Old Uncle Ned. New York, 1889. White and Allen. Written and composed by Stephen Collins Foster. Illustrated by G. W. Brenneman.

Massa's in the Cold, Cold Ground. Troy, N. Y., 1890. Nims and Knight. Written and composed by Stephen Collins Foster. Illustrations by Charles Copeland.

Old Folks at Home. Troy, N. Y., 1890. Nims and Knight. Written and composed by Stephen Collins Foster. Illustrations by Charles Copeland.

Massa's in the Cold, Cold Ground. Philadelphia, 1892. Premium Department of *The Ladies' Home Journal.* Written and composed by Stephen Collins Foster. Illustrations by Charles Copeland.

My Old Kentucky Home. Philadelphia, 1892. Premium Department of *The Ladies' Home Journal.* Written and composed by Stephen Collins Foster. Illustrations by Mary Hallock Foote and Charles Copeland.

The Old Folks at Home. Boston, 1892. Charles E. Brown & Co. Written and composed by Stephen Collins Foster. Illustrated by G. W. Brenneman.

Old Uncle Ned. Boston, 1892. Charles E. Brown & Co. Written and composed by Stephen Collins Foster. Illustrated by G. W. Brenneman.

Nelly Was a Lady. Philadelphia, 1892. Premium Department of *The Ladies' Home Journal.* Written and composed by Stephen Collins Foster. Illustrations by Charles Copeland.

Song Collections

The Carcanet: A Collection of Modern Musical Gems. New York, 1881. Wm. A. Pond & Co.

Minstrel Songs Old and New. Boston, 1882. Oliver Ditson & Co.

Our War Songs North and South. Cleveland, O., 1887. S. Brainard's Sons.

Smith, M. F. H., compiler. *The Sparkling Stream: a Collection of Temperance Melodies.* New York, 1895. Hamilton S. Gordon.

Page, N. Clifford, editor. *Twenty Songs by Stephen C. Foster.* Boston, 1906. Oliver Ditson Company. "The Half Dollar Music Series."

Page, N. Clifford, editor. *Twenty Songs by Stephen C. Foster*. Boston, 1906. Oliver Ditson Company. "The O. D. Music Series."

Burleigh, H. T., editor. *Negro Minstrel Melodies*. New York, 1909. G. Schirmer, Inc.

Martens, Frederick H., author; Page, N. Clifford, composer. *Old Plantation Days*. Boston, 1918. C. C. Birchard and Company.

Foster Melodies Medley. Official Kentucky Souvenir. (The Old Kentucky Home, Bardstown, Ky.) Arrangement copyrighted, 1921, by Winifred Callahan, Louisville, Ky.

Milligan, Harold Vincent, editor. *Album of Songs by Stephen C. Foster*. New York, 1921. G. Schirmer, Inc.

Reinecke, Zudie Harris, arranger. *The Ten Best Foster Songs*. Louisville, Ky., 1923. *The Courier-Journal* and *The Louisville Times*. Especially arranged and dedicated to W. H. A. S.

Martens, Frederick H., and Engel, Carl. *'Way Down South in Dixie*. Boston, 1924. C. C. Birchard & Company.

American War Songs. Philadelphia, 1925. Privately printed for the Colonial Dames of America.

Staton, Kate E., compiler. *Old Southern Songs of the Period of the Confederacy*. New York, 1926. Samuel French.

Two Stephen C. Foster Songs. ("Long-Ago Day" and "This Rose Will Remind You.") New York, 1931. J. Fischer & Bro.

Schauffler, Henry A., author of book; Nevin, Gordon Balch, composer of music. *Following Foster's Footsteps*. New York, 1933. J. Fischer & Bro.

Howard, John Tasker, editor. *A Program of Stephen Foster Songs*. New York, 1934 (in press). J. Fischer & Bro.

SOURCE MATERIAL

Records and Documents, Letters, First and Later Editions of Foster Music, etc.

In the Foster Hall Collection

Documents

Book of Original Manuscripts. Holograph manuscripts of Stephen Collins Foster, covering the period 1851 to 1860.

Holograph Manuscripts of Stephen Collins Foster.

Record Book of William B. Foster, 1839 to 1852.

Buchanan Glee Club Minute Book, 1856.

Account Book of Stephen Collins Foster, 1855 to 1860.

Holograph Letters of Stephen Collins Foster.

Letters and Memoranda Relating to the Death of Stephen Collins Foster, 1864.

Letters from the Immediate Family of Stephen Collins Foster.
Letters and Manuscripts of Morrison Foster.
Letters of John Rowan.
Letters from Descendants (direct and collateral) concerning Stephen Collins Foster.
Documents of Horace Waters, E. A. Daggett, C. M. Tremaine, Charles W. Harris and Stephen T. Gordon concerning the Publication of the Music of Stephen Collins Foster.
Letters and Manuscripts of George Cooper.
Miscellaneous Letters and Manuscripts Indirectly Relating to Stephen Collins Foster.

Editions of Foster Music

First Editions of the Music of Stephen C. Foster.
Editions of the Music of Stephen C. Foster, Published Before 1864; 1864-1900; 1900 to the Present.
Miscellaneous Variations on the Melodies of Stephen C. Foster, Published Before 1864; 1864-1900; 1900 to the Present.
Hymn Books Containing Foster Melodies, Published Before 1864; 1864-1900; 1900 to the Present.
School Song Books Containing Foster Melodies, Published Before 1864; 1864-1900; 1900 to the Present.
Miscellaneous Song Books Containing Foster Melodies, Published Before 1864; 1864-1900; 1900 to the Present.
Miscellaneous Arrangements and Transcriptions of the Melodies of Stephen C. Foster, Published Before 1864; 1864-1900; 1900 to the Present.
Political Songsters, Published Before 1864; 1864-1900; 1900 to the Present.
College Song Books Containing Foster Melodies, Published Before 1864; 1864-1900; 1900 to the Present.
Temperance Songsters, Published Before 1864; 1864-1900; 1900 to the Present.
Patriotic Song Books Containing Foster Melodies, Published Before 1864; 1864-1900; 1900 to the Present.
War Song Books Containing Foster Melodies, Published Before 1864; 1864-1900; 1900 to the Present.
Civil War Songsters.
Broadsides Containing the Words of Foster Songs.
Illustrated Song Pantomimes of Popular Foster Melodies.
"Answer Songs."
"Companion Songs."
Editions of the Music of Stephen C. Foster, Published in England Before 1864; 1864-1900; 1900 to the Present.
English Song Books Containing Foster Melodies, Published Before 1864; 1864-1900; 1900 to the Present.

Arrangements and Transcriptions of the Melodies of Stephen C. Foster, Published in England Before 1864; 1864-1900; 1900 to the Present.

Editions of the Music of Stephen C. Foster, Published in Germany 1864-1900; 1900 to the Present.

Arrangements and Transcriptions of the Melodies of Stephen C. Foster, Published in Germany, 1864 to 1900; 1900 to the Present.

Phonograph Records of the Songs of Stephen C. Foster.

Piano Records of the Melodies of Stephen C. Foster.

Organ Records of the Melodies of Stephen C. Foster.

Reports on Research

Copley, Mrs. Katherine W. Reports on Foster Research at the Library of Congress.

Gordon, R. W. Preliminary Report on Stephen C. Foster's "Oh! Susanna," August, 1931.

Copyright Records of the Works of Stephen Foster.

List of Fosteriana in the British Museum, London.

Catalogue of Fosteriana in the Carnegie Library, Pittsburgh. (Included with an article, "Stephen Collins Foster, 1826-1864," in the Monthly Bulletin of the Carnegie Library of Pittsburgh, June, 1918.)

List of Fosteriana in the Grosvenor Library, Buffalo, N. Y.

List of Fosteriana in the New York Public Library.

List of Fosteriana in the Public Library, Cincinnati, Ohio.

Reports on Genealogical Studies of the Foster Family Made by Foster Hall.

Reports on Research in Life of Stephen Collins Foster Made by Foster Hall.

Studies of the Pittsburgh City Directories, 1850-1860.

Whittlesey, Walter R. Reports on Foster Research at the Library of Congress.

Thematic Index of the Melodies of Stephen Foster.

Miscellaneous Data

Almanacs, Patent Medicine Circulars, and Other Forms of Advertising Utilizing Foster Melodies.

Catalogues of Foster Music by Various Publishers Before 1864; 1864-1900; 1900 to the Present.

Genealogies of the Foster Family.

Material Relating to the Publishers of Stephen Collins Foster's Music.

Minstrel Playbills.

Newspaper and Magazine Articles Concerning Stephen Foster Published Before 1864; 1864 to the Present.

Parodies and Burlesques on Foster Songs.
Photographs of Relatives and Descendants of Stephen Collins Foster.

Records of Tributes to Stephen Foster

Addresses Made at Celebrations Honoring Stephen Foster.
Miscellaneous Programs Issued for Organizations Honoring Stephen Foster.
Miscellaneous Programs of Minstrel Shows Using Foster Melodies.
Miscellaneous Programs of Musical Societies Using Foster Melodies.
Miscellaneous Programs of Organizations Honoring Stephen Foster.
Music Dedicated to Stephen Foster.
Plays and Operettas Based on the Life of Stephen Foster.
Radio Programs Using Foster Melodies.

At the Library of Congress

First Editions of the Music of Stephen C. Foster.
Holograph List of Royalties Received by Stephen Foster, January 27, 1857.
Holograph Manuscripts of Stephen Collins Foster.
Holograph Letters of Stephen Collins Foster.
Agreement Between Firth, Pond & Co. and Stephen Collins Foster, February 9, 1858.
Agreement Between Firth, Pond & Co. and Stephen Collins Foster, December 21, 1854.

In Other Collections

Correspondence Between Morrison Foster and Publishers Regarding Renewal of Copyright on Songs of Stephen Foster (together with Royalty Statements). In the Possession of Mrs. Evelyn Foster Morneweck of Detroit, Michigan.
Foster Family Letters. In the Possession of Mrs. Evelyn Foster Morneweck of Detroit, Michigan.
Scrap Book Compiled by Morrison Foster. In the Possession of Mrs. Evelyn Foster Morneweck of Detroit, Michigan.
Holograph Manuscript of Stephen Collins Foster. Henry E. Huntington Library, San Marino, California.
Holograph Letters of Stephen Collins Foster. Henry E. Huntington Library, San Marino, California.
Foster Family Letters. In the Possession of Mr. Charles Manning, Pittsburgh, Pennsylvania.
Holograph Manuscript of Stephen Collins Foster. Foster Memorial Home, Pittsburgh, Penn.
First Editions of the Music of Stephen C. Foster. Public Library of the City of Boston.

Items in Contemporary Newspapers and Magazines

"Editorial Notes—Music." *Putnam's Monthly* (New York), May, 1854.

"The Late Stephen C. Foster." *Littell's Living Age* (Boston), February 13, 1864. (Reprinted from the New York *Evening Post*.)

Notice of Death of Stephen Foster. *Frank Leslie's Illustrated Newspaper* (New York), February 6, 1864.

Notice of Death of Stephen Foster. *New York Musical Pioneer* (New York), February, 1864.

Notice of Death of Stephen Foster. *Western Musical World* (Cleveland), February, 1864.

"Sketch of the Life of the Late Stephen C. Foster." *The New York Clipper* (New York), February 3, 1864.

"Stephen C. Foster." *Clark's School Visitor* (Philadelphia), April, 1864.

"Stephen C. Foster, the Composer." *The Saturday Evening Post,* February 6, 1864.

"Popular Songs." *Dwight's Journal of Music* (Boston), June 27, 1857.

Thackeray, W. M. "Charity and Humor." *Harper's New Monthly Magazine* (New York), June, 1853.

"Two New Melodies for Children." *Clark's School Visitor* (Philadelphia), May, 1863.

"Who Writes Our Negro Songs?" *Western Fireside* (Madison, Wisconsin), April 25, 1857.

"Who Writes Our Songs?" *Littell's Living Age* (Boston), May 14, 1859. (Reprinted from the New York *Evening Post*.)

"Who Writes Our Songs?" *Cosmopolitan Art Journal,* June, 1859. Reprinted from the *Evening Post*.

Issues of Contemporary Periodicals Containing Reference to Stephen Foster

The American Monthly Musical Review and Choir Singers' Companion (New York), July, 1850-December, 1852.

The Baltimore Olio (Baltimore), 1850.

Clark's School Visitor (Philadelphia), June, 1864.

Demorest's Illustrated News (New York), May 7, 1864.

Demorest's Illustrated News (New York), June 11, 1864.

Demorest's Illustrated News (New York), August 6, 1864.

Demorest's Illustrated News (New York), June 4, 1864.

Dwight's Journal of Music (Boston), October 2, 1852; September 7, 1861.

Godey's Lady's Book (Philadelphia), 1862.

Godey's Lady's Book (Philadelphia), 1863.
Godey's Lady's Book (Philadelphia), May, 1864.
Graham's Magazine (Philadelphia), 1851.
The Illustrated London News (London), July 12, 1856. (Reference to Foster's songs in Crimean War.)
The Knickerbocker, or New-York Monthly Magazine (New York), March, 1849.
Life Illustrated (New York), February 6, 1858.
Life Illustrated (New York), March 12, 1859.
The Musical Review and Choral Advocate (New York), 1853.
Musical World (New York), September 9, 1854, to December 30, 1854.
Musical World (New York), April 30, 1859.
The Musical World and New York Musical Times (New York), September 4, 1852, to September 2, 1854.
The New Mirror (New York), 1843-1844.
The New York Clipper (New York), March 12, 1864.
New York Musical Pioneer and Chorister's Budget (New York), 1855-1856.
Notes and Queries (London), 1863, 1864.
The Pittsburgh Mercury, July 12, 1826. (Contains an account of July 4 celebration occurring at time of Stephen Foster's birth.)
Putnam's Monthly Magazine (New York), January to July, 1856.
Vincent, Francis, editor. *Vincent's Semi-Annual United States Register* (Philadelphia), 1860. Francis Vincent.
Waverly Magazine (Boston), June 16, 1860.

Miscellaneous Source Material

Ayres, George B. *New Descriptive Hand-Book of the Pennsylvania Railroad.* Pittsburgh, 1859. W. S. Haven.
Bowen, Eli. *The Pictorial Sketch-Book of Pennsylvania.* Philadelphia, 1852. Willis P. Hazard.
Day, Sherman. *Historical Collections of the State of Pennsylvania.* Philadelphia, 1843. George W. Gorton.
The Pittsburgh Directory for 1815. Pittsburgh, 1815.
Smith, Joseph, D.D., *History of Jefferson College.* Pittsburgh, 1857. J. T. Shyrock.
Thurston, George H. *Directory of Pittsburgh and Vicinity for 1859-'60.* Pittsburgh, 1859. George H. Thurston.
Williams, C. S., compiler. *Williams' Cincinnati Directory and Business Advertiser for 1849-50.* Cincinnati, 1849. C. S. Williams. liams.
  Williams' Cincinnati Guide and General Business Directory for 1848-9. Cincinnati, 1848. C. S. Williams & Son.

INDEX

"Oh! Susanna," 2, 300; written for "Knights of the S. T.," 119; where written, 136 ff.; given to Peters, 137, 138; first appearance; starts Stephen on vocation of song-writer, 138; the marching song of the forty-niners, 138, 145; question of who first printed, no copyright entry in the Library of Congress, 139; copyright, 140; chronology, 141; published by C. Holt, Jr., 141, 143, 144; sung in foreign lands, 144; used as a quick-step, 146; issued as "Music of the Original Christy Minstrels," and as "Songs of the Sable Harmonists," 180; variations given by William Vincent Wallace, 223; *see also* "Susanna."

"Oh! Susanna Quick Step," arranged by Edward L. White, 142; published by F. D. Benteen, 143

"Old Black Joe," inspiration of; first published in 1860, 160; composition, 301; copyrighted, 322, 327

"Old Dog Tray," 241; title-page bears Christy's name, 187; Christy pays $10 for privilege of first singing, 187, 198; anecdote, 229-30; original publication, 245; earnings, 267

"Old Folks Are Gone, The," by G. F. Root, 203

"Old Folks at Home," 244, 363; earnings, 2, 268, 321, 353, 356; title-page, 181; amount Christy paid for privilege of first singing, 187, 196, 198, 199; bears Christy's name, 188, 196; choosing name of river, 191; one of the world's most famous songs, 193; music analyzed, Henry Kleber said to have helped with, 194; copyright, 195, 246, 350; reharmonization fails to richen, 195; title-page, Foster's name omitted, 195, 196; issued as written and composed by Christy, 195, 196, 198; transaction with Christy questioned, 197, 198; royalties for Firth, Pond & Co., 196, 199, 200; complications in copyright renewal, 197; popularity in England, sung by soldiers in Crimean War, 201; advertisement and news item in *Musical World,* 202; imitations, 202 ff.; Foster's opinion of, 213; popularity, 214-15; sung by Anna Zerr, 216; sung to Sunday School

words, 218; earnings, 267; publishers' claims, 268; first played on Mrs. Woods' piano, 286; a masterpiece, 302; sung by Christine Nilsson, 349; renewal of copyright, 351 ff.

"Old Folks Quadrilles," 224

"Old Home Ain't What It Used to Be, The," 205

"Old Kentucky Home," Bardstown, Ky., 36

"Old Memories," 229; original publication, 245; earnings, 267

"Old Uncle Ned," written for "Knights of the S. T.," 119; given to Peters, 137, 138

Olio, The, 137, 155

Oliver Ditson & Co., 350; royalties paid, 357

"Once I Loved Thee, Mary Dear," 185; original copyright, 246; earnings, 267

O'Neill, Peggy, 50

"Open Thy Lattice, Love," Stephen's first published song, 115; comparison of original MS. with first published version, Knight's music compared with Stephen's, 116

Original Georgia Minstrels, 205

Ostinelli, Louis, 149

Ostinelli, Sophia Hewitt, 149

Our American Music, 269

"Our Bright Summer Days Are Gone," 325; rejected by Firth, Pond & Company, 321, 322; bought by Daly, 322; copyrighted, 327

"Our Darling Kate," 330

"Our Willie Dear is Dying," copyrighted, 322

"Over the Calm Lake Gliding," 228

Park, James H., 70, 358

"Parthenia to Ingomar," earnings, 282, 303; composed on boat, 288, 292

Pearce, Mrs., 34, 35

Pedee river, 191

Penn Cotton Mills, 62

Pennsylvania Railroad, 338

Pentland, Susan E., 106, 129, 287; "Open Thy Lattice Love," dedicated to, 116; Stephen's friendship with; her marriage to Andrew Robinson, 158; account of the trip to New Orleans, 169; "Willie My Brave" dedicated to, 192; wedding, 222; visit to Foster, 319

Perkins, John A., 96; quoted, 99, 100

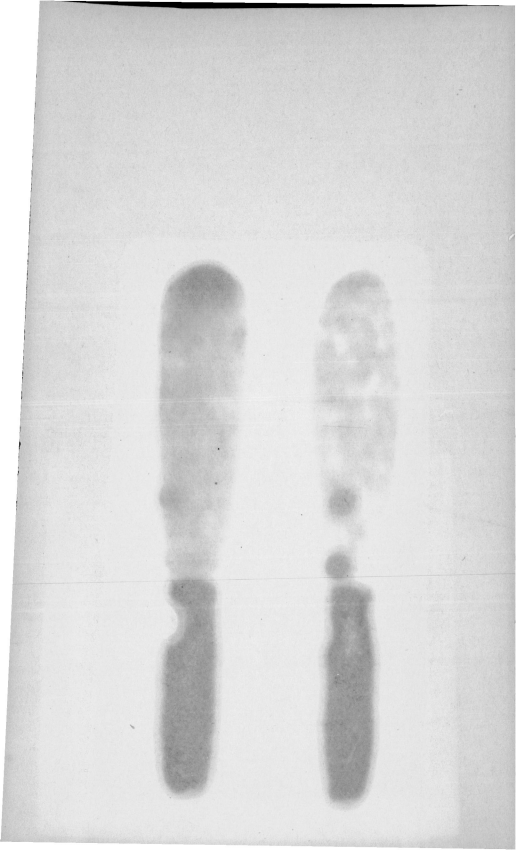